Abolition in Sierra Leone

Tracing the lives and experiences of 100,000 Africans who landed in Sierra Leone having been taken off slave vessels by the British Navy following Britain's abolition of the transatlantic slave trade, this study focuses on how people, forcibly removed from their homelands, packed on to slave ships, and settled in Sierra Leone, were able to rebuild new lives, communities, and collective identities in an early British colony in West Africa. Their experience illuminates both African and African diaspora history by tracing the evolution of communities forged in the context of forced migration and the missionary encounter in a prototypical post-slavery colonial society. A new approach to the major historical field of British antislavery, studied as a history not of legal victories (abolitionism) but of enforcement and lived experience (abolition), Richard Peter Anderson reveals the linkages between emancipation, colonization, and identity formation in the Black Atlantic.

RICHARD PETER ANDERSON is Lecturer in colonial and postcolonial history at the University of Exeter. He has published in journals including *Slavery & Abolition*, *African Economic History*, and *History in Africa*. He is co-editor of *Liberated Africans and the Abolition of the Slave Trade, 1807–1896* (forthcoming) with Henry Lovejoy.

AFRICAN IDENTITIES: PAST AND PRESENT

GENERAL EDITORS

Toyin Falola, *The University of Texas at Austin*
Carina Ray, *Brandeis University*

African Identities: Past and Present offers scholars a unique publishing platform for exploring the multivalent processes through which collective identities have come into being. Books in this series probe the work that African identities have been made to do, the varied investments that historical and contemporary actors have made in them, and the epistemological dilemmas and intellectually fraught politics of writing about such contingent categories of being. The focus on African identities makes clear the series' commitment to publishing histories of the complex and ongoing processes of identity formation through which Africans have taken on shared senses of being. This series calls upon its authors to unpack the flexible, fluid, contingent, and interactive nature of collective African identities, while also exploring how historical actors have alternatively sought to delimit, expand or otherwise challenge the boundaries of such identities.

Abolition in Sierra Leone

Re-Building Lives and Identities in
Nineteenth-Century West Africa

RICHARD PETER ANDERSON
University of Exeter

CAMBRIDGE
UNIVERSITY PRESS

CAMBRIDGE
UNIVERSITY PRESS

University Printing House, Cambridge CB2 8BS, United Kingdom

One Liberty Plaza, 20th Floor, New York, NY 10006, USA

477 Williamstown Road, Port Melbourne, VIC 3207, Australia

314–321, 3rd Floor, Plot 3, Splendor Forum, Jasola District Centre, New Delhi – 110025, India

79 Anson Road, #06–04/06, Singapore 079906

Cambridge University Press is part of the University of Cambridge.

It furthers the University's mission by disseminating knowledge in the pursuit of education, learning, and research at the highest international levels of excellence.

www.cambridge.org
Information on this title: www.cambridge.org/9781108473545
DOI: 10.1017/9781108562423

© Richard Peter Anderson 2020

This publication is in copyright. Subject to statutory exception and to the provisions of relevant collective licensing agreements, no reproduction of any part may take place without the written permission of Cambridge University Press.

First published 2020

Printed in the United Kingdom by TJ International Ltd, Padstow Cornwall

A catalogue record for this publication is available from the British Library.

Library of Congress Cataloging-in-Publication Data
Names: Anderson, Richard (Richard Peter), author.
Title: Abolition in Sierra Leone : re-building lives and identities in nineteenth-century West Africa / Richard Peter Anderson.
Other titles: African identities: past and present.
Description: New York : Cambridge University Press, 2019. | Series: African identities: past and present | Includes bibliographical references and index.
Identifiers: LCCN 2019038219 (print) | LCCN 2019038220 (ebook) | ISBN 9781108473545 (hardback) | ISBN 9781108461870 (paperback) | ISBN 9781108562423 (epub)
Subjects: LCSH: Freedmen–Africa, West–History–19th century. | Forced migration–Africa, West–History–19th century. | Ethnicity–Africa, West–History–19th century. | Africa, West–History–To 1884.
Classification: LCC HT1323 .A53 2019 (print) | LCC HT1323 (ebook) | DDC 306.3/62096609034–dc23
LC record available at https://lccn.loc.gov/2019038219
LC ebook record available at https://lccn.loc.gov/2019038220

ISBN 978-1-108-47354-5 Hardback

Cambridge University Press has no responsibility for the persistence or accuracy of URLs for external or third-party internet websites referred to in this publication and does not guarantee that any content on such websites is, or will remain, accurate or appropriate.

For my parents

Contents

List of Illustrations	page viii
Acknowledgments	x
Notes on the Text	xii
List of Abbreviations	xiv
Introduction: Sierra Leone: African Colony, African Diaspora	1
1 Liberated African Origins and the Nineteenth-Century Slave Trade	30
2 Their Own Middle Passage: Voyages to Sierra Leone	66
3 "Particulars of disposal": Life and Labor after "Liberation"	96
4 Liberated African Nations: Ethnogenesis in an African Diaspora	127
5 Kings and Companies: Ethnicity and Community Leadership	167
6 Religion, Return, and the Making of the Aku	192
7 The Cobolo War: Islam, Identity, and Resistance	227
Conclusion: Retention or Renaissance? Krio Descendants and Ethnic Identity	260
Appendices	267
Select Bibliography	276
Index	286

Illustrations

Figures

4.1 Yoruba "national marks" compiled by Robert Clarke, Senior Assistant Surgeon to the Colony of Sierra Leone, 1843	page 162
6.1 "Mr. Beale Seizing the Egugu"	223

Maps

1.1 Coastal origins of Liberated Africans landed at Freetown, 1808–1863	page 32
1.2 The Oyo Empire and Yoruba-speaking territories, c. 1823	53
3.1 Sierra Leone peninsula and the Liberated African villages, c. 1853	100

Tables

1.1 Slaves disembarked at Sierra Leone versus total disembarked in the Americas, 1808–1865	page 31
1.2 Liberated Africans landed at Freetown by region of embarkation, 1808–1863	33
1.3 Primary ports of receptive embarkation	34
1.4 Most widely spoken receptive languages in *Polyglotta Africana*	38
1.5 "Country" of receptives from Bight of Biafra ports in Liberated African registers, 1821–1822	48
2.1 Average voyage length to Sierra Leone versus slave ship voyages to the Americas, 1808–1863	80
2.2 Mortality between interception and emancipation, 1819–1863	81
3.1 Recaptives sent to major villages, 1811–1848	112

List of Illustrations

3.2 Port and coastal origins of recaptives sent to largest
    Liberated African villages, November 1816–June 1848   116
3.3 Recaptives from Bight of Benin sent to Liberated
    African villages, November 1816–June 1848   118
5.1 Ethnic designations of "Seventeen Nations" and 1848
    census   190
5.2 Members of the "Seventeen Nations"   191

Acknowledgments

This book was written in Sierra Leone, Canada, the United States, England, and Brazil and was shaped by colleagues and mentors in these countries and beyond. The project began as a doctoral dissertation at Yale University. I had the privilege of having a doctoral advisor in Robert Harms, who shared his vast knowledge of pre-colonial Africa and the history of the slave trade while being the most supportive of mentors. At Yale I had many other mentors in Edward Rugemer, Daniel Magaziner, Stuart Schwartz, David Blight, Anne Eller, and Marcela Echeverri.

Research for this book was supported by grants and fellowships from Yale's Gilder Lehrman Center for the Study of Slavery, Resistance, and Abolition, the Fox International Fellowship, the Social Sciences and Humanities Research Council of Canada (SSHRC), and the Commonwealth Scholarship Commission. Many archivists and librarians assisted in research across three continents. I am particularly grateful to Albert Moore, Abu Koroma, and Joanes Caulker in the Sierra Leone Public Archives in Freetown.

I completed much of this book's revision during an SSHRC postdoctoral fellowship with Paul Lovejoy at the Harriet Tubman Institute, York University. Michele Johnson, Deborah Neill, Annie Bunting, José C. Curto, and Denise Challenger helped make the Tubman Institute such a stimulating intellectual environment. I completed the book as a Commonwealth Rutherford Fellow at the University of Leicester and I am greatly indebted to Clare Anderson for this opportunity.

The project has benefited from the assistance of a number of scholars. David Eltis generously brought me in to the African Origins Project, sharing vast resources of data, and his encyclopedic knowledge of the slave trade and its abolition. The Origins Project team of Philip Misevich, Paul Lachance, Daniel B. Domingues da Silva, Alex Borucki, and Nafees M. Khan graciously welcomed me to the project. Origins

Acknowledgments

Project member Olatunji Ojo has been a constant source of expertise on all matters pertaining to Yoruba history.

I received tremendous encouragement from other historians of Sierra Leone, including Emma Christopher, Bronwen Everill, Maeve Ryan, and Padraic Scanlan. Allen M. Howard has shared his tremendous knowledge of the region through many conversations. Richard Huzzey and Sean Kelley have been equally generous through our many exchanges. Manuel Barcia, Kristin Mann, Christine Whyte, and Kyle Prochnow read portions of the manuscript. I deeply appreciate their suggestions, encouragement, and corrections. Toyin Falola and Carina Ray have been encouraging and supportive series editors, while Maria Marsh at Cambridge has been equally supportive and patient.

While writing this book I met my wife, Maria Clara Carneiro Sampaio, and she has been a constant source of love and support. This book is dedicated to my parents for always being there, even when we are oceans apart.

Notes on the Text

The subject of this book is a population of formerly enslaved Africans referred to in the scholarship as Liberated Africans or recaptives. Many studies state that Liberated Africans were originally termed recaptives. Yet as Christopher Fyfe points out, this usage is anachronistic.[1] "Captured negroes" was the first term adopted following the 1807 Abolition Act, and remained in currency until Freetown's Captured Negro Department was renamed the Liberated African Department in 1822. While the very first page of the first register of freed Africans from November 1808 refers to "Liberated Africans," the term was not widely used in Sierra Leone or by British authorities elsewhere during the first decade of suppression, and it was not until 1820 that the term "Liberated Africans" made its first appearance in Parliamentary Papers.

An 1816 report by Edward Bickersteth, the Assistant Secretary of the Church Missionary Society sent to inspect the mission in 1816, contains what may be first use of phrase "Recaptured Negroes."[2] But while the adjective "recaptured" was in use by the 1820s, there is no record of the noun "recaptive" before the 1880s. It might therefore inappropriate in a study on identity to employ this anachronistic term. Yet "recaptives" is used herein for two reasons. First, the term conveys the two key moments – that of enslavement and the subsequent intervention of the British Navy – that defined the lives of those who disembarked from slave ships at Freetown. Second, employing the term "Liberated African" uncritically fails to consider

---

[1] Christopher Fyfe, *A History of Sierra Leone* (London: Oxford University Press, 1962), 114.
[2] *Proceedings of the Church Missionary Society for Africa and the East, Seventeenth Year: 1816–1817* (London: L. B. Seeley), 161.

Notes on the Text

the very circumscribed freedom that many recaptives faced in this colonial setting.[3]

A further complication arises from the various meanings of the term Sierra Leone over time. Chapter 1 employs the term Sierra Leone in reference to a region of coast, defined by Philip Curtin and adopted by the *Voyages* database as stretching from Guinea-Bissau to just west of Cape Mount (Liberia).[4] But the term does not represent a political or ethnolinguistic region except in the documents of slave traders, nor does it correspond in any meaningful way to pre-colonial African history.[5] The term also does not correspond to the present-day borders of Sierra Leone, which expanded dramatically with Britain's declaration of a protectorate in 1896. To avoid confusion, the text usually refers to the "colony" or "peninsula" of Sierra Leone, today the Western Area and one of four principal regions in the post-colonial state of Sierra Leone.

The social and cultural history of recaptives means engaging with several African languages. Many of these languages were being studied and transcribed for the first time in Sierra Leone in this period. I have employed modern usage, including tone marks, except when quoting contemporary documents, in which the spelling and orthography of these languages were often only in their formative stages.

---

[3] My reasoning echoes Sharla Fett, who argues in the case of Liberia and American slave trade suppression that "recaptive" and "recaptured" serve "both as a more accurate descriptor [than 'liberated'] of the social experience of slave ship rescue and as a useful metaphor for the conflicting representational claims made on the bodies of slave ship refugees." Sharla M. Fett, *Recaptured Africans: Surviving Slave Ships, Detention, and Dislocation in the Final Years of the Slave Trade* (Chapel Hill: University of North Carolina Press, 2017, 4).

[4] P. E. H. Hair, "The Spelling and Connotation of the Toponym 'Sierra Leone' since 1461," *Sierra Leone Studies*, New Series, 18 (1966): 43–58.

[5] Paul E. Lovejoy, "The Trans-Atlantic Slave Trade Database and the History of the Upper Guinea Coast," *African Economic History*, 38 (2010): 1–28.

Abbreviations

CMS	Church Missionary Society Archives, University of Birmingham
CO	Records of the Colonial Office, The National Archives, Kew
FO	Records of the Foreign Office, The National Archives, Kew
HCA	Records of the High Court of Admiralty, The National Archives, Kew
LADLB	Liberated African Department Letterbook, Sierra Leone Public Archives, Fourah Bay College, Freetown
MMS	Methodist Missionary Society Archives, School of Oriental and African Studies, London
SLPA	Sierra Leone Public Archives, Fourah Bay College, Freetown

Introduction
Sierra Leone: African Colony, African Diaspora

The history of Sierra Leone is one of departures and arrivals. Between 1581 and 1867, European slave traders carried away an estimated 389,000 Africans from the regions in and around what now constitutes the country of Sierra Leone.[1] In the late eighteenth century, as Britain began contemplating the legal abolition of the slave trade, Sierra Leone became the destination for a reverse migration of enslaved Africans and their descendants who sought to return from the Americas. Between 1787 and 1800 more than two thousand formerly enslaved men, women, and children sailed from Britain, Nova Scotia, and Jamaica to populate a nascent colony financed by British abolitionists and like-minded businessmen. On the coast of West Africa these three waves of colonists hoped to create what abolitionist Granville Sharp called a "province of freedom."

Starting in 1808, Sierra Leone's fledgling settler population was joined by a fourth, much larger wave of forced migrants who never reached the Americas. Britain's 1807 Act to Abolish the Slave Trade led to the deployment of the Royal Navy to intercept slave ships along three thousand miles of West African coastline. Freetown became the epicenter of Britain's judicial and military campaign against the slave trade, serving as a base for the Navy's squadron and the point of disembarkation for Africans on captured vessels. Between 1808 and 1863, an estimated 99,752 Africans disembarked from slave vessels at Freetown's waterfront. As many as 72,284 resettled in the Sierra Leone colony; the rest were forcibly relocated to fulfill the labor and defense needs of Britain's Atlantic empire.[2]

---

[1] David Eltis and David Richardson, *Atlas of the Transatlantic Slave Trade* (New Haven, CT: Yale University Press, 2010), 18–19.

[2] For the calculation of these estimates, see Chapter 1 and Richard Anderson, "The Diaspora of Sierra Leone's Liberated Africans: Enlistment, Forced Migration, and 'Liberation' at Freetown, 1808–1863," *African Economic History*, 41 (2013): 101–138.

Known first as Captured Negroes, and after 1821 as Liberated Africans, these ostensibly freed captives were drawn from countless societies across West and West Central Africa. Once legally emancipated before Freetown's Vice-Admiralty Court and Courts of Mixed Commission, these Africans of diverse origins began new lives along the narrow Sierra Leone peninsula, a laterite outcropping some twenty-five miles long by ten miles wide. The result was one of the most geographically concentrated African diasporic communities of the nineteenth century and one of the most ethnolinguistically heterogeneous societies in the Atlantic world.

This book explores the origins, experiences, and identities of this population released by the British Navy. It is at once a history of colonial Africa and of the African diaspora. The diverting of freed slaves to Sierra Leone was the third largest movement of Africans in the nineteenth-century Atlantic, exceeded only by the Brazilian and Cuban slave trades. As a place of disembarkation for Africans on slave ships after 1807, Freetown was exceeded only by Rio de Janeiro, Bahia, Havana, and Pernambuco. Sierra Leone became one of the largest communities of Africans forcibly displaced by the transatlantic trade, albeit a vastly different colonial setting than on the other side of the Atlantic. The Sierra Leone colony was also Britain's first permanent colonial endeavor in sub-Saharan Africa and the location of some of the earliest Protestant missions to the continent. The society that emerged in Sierra Leone was simultaneously part of the African diaspora and early colonial Africa.

Sierra Leone: Abolition and Imperialism

The historiography on Sierra Leone has been reinvigorated over the past decade. The 2007 bicentennial of the 1807 Abolition Act has prompted new attention from imperial and naval historians, while the conclusion of Sierra Leone's civil war (1991–2002) enabled foreign researchers to return and undertake fieldwork and archival research.[3] At the same time, Gibril Cole, C. Magbaily Fyle, Mac Dixon-Fyle, and

---

[3] Alexander X. Byrd, *Captives and Voyagers: Black Migrants across the Eighteenth-Century British Atlantic World* (Baton Rouge: Louisiana State University Press, 2008); Paul E. Lovejoy and Suzanne Schwarz (eds.), *Slavery, Abolition, and the Transition to Colonialism in Sierra Leone* (Trenton, NJ: Africa World Press, 2014).

Joseph J. Bangura have continued the rich tradition of Sierra Leonean scholars writing the history of their country.[4] Several recent studies have looked at Sierra Leone as a case study in imperial history, examining how policies foreshadowed both post-emancipation societies around the Atlantic and later British colonies in Africa.[5] Sierra Leone has resumed its place in the history of British antislavery, with historians increasingly acknowledging the role of the colony in the burgeoning antislavery movement of late eighteenth-century Britain.[6]

Despite the historiographical effervescence on Sierra Leone's place in British abolition, the broader historiography of abolitionism has remained focused on the historical processes leading up to the 1807 Act: Why Britain? Why at that moment?[7] There has been a great deal of research on *abolitionism* as a humanitarian campaign, and far less on *abolition* as the implementation of that campaign's parliamentary success.[8] A peculiar feature in this historiography is the scant attention on Africans for whom the Abolition Act and its naval enforcement was meant to help. This study, by contrast, explores the human

---

[4] Joseph J. Bangura, *The Temne of Sierra Leone: African Agency in the Making of a British Colony* (Cambridge: Cambridge University Press, 2017); Gibril Cole, *The Krio of West Africa: Islam, Culture, and Colonialism in the Nineteenth Century* (Athens: Ohio University Press, 2013); Mac Dixon-Fyle and Gibril Cole (eds.), *New Perspectives on the Krio of Sierra Leone* (New York: Peter Lang, 2006).

[5] Michael J. Turner "The Limits of Abolition: Government, Saints, and the 'African Question,' c. 1780–1820," *The English Historical Review*, 112.446 (April 1997): 319–357; Padraic X. Scanlan, *Freedom's Debtors: British Antislavery in Sierra Leone in the Age of Revolution* (New Haven, CT: Yale University Press, 2017).

[6] Christopher Leslie Brown, *Moral Capital: Foundations of British Abolitionism* (Chapel Hill: University of North Carolina Press, 2006); Bronwen Everill, *Abolition and Empire in Sierra Leone and Liberia* (London: Palgrave Macmillan, 2013).

[7] The literature on British abolition is vast. See in particular Eric Williams, *Capitalism and Slavery* (Chapel Hill: University of North Carolina Press, 1944); Seymour Drescher, *Abolition: A History of Slavery and Antislavery* (Cambridge: Cambridge University Press, 2009); Drescher, *Econocide: British Slavery in the Era of Abolition* (Pittsburgh: University of Pittsburgh Press, 1977); David Brion Davis, *The Problem of Slavery in the Age of Revolution* (Oxford: Oxford University Press, 1999); Brown, *Moral Capital*. For the history of British antislavery after abolition, see Richard Huzzey, *Freedom Burning: Anti-Slavery and Empire in Victorian Britain* (Ithaca, NY: Cornell University Press, 2012).

[8] Padraic X. Scanlan, "MacCarthy's Skull: The Abolition of the Slave Trade in Sierra Leone, 1792–1823," unpublished PhD dissertation, Princeton University, 2013, 6.

consequences for the supposed beneficiaries of this campaign, in other words, the immediate human impact of abolition. The emphasis is not on Sierra Leone as a case study in British imperial history; it is, rather, a history of a particular kind of African diaspora formed from British imperial and abolitionist policies. The central theme of this book is how Africans, forcibly removed from their homelands, rebuilt new lives, communities, and collective identities in an early British colony in Africa.

The lives and experiences of receptives provide unique comparative insights within the field of studies on post-emancipation societies. The "age of emancipation" has become a major field within the historiography on slavery and the Black Atlantic.[9] In the nine decades after 1800, between seven and eight million people around the Atlantic world passed through a variety of emancipation processes.[10] Sierra Leone was an early site of the "mighty experiment" where Britain hoped to display the advantages of free labor in tropical agriculture. While most slave societies in the age of emancipation comprised different proportions of African and colony-born slaves, all Liberated Africans were born in Africa and thus provide an African perspective on responses to emancipation and the meaning of "liberation."[11]

[9] Frederick Cooper, Thomas C. Holt, and Rebecca J. Scott, *Beyond Slavery: Explorations of Race, Labor, and Citizenship in Postemancipation Societies* (Chapel Hill: University of North Carolina Press, 2000); Howard Temperley (ed.), *After Slavery: Emancipation and Its Discontents* (London: Frank Cass, 2000); Rebecca J. Scott, *Slave Emancipation in Cuba: The Transition to Free Labor, 1860–1899* (Princeton: Princeton University Press, 1985); Scott, *Degrees of Freedom: Louisiana and Cuba after Slavery* (Cambridge, MA: Harvard University Press, 2005); Thomas C. Holt, *The Problem of Freedom: Race, Labor, and Politics in Jamaica and Britain, 1832–1938* (Baltimore: Johns Hopkins University Press, 1992); Seymour Drescher, *The Mighty Experiment: Free Labor versus Slavery in British Emancipation* (New York: Oxford University Press, 2002).

[10] Daniel Domingues da Silva, David Eltis, Philip Misevich, and Olatunji Ojo, "The Diaspora of Africans Liberated from Slave Ships in the Nineteenth Century," *Journal of African History*, 55.3 (November 2014): 348.

[11] For Liberated Africans in the British Caribbean, see Monica Schuler, "*Alas, Alas, Kongo*": *A Social History of Indentured African Immigration into Jamaica, 1841–1865* (Baltimore: Johns Hopkins University Press, 1980); Schuler, "Liberated Central Africans in Nineteenth-Century Guyana," in Linda M. Heywood (ed.), *Central Africans and Cultural Transformations in the American Diaspora* (Cambridge: Cambridge University Press, 2002); and Roseanne Marion Adderley, *New Negroes from Africa: Slave Trade Abolition and Free African Settlement in the Nineteenth Century Caribbean* (Bloomington:

The nineteenth century is often heralded as an age of abolition. But it was also an age of massive forced migrations. The trans-shipment of Liberated Africans to face adjudication before British courts was one such strand, a redirection of the coerced labor migrations originally destined for Brazil and the Caribbean. As a by-product of the transatlantic slave trade, Sierra Leone's recaptives represented part of a broader African diaspora in the Atlantic, albeit under different conditions and circumstances on arrival. The combination of a large population of African birth arriving between 1808 and 1863, and the unique colonial project of forging a Christianized "free" labor society, makes Sierra Leone a fruitful comparative case study in the social and cultural history of the African diaspora. Scholars of the diaspora have largely chosen to work on migrations to the Americas rather than diasporas within Africa. As Pier Larson points out, this emphasis on transatlantic diasporas at the expense of diasporas in the Indian Ocean and within Africa effaces the diverse experiences of millions of Africans in diaspora.[12] This book argues that the concept of diaspora applies to Sierra Leone's Liberated African communities in ways that illuminate processes of ethnogenesis across the Black Atlantic.

David Northrup was the first to suggest that Sierra Leone's recaptive community offered a fruitful comparative case study to African identity formation in the Americas. Like slaves in the Americas, Liberated Africans experienced the trauma of enslavement, forced migration, and disembarkation in an alien, colonial landscape. But the differences between the experiences of Liberated African and their New World counterparts are equally insightful. For Liberated Africans, the key factors in community formation were the relative state of freedom combined with far more robust attempts to convert them and to instruct their children in an Anglican fashion. As Northrup points out, "recaptives' greater freedom shows how the process of community and identity formation operated when removed from the coercive

---

Indiana University Press, 2006). For Brazil, see Beatriz G. Mamigonian, *Africanos Livres: A Abolição do Tráfico de Escravos no Brasil* (São Paulo: Companhia das Letras, 2017).

[12] Pier M. Larson, "Horrid Journeying: Narratives of Enslavement and the Global African Diaspora," *Journal of World History*, 19.4 (2008): 443.

power of the slave master."[13] At the same time, the important administrative and ecclesiastical role played by Protestant missionaries and their attempts to extirpate "idolatry" and Islam were impediments to this freedom.

The study of ethnogenesis in the New World is often plagued by scanty evidence, recorded by outside observers, and from late in the process.[14] By contrast, Sierra Leone provides perhaps the best-documented diasporic community in the Black Atlantic due to the recordkeeping of Freetown's Liberated African Department and the copious records of the Church Missionary Society, Wesleyan Methodists, and eyewitness accounts of contemporary observers. In contrast to the Americas where African origins are often difficult to unravel, Sierra Leone sources allow a study of people's regional origins and often the specific home states, towns, or even villages. This level of detail in tracing origins allows an examination of the processes of identity formation among different cohorts of Liberated Africans during fifty-six years of settlement.

This detailed documentation pertains not only to the mass migration of Africans on intercepted vessels but to individual life histories. Most of the estimated 12.5 million victims of the transatlantic trade left no account of their lives and experiences. Yet a disproportionate number of recaptives did exactly that. The documentary record of Sierra Leone as a diaspora born of the slave trade is at its richest in the personal narratives left by those who experienced the journey. This includes the well-known narratives of Samuel Crowther, Joseph Wright, and others among Freetown's educated Christian converts. But there remains a treasure trove of less known and unpublished life stories. These narratives recount experiences of warfare and enslavement that were common in nineteenth-century West Africa, but also unique life trajectories as unwilling migrants entering a peculiar colonial experiment. Whenever possible, these individual narratives take a central place within this study.

Missionary records, when approached with requisite caution, are similarly rich sources for how Liberated Africans interacted with each other, the degree to which they perpetuated the religious and cultural

[13] David Northrup, "Becoming African: Identity Formation among Liberated Slaves in Nineteenth-Century Sierra Leone," *Slavery and Abolition*, 27.1 (April 2006): 3.
[14] Ibid., 3.

practices of their homelands, and how they responded to the offering and imposition of Christianity and European culture. Sources written by individuals in institutions antagonistic to African religions and cultures unintentionally became records of cultural vitality. Moreover, many receptive converts became missionaries, catechists, and schoolmasters, meaning that they often documented the religions of their homelands in the Liberated African diaspora.

This study builds on Northrup's argument for studying Liberated African identity formation as a comparative case study in diasporic ethnogenesis. It largely substantiates Northrup's arguments regarding receptive identity formation, though with some considerable caveats. Northrup has suggested that the dynamics of Liberated African society are best understood as a complementary process of "Africanization" and "creolization."[15] This terminology posits two simultaneous and connected transformations in terms of evolving identities and the impact of European education and proselytization. Northrup's conception of "Africanization" seeks to describe "the construction of radically altered senses of their African identities."[16] But as Northrup concedes, few (if any) first-generation Liberated Africans saw themselves primarily as "Africans" or possessed an inchoate pan-African consciousness.[17] His definition of creolization in Sierra Leone focuses primarily on the acquisition of the English language and of Christianization. This conception of creolization excludes the sizable population of Liberated Africans – including many Muslims – who consciously abstained from official attempts to impose an Anglophone, Christian society.

Within Sierra Leone historiography the dominant narrative remains the rapid acculturation of Liberated Africans into a creole (or Krio)

---

[15] The ideas Northrup first presented in "Becoming African" are elaborated on in David Northrup, "Identity among Liberated Africans in Sierra Leone," in Jorge Cañizares-Esguerra, Matt D. Childs, and James Sidbury (eds.), *The Black Urban Atlantic in the Age of the Slave Trade* (Philadelphia: University of Pennsylvania Press, 2013), 21–41; and Northrup, *Africa's Discovery of Europe*, 3rd edition (New York: Oxford University Press, 2014), 173–189.

[16] Northrup, "Identity among Liberated Africans," 24.

[17] The problem with this terminology is that it suggests that Liberated Africans were primarily beginning to see themselves as "Africans." Yet what Northrup is really describing is a process in which Liberated Africans "alienated from the rural villages of their homelands ... began to reidentify themselves with the broader population whose fate they shared." Northrup, *Africa's Discovery of Europe*, 174.

society through Anglo-Christian education. More recently, though, Sierra Leonean scholars such as Gibril Cole have reaffirmed the important role of Islam in the development of colonial society. Placing Islam at the center of Sierra Leone historiography is an important corrective in studying a country with a Muslim majority. This study similarly places Yoruba *orisa* worship as central to a large contingent within Sierra Leonean society, and considers the interplay between Christianity, Islam, and African cosmologies in identity formation.

More broadly, scholars of the African diaspora including James Sweet, Toby Green, and Megan Vaughan have reconceptualized the concept of creolization as a far more complex and dynamic set of sociocultural changes than the unidirectional adoption of certain Western and European linguistic, aesthetic, and cultural practices by Africans removed from their societies of birth.[18] While this study does not attempt to contribute to the extensive historiography on creolization, it does highlight one particular challenge within the literature: the lack of chronological specificity in tracing such processes of cultural and societal change over decades and centuries.[19] This book presents a more geographically and temporally specific case study. Liberated Africans arrived over a period of fifty-six years and settled across a single peninsula. Assessing this group of Africans who experienced enslavement, emancipation, and colonization affords a more nuanced investigation into whether creolization involved people dramatically

---

[18] Ira Berlin, "From Creole to African: Atlantic Creoles and the Origins of African-American Society in Mainland North America," *William and Mary Quarterly*, 53.2 (1999): 251–288; Linda Heywood and John Thornton, *Central Africans, Atlantic Creoles, and the Foundation of the Americas, 1586–1660* (New York: Cambridge University Press, 2008); Jane Landers, *Atlantic Creoles in the Age of Revolutions* (Cambridge, MA: Harvard University Press, 2010); Megan Vaughan, *Creating the Creole Island: Slavery in Eighteenth Century Mauritius* (Durham: Duke University Press, 2005). A further complication arises from whether "creolization" is taken as a metaphor for cultural mixtures, or more concretely for the emergence of a creolized language. The latter approach is adopted by Pier M. Larson, *Ocean of Letters: Language and Creolization in an Indian Ocean Diaspora* (Cambridge: Cambridge University Press, 2009); and Toby Green, *The Rise of the Trans-Atlantic Slave Trade in West Africa* (New York: Cambridge University Press, 2012).

[19] As Sidbury and Cañizares-Esguerra remark, "it sometimes seems that generalization [about creolization and ethnogenesis] leap ahead of the careful empirical mapping of experiences on which they should be based." James Sidbury and Jorge Cañizares-Esguerra, "Mapping Ethnogenesis in the Early Modern Atlantic," *William and Mary Quarterly*, 68.2 (April 2011): 182.

realtering their lifeways and terms of self-identification, or if this was a cross-generational process.

The various uses of "creole" and "creolization" are further complicated by the fact that the descendants of Liberated Africans in Sierra Leone are known as the Krio or Creole people.[20] The term has assumed ethnic connotations to describe a population of mixed ancestry in and around Freetown. Sierra Leonean scholars such as Akintola Wyse and Gibril Cole insist that the term "Krio" derives not from "creole" but from the Yoruba language, attributing it variously to the Yoruba akiriyo ("those who go about paying visits") or kiri ("to trade").[21] The etymology of the term is not in itself important, except for its implications for historical analysis. By attributing a different etymology to Krio, the meaning of the term is detached from colonial birth. The corollary is that Liberated Africans could have conceivably self-identified as "Krio," whereas earlier scholarship suggested that the term applied only to their "creole" offspring. The consensus largely remains that an overarching "Krio" or "creole" identity, encompassing the descendants of Liberated Africans and settlers, only emerged in the last decades of the nineteenth century.

While this study explores processes of cultural and social adjustment that are often labeled as creolization, it is not a study of the Krio/Creole.[22] The following chapters focus primarily on those who experienced enslavement in Africa and British naval interdiction. In doing so,

---

[20] See David Skinner and Barbara E. Harrell-Bond, "Misunderstandings Arising from the Use of the Term 'Creole' in the Literature on Sierra Leone," *Africa*, 47.3 (1977): 305–319; A. J. G. Wyse, "On Misunderstandings Arising from the Use of the Term 'Creole' in the Literature on Sierra Leone," *Africa*, 49.4 (1979): 405–415; Christopher Fyfe, "The Term 'Creole': A Footnote to a Footnote," *Africa*, 50.4 (1980): 422; David Skinner and Barbara E. Harrell-Bond, "Creoles: A Final Comment," *Africa*, 51.3 (1981): 787.

[21] Akintola Wyse, *The Krio of Sierra Leone: An Interpretive History* (Washington, DC: Howard University Press, 1991); Cole, *Krio of West Africa*, 18–19. The Krio/creole debate is a rather fruitless discussion that cannot be fully engaged with here. The argument that "Krio" derives from Yoruba is unconvincing for several reasons, not the least of which is that neither Wyse nor Cole provide any evidence from the nineteenth century. For the latest contribution to this debate, see Ian Hancock, "On the Origin and Application of the Word Krio," *The Journal of Sierra Leone Studies*, 5.2 (March 2016).

[22] For the history of the Krio, see Leo Spitzer, *The Creoles of Sierra Leone: Responses to Colonialism, 1870–1945* (Madison: University of Wisconsin Press, 1974); Wyse, *Krio of Sierra Leone*; Dixon-Fyle and Cole (eds.), *New Perspectives on the Krio*; Cole, *Krio of West Africa*.

this study disaggregates how Liberated Africans and their descendants – generations of significantly different socialization and life histories – identified among their contemporaries, and with institutions of church and state. Among this generation there is no evidence that they referred to themselves as "Krio" or "creole," or saw themselves as a single, unified people.

Like enslaved Africans throughout the diaspora, Liberated Africans self-identified in ways that enable an analysis of identity formation. They used a range of ethnonyms and "national" designations, including Aku, Igbo, Calabar, Popo, Cosso, Congo, Hausa, Moko, and others. These terms were common in Sierra Leone not just because they indicated where people came from and the languages they spoke, but also because they reflected how people self-identified. These designations were often new, diasporic coinages that demonstrate that people did not self-identify as they had previously done in their homelands. Many of the descriptive terms – from Aku to Cosso to Moko – had no saliency in the regions from where Liberated Africans of these "nations" had come from. Even terms of an older genealogy such as Hausa took on different meanings in a new setting. Group identities were defined and redefined through the process of forced migration, resettlement, quotidian interactions among recaptives, and the relationship with missionaries and the colonial state.

Ethnicity and Identity

The following chapters examine patterns of ethnic identification in the context of diaspora and the colonial and missionary encounter. Ethnicity has been a topic of great discussion within the historiographies of Africa and the diaspora, yet these two fields have approached the topic in very different ways. Africanists have interrogated the degree to which colonial administrators, along with missionaries and ethnographers, created or augmented identities as a technique for ruling. Studies of the slave trade and the diaspora have looked at the prevalence of certain ethnicities in diasporic societies, and the dynamic realignment of identities that forced migrations engendered. Scholars of the diaspora have used records mentioning certain ethnic groups to trace the origins of slaves in Africa to specific regions of the Americas, and their subsequent cultural impacts. But much like the best work by historians of Africa, scholars of the diaspora approach Euro-American documents that contain "ethnic" information regarding Africans with a hermeneutic of suspicion in order to provide a careful reading of how Africans in diaspora viewed themselves and others in colonial society.

Paul Lovejoy has argued that the scale of the transatlantic trade over three hundred years "enabled the maintenance and transformation of cultures and traditions in what can be thought of as a series of overlapping diasporas, in which ethnicity was a factor in the identity of those enslaved and their descendants."[23] Analyzing ethnicity as a facet of identity involves the double challenge of forming a workable definition of ethnicity – a difficult task for the present, let alone the past – and then interrogating the veracity of certain ethnic labels while exploring how these identities changed over time. Both Lovejoy and Michael Gomez provide definitions of ethnicity that are precise while fully recognizing the diverse bases of ethnic affiliation and belonging. Lovejoy has defined ethnicity as "a characteristic of a group of people, in which groups sharing common ethnicity are usually perceived to be largely biographically self-perpetuating, to share fundamental cultural values, to comprise a common field of communication and interaction, and to identify themselves and be identified by others as constituting a recognizable group."[24] Gomez has similarly defined ethnicity as "networks of sociocultural communications" that "at times can be interchanged with community, but lacks elasticity: bound by language, culture, territorial association, and historical derivation." Gomez adds that implicit in the concept of ethnicity is the determination of that which is unique about a group of people.[25]

This book employs the concept of ethnicity as defined by Lovejoy and Gomez. But I am simultaneously mindful of recent critiques of the concept of ethnicity and its invocation by historians of Africa and the diaspora. Joseph Miller argues that ethnicity in Africa "provides only the most limited and misleading approximation of the creative, fluid series of identities that people in fact constructed to replace the ties

---

[23] Paul E. Lovejoy, "Ethnic Designations of the Slave Trade and the Reconstruction of the History of Trans-Atlantic Slavery," in Lovejoy and David V. Trotman (eds.), *Trans-Atlantic Dimensions of Ethnicity in the African Diaspora* (London: Continuum, 2003), 9.
[24] Ibid., 10.
[25] Michael Gomez, *Exchanging Our Country Marks: The Transformation of African Identities in the Colonial and Antebellum South* (Chapel Hill: University of North Carolina Press, 1998), 6.

disrupted by their enslavement."[26] The issue, as Miller points out, is the inconsistent meaning ethnicity has taken as scholars appropriate the term for their own purposes. Philip Morgan adds that ethnicity is often used as a stand-in for some kind of group (*ethnos*) as a residual term when too little is known about the actual group to label it more precisely.[27] Chapman, McDonald, and Tonkin note that the term emerged from the long-standing trend of English sociolinguistics to look to Romance languages (in this case the Greek *ethnos*) to "fancify a plain idea or expression." The result was a somewhat murky intellectual term that tries to delimit human groups.[28]

The concept of ethnicity, even when used cautiously by scholars, often retains a familiar bias toward "difference" and "otherness." But David Eltis, rather than seeing ethnicity as a particularly African trait, and one imposed under colonialism, has argued that ethnicity characterized both the European and African worlds.[29] In other words, the conception of ethnicity was neither "Western" nor "modern."[30] Rather, it was what John Comaroff has referred to as "the act of drawing boundaries among populations."[31] The conclusions of Chapman, McDonald, and Tonkin, however, hold that ethnicity "is a term that only makes sense in a context of relativities, of processes of identification, and that nevertheless aspires to concrete and positive status both as an attribute and as an analytical 'concept.'"[32]

Historians of colonial Africa have remained justifiably skeptical of "ethnicity" and "nation" in Africa and the African diaspora in the centuries before the Scramble for Africa. Broadly, this literature argues

---

[26] Joseph Miller, "Retention, Reinvention, and Remembering: Restoring Identities through Enslavement in Angola and under Slavery in Brazil," in José C. Curto and Paul E. Lovejoy (eds.), *Enslaving Connections: Changing Cultures of African and Brazil during the Era of Slavery* (Amherst, NY: Humanity Books, 2004), 87.

[27] Philip D. Morgan, "Cultural Implications of the Atlantic Slave Trade: African Regional Origins, American Destinations and New World Developments," *Slavery and Abolition*, 18 (1997): 135.

[28] Elizabeth Tonkin, Maryon McDonald, and Malcolm Chapman (eds.), *History and Ethnicity* (London: Routledge, 1989), 11.

[29] David Eltis, *The Rise of African Slavery in the Americas* (Cambridge: Cambridge University Press, 2000).

[30] Lovejoy, "Ethnic Designations," 12.

[31] John L. Comaroff, "The End of Anthropology, Again: On the Future of an In/Discipline," *American Anthropologist*, 112.4 (2010): 531.

[32] Tonkin et al., *History and Ethnicity*, 16.

Ethnicity and Identity 13

that before colonialism Africans did not belong to fixed ethnic groups, but participated in fluid, overlapping social networks of kin, agemates, clients, neighbors, and chiefdoms.[33] Many of these works draw their case studies from southern or eastern Africa, but often make generalizations about the continent. Within West Africa, Jean-Loup Amselle's conclusions based on extensive fieldwork in Mali, Guinea, and Côte d'Ivoire were that societies, cultures, or ethnic groups called Fulani, Bambara, Mandingo, Senufo, or Minyanka, "far from constituting isolated identities, comprise systems or paradigms." Amselle argues that it was only with colonial conquest that distinct ethnic groups with these designations emerged, along with distinct political and religious systems. Missionaries, district officials, and fieldworkers "congealed identities" that were subsequently reappropriated by local social actors in a process of "working misunderstanding." These terms became "onomastic emblems" that actors appropriated and abandoned in aleatory fashion according to political contingencies.[34]

Some scholars of African history have argued that historians of the slave trade have reified colonial categories, though the existence of these ethnic designations is found long before these regions of Africa were formally colonized. Thomas Spear points out that the "strict constructivism" school of ethnic "invention" in colonial Africa is unable to account for pre-colonial ethnicities and fails to consider the limitations of invented traditions.[35] Attempts to identify people with ethnic categories in West Africa dates back not only before colonial rule, but also to the opening of the Atlantic trade.[36] Arguments that

---

[33] See, e.g., Leroy Vail (ed.), *The Creation of Tribalism in Southern Africa* (Berkeley: University of California Press, 1989); Mahmood Mamdani, *Citizen and Subject: Contemporary Africa and the Legacy of Late Colonialism* (Princeton: Princeton University Press, 1996).

[34] Jean-Loup Amselle, *Mestizo Logics: Anthropology and Identity in Africa and Elsewhere* (Stanford: Stanford University Press, 1998), xi–xiii, 43.

[35] Thomas Spear, "Neo-Traditionalism and the Limits of Invention in British Colonial Africa," *Journal of African History*, 44 (2003): 18.

[36] The etymologies of terms like "Hausa," "Bamabara," and "Yoruba" have been traced to questions of the legitimacy of enslavement and classifying people for purposes of protection and oppression. Paul E. Lovejoy, "Enslaved Africans in the Diaspora," in Lovejoy (ed.), *Identity in the Shadow of Slavery* (London: Continuum, 2000), 11; Paul Nugent, "Putting the History Back into Ethnicity: Enslavement, Religion, and Cultural Brokerage in the Construction of Mandinka/Jola and Ewe/Agotime Identities in West Africa, c. 1650–1930," *Comparative Studies in Society and History*, 50.4 (October 2008): 920–948.

European colonizers "invented" ethnic identities give colonial officials far too much credit as social engineers. Worse still, such interpretations treat African populations as incredibly credulous, willing to accept whatever label and grouping European colonizers projected on them. Moreover, it is now recognized that regular social and economic intercourses and population movements were similarly active in forming and transforming identities in the pre-colonial era.[37] This was certainly so in the nineteenth century, a period in which the homelands of many Liberated Africans faced unprecedented violence, dislocation, and political crisis.

Parés reflects many current perspectives in arguing that an ethnic community "is not a physical or geographical entity but a symbolic and dynamic construction, and given the situational and relational nature of ethnic identification, the boundaries of these kinds of social entities are always permeable and diffuse."[38] Similarly, Mariana Candido observes that in West Central Africa people often adopted new identities when confronted with an expansionist state, being incorporated into those powerful entities, enslaved, or forced to relocate. Candido concludes that identities related to state or language affiliation "were superimposed on those of village and lineage, showing how people had multiple identifies rather than the one since attributed to them by Europeans who could not conceive of identities as flexible and socially constructed."[39]

The study of ethnicity has thus been placed within larger discussions of identity or, rather, *identities* as fluid, multiple, and overlapping. Yet as Frederick Cooper and Rogers Brubaker argue, the term "identity," as used in social science literature, faces many of the same conceptual issues as ethnicity. First is the assumption that identity is something that all people have, seek, construct, and negotiate.

---

[37] Femi James Kolapo "Ethnicity and Identity at the Niger–Benue Confluence during the Nineteenth Century Nupe Jihad," in Olatunji Ojo and Nadine Hunt (eds.), *Slavery in Africa and the Caribbean: A History of Slavery and Identity since the 18th Century* (New York: I. B. Taurus, 2012), 10.

[38] Luis Nicolau Parés, "The Hula 'Problem': Ethnicity on the Pre-colonial Slave Coast," in Toyin Falola and Matt D. Childs (eds.), *The Changing Worlds of Atlantic Africa: Essays in Honor of Robin Law* (Durham, NC: Carolina Academic Press, 2009), 323–346.

[39] Mariana Candido, *An African Slaving Port and the Atlantic World: Benguela and Its Hinterland* (Cambridge: Cambridge University Press, 2013), 13.

Second, the idiom of identity "saddles us with a blunt, flat, undifferentiated vocabulary" when used to conceptualize all forms of affiliations, experiences of commonality, and forms of belonging.[40] Cooper and Brubaker add that social scientists have problematically conceptualized identity as both "strong" and "weak." Strong conceptions of identity posit that identity is something all people or all groups have (or ought to have), that people or groups can have an identity without being aware of it, and that collective identities imply strong notions of group boundedness and homogeneity. This tendency is apparent in many earlier works on ethnicity in Africa. More recent theorizing of identities as multiple, fragmented, and fluid has moved away from facile assertions of identity as sameness over time. Yet definitions of identity often become too convoluted in explaining what identity actually is. The recent emphasis on multiple, fluid, and overlapping, identities that were continuously reimagined suggests a chameleon-like quality of constant reinvention. It also raises the question: Did Africans in the diaspora spend as much time thinking about who they were as recent social histories of the diaspora suggest?

Immanuel Wallerstein has defined identity as "the dynamic product of a dialectical interaction between self-definition and ascribed or imposed definitions."[41] Because identity is a dynamic process, Cooper and Brubaker have suggested a series of terms that potentially avoid heterogeneous understandings of "identity." First, they propose the active term *identification*, a noun which invites us to specify the agents that do the identifying and consider the contexts in which one identifies oneself.[42] *Identification* also connotes a basic distinction between self-identification and the identification and categorization of oneself by others. Peter Mark adds that "no community, no social group, can articulate its identity independently of the outside world" and that those "who are not members of a given group map help to create

---

[40] Frederick Cooper, *Colonialism in Question: Theory, Knowledge, History* (Berkeley: University of California Press, 2005), 60.
[41] Immanuel Wallerstein, "Ethnicity and National Integration in West Africa," *Cahiers d'Etudes Africaines*, no. 3 (October 1969): 129–138.
[42] Cooper, *Colonialism in Question*, 71.

and revise the identity of the group." Mark concludes that identity thus "entails a dialogue or a discourse between members of the group in question and members of other groups with whom they enter into contact."[43]

Cooper and Brubaker have further suggested that *self-understanding* is a preferable alternative to *identity*, since it is a situational term that better designates one's sense of who one is. This study invokes the terminology of identification and self-understanding since identity can be understood only in terms of the interplay between self-definition and ascribed or imposed definitions. This interplay between self-understanding and identification was evident in the context of nineteenth-century Sierra Leone. Colonial and missionary officials sought to identify and categorize the populations they governed, based primarily on language. In their inquiries they uncovered a range of terms that people used to self-identify and to identify others. For the Liberated Africans themselves, like all victims of transatlantic slavery, the alienation of enslavement and the forced migration over land and sea to a British colony was an experience that forced them to consider how they understood themselves and their surroundings.

These "uprootings and regroundings" were fundamental to processes most commonly described as "identity formation" and "ethnogenesis," as individuals came to identify as members of an ethnolinguistic community in new and often broader, more-encompassing ways.[44] This process was shaped by the palimpsest memories of home, violence, and enslavement combined with the exigencies of seeking out support systems in an alien, colonial setting. This is a study about how people saw themselves in new ways based on experiences and new contexts. The experiences were the anguish of enslavement and the Middle Passage; the context was Britain's first colony in tropical Africa and one of missionary Protestantism's first fields of operation.

---

[43] Peter Mark, *"Portuguese" Style and Luso-African Identity: Precolonial Senegambia, Sixteenth–Nineteenth Centuries* (Bloomington: Indiana University Press, 2002), 2–3.
[44] Byrd, *Captives and Voyagers*, 7.

Chapter Outline

The Introduction traverses the early history of the colony from its founding in 1787 to 1807. This history has received ample treatment elsewhere.[45] Rather than re-rehearse the colony's early history at length, the Introduction emphasizes the origins and cultures of Sierra Leone's colonists in the years prior to the arrival of the first Liberated Africans. The historiography on Sierra Leone presents a dichotomy between the first three waves of immigrants from London, Nova Scotia, and Jamaica, referred to collectively as "settlers" and the later involuntary arrival of Liberated Africans. The standard interpretation of nineteenth-century Sierra Leone is that the three cohorts of voluntary migrants formed a cohesive society into which Liberated Africans were "incorporated" or "absorbed." The Introduction argues that this common narrative of Liberated African incorporation and socialization into a pre-existing settler society is untenable, given the preponderance of emancipated Africans arriving on an annual basis and the nature of their interaction with settlers.

Chapter 1 traces the geographic origins of Liberated Africans landed at Sierra Leone. The chapter draws on a unique collection of Liberated African registers found in the Sierra Leone Public Archives, which contain the names of 81,745 Africans landed at Freetown. The strength of this source is that African naming practices are often very regionally specific, and identifying their regions of origin greatly expands our knowledge of how the slave trade operated within Africa.[46] This chapter combines this methodology with other

---

[45] See Suzanne Schwarz, "From Company Administration to Crown Control: Experimentation and Adaptation in Sierra Leone in the Late Eighteenth and Early Nineteenth Centuries," in Lovejoy and Schwarz (eds.), *Slavery, Abolition, and the Transition to Colonialism in Sierra Leone*, 163–188. For foundational studies on Sierra Leone, see Fyfe, *History of Sierra Leone*; Arthur T. Porter, *Creoledom: A Study of the Development of Freetown Society* (Oxford: Oxford University Press, 1963); John Peterson, *Province of Freedom: A History of Sierra Leone, 1787–1870* (London: Faber & Faber, 1969).

[46] For a discussion of these sources and methodology, see Richard Anderson, Alex Borucki, Daniel Domingues da Silva, David Eltis, Paul Lachance, Philip Misevich, and Olatunji Ojo, "Using African Names to Identify the Origins of Captives in the Transatlantic Slave Trade: Crowd-Sourcing and the Registers of Liberated Africans, 1808–1862," *History in Africa*, 40.1 (2013): 165–191; and David Eltis and G. Ugo Nwokeji, "The Roots of the African Diaspora: Methodological Considerations in the Analysis of the Names in the Liberated

missionary and colonial documents such as census data, missionary school registers, and linguistic studies conducted in nineteenth-century Sierra Leone. I argue that the overwhelming majority of Liberated Africans came from a limited number of identifiable ethnolinguistic groups, principal among which were speakers of the Yoruba, Igbo, Gbe, Hausa, Mende, and Efik languages. Based on these sources, I estimate that perhaps 33,000 Liberated Africans, or approximately one-third of all Africans landed at Freetown, were Yoruba speakers enslaved in the aftermath of the fall of the Oyo Empire. Igbo speakers were similarly prominent among those brought on slave ships from the Bight of Biafra, and constituted perhaps one-fourth of those landed at Freetown.

Chapter 2 complements the previous chapter by switching the level of analysis from macro to micro history. It follows the forced migration of enslaved Africans from their homelands through their sale into the Atlantic trade and their interception by the British Navy. I argue that the voyages of Liberated Africans to Sierra Leone were in many ways analogous to those experienced on unimpeded voyages to the Americas in the nineteenth century in terms of duration and the omnipresence of death and disease. I also introduce the argument, further elaborated on in subsequent chapters, that this experience was a crucible during which "shipmates" forged deep, lasting connections. Historians of the African diaspora have acknowledged the importance of "shipmate bonds" in diasporic societies. Yet the ability to trace specific groups of captives who experienced the Middle Passage together has been hampered by a dearth of documentary evidence within the Americas. In the case of the Sierra Leone peninsula, there are numerous documented cases that show the centrality of shipmate bonds and how such bonds both intersected and transcended ethnolinguistic ties.

Chapter 3 continues the narrative arc of Liberated Africans' journeys from homeland to diaspora. It traces the settlement of emancipated men, women, and children in the colony, emphasizing the cultural implications of particular settlement policies in operation at different times. Most Liberated Africans were sent to one of twenty-six villages established across the Sierra Leone peninsula in the vicinity of Freetown. The Liberated African registers record settlement for tens of

African Registers of Sierra Leone and Havana," *History in Africa*, 29 (2002): 368.

thousands of Liberated Africans, allowing us to trace captives from particular ports of embarkation to particular villages in Sierra Leone. This detailed documentation of settlement is unique within the African diaspora and offers insights into the quotidian interactions through which diasporic identities were born.

While the first three chapters explore the regional origins of Liberated Africans and the experiences of their forced migrations to Sierra Leone, the later chapters explore the new communities and identities these migrants forged. Chapter 4 investigates the multifarious "nations" that were at the center of Liberated African identity formation and political life. Within Liberated African society, Africans formed communities based on common language and experience, referred to in colonial and missionary documents as "nations." The chapter scrutinizes common national terms, looking at their varying meanings from the perspectives of Liberated Africans, missionaries, and colonial officials. The chapter's discussion fits within larger debates over the meaning of ethnicity in colonial Africa and the diaspora and how identity was shaped by particular imperial contexts. In the Americas, the slave work regime, impediments to mobility and communication, mortality, and the challenges of marriage and family formation circumscribed the vitality of diaspora "nations." In Sierra Leone, the relative freedom of communication, movement, and assembly allowed members of these nations the ability to congregate and organize in ways impossible in a slave society.

Missionaries and colonial officials also shaped the emergence and consolidation of ethnolinguistically defined "nations" within colonial society, though in an ancillary role to Liberated Africans themselves. The efforts of missionaries to study and classify languages contributed to both identification of nations and their consolidation of self-ascription. Over time, Church Missionary Society (CMS) missionaries came to see Liberated Africans as a resource to unlock the linguistic complexities of sub-Saharan Africa. Sierra Leone became a linguistic laboratory in which missionaries undertook pioneering work in the study of many West African languages. This chapter examines the intersection of ethnicity and ethnogenesis in the context of diaspora and the colonial and missionary encounter.

After exploring the etymology and meaning of national categories in Sierra Leone, Chapter 5 looks at the leadership and organization of these nations. Within the historiography, African diaspora "nations" are often interpreted as nostalgic recreations of particular homelands, defined by linguistic affinity. This chapter demonstrates how national organizations in Sierra Leone were not simply about perpetuating language and culture in exile, but were forms of communal welfare born out of the exigencies of displacement to an unfamiliar setting. "National" identities were also political identities as Liberated Africans were able to politically mobilize to a greater degree than slaves in the Americas. This chapter explores how these groups organized for particular purposes, how they were led, and how they made demands on the colonial government.

Chapter 6 focuses more specifically on the nation that colonial and missionary officials agreed was the most conspicuous within Sierra Leonean society: the Aku. Most studies of Sierra Leone have asserted that "Aku" was a colonial term for Yoruba peoples from present-day Nigeria and have echoed contemporary observations treating them either implicitly or explicitly as a majority among the Liberated African population. While the opening chapter of this study disproves this assertion, it nevertheless raises the question of why colonial officials and historians alike have shared this perception about the size and singular influence of the Yoruba population in the colony.

This chapter considers the role of language in shaping Aku identity, and the interaction between Islam, Christianity, and "traditional" *oriṣa* worship in defining the Aku. It then traces the shifting relationship between diaspora and homeland, as Aku merchants and missionaries returned to coastal towns near their ancestral homes after 1838, bringing with them a broader sense of Yoruba ethnicity. The chapter contributes to the historiography tracing the tremendous linguistic, cultural, and religious impact of Yoruba speakers around the Atlantic basin and the role of diaspora and return in the formation of Yoruba identity.[47] Scholars of Yoruba identity have helped reconceptualize the relationship between homeland and diaspora. J. Lorand Matory, Robin Law, and Kristin Mann have called for a nonlinear interpretation of diasporas, in which a dialectical approach is taken to the relationship between diasporas and homelands around the Atlantic perimeter.[48] This chapter argues that what it meant to be Aku in Sierra

---

[47] Toyin Falola and Matt D. Childs (eds.), *The Yoruba Diaspora in the Atlantic World* (Bloomington: University of Indiana Press, 2004).
[48] James Lorand Matory, *Black Atlantic Religion: Tradition, Transnationalism, and Matriarchy in the Afro-Brazilian Candomblé* (Princeton: Princeton

Leone and what it meant to be Yoruba in Yorubaland were defined and reinforced through a dialogue along the West African coast.

Chapter 7 follows the buildup, instigation, suppression, and legacies of the Cobolo War, an 1832 conflagration that marked the largest flashpoint between Liberated Africans and the colonial state. During the "war" a group of "Mahomedan Aku" (Yoruba Muslims), who had previously vacated the colony, temporarily defeated a colonial militia instructed to bring the émigrés back to Freetown. The actions of these Aku Liberated Africans were contemporaneous with a pattern of violent resistance to colonial oppression instigated by Yoruba speakers around the Atlantic world in the 1820s and 1830s. Although eventually defeated, the conflict at Cobolo had long-standing legacies. In the months and years after the battle – and a failed attempt to try the leaders for treason – British officials embarked on a campaign of intimidation and repression, repeatedly attempting to expel a community seeking religious autonomy in a Christian colony. This chapter traces the relationship between Muslim and ethnic identity in the context of colonial oppression, the role of Islam in shaping the conceptual meaning of "Aku," and the endurance of Muslim Liberated African communities over generations.

The Conclusion moves chronologically forward, exploring the connections that the colony-born offspring of Liberated Africans felt toward their parents' societies of birth, their forms of communal association, and their cultural and religious practices. While the emphasis of the study is on the generation that experienced the Middle Passage, themes such as community and identity do not lend themselves well to concrete end dates. The Conclusion argues not only that certain customs and forms of communal identification survived the westernizing and Christianizing influences of colonial life, but that the late nineteenth century saw a resurgence of such customs and associations. At a time of growing disillusionment with the British colonial project, the first- and second-generation offspring of those who came to Freetown on slave ships looked to the languages, dress, and community organizations of their forebears. This Conclusion argues that processes of ethnogenesis and creolization cannot simply be seen as a linear

---

University Press, 2005); Robin Law and Kristin Mann, "West Africa and the Atlantic Community: The Case of the Slave Coast," *William and Mary Quarterly*, Third Series, 56.2 (April 1999): 307–334.

process in which certain vestiges can be traced across generations to certain regions of the African continent.

Background: Sierra Leone, 1787–1807

While this study focuses on the years 1808–1863 and on the population of Liberated Africans who formed a majority of Sierra Leone's inhabitants in this period, it is necessary to first trace the earlier history of the colony into which they arrived. In 1787, Granville Sharp and the Committee for the Relief of the Black Poor in London founded a "Province of Freedom" in West Africa. The colony's British proponents viewed it as a practical experiment in creating a post-slave society two decades before Britain's abolition of the slave trade was achieved. The first colonists were some four hundred black Londoners, collectively known as the "black poor." Many were runaways or refugees of Great Britain's war in America, living destitute in the imperial capital.[49] Others had been enslaved to returning West Indian planters or to seamen discharged in London after serving on British ships. These black Londoners and their British benefactors negotiated a plan for a settler colony, choosing the western coast of Africa as the preferred location.

The 377 survivors of the 411 who embarked in England arrived at the Sierra Leone estuary in May 1787. They disembarked on the southern side of the river mouth that forms Africa's largest natural harbor. The early settlement fared poorly, depleted by death and desertion before being razed in a dispute with the local Temne leader, King Jimmy, in December 1789. Those who survived scattered into the surrounding countryside. Destroyed within three years of its foundation, Granville Sharp resurrected the colony as a stock company, finding support among abolitionists willing to invest in an African settlement to foster "legitimate" trade.

The need to repopulate the colony was met, fortuitously, by the arrival in London of Thomas Peters, a representative of the Black Loyalist community of Nova Scotia and New Brunswick, which was seeking to relocate to a more favorable part of the British Empire.

---

[49] For the "black poor," see Stephen J. Braidwood, *Black Poor and White Philanthropists: London's Blacks and the Foundation of the Sierra Leone Settlement, 1786–1791* (Liverpool: Liverpool University Press, 1994), and more recently, Byrd, *Captives and Voyagers*.

The directors of the Sierra Leone Company received Peters's petition enthusiastically, sending the abolitionist naval lieutenant John Clarkson to Halifax to recruit emigrants. The subsequent migration of some 1,200 settlers from Nova Scotia and New Brunswick to Sierra Leone in 1792 was the seminal moment in the colony's early history. Most migrants were former American slaves who had sided with the British during the American Revolution. Even before departing for Sierra Leone, they had traversed a fraught passage from southern plantations, primarily to New York City and Charleston, and boarded government ships as the British evacuated in 1783.[50]

The Nova Scotians refounded the abandoned Granville Town; some scattered survivors of the first settlement returned. The new colony was dedicated and, as the directors instructed, named Freetown. Like its predecessor, the new venture was hindered by climate, unpreparedness, dissent, and the tensions inherent in "purchasing" land from the surrounding Temne population. But the number of new colonists, relatively balanced sex ratios, and the shared experience of multiple migrations helped them create a more enduring settlement.

This larger population put the settlement on more secure footing, even more so with the arrival of 551 Jamaican Maroons in November 1800. The Maroons of Trelawney Town, in the mountainous northwest of Jamaica, had maintained their own communities beyond British control before they were defeated in the Maroon War of 1795–1796. In the shadow of the recent and ongoing slave revolt on neighboring Saint-Domingue, a concerned Jamaican assembly and plantocracy sent them to Nova Scotia in 1796. Like the Black Loyalists, they successfully petitioned the British government for passage elsewhere. Maroons in Nova Scotia agitated for a new location, for reasons more related to climate than sentiment toward Sierra Leone.[51] Like the Black Poor and Nova Scotians before them, the coalescence of their desires and British intentions brought them to West Africa.

---

[50] The "Black Loyalists" have been studied extensively by James St. G. Walker, *The Black Loyalists: The Search for a Promised Land in Nova Scotia and Sierra Leone 1783–1870* (London: Longman, 1976); Ellen Gibson Wilson, *The Loyal Blacks* (New York: Capricorn Books, 1976); and Maya Jasanoff, *Liberty's Exiles: American Loyalists in the Revolutionary War* (New York: Knopf, 2011).

[51] See Ruma Chopra, *Almost Home: Maroons between Slavery and Freedom in Jamaica, Nova Scotia, and Sierra Leone* (New Haven, CT: Yale University Press, 2018).

These three waves of migrants had varying connections to the African continent. While some Black Poor had been born in Africa, the idea of a "return" rarely appears in documents as a motivation for placing the colony in West Africa, as opposed to Nova Scotia or the West Indies.[52] Among the Nova Scotians, perhaps one-quarter of those who traveled to Sierra Leone had been born in West or West Central Africa. One settler, Frank Peters, was born near the future site of Freetown, while another, John Kizell, was enslaved and sold at the nearby Sherbro when he was only twelve.[53] John Gordon, a Methodist leader among the Nova Scotians, was a Koranko, born 130 miles inland and sold at Bunce Island in the Sierra Leone River estuary when he was about fifteen. But the majority of those referred to as Nova Scotians had been born into the slave societies of Virginia, Maryland, South Carolina, or Georgia.[54] Even those born in Africa had likely left while young and spent two or three decades in the Americas. Despite William Wilberforce's suggestion that it would be tactful to refer to the Nova Scotians as "Africans" instead of "Blacks or Negroes," they called themselves Nova Scotians and often referred to a Britain they had never seen as "home."[55]

Place of birth and experiences of slavery were not the only distinctions between settlers and the later-arriving Africans rescued from slave ships. The Nova Scotians comprised communities of Baptist, Wesleyan Methodist, and Huntingdonian Methodist congregations. By contrast, the Maroons, especially the older part of the population, were indifferent to Christianity, and much has been made of their rejection of monogamy. As Walker notes, the cultural contrasts and Nova Scotian sense of superiority led the groups to remain in their own distinct sections of town with minimal social mixing.[56] This animosity was established immediately. The Maroon transport ship arrived in Freetown harbor during an incipient rebellion of Nova Scotians against the government. Though it was a rebellion against government taxation, laws, and land rights – concerns that the Maroons would

---

[52] Braidwood, *Black Poor and White Philanthropists*, 84.
[53] Wilson, *Loyal Blacks*, 219, 242.
[54] James Sidbury, "'African' Settlers in the Founding of Freetown," in Lovejoy and Schwarz (eds.), *Slavery, Abolition, and the Transition to Colonialism in Sierra Leone*, 129, 136.
[55] Wilson, *Loyal Blacks*, 241. [56] Walker, *Black Loyalists*, 251.

Background: Sierra Leone, 1787–1807

have shared – the Maroon leadership decided to fight the rebels in order to ensure the immediate allocation of their own promised land.

By 1807 the colony was the product of three waves of voluntary migrants, as well as those who gravitated over land to the new settlement. In that year, two pieces of legislation dramatically altered the colony's trajectory. The British Parliament passed the Act to Abolish the Slave Trade in March 1807. Within five months, royal assent was given to a bill transferring the indebted Sierra Leone colony to British Crown control. The establishment of a British Crown Colony in 1808 effectively represented the beginning of the creation of the British Empire in Tropical Africa. The colony, at the time of transfer to the Crown, was focused around Freetown and its approximately 2,000 inhabitants. Alongside the "settler" population was a regular ebb and flow of traders, including many Muslims.[57]

The ceremony transferring power to the British government took place on New Year's Day, 1808. Soon after, Freetown became the base for a Vice-Admiralty Court and, from 1819 onward, Courts of Mixed Commission.[58] An order-in-council of March 16, 1808, established the Vice-Admiralty Court "for the trial and adjudication of any captures of slaves offered as prizes." The Africans on board were to be enlisted, apprenticed to members of the settler population, or "disposed of according to the true meaning of the Abolition Act."[59] This "true meaning" was not elaborated on, leaving its interpretation to Sierra Leone's governors over the next half-century. Ships of the Royal Navy patrolled the West African coast, and Freetown became the base for a permanent West Africa squadron. In the history of British abolition, Sierra Leone was where humanitarian campaign became human experience. This experience was simultaneously an act of emancipation and colonization, as freed slaves were expected to conform to the

---

[57] See Barbara E. Harrell-Bond, Allen M. Howard, and David E. Skinner, *Community Leadership and the Transformation of Freetown (1801–1976)* (The Hague: Mouton Press, 1978).

[58] For the courts' operations, see Leslie Bethell, "The Mixed Commissions for the Suppression of the Transatlantic Slave Trade in the Nineteenth Century," *Journal of African History*, 7.1 (1966): 79–93; Tara Helfman, "The Court of Vice Admiralty at Sierra Leone and the Abolition of the West African Slave Trade," *The Yale Law Journal*, 115.5 (March 2006): 1122–1156.

[59] Order-in-Council, March 16, 1808, reprinted in the appendix to *African Institution, Fourth Report of the Directors of the African Institution: Read at the Annual General Meeting on the 28th of March, 1810* (London, 1810), 62.

settlement, labor, and ecclesiastical expectations of a benevolent Britain.

The historiographical narrative of Liberated African arrival, settlement, and adaptation to their new surroundings has largely revolved around the terminology of "incorporation" or "absorption" into a pre-existing, westernized settler society.[60] Some historians frame this process as a conscious effort on the part of the emancipated to "gain entry into settler society."[61] There are two crucial problems with this interpretation. The first is the supposition that a cohesive "settler" society existed by 1808. Fyfe, for example, concludes that "by 1808 when the Granville Town Settlers had been twenty-one years in Sierra Leone, the Nova Scotians sixteen, the Maroons eight, they formed together a distinctive community of their own, neither wholly European nor wholly African."[62] Yet as Lovejoy and Schwarz point out, the settlement had "rapidly developed as a multi-ethnic society, as it was the focal point for inward migration by people of African origin and descent dispersed in the British Atlantic world."[63]

This dichotomy of "settlers" versus Liberated Africans ignores the diverse backgrounds and experiences of the first three waves of colonists and those who reached the colony over land. That the Maroons were overwhelmingly of Akan descent and spoke this language within their isolated settlements in Jamaica highlights the limitations of grouping them with the Black Poor and Black Loyalists as "settlers" in contradistinction to Liberated Africans. Indeed, in Sierra Leone British colonial attitudes toward Maroons reflected Anglo-American attitudes toward "Coromantee" (an English term for enslaved Akan-speakers) as enterprising and physically and mentally tough. Acknowledging this distinction is not meant to perpetuate an image of Maroons as the most "purely African" of African Americans – ostensibly

---

[60] Fyfe notes that the term "Settlers" was at time used for the Nova Scotians alone, but he, like many others, used it to describe both Nova Scotian and Maroon. He did so while noting, "Though there was occasional intermarriage and some Maroons went to Nova Scotian churches, they tended to remain hostile communities divided by the memory of their first encounter." Fyfe, *History of Sierra Leone*, 99.
[61] Wyse, *Krio of Sierra Leone*, 5.   [62] Fyfe, *History of Sierra Leone*, 104.
[63] Paul E. Lovejoy and Suzanne, "Sierra Leone in the Eighteenth and Nineteenth Centuries," in Lovejoy and Schwarz (eds.), *Slavery, Abolition, and the Transition to Colonialism in Sierra Leone*, 13.

untainted by the legacies of slavery.[64] Rather, it is to point out the varying experience of having lived in London versus the Maroon communities of rural Jamaica.

The sheer scale of the Liberated African forced migration meant that they could never be incorporated into settler society. By 1811 the population discharged from slave vessels outnumbered Nova Scotians and Maroons combined; the number of enslaved landed in 1816 alone exceeded the entire settler population.[65] By 1820 Liberated Africans constituted 62 percent of Sierra Leone's 12,500 inhabitants. The earlier "settler" immigrants, by contrast, formed only 13 percent.[66] The notion of Liberated African incorporation into settler society within the historiography persists despite the overwhelming demographic and cultural evidence recorded in colonial and missionary sources.[67] For more than three decades the average annual arrival of captives from the Bight of Benin alone rivaled the original settler population. In total, a greater percentage of those who reached Sierra Leone from Atlantic vessels embarked at the ports of Lagos, Bonny, Ouidah, Old Calabar, the Gallinhas, Badagry, and Cabinda, than those who arrived from the Americas and Britain. In other words, Lagos and Bonny, not Halifax and London, were the main ports of departure for those reaching Sierra Leone in its first century of existence.

The narrative of incorporation and absorption persists partly because historians have often characterized the Africans brought to Sierra Leone on captured slave ships as amorphous crowds. Arthur Porter, for example, contended that "the Liberated Africans faced

---

[64] On "Coromantee" and stereotypes of rebelliousness, see Walter C. Rucker, *Gold Coast Diasporas: Identity, Culture, and Power* (Bloomington: Indiana University Press, 2015), 1–9; Jessica A. Krug, "Social Dismemberment, Social (Re)membering: *Obeah* Idioms, Kromanti Identities, and the Trans-Atlantic Politics of Memory, c. 1675–Present," *Slavery & Abolition*, 35.4 (2014): 539.

[65] Christopher Fyfe, "Reform in West Africa: The Abolition of the Slave Trade," in J. F. Ade Ajayi and Michael Crowder (eds.), *History of West Africa*, vol. 2 (New York: Columbia University Press, 1973), 47.

[66] Great Britain, PP 1825 (520) xxv, Sierra Leone, Accounts, Census July 8, 1820.

[67] Arthur Porter, for example, writes, "A Liberated African who was desirous of social mobility in the society as it was then structured had to make the Settler groups his focus of reference, and his process of incorporation into this reference group was facilitated by his success in acquiring the other characteristics which reinforced and strengthened the ascriptive descent status, namely, western education and religion, industrial and economic skills, and western political behaviour." Porter, *Creoledom*, 6.

Settler culture as individuals and isolates," which "rendered the task of acculturation easier to accomplish."[68] While Sierra Leonean–born historians have more recently pointed to the strength of Yoruba cultural heritage in the country, the image persists of Liberated Africans as a heterogeneous "babel of tongues."[69] This interpretation is untenable. As Chapter 1 will show, most Liberated Africans came from a limited number of identifiable ethnolinguistic groups, principal among which were speakers of Yoruba, Igbo, Gbe, Hausa, Mende, and Efik. The number of arriving individuals speaking each of these languages likely far exceeded the settler population of 1807.

Other interpretations stress that settlers provided a "reference point" for those who subsequently arrived in the colony. James Walker, for example, is correct in observing that, for Liberated Africans, "the Nova Scotians represented an achievable social and cultural goal."[70] However, he overstates the process in concluding that "the Liberated African, removed from the source of his own traditional culture, rapidly accepted many aspects of the Nova Scotian alternative and soon became indistinguishable from its originators."[71] The colony's African born-population did not uniformly desire and seek out these goals.[72] If Nova Scotians served as a reference point for Liberated Africans, they often did so from a distance. In 1816, two-thirds of the 10,000 people in the colony lived outside the main town, creating their own communities with minimal interaction with settlers.[73] These communities had little European oversight. What they did have, as Chapter 3 will show, were substantial concentrations of Liberated Africans of similar ethnolinguistic backgrounds.

The argument of the Introduction is therefore threefold. First, the multifarious origins and experiences of Black Poor, Black Loyalists, and Maroons should preclude them being seen as a coherent "settler" society by 1807. Second, the narrative of Liberated African "incorporation" into settler society ignores both the demographic scale of Liberated African arrivals and their patterns of settlement. Third, the

---

[68] Porter, *Creoledom*, 8.   [69] Fyfe, *History of Sierra Leone*, 128.
[70] Walker, *Black Loyalists*, 322.   [71] Ibid., 361.
[72] E. Frances White highlighted Walker's "error by describing the Liberated Africans as imitators of Nova Scotian society." E. Frances White, *Sierra Leone's Settler Women Traders: Women on the Afro-European Frontier* (Ann Arbor: University of Michigan Press, 1987), 26.
[73] Peterson, *Province of Freedom*, 76.

population that arrived in Sierra Leone on intercepted slave ships did not arrive as linguistic and cultural "isolates" malleable to the dominant Anglophone Christian culture of the colony.

The implications of these three arguments is to recalibrate the nineteenth-century history of Sierra Leone away from its founding, if relatively fleeting, pioneer generation. The earliest settlers have been privileged in Sierra Leone historiography to an extent that far outweighs their demographic and cultural influence. Most inhabitants of nineteenth-century Sierra Leone were African born, and had spent no time outside the continent. The following chapters therefore trace the African origins of the vast forced migration that remade the colony of Sierra Leone in the nineteenth century.

1 | *Liberated African Origins and the Nineteenth-Century Slave Trade*

The 99,752 Liberated Africans landed at Sierra Leone from intercepted slave vessels were among 2.8 million Africans who survived the transatlantic slave trade after 1807.[1] Some 450 captured slave vessels were adjudicated in Freetown beginning with the arrival of the US slave ships *Baltimore* and *Eliza* in March 1808, and ending with the disembarkation of 366 people from the *Bela Augusta* in February 1863. A total of 95,640 Africans destined for the Americas were diverted to Freetown from these trans-oceanic vessels.[2] In addition, 4,112 Africans disembarked from intra-African slave trading ships or from raids on coastal barracoons launched from naval vessels.

Where did these Liberated Africans originate from? Answering this question is essential to examining ethnogenesis among Sierra Leone's recaptive population. The capture and adjudication of slave vessels at Freetown engendered a bureaucracy that created voluminous records documenting intercepted slave ships and their captive cargoes. These court records are complemented by colonial census data and linguistic evidence compiled by CMS missionaries. The result is perhaps the best-documented forced migration of Africans to any colony in the Atlantic world.[3]

---

[1] David Eltis and David Richardson (eds.), *Extending the Frontiers: Essays on the New Transatlantic Slave Trade Database* (New Haven, CT: Yale University Press, 2008), 3–68.

[2] Figures for intra-African slaving voyages or naval raids on barracoons are compiled from the Sierra Leone-based registers (volumes 1–9) and the Liberated African Department Miscellaneous Letterbook, 1845–1861, SLPA.

[3] The records of the Mixed Courts at Freetown as well as Havana have provided much of the documentation in analyses of the slave trade in the "illegal era" after 1807. See Philip D. Curtin and Jan Vansina, "Sources of the Nineteenth Century Atlantic Slave Trade," *Journal of African History*, 5.2 (1964): 185–208; P. E. H. Hair, "The Enslavement of Koelle's Informants," *Journal of African History*, 6.2 (1965): 193–203; Philip D. Curtin, *The Atlantic Slave Trade: A Census*, (Madison: University of Wisconsin Press, 1969), 231–263. For the Cuban records, see Henry Lovejoy, "The Registries of the Archives of the Havana Slave

Table 1.1 *Slaves disembarked at Sierra Leone versus total disembarked in the Americas, 1808–1865*

	Liberated Africans landed at Freetown	Slaves landed in the Americas
Senegambia	1,583 (1.6%)	32,041 (1.9%)
Sierra Leone[a]	12,825 (12.9%)	33,212 (2.0%)
Windward Coast	2,542 (2.5%)	3,764 (0.2%)
Gold Coast	1,189 (1.2%)	5,523 (0.3%)
Bight of Benin	38,360 (38.5%)	161,881 (9.8%)
Bight of Biafra	31,471 (31.5%)	115,580 (7.0%)
West Central Africa	7,559 (7.6%)	1,046,238 (63.2%)
Southeast Africa	596 (0.6%)	243,073 (14.7%)
Unknown/other	3,627 (3.6%)	14,771 (0.9%)
Totals	99,752	1,656,083

[a] Calculations for Sierra Leone column by author, estimates for slave trade to the Americas from *Voyages* database.

Coastlines and Ports

At the most basic level, we can compile the coastlines and ports of embarkation for Liberated Africans brought to Sierra Leone. Table 1.1 provides an overview of coastlines of embarkation among recaptives compared with the entirety of the Atlantic slave trade for this period. The coastal origins of Liberated Africans did not fully reflect that of the larger nineteenth-century slave trade. British cruisers intercepted Spanish, Portuguese, and Brazilian vessels, but did not have the legal means to interfere with the slave trade carried out under American and French flags. Even more limiting, the treaties signed with Portugal, and in 1826 with independent Brazil, allowed the navy to detain only Portuguese and Brazilian vessels north of the equator. Thus while the largest single stream of the nineteenth-century slave trade was between Angola and southern Brazil, West Central Africans were always a small minority among recaptives. Slave ship cargoes brought to Sierra Leone for adjudication were overwhelmingly on voyages originally destined for

Trade Commission: Transcription Methodology and Statistical Analysis," *African Economic History*, 38 (2010): 107–136.

32 *Liberated African Origins and the Nineteenth-Century Slave Trade*

Coastal Origins of
Liberated Africans
1808–1863

Senegambia

Sierra Leone

Windward Coast

Gold Coast

Bight of Benin

Bight of Biafra

West Central Africa

Southeast Africa

Senegambia	1,583
Sierra Leone	12,825
Windward Coast	2,542
Gold Coast	1,189
Bight of Benin	38,360
Bight of Biafra	31,471
West Central Africa	7,559
Southeast Africa	596
Unknown	3,627
Total	99,752

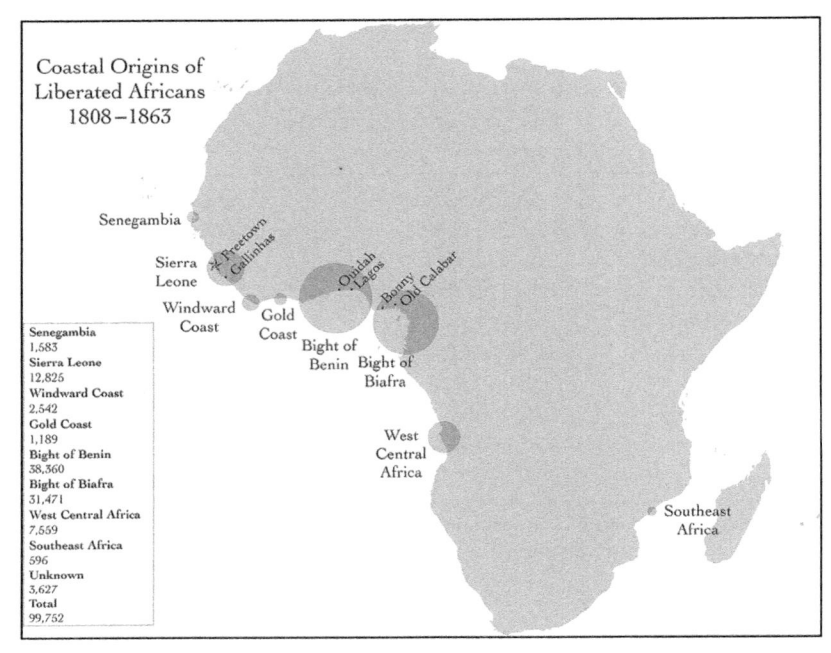

Map 1.1 Coastal origins of Liberated Africans landed at Freetown, 1808–1863
(map by author)

Cuba (chiefly Havana) and northeastern Brazil (chiefly Bahia) from the Bights of Benin and Biafra (Map 1.1).

The arrival of recaptives from different coastlines varied much more by decade than in slave-importing regions in the Americas. Table 1.2 illustrates these coastal origins in five-year intervals between 1808 and 1863. Factors such as the size of the naval squadron, the vessels used, their tactics, and the treaties delimiting their actions in different periods dictated where recaptives arrived from and in what proportion. For example, while fewer than 500 disembarked in 1820, more than 8,500 did so in 1837. In tracing the origins of Sierra Leone's Liberated African population there is an additional consideration: the substantial percentage of recaptives who were immediately sent elsewhere to fulfill the labor and defense needs of Britain's Atlantic empire. The final column of Table 1.2 lists estimates for the number of recaptives who were subsequently forcibly transported within the empire. This out-migration of one

Table 1.2 Liberated Africans Landed at Freetown by Region of Embarkation, 1808–1863[i]

	Senegambia	Sierra Leone	Windward Coast	Gold Coast	Bight of Benin	Bight of Biafra	West Central Africa	Southeast Africa	Unknown	Totals	Subsequent Migrations
1808–1810		1,173	437	380		184			458	2,632	–89
1811–1815	393	1,409	896	146	1,503	2,214	832		130	7,523	–2,138
1816–1820	353	1,384	415		691	1,832			540	5,215	–320
1821–1825	178	1,133	246	132	4,599	3,192	91		153	9,724	–193
1826–1830	312	1,302	323	396	9,115	6,972	3		438	18,861	–1,288
1831–1835	307	1,004		135	2,640	8,507	309			12,903	–2,860
1836–1840	40	2,102	225		6,174	7,769	280		1	17,187	–437
1841–1845		776			3,797	354	2,403		3	7,333	–6,662
1846–1850		1,367			8,534	445	1,911		1,333	13,590	–8,197
1851–1855		584			377	2	106		221	1,290	–1,024
1856–1860		580			930				349	1,859	–285
1861–1863		11					1,624			1,635	–1,043
Totals	1,583	12,825	2542	1,189	38,360	31,471	7,559	596	3,627	99,752	–24,328

[i] The basis for this estimate is the *Voyages* database, which lists 95,640 Liberated Africans disembarked from 450 slave vessels. *Voyages* contains coastal embarkation information for 91,705 liberated Africans landed at Freetown. The estimates are augmented by data on 4,122 Liberated Africans taken from intra-African slaving voyages or naval raids on coastal barracoons. These supplementary figures are compiled from the Sierra Leone-based registers (volumes 1–9) and the Liberated African Department Miscellaneous Letterbook, 1845–1861, SLPA. For the calculation of the "subsequent migration" column See Richard Anderson "The Diaspora of Sierra Leone's Liberated Africans: Enlistment, Forced Migration, and 'Liberation' at Freetown, 1808–1863," *African Economic History*, Volume 41 (2013): 101-138.

in four recaptives landed at Freetown shaped the overall size and ethnolinguistic composition of the colony's population.

Broadly, we can identify three phases of Liberated African arrivals. The first, 1808 to c. 1819, saw recaptives arrive primarily from the Sierra Leone region. Many early recaptives were not actually taken from transatlantic slave vessels by the Royal Navy, but captured through small, armed raids conducted from Freetown against coastal barracoons. During this period the squadron was small and did not venture far from Freetown harbor. The second period of c. 1819–c. 1839 saw the squadron's operations concentrated on the Bights of Benin and Biafra. The final period of 1839–1863 brought sustained arrivals from the Bight of Benin, the end of arrivals from the Bight of Biafra after the demise of that trade, and the emergence of West Central Africa as an embarkation point for recaptives. However, the fact that a majority of recaptives "emancipated" at Freetown after 1848 were sent to the British Caribbean means the most sustained period of settlement within the colony fell in the first four decades of the Squadron's operations.

British cruisers targeted specific ports, informed by the Admiralty's understanding of the trade. The concentration of Britain's patrolling meant that a majority (52.05 percent) of recaptives embarked at only five ports: Lagos, Bonny, Ouidah, Old Calabar, and Gallinhas (Table 1.3). The geographic proximity of Ouidah, Lagos, Bonny, and Old Calabar means that a majority of recaptives embarked along just over three hundred miles of coast in present-day Benin and Nigeria (Map 1.1).

Table 1.3 *Primary ports of recaptive embarkation*

Port	Disembarked	Percentage
Lagos	16,883	16.92
Bonny	14,488	14.52
Ouidah	8,301	8.32
Old Calabar	7,077	7.0.9
Gallinhasa[a]	5,175	5.19
Total	51,924	52.05

[a] The total for the Gallinhas is likely underestimated due to the number of non-transatlantic vessels captured in the region for which no record of port of embarkation exists.

Coastlines and ports alone say little about the societies from which Liberated Africans were taken. Ports were collection sites where goods – and, in the case of the slave trade, people – flowed from afar and were collected for shipment. Additionally, particular political events and instances of warfare might account for large percentages of captives from certain regions at particular periods. Scholars of the transatlantic trade are now looking in unprecedented detail at the historical contexts in which people were enslaved, marched to the coast, and sold to European slave traders. Fortunately, sources produced in Sierra Leone afford us a unique opportunity to look beyond the coast and discern the regional origins of recaptives in West and West Central Africa.

Church Missionary Society School Rosters

The earliest ethnographic information on recaptives comes from a series of school registers compiled by the CMS between 1816 and 1824. The CMS began operating within the colony in 1816, overseeing the increasing demand to educate the growing population of young recaptives. During its first years the mission kept rosters of children in each of their schools. The rosters list the Anglicized names of the students, their age, village of residence, and a column that records their purported "nation." Given the missionary impulse toward translation, it is likely that these terms reflected missionary perceptions of broad African language families. In total, twenty-two registers exist listing more than a thousand students.[4]

The twenty-two registers comprise 2,403 individual entries. Some individuals are registered up to seven times over nine years. Because some children were identified as belonging to two or three nations over

---

[4] Adam Jones previously analyzed fourteen registers compiled between December 1821 and January 1824 in order to assess the composition of the recaptive population in its early years. The analysis below incorporates additional children's rosters from 1816, 1818, and 1819, the earliest documents in which the purported ethnic origins of recaptives are recorded. Adam Jones, "New Light on the Liberated Africans and Their Origins: A List of Children Named after Benefactors, 1821–4," in Adam Jones and Peter K. Mitchell (eds.), *Sierra Leone Studies at Birmingham 1988* (Birmingham: University of Birmingham, 1990), 32–42; Adam Jones "Recaptive Nations: Evidence Concerning the Demographic Impact of the Atlantic Slave Trade in the Early Nineteenth Century," *Slavery & Abolition*, 11.1 (1990): 42–57.

time, the number of "nations" counted (1,066) exceeds the number of children (967). While these ambiguities and inconsistencies are problematic, these records nevertheless provide unique insights into the prevalence of certain ethnic groups among the early receptive population, and the range of ethnonyms used to describe them. Moreover, the fact that individuals are listed on multiple occasions is one of the great values of this series of documents.

Appendix A provides a summary of individual identifications for all rosters compiled between 1816 and 1824, providing proposed linkages between the recorded nations and modern language or dialect groups, broken down by probable coastlines of embarkation. While the rosters list at least eighty-six different "national" categories, over three-quarters of students were categorized into one of thirteen nations: Ebo, 205 (19.2%); Cosso, 189 (17.7%); Accoo, 75 (7.0%); Calabar, 68 (6.4%); Bayong, 57 (5.3%); Bassa, 40 (3.8%); Papa, 33 (3.1%); Congo, 32 (3.0%); Sosoo, 28 (2.6%); Baccumcum, 25 (2.3%); Golah, 24 (2.3%); Haussah, 21 (2.0%); Kissy, 21 (2.0%). The predominance of Ebo (Igbo) and Cosso (a colonial term for Mende, see Chapter 4) reflects the Navy's focus on the Bight of Biafra and the Sierra Leone coastline in the first decade of the squadron's operations. The rosters also highlight the prominence of certain nations from particular coastlines, with Cosso representing 59.8 percent of children likely from Upper Guinea, Ebo representing 54.4 percent from the Bight of Biafra, and Aku – a colonial term for Yoruba speakers (see Chapter 4) – representing 60.5 percent from the Bight of Benin. The rosters represent a subset of the receptive population, even at this early date. Despite these limitations and the imperfect nature of recording, the rosters provide important insights into the origins of receptives in the 1810s and early 1820s.

Koelle's *Polyglotta Africana*

The preponderance of Igbo and Mende receptive children from the Bight of Biafra and Upper Guinea within missionary schools contrasts with the picture provided by two later sources that are well known to historians and have formed the basis of most previous analyses of receptive origins. The first is Sigismund Wilhelm Koelle's *Polyglotta Africana*, an 1854 linguistic survey of African languages in which Koelle compiled ethnographic information from informants in Sierra

Leone.[5] The second is the 1848 census of the Liberated African population of the colony, in which the "nation" of origin for 13,273 recaptives and their offspring are recorded.[6] Both of these documents were compiled in the late 1840s, after the majority of recaptives had arrived in the colony and after the slave trade from many parts of West Africa had terminated.

The Württemberg-born missionary Sigismund Koelle arrived in Sierra Leone in 1847 and spent periods of 1849–1850 collecting linguistic samples within the colony.[7] This involved interviewing 210 informants, often on multiple occasions. Of Koelle's informants – all but two of whom were adult males – 179 can be definitely identified as former slaves, the others being primarily traders or sailors settled in Freetown.[8] Koelle included brief biographical sketches of his informants, listing their place of birth, approximate year and means of their enslavement, and their language and dialect (based on his own linguistic criteria).

Koelle was often obliged to use vague terms such as "many," "few," or "several thousand" when recording his informants' estimates for how many others in the colony spoke their language. These observations are nevertheless informative. Table 1.4 shows the languages with the most speakers in the colony, according to Koelle's informants. Only a few of Koelle's informants felt that their languages were widely spoken in the colony. Koelle's conclusions point to the preponderance by mid-century of languages located in present-day southern Nigeria and Sierra Leone. By contrast, Koelle found no recaptive speaking the languages of the Windward or Gold Coasts.

---

[5] Sigismund Wilhelm Koelle, *Polyglotta Africana: or A Comparative Vocabulary of Nearly Three Hundred Words and Phrases in More than One Hundred Distinct African Languages* (London: Church Missionary House, 1854).

[6] Curtin and Vansina's analysis on the sources of the nineteenth-century slave trade employed Koelle's findings and the 1848 census. Curtin and Vansina, "Sources," 185–208; Curtin, *Atlantic Slave Trade*.

[7] Curtin and Vansina believed most of Koelle's research was conducted in 1849. P. E. H. Hair believed this work was done in 1850. Koelle's other missionary documents (C/A1/O135, CMS) suggest he conducted his interviews intermittently in 1849 and 1850. The dates presented in Appendix D herein are calculated based on these dates.

[8] Hair, "The Enslavement of Koelle's Informants," 193.

Table 1.4 *Most widely spoken recaptive languages in Polyglotta Africana*[a]

Language in Koelle	Modern equivalent[b]	Present-day location	Number in colony
Mende	Mende	Sierra Leone, Liberia	"some hundreds"
Aku	Yoruba	Nigeria and Benin	"several thousand"[c]
"Ibo" dialects	Igbo	East Nigeria	"many"[d]
Nupe	Nupe	Nigeria	"about sixty"
Basa	Kakanda or Basange	Nigeria	"about 100"
Bayon	Banggot or Bate	East Cameroon	"about fifty"
Sunde	Nsundi/Sundi	Congo	fifty
Barba	Bariba/Bargu	Benin	"about fifty"
Anan/Kalaba	Anang/western Ibibio	East Nigeria	"at least two hundred"
Konguan	Anyang/Banyangi	West Cameroon	"about 100"

[a] Koelle had many informants of Mandinka dialects who combined represented a substantial presence in the colony. However, he noted that his informants and their countrymen were "all of them travelers or traders, not liberated slaves." Koelle, *Polyglotta Africana*, 3.

[b] Compiled from Curtin and Vansina "Sources," 185–208; David Dalby, "Provisional Identification of Languages in the Polyglotta Africana," *Sierra Leone Language Review*, 3 (1964): 83–90.

[c] This observation was made by Koelle's Oyo informant. In addition, his Egba, Ìjẹ̀ṣà, and Ijebu informants similarly referred to "many" or a "great many" countrymen.

[d] This vague reference comes partly from the fact that Koelle was trying to discern as many "Ibo" dialects as possible, while being adamant that they "never had heard" the name Igbo before arriving in Sierra Leone.

The 1848 Census

A broader overview of the most prevalent languages in the colony is the 1848 colonial census, which records the supposed ethnolinguistic identity of individuals. Though censuses had been taken in the colony since 1811, the 1848 census was the first to record the "nation" of the population. The census counted a total population of 46,511. Liberated Africans accounted for 20,619, with an additional 19,624 listed as their colony-born offspring. Governor Benjamin Pine instructed that the census distinguish "persons actually liberated from slavery, and their descendants ... and also that the former class should be subdivided according to the nations or tribes of which it is composed."[9] Miscommunications between the governor and the census takers meant that information for "nations and tribes" was often recorded haphazardly for both recaptives and their descendants, resulting in a return of 13,273 individuals (Appendix B). The miscommunication also resulted in these data being recorded for Freetown but not the surrounding districts.

The census has other known drawbacks. Curtin and Vansina noted that the "nations" in the census was far less accurate than Koelle's inventory, and that most of the names were categories used for slaves in the West Indies at an earlier period.[10] The census has other issues that can obscure as much as it reveals. For instance, the relatively small number of Igbo enumerated (2,677) compared with Aku (7,114) led Curtin to conclude that the Igbo, "who had once been such an important source of the eighteenth-century slave trade," were now less prevalent victims of the slave trade.[11] But recaptives who likely embarked at the Bight of Biafra were underrepresented within the census. Even if we add all identified Hausa to the recorded Igbo, Calabar, and Moko population who embarked at Biafran ports, these groups combined represented only 20.7 percent of the population. This contrasts to the 63.7 percent of the population identified as Aku, Paupah (Popo/Ewe), Kakajna (Nupe), or Binnee (Benin), and likely embarked in the Bight of Benin.

One problem with both the census and Koelle's *Polyglotta* is that they are snapshots in time, compiled in the late 1840s. Recaptives from different parts of the African continent arrived in different proportions throughout the nineteenth century. Moreover, many subsequently left, voluntarily or not, while there were differing levels of mortality after disembarkation. Ali Eisami Gazirmabe, Koelle's Kanuri informant, noted that the number of Kanuri speakers in Sierra Leone "when greatest, amounted to about 200" but by the late 1840s had been "reduced to thirty."[12]

---

[9] Report of the Annual Blue Book of Sierra Leone for the Year 1848 CO 267/209.
[10] Curtin and Vansina, "Sources," 207.   [11] Curtin, *Atlantic Slave Trade*, 260.
[12] Koelle, *Polyglotta Africana*, 10.

Names and African Origins

A final source for tracing the origins of Liberated Africans comes from the registers of the names of 81,745 Africans landed at Freetown compiled by the colony's Liberated African Department.[13] The strength of these sources, as highlighted by David Eltis, Ugo Nwokeji, Daniel Domingues da Silva, Philip Misevich, and Henry Lovejoy, is that African naming practices are often very regionally specific and can therefore provide further evidence about the geographic origins of the African diaspora. This methodology has formed the basis of the *African Origins Project*, an online database designed to identify the ethnolinguistic provenance of names recorded in the registers.[14] David Eltis and Ugo Nwokeji, the pioneers of this methodology, argue that "in contrast to many plantation records in the Americas, the ethnic basis of many of the names is recognizable, and makes it possible to identify broad ethnic groupings, and in some cases, sub-groupings."[15]

Receptives were drawn from societies with ritualized traditions associated with naming practices. Samuel Johnson, the famed Yoruba historian born in the Sierra Leone village of Hastings, devoted a chapter of his monumental *History of the Yorubas* to Yoruba naming practices. Johnson noted that "the naming of a child is an important affair amongst the Yoruba," among whom "names are not given at random because of their euphony or merely because a distinguished member of the family or community was so named, but of a set purpose from circumstances connected with the child itself, or with

---

[13] Liberated African Registers and Duplicate Registers: 1–3772 (1808–1812), 3773–6274 (1812–1814), 4684–7507 (1814–1815), 6289–8528 (1814–1816), 7508–9758 (1815–1816), 8529–9758 (1816–1817), 9759–11908 (1816–1819), 10115–15143 (1816–1822), 11909–15967 (1819–1822), 15144–19888 (1822–1825), 19889–24205 (1825–1827), 20514–25422 (1827), 25423–30708 (1827–1829), 30709–37429 (1829–1830), 37430–43537 (1829–1833), 50762–54382 (1835–1836), 54157–57571 (1837), 57572–64406 (1837–1839), 64407–67635 (1839), 75378–84307 (1845–1848), SLPA.

[14] See www.african-origins.org/. The development of the *Origins Project*, including the transcription and systematic comparison of the various Liberated African registers is explained in Anderson et al. "Using African Names to Identify the Origins of Captives in the Transatlantic Slave Trade," 188–189; Henry Lovejoy "Old Oyo Influences on the Transformation of Lucumí Identity in Colonial Cuba," PhD dissertation, University of California, Los Angeles, 2012; Daniel B. Domingues da Silva, *The Atlantic Slave Trade from West Central Africa, 1780–1867* (Cambridge: Cambridge University Press, 2017).

[15] Eltis and Nwokeji, "The Roots of the African Diaspora," 368.

reference to the family fortunes at the time."[16] Such naming traditions were apparent among recaptives. The recaptive preacher Joseph Boston May was originally named Ifacayeh (Ifákayé, "Ifá covers the world") by his father, a *babaláwo* in the Oyo town of Iware.[17] Likewise, John Weeks Okrafor-Smart, a recaptive carpenter in Regent village, was born Okoroafor, an Igbo name given to males born on the market day of Afor.[18] The potential to identify the meanings of tens of thousands of names therefore presents new insights into the origins of recaptives and the slave trade from the ports and regions from which they were drawn.

The *African Origins Project* is still in its initial stages. The findings of this chapter will thus face a constant process of reassessment. At present, the *Origins* database contains tentative ethnolinguistic associations for 26,466 individuals landed at Freetown between 1808 and 1848.[19] The earlier work of Eltis and Nwokeji, as well as subsequent research by Philip Misevich, mean that the fullest information so far on ethnolinguistic associations is available for Upper Guinea and southeastern Nigeria.[20] However these data represent only 30 percent of those landed at Freetown whose names were recorded.

Since the majority of recaptives landed at Sierra Leone entered the transatlantic slave trade through only five ports, understanding the catchment regions these ports drew on tells us much about the demographic profile of recaptive society. For example, 5,393 of the 14,947 recaptives who embarked at Lagos have been identified by language of origin. The preliminary results show that among those whose language has been identified, 92.84 percent of Africans departing Lagos were Yoruba speakers. "Yoruba speakers" and similar phrasing is used here

---

[16] Samuel Johnson, *The History of the Yorubas: From the Earliest Times to the Beginning of the British Protectorate* (Lagos: C. M. S. Bookshops, 1921), 79.

[17] Leo Spitzer, *Lives in Between: Assimilation and Marginality in Austria, Brazil, West Africa, 1780–1945* (Cambridge: Cambridge University Press, 1989), 40–45, 207.

[18] Victor S. Weeks Okrafo-Smart, *Okrafo: Over a Century in the Lives of a Liberated African Family, 1816–1930* (Nottingham: Palm Tree Publishers, 2006).

[19] www.african-origins.org/african-data/. Data accessed and downloaded October 30, 2017.

[20] Philip Misevich, "The Origins of Slaves Leaving the Upper Guinea Coast in the Nineteenth Century," in Eltis and Richardson (eds.), *Extending the Frontiers*, 155–175.

since, as Chapter 4 will show, a recaptive with a Yoruba name would likely not have self-identified as "Yoruba" in this era.

The complexities of recaptive self-identification are analyzed in Chapter 4. But that analysis first requires an overview of the homelands and linguistic regions from which recaptives were drawn. The sources presented above – the CMS school rosters, 1848 census, Koelle's *Polyglotta Africana*, and ethnolinguistic data discerned from the registers of Liberated Africans – allow a composite picture of recaptive origins beyond ports and coastlines of embarkation. The remainder of this chapter looks at the provenance of Liberated Africans from Upper Guinea, the Bight of Benin, and Bight of Biafra, since the overwhelming majority of Liberated Africans came from these regions.

Sierra Leone and the Upper Guinea Coast

Many of the earliest recaptives came from the region near the colony as Britain's naval campaign greatly impacted slave trading along the Sierra Leone coast. Freetown's founding forced slave dealers away from the Sierra Leone River – particularly the slave trading fort of Bunce Island – and saw the rise of the trade from the Rio Pongo to the north of Freetown, and especially at the Gallinhas and Sherbro to the south.[21] By 1824, the British considered the Gallinhas "the only notorious haunt for slave-ships betwixt Sierra Leone and Cape Coast."[22] Recaptives from this region included those taken from transatlantic slave voyages, intra-African slaving voyages along the coast, and raids by the Royal Navy on coastal barracoons. The transatlantic trade from the Sierra Leone coast finally declined in the 1840s.[23] However, the interception of coastal slaving ships and canoes meant that recaptives from the region continued to arrive through 1863.

Liberated Africans from this region appear to have originally resided in or near coastal areas. While slaves from the Upper Guinea coast prior to 1807 had been drawn from a catchment area more than a hundred miles inland, the growing trade at ports in southern Sierra

---

[21] Philip Misevich, "The Mende and Sherbro Diaspora in Nineteenth-Century Southern Sierra Leone," in Misevich and Kristin Mann (eds.), *The Rise and Demise of Slavery and the Slave Trade in the Atlantic World* (Rochester: Rochester University Press, 2016), 249.
[22] Gregory and Hamilton to Foreign Office, May 15, 1824, FO 84/28.
[23] Misevich, "Origins of Slaves Leaving the Upper Guinea Coast," 160.

Leone fed primarily on people living within sixty miles of the coast.[24] Philip Misevich has analyzed the names of 8,871 Africans in the Liberated African registers from Freetown, Havana, and Rio de Janeiro, who embarked at the ports of southern Sierra Leone between 1808 and 1844. Misevich's estimates indicate a high concentration of Mende- and Sherbro-speaking peoples, which together represent more than half of all southern Sierra Leone captives. The most common names were identified as Mende/Sherbro (2457/54 percent), Kissi/Kono/Koranko (857/19 percent), Temne (416/9 percent), Limba (204/4 percent), Fulbe (178/4 percent), Mandinka (119/3 percent), Vai (73/2 percent), and Loko (68/1 percent).[25] Preliminary results from the Freetown sample for the years 1808–1848 corroborate these findings. Of 3,681 names identified so far from Sierra Leone ports, 1,362 (37.5 percent) have been identified as Mende. The CMS children's rosters noted the early prevalence of Mende or "Cosso" in the colony, referring to 189 children, who represented 59.8 percent of those from Upper Guinea and 17.7 percent of all children identified by "nation."

By 1848, the colonial census listed "Koosoos" as the fifth largest "nation" in the colony, or 4.9 percent of the counted population. Koelle's Mende informant, Sam Chapman of Freetown, could only estimate that "some hundreds of his countrymen" lived in the colony. Koelle also obtained information from Kono, Kpelle, Bandi, Vai, and Kissi informants, who, when asked, gave more modest estimates of the number of their countrymen. Mende speakers therefore formed a sizable portion of the receptive population, from the early days of the antislavery squadron through the demise of the transatlantic trade. They were joined by smaller numbers of Koranko/Kissi/Kono, Mandinka, Susu/Yalunka, Temne, and Fulbe.

Bight of Biafra

The movement of recaptives from the Sierra Leone coastline was matched in the first decade of the squadron's operation by Liberated

---

[24] Philip Misevich, "'On the Frontier of 'Freedom': Abolition and the Transformation of Atlantic Commerce in southern Sierra Leone, 1790s to 1860s," PhD dissertation, Emory University, 2009, 5, 19. Misevich suggests that a drop in prices after 1807 made it less profitable to transport slaves from further inland.

[25] Misevich, "The Mende and Sherbro Diaspora," 254.

Africans arriving from the Bight of Biafra. Ultimately 31,471 recaptives embarked at ports in the Bight of Biafra, primarily at Bonny and Old Calabar. Contemporary observers and more recent scholars have generally recognized the Igbo people of the Bight of Biafra interior as the second largest "nation" among Sierra Leone recaptives.[26] The 1848 census recorded 1,231 "Eboos," dwarfed only by the large number of "Aku." The visibility of Igbo within the colony in the 1840s is not surprising, given that some 16,276 recaptives arrived in Sierra Leone from the Bight of Biafra in the 1830s, more than from any other coastline. Moreover, captives from the Bight of Biafra formed a relatively constant stream of arrivals from 1810 until the demise of the Biafran trade in the 1840s.

An analysis of this Igbo migration to Sierra Leone cannot simply refer to "the Igbo" as a percentage of recaptured slaves from the Bight of Biafra. There is a contested historiographical discussion over the meaning of "Igbo" in the era of the slave trade, despite the existence of such philological terms as "Eboe" "Hackbu," or "Heebo" (i.e., Igbo) in the writings of early European traders and visitors to the Bight of Biafra.[27] The debate is not whether the Igbo ethnic group as it exists in the twenty-first century existed as such in the era of the transatlantic slave trade, but whether there were any people who identified themselves as Igbo and, if so, when they began to do so.[28] This debate has considered whether this recognition first took place within those societies that later constituted Igboland, or within the diaspora. Koelle noted that the Igbo within Sierra Leone did not refer to themselves as such, but by more localized identities. He collected vocabularies of five main Igbo dialects and ten "countries" whose people were called Igbo in Sierra Leone.[29] For the purposes of this chapter, I refer to "Igbo speakers" with a discussion of how documents regarding "the Igbo" in Sierra Leone can inform the debate regarding Igbo ethnogenesis more fully explored in Chapter 4.

[26] See, e.g., Northrup, "Identity among Liberated Africans," 28.
[27] Raphael Chijioke Njoku and Toyin Falola, "Introduction," in Falola and Njoku (eds.), *Igbo in the Atlantic World: African Origins and Diasporic Destinations* (Bloomington: Indiana University Press, 2016), 3.
[28] G. Ugo Nwokeji, *The Slave Trade and Culture in the Bight of Biafra: An African Society in the Atlantic World* (New York: Cambridge University Press, 2010), xv.
[29] Koelle, *Polyglotta Africana*, 8–9.

Questions regarding Igbo ethnicity in the nineteenth century are often treated in conjunction with the meaning of other ethnonyms of present-day southeastern Nigeria. One of the most common in the African diaspora is "Calabar," a term that features heavily in documents from Sierra Leone. Much like the term Igbo, Calabar cannot be taken unequivocally as referring to an African ethnic or linguistic group, since the term refers to one of two ports within the Bight of Biafra: Elem Kalabari (or New Calabar) and Old Calabar. Moreover, slaves sold along the westerly half of the Bight of Biafra, and specifically the ports of Bonny and Elem Kalabari, often came from the interior and not the coast itself.[30] Thus, any term that suggests a coastal origin of enslaved Africans from this region must be scrutinized.

As an ethnonym in New World documents, "Calabar" had shifting, conflicting, and ambiguous uses over time. In certain diasporic settings the term referred to captives sold through the port of Elem Kalabari, an Ijo-speaking trading community on the Niger Delta. Elsewhere the term meant captives sold from the more westerly Efik-speaking port of Old Calabar, a cluster of settlements on the Cross River estuary. The term Caravali/Carabali is recorded as early as 1547 in documents from Hispaniola in reference to people from the Bight of Biafra, and is generally assumed to derive from Elem Kalabari. Alonso de Sandoval, a Jesuit missionary collecting information on Africans in seventeenth-century Peru, provides the earliest source elaborating the meaning of "Calabar." Sandoval noted that the *Caravalies* were inhabitants of the lower Niger Delta, but also of two distinct types. The "native or pure Caravalies" were those with whom Europeans traded, readily definable based on name and location with the Elem Kalabari.[31] The "pure Caravalies" were distinguishable from the "Caravalies particulares," a heterogeneous collection of "forty or fifty villages of various or different groups" who were labeled Caravalies due to their trade with their "pure" counterparts.

By the late eighteenth century, the term "Calabar" became more strongly associated with Old Calabar, as British slave traders focused their extensive commerce on the Cross River area. The term thus derived from European traders, and over time variants of "Caravali"

---

[30] Paul Lovejoy, *Transformations in Slavery: A History of Slavery in Africa*, 3rd edition (Cambridge: Cambridge University Press, 2011), 58–59.
[31] David Northrup, "Igbo and Myth Igbo: Culture and Ethnicity in the Atlantic World, 1600–1850," *Slavery & Abolition*, 21.3 (2000): 7.

came to refer to enslaved Africans leaving Old Calabar rather than Elem Kalabari.[32] As Northrup points out, the transfer of "Calabar" from Elem Kalabari to the distant and linguistically different port of Old Calabar "is a vivid reminder of the imprecision of such terminology."[33]

The meanings of "Calabar" is more than an etymological discussion since in Sierra Leone it became a term of self-ascription. In the colony, "Calabar" clearly referred to captives sold through Old Calabar or even Bonny, rather than Elem Kalabari. Besides the abovementioned shift in Anglophone usage, the number of recaptives who embarked at Old Calabar (7,077) far outnumbered those who embarked at Elem Kalabari (1,524). But could "Calabar" simply be a term imposed on captives sold through the port? A British mariner purchasing slaves at Old Calabar in 1790 explained a process by which 150 slaves of "fourteen different tribes or nations" became "Calabars" when exported.[34] If this were true in the mindset of enslavers, it is unclear that enslaved Africans felt likewise.

Other hints as to what Calabar meant in Sierra Leone come from Koelle's "Kálaba" informant and the inventory of words Koelle designated as "Kálaba." Koelle noted that "Kálaba" was a term used by Europeans for a group he classified linguistically as the "Annang," a language that has subsequently come to be called Efik-Ibibio or Efik.[35] Northrup speculates that Koelle's decision to call the language Anang perhaps indicates how numerous people from this dialect of Efik were among recaptives in Sierra Leone. He adds that the Anang, located at the western end of Efik-speaking lands, would have been more likely to furnish slaves through Bonny than through Old Calabar.[36]

---

[32] Renée Soulodre-La France, "'I, Francisco Castañeda, Negro Esclavo Caravali': Caravali Ethnicity in Colonial Granada," in Lovejoy and Trotman (eds.), *Trans-Atlantic Dimensions of Ethnicity in the African Diaspora*, 101–102.

[33] Northrup, "Igbo and Myth Igbo," 10.

[34] William Butterworth [pseudonym for Henry Schroeder], *Three Years Adventures of a Minor in England, Africa, the West Indies, South-Carolina and Georgia* (Leeds: Thomas Inchbold, 1831), 85.

[35] Curtin and Vansina identified Koelle's Anan/Kalaba as the Anang or Western Ibibio, while Dalby's categorized the Anan linguistic samples as Ibibio-Efik. Curtin and Vansina "Sources," 206; Dalby, "Provisional Identification of Languages in the Polyglotta Africana," 88.

[36] Northrup, "Igbo and Myth Igbo," 10.

The debate over what Igbo, Calabar, and other ethnic labels actually meant in terms of identity – and what evidence from Sierra Leone has to say about this debate – will be addressed in Chapter 4. For now, the relevant distinction is that linguistically Igbo and Ibibio lie on opposite sides of one of the major dividing lines of the Niger–Congo language family. While Igbo is the easternmost extension of the Kwa subfamily of Niger–Congo languages, Ibibio is one of the westernmost extensions of the Benue–Congo subfamily.[37] Beyond this linguistic divide the terms, as used within Sierra Leone, demarcated a different proximity to the coast.

Igbo and Calabar were the two most common ethnonyms in Sierra Leone attributable to the Bight of Biafra. The earliest reference to both "Ebo" and "Calabar" in the colony comes from the first CMS student roster for the school at Leicester Mountain in 1816. Of 250 students in attendance, 95 were listed as "Ebo," more than any other "country."[38] A further twenty-one were listed as "Calabar" or "Calaba." However, many of these students in 1816 were subsequently identified differently, and the prevalence of "Ebo" in this early list may say more about the challenges of German and English missionaries establishing new schools for such a heterogeneous student population. Nevertheless, the persistent record of Ebo in the 1819–1824 rosters suggests their strong presence among the early recaptives from the Bight of Biafra.

More evidence for the Bight of Biafra comes from material recorded in the Liberated African registers in 1821–1822. For this brief period, clerks made efforts to record the "name of country" for some 1,659 recaptives.[39] The clerks registered more than 200 different "countries," most of them unrecognizable in terms of modern ethnonyms. However, this is not so for the records of seven vessels intercepted in the Bight of Biafra. The registers record the "country" of 1,008 recaptives from the Bight of Biafra; 720 on four redirected voyages from Bonny and 288 on three redirected voyages from Old Calabar

---

[37] David Northrup, *Trade without Rulers: Pre-colonial Economic Development in South-eastern Nigeria* (Oxford: Clarendon Press, 1978), 14.
[38] "A List of the Boys & Girls Supported by the Church Missionary Society at Leicester Mountain," CA1/E5A/68/N, CMS.
[39] Foreign Office orders in May of 1821 stated that "in registering the slaves emancipated by the court the nations or countries to which such slaves are natives be recorded." May 14, 1821, Spanish Minute Book 1819–1828, FO 315/26. The orders were followed briefly and inconsistently.

48   Liberated African Origins and the Nineteenth-Century Slave Trade

Table 1.5 *"Country" of recaptives from Bight of Biafra ports in Liberated African registers, 1821–1822*[a]

	Bonny	Old Calabar	Bight of Biafra total
Igbo	530 (73.6%)	161 (55.9%)	691 (68.5%)
Calabar	145 (20.1%)	120 (41.7%)	265 (26.3%)
Hausa	8 (1.1%)	1 (0.3%)	9 (0.9%)
Other	37 (5.1%)	6 (2.1%)	43 (4.3%)
Total	720	288	1,008

[a] These totals are derived from registers contained in FO 84/9, FO 84/15, and FO 315/31. Discrepancies between FO 84 and FO 315 mean that my figures differ from those earlier presented by Northrup, *Trade without Rulers*, 60–62.

(Table 1.5). Here, more than two-thirds of the Africans on board are identified as Igbo.

As Northrup points out, these data cannot be used to represent the total Biafran slave trade without two reservations. First is the number of persons who were likely not of Igbo or Ibibio origin, including Hausa and other populations to the north. Second, the ratio of Ibibio to Igbo is likely too high since the Ibibio population was likely much smaller than the Igbo. Northrup estimates that by the late eighteenth century Old Calabar's slave exports may well have been over half Igbo. Eltis has estimated that, east of the Niger probably 70 percent of deportees in the nineteenth century were Igbo.[40] Preliminary results from the *African Origins Project* suggest perhaps an even higher percentage of Igbo. Among recaptives embarked in the Bight of Biafra, 7,760 (77.1 percent) of 10,065 identified names have been classified as Igbo, as well as 408 classified as Ibibio and 95 as Efik. The percentage of Igbo corroborates with these earlier estimates, though the small number of names classified as Ibibio and Efik is likely underrepresented.

[40] Northrup, *Trade without Rulers*, 60–62. Eltis adds that "the Agbaja and Isuama Igbo were the largest groups both in the Sierra Leone of the 1840s and in southeastern Nigeria in 1921 [according to the 1921 Nigerian census]. A further 20% were Ibibio, with the people of the Anang and Arochukwu areas particularly prominent." David Eltis, "The Slave Trade in Nineteenth-Century Nigeria," in Toyin Falola and Ann O'Hear (eds.), *Studies in the Nineteenth-Century Economic History of Nigeria* (Madison: African Studies Program, University of Wisconsin, 1998), 87.

The final piece of evidence is the 1848 census, which listed 1,231 Eboos (Igbo), 470 Mokos (Ibibio), and 319 Calabahs (Ibibio/Efik) among 13,273 recaptives in Freetown. If we exclude the 657 Hausa enumerated in the census (some of whom likely arrived through Bight of Biafra ports), the percentages of recaptives likely from the Bight of Biafra are 60.9 percent Igbo, 23.3 percent Moko, and 15.8 percent Efik. The ratios here are closer to the Liberated African register sample than the preliminary *Origins* findings. However, the overall percentage of "nations" attributable to the Bight of Biafra in the 1848 census is far less than the data for coast and port of origin would suggest. Overall, "Eboo," "Moko," and "Calabah" comprised 15.2 percent of the census population, and Eboo alone only 9.3 percent. Northrup has suggested that this surprisingly small percentage of Igbo is because a disproportionate number of those who left Sierra Leone in the 1840s to work elsewhere in West Africa or in the West Indies were Igbo. This out-migration certainly must be taken into account. However, there is little evidence to suggest that this movement was disproportionate, especially compared with the Yoruba exodus, whose numbers nevertheless remained large in Sierra Leone through the 1840s.

A further explanation lies in varying levels of mortality after disembarkation. Recaptives from the Bight of Biafra experienced a uniquely high mortality rate of approximately 20 percent between interception and disembarkation. This was also true of slave voyages to the Americas, owing primarily to the disease environment along this region's coastline. In Sierra Leone the high rate of mortality during the voyage persisted after disembarkation. The Liberated African registers record 2,741 recaptives dying in the days between their disembarkation and the adjudication of their vessel, a period ranging from days to several weeks. Among these fatalities, 1,979 (72.2 percent) of the deceased were from ports in the Bight of Biafra. Captives from Bonny seem to have faced a particularly arduous experience, accounting for 1,190 deaths in the Liberated African yard, more than four out of every ten people who died while being overseen by the Liberated African Department.[41] After fourteen years working in the department, Thomas Cole was all too aware that "the condition of a body of captured slaves on

[41] The registers also record 1,187 recaptives immediately sent to the Liberated African Hospital at Kissy. The registers do not record whether they survived. Of the 1,187 entrants, 603 were from ports of the Bight of Biafra, of whom 368 embarked at Bonny.

their first landing at Sierra Leone, especially those from the rivers 'Calabar' and 'Bonny' and other parts near the equator, is deplorable in the extreme."[42] These quantitative data and qualitative observations suggest the need to consider how different mortality rates shaped diasporic communities. Nevertheless, the large number of recaptives from the Bight of Biafra suggests that perhaps one in four of Africans who disembarked at Freetown spoke Igbo, and were surpassed only by the movement of Yoruba speakers to the colony.[43]

Bight of Benin

Special attention must be paid to the Bight of Benin since more Liberated Africans (38,360) embarked along this coastline than any other, with Lagos the largest single port of embarkation among recaptives. Moreover, most histories of Sierra Leone have presented the Yoruba-speaking peoples of the Bight of Benin as an outright majority among recaptives. Christopher Fyfe, for example, contended that "by the late 1820s most recaptives were from the Yoruba country, known in Sierra Leone as 'Aku.'"[44] John Peterson similarly concludes that "the Yoruba wars which broke out early in the nineteenth century provided Sierra Leone with a dominant Yoruba group in its Liberated African population."[45] This perception of a Yoruba-speaking majority is not unfounded; its origins lie with many contemporary observers. Hannah Kilham, a Quaker educator who visited the colony in 1827, concluded that Yoruba "is said to be spoken by more than half the Liberated Africans in Sierra Leone."[46] The prominent abolitionist Thomas Fowell Buxton observed from afar in 1839 that "the Aku language had been found to be understood by the great majority of the captured negroes."[47] Additionally, both Koelle's statements and the 1848 census suggest an "Aku" majority. These reports are not necessarily

---

[42] Cole to John Russell, August 11, 1849, CO 267/162.
[43] This estimate combines the estimate of 77.1 percent of recaptives from the Bight of Biafra having Igbo names with the percentage of recaptives from the Bight of Biafra in relation to all those landed at Sierra Leone (31,471/99,752 = 31.55%).
[44] Fyfe, *History of Sierra Leone*, 170.   [45] Peterson, *Province of Freedom*, 169.
[46] Hannah Kilham, *Report on a Recent Visit to the Colony of Sierra Leone* (London: William Philipps, 1828), 9.
[47] Thomas Fowell Buxton, *The African Slave Trade and Its Remedy* (London: J. Murray, 1840), 499 note.

inaccurate, but all are snapshots in time based on individual observations and colonial perceptions.

Evaluating the scale of this Yoruba migration raises the further complication of what "Yoruba" meant in the nineteenth century and prior. As Robert Smith, Robin Law, and J. D. Y. Peel have shown, the region of Nigeria that we now refer to as Yorubaland and the people referred to as *the* Yoruba did not see themselves as such prior to colonization and the missionary encounter of the latter nineteenth century.[48] This issue of self-definition and self-understanding is addressed more comprehensively in Chapters 4 and 6, and I here refer to "Yoruba speakers" on the basis of their shared language, cosmologies, origin myths, and the common experiences of warfare in this period. This chapter refers anachronistically to the major kingdoms and polities that would later be referred to as Yoruba "subgroups." Among these subgroups, the evidence suggests that the Oyo, Egba, Ìjèṣà, and Ijebu were the most prevalent among recaptives. The findings presented below suggest that perhaps 33,000 recaptives, approximately one-third of all Africans liberated at Freetown, were Yoruba speakers. This conclusion reaffirms the historiographical consensus that the Yoruba were the most numerous ethnolinguistic group among recaptives, though not an outright majority among those liberated from slave ships at Freetown.

The large presence of Yoruba speakers in Sierra Leone was the result of developments both internal and external to Yoruba societies. In the years after the Napoleonic Wars, Britain's naval squadron targeted the Bights of Benin and Biafra. Their patrols coincided with a period of political change and violence within the Bight of Benin interior. The collapse of the Oyo Empire in the early nineteenth century and the subsequent Yoruba wars brought unprecedented numbers of Yoruba speakers to the New World as slaves. The visibility of Yoruba in the African diaspora – particularly in northeastern Brazil and Cuba – reflected the emergence of Lagos as a major slave-trading port in the 1790s. The proximity of Lagos to the Yoruba interior increased the violence associated with slaving, helping to reinforce a pattern of slave

---

[48] Robert S. Smith, *Kingdoms of the Yoruba*, 3rd edition (Madison: University of Wisconsin Press, 1988), 7; Robin Law, "Ethnicity and the Slave Trade: 'Lucumi' and 'Nago' as Ethnonyms in West Africa," *History in Africa*, 24 (1997): 205–206; J. D. Y. Peel, *Religious Encounter and the Making of the Yoruba* (Bloomington: University of Indiana Press, 2000), 26.

capturing and regional interstate rivalries.⁴⁹ As the analysis above shows, there are few references to Yoruba in Sierra Leone prior to 1818, though there are many references to Hausa and northern populations of the Bight of Benin during the first decade of the squadron's operations. The coincidence of the collapse of the Oyo Empire (c. 1817–1836) and the presence of British naval ships patrolling the ports of Lagos and Ouidah dramatically altered the composition of recaptive society, bringing large numbers of Yoruba speakers to the colony's shores.

Yorubaland, as missionaries would later term it, was a system of mostly smaller polities, with Oyo the most dominant. Oyo was both the largest and most populous of the Yoruba kingdoms, the result of centuries of imperial expansion. At its late eighteenth-century height, the Oyo kingdom stretched ten thousand square miles and controlled between a third and a half of the Yoruba-speaking territories (Map 1.2). The kingdom's location within the Benin gap – a break in the coastal forest unique to the region – facilitated its involvement in both the trans-Saharan trade and the Atlantic trade, and led to a projection of Oyo cultural values and the usage of Yoruba as a regional lingua franca.⁵⁰ Besides trade, Oyo solidified its authority through its cavalry, sophisticated imperial administration, and the royal Ṣàngó cult. The surrounding region, speaking the Oyo dialect and under tight control by the Aláàfin ("lord of the palace"), was subsequently referred to by Samuel Johnson and other Sierra Leoneans of Oyo descent as "Yoruba proper."

The Oyo Empire reached the height of its size and power in the 1780s, after which it faced attacks on its northern frontier from the neighboring Bariba and Nupe. The reasons for Oyo's decline are complex, though Robin Law has concisely summarized them as a "combination of metropolitan dissension, provincial disaffection, and Muslim rebellion."⁵¹ Decades of internal political conflict reached a head during a succession dispute involving Afonja, the ruler of Ilorin, who was also the Are ona Kakamfo (commander of the provincial army), Oyo's highest military title. Afonja, who held ambitions of dominating the state, launched a successful coup d'etat against Aláàfin

---

⁴⁹ Olatunji Ojo, "The Organization of the Atlantic Slave Trade in Yorubaland, ca.1777 to ca. 1856," *International Journal of African Historical Studies*, 48.1 (2008): 80.

⁵⁰ Matory, *Black Atlantic Religion*, 51.   ⁵¹ Law, *Oyo Empire*, 297.

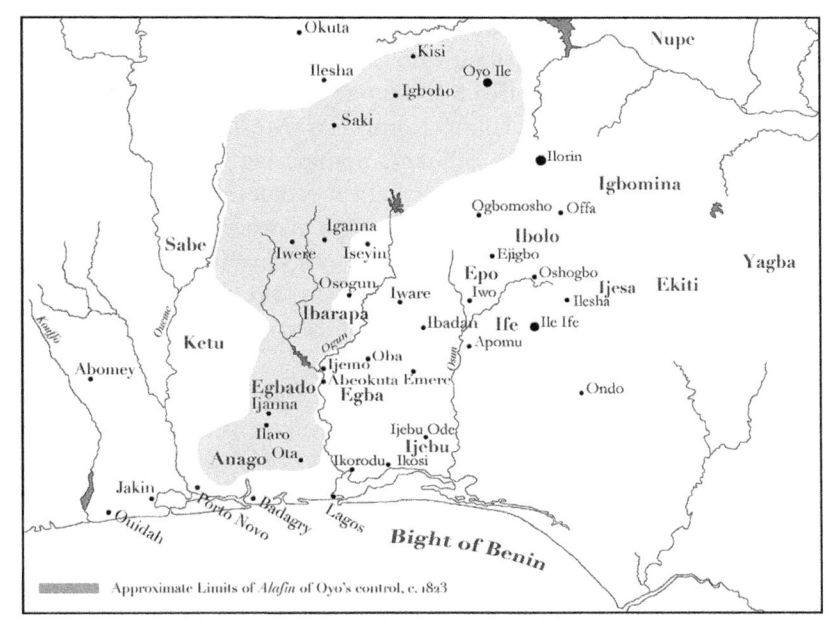

Map 1.2 The Oyo Empire and Yoruba-speaking territories, c. 1823
Map by author, based on map in Robin Law, *The Oyo Empire c. 1600–c. 1836: A West African Imperialism in the Era of the Atlantic Slave Trade* [Oxford: Clarendon Press, 1977], 279

Awole, leading Awole to commit suicide c. 1796.[52] Afonja expected that the Oyo Mesi would install him as Aláàfin; when they instead chose a less militant successor, Afonja repudiated his allegiance to Oyo and instead sought to create his own kingdom from his base at Ilorin.

A stalemate existed between Oyo and Ilorin for several years until Afonja decided to invoke a Muslim rebellion in his support. To the north of Oyo, militant Muslims, mainly Fulani under the reformer Uthmān dan Fodio, had launched a jihad in 1804 that brought most of Hausaland under the control of a Muslim Caliphate with its capital at Sokoto. The jihad overthrew the Hausa states by 1808 and spread into Nupe by 1810. Afonja, though not a Muslim himself, realized that many groups within Oyo would respond to the call for a jihad. He

[52] Robin Law, "The Chronology of the Yoruba Wars of the Early Nineteenth Century: A Reconsideration," *Journal of the Historical Society of Nigeria*, 2 (1970): 215.

secured an alliance with a group of Muslim Fulani led by the influential Muslim preacher Mallam Alimi, who declared a jihad against "pagan" Oyo. This declaration inspired a revolt of Hausa slaves in Oyo, as well as Oyo Muslims and local Fulani pastoralists. Muslim slaves formed a substantial part of the Oyo military, dominating the army's highly effective cavalry. They had increasingly become involved in Oyo's politics and were called on against the Oyo aristocracy. Ali Eisami, a Kanuri recaptive who lived for four years as a slave in Oyo, recounted that "now, all the slaves who went to war, became free; so when the slaves heard these good news, they all ran there, and the Yoruba saw it."[53]

The exact date of the Hausa slave revolt is unclear. Samuel Crowther, who experienced the assault of Afonja and his Fulbe allies on his hometown of Osogun, places the date c. 1817. Law has accepted this date, noting that Crowther was very close to these events and he may have also corroborated his dates with other Oyo recaptives in Sierra Leone.[54] Afonja used Ilorin as his base to launch a series of desultory wars in northern Oyo, leading to chaos and political instability within the kingdom. Yet Afonja fell out with his Muslim Fulani allies, who killed him in 1823 or 1824. Alimi's son Abudusalami took charge at Ilorin and set about creating an Islamic city-state aligned with the Sokoto Caliphate.[55]

The overthrow of Afonja at Ilorin c. 1823 led to further violence, as Sokoto absorbed Ilorin and aimed for the destruction of Oyo. Muslim Hausa and Nupe slaves in Oyo fled to Ilorin and formed a formidable fighting force. Crowther reported, "The enemies who carried on these wars were principally the Eyo [Oyo] Mahomedans – with whom my country abounds – with the Foulahs [Fulbe], and such foreign slaves as had escaped their owners, joined together, making a formidable force of about 20,000 who annoyed the whole country."[56] Oyo's eastern provinces fell, and refugees flooded into the forest regions of the south and east beyond the borders of the kingdom.

---

[53] "Ali Eisami Gazirmabe of Bornu," in Philip D. Curtin (ed.), *Africa Remembered: Narratives by West Africans from the Era of the Slave Trade* (Madison: University of Wisconsin Press, 1967), 212.
[54] Law, "Chronology of the Yoruba Wars," 214–215.
[55] See Ann O'Hear, "Ilorin as a Slave-Trading Emirate," in Paul E. Lovejoy (ed.), *Slavery on the Frontiers of Islam* (Princeton: Marcus Weiner, 2004), 55–68.
[56] "Samuel Ajayi Crowther of Oyo," in Curtin (ed.), *Africa Remembered*, 299.

The disintegration of Oyo was followed soon after by a series of wars in southern Yorubaland. The first victim was the kingdom of Owu, one of the principal Yoruba-speaking states. The catalyst for the conflict was the kidnapping of Oyo traders going to the Ife market town of Apomu. When provincial rulers in Oyo requested that the Olowu of Owu prevent the capture of Oyo subjects as slaves, Owu complied and attacked several Ife towns.[57] Ife declared war on Owu and, after a protracted siege of several years, a victorious Ife–Ijebu alliance captured Owu.

The earliest written reference to the Owu War comes from the Sierra Leone-based missionary John Raban, who interviewed captives of the war while compiling a Yoruba vocabulary.[58] A recently uncovered narrative by Charles Harding, a Liberated African at the Gambia, may provide the only first-hand account of the Owu War (c. 1816/17–1821/22).[59] In his narrative, Harding recounts how he "was born in Western Coast of Africa ockue nation particularly native owoo City ... until when war come to my country ... 6 or 7 years they fight day and night." The dates of the Owu War are debated within the literature. J. F. Ade Ajayi suggests dates of roughly 1820–1825, while Robin Law places the onset of the siege as c. 1816/17, and the fall of Owu as c. 1821–1822.[60] While the start and end dates of the conflict

---

[57] See A. L. Mabogunje and J. Omer-Cooper, *Owu in Yoruba History* (Ibadan: Ibadan University Press, 1971), and Robin Law, "The Owu War in Yoruba History," *Journal of the Historical Society of Nigeria*, 7.1 (1973): 141–147.

[58] John Raban, *The Eyo Vocabulary*, Part II (London: Church Missionary Society, 1831), 10.

[59] Sierra Leone Correspondence, fiche box 25, box no. 280, "Sierra Leone Odds papers," fiche no. 1880, no. 6, MMS.

There have heretofore been no known contemporary accounts of the Owu War. Several sources written in and outside Yorubaland between the 1830s and 1850s do derive testimonies from eyewitnesses. Previously, the earliest known account of the Owu War was recorded from Osifekunde, a freed slave of Ijebu origin, in Paris in 1839/1840. Marie Armand Pascal d'Avezac-Macaya, "Notice sur le Pays et le Peuple des Yébous en Afrique," in *Mémoires de la Société Ethnologique*, 2.2 (1845): 37, translated and annotated in Curtin (ed.), *Africa Remembered*, 247; Law, "The Owu War," 142.

[60] J. F. Ade Ajayi, "The Aftermath of the Fall of Old Oyo," in Ajayi and Crowder (eds.), *History of West Africa*, vol. 2, 129–166; Law, *Oyo Empire*, 275; Law, 'The Chronology of the Yoruba Wars of the Early Nineteenth Century: A Reconsideration,' *Journal of the Historical Society of Nigeria*, 2 (1970): 211–222; Law, 'The Owu War in Yoruba History', *Journal of the Historical Society of Nigeria*, 7.1 (1973): 142–143.

are debated, it is generally agreed that the siege of Owu lasted about five years.

The Owu War was a catalytic event in the expansion of warfare in Yoruba territories, producing a wave of captives who reached Freetown in the mid-1820s. Following the fall of Owu, the victorious alliance of Ife, Ijebu, and refugee Oyo did not disband but moved westward against the Egba territories. Mabogunje and Omer-Cooper suggest that the spread of warfare into Egba territory resulted from the Ijebu slave traders' vested interest in continued conflict and the large number of Oyo refugees who had no homes to return to and could not easily be disbanded.[61] The Egba's supposed support of Owu during the siege provided the allied army with a useful pretext to move against the Egba.[62]

The Egba constituted a loose federation. Their forest homelands were grouped into three territories: the Egba Agura, Egba Alake, and Egba Oke Ona.[63] They had been a dependency of Oyo, though they were one of the first to assert their independence from the faltering empire in the 1770s or 1780s.[64] But independence meant assuming responsibility for their external defense. Moreover, the united front the Egba showed against Oyo did not persist, and local outbreaks of civil war preceded the wider conflagration of the Owu War. This lack of political unity facilitated the demise of the Egba, who made little to no attempt at coordinated resistance when faced with allied forces of Ife, Ijebu, and refugee Oyo.

The testimony of one Egba recaptive, James Barber, provides much of the chronological detail of the Egba's demise.[65] A native of Ijemo, Barber was enslaved when the allied forces captured his town. He later

---

[61] Mabogunje and Omer-Cooper, *Owu in Yoruba History*, 57. As Law points out, many of these "refugees" comprised war chiefs and their marauding band of followers. Law, "Owu War," 147.

[62] The Egba had in fact remained neutral in the conflict due to both the animosity toward Owu and the divisive impact of the Muslim infiltration of the Fulani. Saburi O. Biobaku, *The Egba and Their Neighbours, 1842–1872* (Oxford: Clarendon Press, 1957), 13.

[63] Biobaku, *Egba and Their Neighbours*, 4–6; Ajayi, "Aftermath of the Fall of Old Oyo," 130.

[64] Biobaku, *Egba and Their Neighbours*, 9; I. A. Akinjogbin, "The Oyo Empire in the Eighteenth Century – A Reassessment," *Journal of the Historical Society of Nigeria*, 3.3 (1966): 458.

[65] Law, "Chronology of the Yoruba Wars," 219.

told the missionary E. C. Irving that "he was taken captive at the destruction of that place [Ijemo], and followed his new master into the Ijebu country. He was with the army that besieged Ikereku, before being sold as a slave. The town, he states, was destroyed in 1826, as it was the year previously to his being liberated at Sierra Leone, which he knows to have been 1827."[66] Another Egba recaptive, named Thomas King, recounted that his hometown of Ẹmẹrẹ was destroyed in November 1825. On his way to Lagos, King passed through the abandoned town of Kesi, which he stated was destroyed about two years earlier.[67]

Joseph Wright, a recaptive of the Egba Alake, provides the most complete account of warfare and enslavement in the Egba forests. Wright was likely from Oba, one of three Egba towns captured in a single day by the Ife–Ijebu forces in late 1826 or early 1827. Wright made clear that "[t]hese people that raised up this war … are not another nation. We are all one nation speaking one language." The siege of Oba "shut us from all business. They fought us with all their strength and we fought against them with all our might, but not with hope of escape…. At last the famine overcame us, so that the chosen men of war could not forebear."[68] After seven months of siege, the Egba fighters undertook a mission to procure food, leaving Oba vulnerable "because there remained but women and young men and boys in the town." The Ife–Ijebu forces soon breached the city's walls, and "satisfied themselves with little children, little girls, young men, and young women." Wright was presented to a war chief, sold, and transported downriver to Lagos. By 1829 most of the Egba towns were destroyed, leaving only a succession of small refugee groups and dispersed bands of fighting men. The scattered Egba established a new city at Abeokuta in c. 1830, a fortified site near the Ogun River. The city became a general refuge for Egba and Owu, growing far larger than the villages they left behind.

The final collapse of Oyo in the early 1830s provided yet more captives for the transatlantic trade. In alliance with the Nupe town of

---

[66] "Journal of the Late Dr. Irving R.N., on a Visit to the Ijebu Country," in *The Church Missionary Intelligencer*, 7 (1856): 70.
[67] King, Journal Extracts for the quarter ending June 25, 1850, CMS/CA2/O61/36. King noted that Kesi was "the town of Andrew Wilhelm," a catechist with the CMS.
[68] "Joseph Wright of the Egba," in Curtin (ed.), *Africa Remembered*, 323.

Ogodo, the Fulani of Ilorin took and plundered Oyo c. 1831–1833, forcing the Aláàfin to make a nominal confession to Islam. A final Oyo attempt to counterattack Ilorin was unsuccessful and the capital of Oyo Ile (Old Oyo) was abandoned around 1836. The Aláàfin moved the kingdom south and refounded the capital at modern Oyo. Two decades of warfare had fundamentally altered the political and demographic map of Yoruba territory.

In the years between the revolt of the enslaved Hausa (c. 1817) and the abandonment of Old Oyo (c. 1836), the British navy captured sixty-eight slave vessels in the Bight of Benin, diverting to Freetown 19,962 Africans, of whom 9,884 were embarked at Lagos. Over 94 percent of recaptives diverted to Freetown from the Bight of Benin embarked after the jihad reached Ilorin in 1817, likely placing their enslavement within the chronology of the fall of Oyo, the Owu war, and the destruction of Egba communities. Large numbers of recaptives from the Bight of Benin also arrived in Freetown from 1836 to 1838 (4,819) and from 1845 to 1850 (10,238).

At the coast, the slave trade in the Bight of Benin persisted through the 1840s and British naval patrols continued to capture vessels. The cycles of violence inland and British vigilance offshore contributed to the large and sustained influx of Yoruba speakers to Freetown over more than three decades. References to Yoruba (Aku) in Sierra Leone grew accordingly in the middle 1820s. While outnumbered by Igbo, Calabar (Efik/Ibibio), and Cosso (Mende) before the 1820s, the Aku were soon recognized as the largest "nation" in the colony. Recaptive arrivals from the Bight of Benin fell off after Britain's bombardment of Lagos in 1851 and the closure of the Brazilian trade in 1851–1852.

The best-represented Yoruba subgroups in Sierra Leone were from those regions that experienced the greatest violence. Koelle interviewed seventeen recaptives who spoke what he classified as twelve different dialects of Aku. Most of his informants were captured in war, though Koelle does not provide detail as to whether these men (usually of fighting age) were combatants or simply captured in attacks. They do however give a sense of the scale of the Yoruba presence in the colony c. 1849–1850 and the preponderance of captives from the major regions of violence within Yorubaland.

While most of Koelle's non-Yoruba informants could provide rough estimates of how many of their countrymen were in the colony, the scale of the Yoruba presence did not allow this. Koelle's Oyo informant, who had been in the colony for twenty-eight years, believed there were "several thousand" speaking the Oyo dialect. The missionary's Egba and Ìjẹ̀sà informants could only state that there were a "great many" speaking those dialects, while there were also "many" Ijebu. Most Yoruba-speaking recaptives therefore seem to have been enslaved within the Oyo kingdom, the southerly Owu kingdom, Egba territories, or the kingdom of Ijebu (Appendix C). Koelle's data corroborate the recent findings of the *African Origins Project*, in which the Egba, Ijebu, and Oyo subgroups have been most often identified.

Most of Koelle's informants taken in war had been in the colony between fifteen to twenty-four years, placing their arrival between c. 1825 and c. 1835. While some of Koelle's Aku informants noted they were captured by Fulani or Nupe, or sold on account of adultery, many were taken in conflicts, raids, and reprisals between Yoruba subgroups. Seven of Koelle's seventeen Aku informants explicitly stated that they were captured in war or kidnapped by other Yoruba speakers. Thomas Cole, from the Egba town of Igbore, stated that he was "taken by the Dsebus [Ijebu] and sold" twenty-five years earlier. Conversely, Koelle's Ijebu informant was "taken in war by the Egbas" about five years later. Both were likely therefore captured in the series of conflicts played out between the two regions in the 1820s.

Preliminary results from the *African Origins Project* highlight the centrality of Yoruba speakers in the Bight of Benin slave trade in the period after British abolition. Some 7,352 of the 8,431 names identified in the Sierra Leone registers for slave ships from the Bight of Benin have been identified as Yoruba. As the project progresses, more specific identifications will afford an increasingly nuanced perspective on the relative number of Oyo, Egba, Ijebu, and other Yoruba subgroups. All sources corroborate the mass arrival of Yoruba speakers among slaves landed at Freetown, though they differ in recording the scale of Yoruba in relation to other ethnic groups. The evidence clearly shows they were the largest ethnolinguistic group in the colony, though not an outright majority. The absence of early references to Yoruba speakers before 1817 suggests that over a twenty-year period coinciding with the fall of Oyo, Yoruba speakers went from being one of many speech communities in the colony to being the predominant.

The Central Sudan and Sierra Leone's Muslim Diaspora

Beyond the Yoruba element in receptive society was the number who made the longer journey from the Central Sudan through the ports of the Bight of Benin. In the late eighteenth and early nineteenth century, Oyo dominated the export trade from the Bight of Benin, funneling slaves from the far interior to the coast in increasing numbers.[69] Records in Sierra Leone for the years prior to Oyo's collapse show early references to "Housso" (Hausa) and "Foulah" (Fulbe) in the colony.[70] The recaptives that reached Freetown from the Bight of Benin reflected the near simultaneous outbreak of warfare in the Central Sudan and Yorubaland. The religious war led by Uthmān dan Fodio broke out in 1804 after decades of tension within Hausaland. As Mahdi Adamu points out, most slaves in the Central Sudan were acquired as prisoners of war, and Hausaland and Borno did not follow the social laws of Islam forbidding the enslavement of Muslims.[71] Koelle's Nupe informant, for example, was captured in war with the Fulani and reached Freetown around 1815.

Koelle's informants from the Central Sudan noted small numbers of their fellow language speakers, among them the Igala (13), Nupe (303), Borno or Kanuri (36), Buduma (1), Fika (5), Karekare (2), Bede and Ngizim (16), Hausa (8), and Fulani (unknown number). The 1848 census reported only 657 Hausa and 163 Nupe out of 13,273 Liberated Africans recorded. From these two sources, Lovejoy concludes that there were at least 1,240 people from the Central Sudan in Freetown, or less than 10 percent of the liberated slave population.[72]

The relative presence of Yoruba, Hausa, Nupe, and Kanuri raises the additional question of the Muslim contingent among recaptives from the Bight of Benin. Sierra Leone's Liberated Africans included a visible population of enslaved Muslims. Britain's navy patrolled the West African coast during a period in which jihad intensified the practice

---

[69] Paul E. Lovejoy, "Background to Rebellion: The Origins of Muslim Slaves in Bahia," *Slavery and Abolition*, 15.2 (1994): 156.

[70] "A List of the Boys & Girls Supported by the Church Missionary Society at Leicester Mountain," 1816, CA1/E5A/68/N, CMS.

[71] Mahdi Adamu, "The Delivery of Slaves from the Central Sudan to the Bight of Benin in the Eighteenth and Nineteenth Centuries," in Henry A. Gemery and Jan S. Hogendorn (eds.), *The Uncommon Market: Essays in the Economic History of the Atlantic Slave Trade* (New York: Academic Press, 1979), 167.

[72] Lovejoy, "Background to Rebellion," 159–160.

of Islam among elites, merchants, and the general population in West Africa. Liberated Africans came from regions of long-standing Muslim practice and Islamic expansion. The fact that the British Navy patrolled West African ports – while the ports of West Central Africa remained legally off-limits – meant that Muslims were a conspicuous element among Liberated Africans.

It is difficult to estimate with any precision the percentage of Liberated Africans who were Muslims prior to their enslavement.[73] One proxy for this – albeit a potentially imprecise one – is the recording of Muslim names within the Liberated African registers. As Domingues da Silva et al. explain, the adoption of Islamic names, especially those drawn from the Qur'an or other works of leading Islamic scholars, was one way in which Muslims identified themselves. The authors acknowledge that not every African with an Arabic name was necessarily a Muslim, just as not every African Muslim had an African name. But they conclude that "the association between name and religious affiliation seems plausible, as several scholars have noted that Africans with Arabic names in the nineteenth century were frequently Muslims or lived under the influence of Islam."[74]

Based on this methodology, Domingues da Silva et al. estimate that just 4.5 percent of Liberated Africans originating in West Africa between 1808 and 1848 had an identifiable Islamic name. Moreover, no less than 78 percent of those with Islamic names in their large sample were males. Traditional Arabic names in sub-Saharan Africa were most common in the Liberated African registers. Prophet Muhammad's name commonly appears as "Mohammed," "Mohammedu," "Mahmadoo," "Mahama," and "Majamah," while the name of the prophet's daughter, Fatimah, appears as "Fatamah," "Fahtama," "Fatima," "Fatuma," and other variations. Other common names, such as Abu Bakr, Ahmad, Bukhari, Ibrahim, Sulayman, and Uthman, also appear in different forms.[75]

---

[73] Harrell-Bond, Howard, and Skinner have previously suggested (though it is unclear on what basis) that among the Liberated Africans "there were many – perhaps up to 10 percent – who were followers of Islam before their resettlement in Sierra Leone." Harrell-Bond et al., *Community Leadership*, 106.
[74] Domingues da Silva, B. Daniel, David Eltis, Nafees Khan, Philip Misevich, and Olatunji Ojo, "The Transatlantic Muslim Diaspora to Latin America in the Nineteenth Century," *Colonial Latin American Review*, 26.4 (2017): 529.
[75] Ibid., 7.

The name data indicate that Muslim Liberated Africans most likely departed Upper Guinea and the Bight of Benin. Probably a higher proportion of Liberated Africans from the Upper Guinea coast were Muslims, but the greatest total number of Muslim Liberated Africans were from the Bight of Benin due to the British Navy's constant patrolling of this coastline following the start of the jihad in the Hausa states and Nupe and especially after its spread to Oyo in 1817.

The name analysis and other data all suggest that only a small percentage of captives carried into the transatlantic trade were Muslims. Opposition to the enslavement of freeborn Muslims was a central factor in the jihad movement of the late eighteenth and early nineteenth century. Lovejoy has argued that this was a significant inhibiting factor in the provision of slaves to the Americas, and that Muslims were accordingly underrepresented in terms of the number of slaves exported, particularly in the nineteenth century.[76] Lofkrantz has shown how the protection of freeborn Muslims was not always possible.[77] War inevitably led to extensive enslavement, including of many Muslim captives, some of whom entered the Atlantic slave trade despite the goals of Muslim leaders to protect the Muslim community.

The biographical accounts of Muslim Liberated Africans demonstrate how Muslims could still be enslaved despite the intentions of the jihad leadership. Ali Eisami, born to a Muslim cleric in Borno, was enslaved in 1808 when the jihad forces sacked the Borno capital. A Sergeant Frazer, serving in the Second West India Regiment in Freetown, told one of his officers in 1821 that he was "born in Houssa [Hausa], and resided there for a long time, was taken prisoner in Goingia [Gonja], and brought to the Gold Coast, where he was sold."[78] Similarly, the Liberated African Pasco, whose birth name was Abubakar, told how he was born in Gobir but was "kidnapped by a marauding party of Falatahs [Fulbe], and sold to a Gonja trader"

---

[76] Paul E. Lovejoy, *Jihād in West Africa during the Age of Revolutions* (Athens: Ohio University Press, 2016), 31, 133–166. Lovejoy concludes that "admittedly based on some extent of conjecture, fewer than 10 percent of Africans taken to the Americas came from Muslim areas, and even fewer were actually Muslims."

[77] Jennifer Lofkrantz, "Protecting Freeborn Muslims: The Sokoto Caliphate's Attempts to Prevent Illegal Enslavement and Its Acceptance of the Strategy of Ransoming," *Slavery & Abolition*, 32.1 (2011): 109–127.

[78] "Narrative of a Journey from Egypt to the Western Coast of Africa, by Mahomed Misrah. Communicated by an Officer Serving in Sierra Leone, April 8, 1821," *Quarterly Journal*, October 1822, 16.

sometime before 1815.[79] From Gonja, Abubakar was resold "to a native of Ashantee... and sold to the master of a Portuguese schooner, then lying at Whydah."

The number of Liberated Africans identified as "Hausa," "Tapa" (i.e. Nupe), and "Borno" demonstrates that enslaved Muslims were entering the transatlantic trade after the dual impact of Sokoto's establishment in 1804 and British abolition in 1807. Many enslaved Muslims in Yoruba territories – often from the Central Sudan – were exported when their presence was viewed as a threat. This included Ali Eisami, who was enslaved to the "son of the Katunga king" at Oyo.[80] When Afonja incited his rebellion and offered freedom to slaves who joined his forces, Eisami's Yoruba master sold him to the coast at Porto Novo to prevent his escape. Eisami was likely one of many slaves within Oyo who were sold into the transatlantic trade in the wake of the jihad, of whom many likely reached Sierra Leone.

The large contingent of Yoruba speakers who reached Sierra Leone would have included a conspicuous number of Muslims among their ranks. The earliest CMS school registers include "Accoo" children with Muslim names, such as "Abdool Messeeh", a sixteen-year-old at school in Regent in 1821.[81] Islam had reached Yoruba territory from the north by at least the seventeenth century, carried by soldiers, settlers, and traders in particular. By the nineteenth century, Muslim communities were established in market and port towns such as Owu, Badagry, and in particular the Oyo capital.[82] These early Muslim communities – based almost entirely within the Oyo Empire – comprised Yoruba and non-Yoruba, including slaves such as Ali Eisami. The earlier arrival and influence of Islam in comparison to Christianity among the Yoruba is reflected in the Yoruba saying *Ile la ba Ifa, ile la ba Ilame, osagangan ni ti Igbagbo* (We met Ifá at home, we met Islam at home, but only later in the day did we encounter Christianity). Still,

---

[79] Richard Lander, *Records of Captain Clapperton's Last Expedition to Africa*, vol. 1 (London: Henry Colburn and Richard Bentley, 1830), 204–206.

[80] Eisami may be referring to the son of former Aláàfin or a claimant, the office of Aláàfin likely being vacant at this time. Despite the ambiguity, it is clear Eisami was purchased by a prominent member of Oyo society. Curtin (ed.), *Africa Remembered*, 212.

[81] List of African children named after benefactors, made out by Mr. James Norman, up to December 29, 1821, CMS/CA1/M1.

[82] For the broader chronology, see T. G. O. Gbadamosi, *The Growth of Islam among the Yoruba, 1841–1908* (London: Longman, 1978).

it is unlikely that at the beginning of the nineteenth century Islam had been adopted by more than a small minority of the Oyo–Yoruba and hardly at all by non-Oyo.[83]

The only other estimates for the percentage of Liberated Africans who practiced Islam comes from colonial census data. Given the state's official hostility to Islam, estimates for the number of Muslims within the colony are likely imprecise or understated. Acting-Governor Pine's annual report for 1848 concluded that "the Mahomedans residing in this colony are in number about 2000" (out of an estimated population of 45,006).[84] That year's census estimated their number at 2,439 out of a population of 46,511.[85] Other census data present a similar picture, though most colonial censuses did not attempt to enumerate the population based on religion.

Conclusion

Sierra Leone's recaptive population is perhaps the best-documented African diasporic population in the Atlantic world. Nevertheless, conclusions on the composition of recaptive society have varied greatly. Gwendolyn Midlo Hall has concluded that "Africans arriving in some regions in the Americas were not nearly as varied as Africans who were disembarked and resettled within a limited time period in Sierra Leone from recaptured ships."[86] Indeed, the West Africa squadron diverted to Freetown captives of both the slave trades to northeastern Brazil and Cuba, the latter being by the 1800s perhaps the most regionally diverse branch of the transatlantic trade throughout its history. Yet the Royal Navy's emphasis on certain ports, and the political and military developments inland from them, meant that a handful of ethnic groups were prevalent among those disembarked. At the same time, the common contemporary and historiographical view of a Yoruba majority is likely exaggerated, though Chapter 6 will explore the combination of

[83] J. D. Y. Peel, *Christianity, Islam, and the Oriṣa: Three Traditions in Comparison and Interaction* (Oakland: University of California Press, 2016), 151.
[84] Benjamin Pine, Report on the Annual Blue Book of Sierra Leone for the year 1847, enclosed in dispatch no. 88 of October 27, 1848, CO 267/204.
[85] Report of the Annual Blue Book of Sierra Leone for the Year 1848, CO 267/209.
[86] Gwendolyn Midlo Hall, *Slavery and African Ethnicities in the Americas: Restoring the Links* (Chapel Hill: University of North Carolina Press, 2005), 166.

Conclusion

demographic, political, religious, and cultural factors that led many nineteenth-century (and subsequent) observers to believe this.

A sizable percentage of recaptives were from the region that now constitutes the nation of Sierra Leone, particularly in the early years of the squadron from 1808 to 1819. Eventually, their numbers were eclipsed by the much larger movement of peoples from the Bights of Benin and Biafra, especially Yoruba and Igbo speakers. By contrast, few recaptives were drawn from the expanses of African coast between Cape Mount (in present-day Liberia) and the Volta River (eastern Ghana), between the Wouri River (Cameroon) and Cabinda, or south of Ambriz. West Central Africans were a minority, and perhaps in no other African diaspora in the Atlantic were they so underrepresented. Sierra Leone's recaptive population thus reflected the scale and diverse regional origins of the nineteenth-century slave trade, but also the concentration of the trade at certain ports and the historical processes and mechanisms of enslavement in their hinterlands.

2 | *Their Own Middle Passage*
Voyages to Sierra Leone

A quarter-century after he had been torn from his family and sold into transatlantic slavery, Thomas King, a CMS pastor and Egba Liberated African, recalled "the morning of that unhappy day that I was separated from my parents about the year 1825 in the beginning of November." On that morning, the young man had

> left home about eight o'clock for farm about three miles distance from home, in order to get some corn … No sooner had I got to the farm, and just cut sufficient corn for my load, than the repeated reports of muskets at the town gate acquainted me of my dangerous situation. All my endeavour to escape had utterly proved a failure, as I was surrounded by a number of men, who were very eager, as to whose lot my capture should fall. At last, as a kid among many chasing wolfs, I was caught by one of them. It was a day of inexpressible sorrow to me.

King – whose birth name is unknown – grew up in the Egba town of Ẹmẹrẹ. As war descended on the towns of the Egba forest, Ẹmẹrẹ fell to the marauding Ife, Ijebu, and refugee Oyo forces in late 1825. King's captors swiftly moved their prisoners of war; he recounted how "before a fortnight after my capture, I was sold to one of the Havannah slave traders at Lagos" where he remained for about three weeks. Here, "the sad intelligence that our town was reduced to ashes reached us. A few days later, with heavy hearts and sad countenances, we took leave of our shores without the slightest hope of visiting it any more."[1]

King was likely sold to the slave traders of the Havana-bound ship *Iberia*, which departed Lagos on December 27, 1825, with the young man and 421 others confined below deck.[2] After being intercepted at sea, the vessel and its captive cargo, under the guidance of the crew of

---

[1] King, Journal Extracts for Quarter ending June 25, 1850, CMS/CA2/O61/36; "How Thomas King Became a Slave," *Church Missionary Gleaner*, May 1851, 138–141.
[2] *Voyages*, http://slavevoyages.org/voyage/2368/variables.

HMS *Brazen*, arrived in Freetown Harbor in late January 1826.[3] The 417 survivors of the twenty-six-day journey were dispersed to the Liberated African villages; 30 died of smallpox soon after.[4]

Thomas King's experiences were like those of tens of thousands of Liberated Africans. For them, the arduous journeys to liberation occurred over thousands of miles of land and ocean. They were subjected to weeks of disease, cramped conditions, and uncertainty over their destination and the duration of their confinement. This chapter argues that these shared experiences of enslavement, the Middle Passage, naval interception, and relocation were fundamental to how Liberated African society was forged. The society that emerged in nineteenth-century Sierra Leone was far more than the relative demographic inputs of Africans of various regions and cultures; it was also the result of improbable journeys and traumatic memories. The chapter first elucidates the experiences of enslavement and forced migration, drawing on the personal narratives of recaptives and British naval men. The chapter then considers how the experience of forced migration and shared misery on board slave ships forged lasting bonds between individuals and entire communities that endured in Sierra Leone.

Both first-hand accounts, written by Africans and Britons, as well as quantitative data make it clear that the navy's interventions did little to immediately alleviate the plight of the Africans for whom the squadron was intended to help. Interception and transportation to Sierra Leone were not triumphant moments of emancipation. Rather, recaptives underwent their own "Middle Passage," analogous to slaving journeys to the Americas in terms of voyage length, uncertainties over their future, and the omnipresence of disease and death. Like slaves disembarked in the New World, recaptives were torn from families, commoditized, placed in deadly conditions, and transported to unfamiliar settings. In this process the oceanic voyage was the middle stage in a journey from their societies of birth to Sierra Leone. First came their journeys to the coast; second their embarkation on a slave ship and interception by the British; last was the drawn-out process of disembarkation and acclimatizing physically and socially to their new environment, not unlike the process of "seasoning" that Africans faced in

---

[3] Schooner *Iberia*, January 31, 1826, FO 315/36.
[4] Liberated African Department Statement of Disposals, 1821–1833, SLPA.

the Americas. Each phase was marked by adversity, even if the lives these recaptives subsequently led was far different from those of their counterparts on the other side of the Atlantic.

Arguing that recaptives underwent their own Middle Passage requires an elaboration on the famous term. "Middle Passage" has historically referred to the shipping patterns of Europeans trading in human beings. It is a Eurocentric description of the slave trade from the vantage of the slave ship. In recent years historians have appropriated the term to describe the conditions and experiences common to forced migrations in the early modern and modern periods. African historians have added to and changed the meaning of "Middle Passage," recognizing that the march to the coast was often as long and deadly as the ensuing oceanic voyage, and therefore deserving of equal consideration. Paul Lovejoy has encouraged scholars of the slave trade to "place the 'middle passage' in the middle," arguing that "what happened before the shipboard trauma had ramifications affecting the historical development of the African diaspora, the other side of the 'middle' for the enslaved."[5]

At the same time, a growing body of scholarship on comparative forced migrations has explored the Middle Passage conceptually as "the structuring link between expropriation in one geographic setting and exploitation in another."[6] Christopher, Pybus, and Rediker have explored the social and cultural transformations associated with the movement of indentured servants, transported convicts, and coerced migrants around the globe. They argue that the experience of dislocation and alienation were a shared facet of all such journeys. Certainly, their emphasis on "the sense of disarticulation from all that was previously known" applies equally to the voyages of recaptives as it does to their chosen case studies.[7] A central question of this and subsequent chapters is the social consequences for Liberated Africans being physically compelled to move, by both slave traders and the British Navy.

---

[5] Paul E. Lovejoy, "Identifying Enslaved Africans in the Diaspora," in Lovejoy (ed.), *Identity in the Shadow of Slavery*, 2.

[6] Emma Christopher, Cassandra Pybus, and Marcus Rediker (eds.), *Many Middle Passages: Forced Migrations and the Making of the Modern World*, (Berkeley: University of California Press, 2007), 2.

[7] Ibid.

Their Own Middle Passage: Voyages to Sierra Leone

Capturing the experiences of dislocation, alienation, and social transformation among recaptives requires multiple methodologies. Recent studies of the slave trade have argued that the quantitative approach that has dominated the study of the Middle Passage cannot fully convey the horrors of forced oceanic migration.[8] In light of these critiques has been a return to narratives, microhistory, and biography.[9] But these methodologies need not be in opposition, and the reconstruction of individual lives from slavery to liberation should employ all available sources and levels of analysis. This chapter explores both individual life stories of recaptives and how those stories were reflective of the experiences of 100,000 Africans in the nineteenth century.

Thomas King, whose testimony began this chapter, was one of many Liberated Africans who left accounts of their experiences enslavement in Africa. While most of the estimated 12.5 million victims of the transatlantic slave trade left no account of their lives and experiences, a disproportionate number of Liberated Africans did exactly that. The CMS and Methodist Missionary Society (MMS) archives hold some of the most famous narratives of enslavement in West Africa, including those of Samuel Crowther, Joseph Wright, and Ali Eisami. Beyond these famous chroniclers, the archival record on Sierra Leone contains a treasure trove of unexplored narratives and life histories, from brief recollections told to missionaries and travelers, to detailed narratives of lost lives and new beginnings.[10]

These narratives provide first-hand accounts of the revolutionary changes that swept regions of West Africa at the turn of the nineteenth

---

[8] Vincent Brown has argued that the reliance on business records and use of quantification "renders the deadly migration of Africans somewhat like the chalk outline of a murder victim." Vincent Brown, *The Reaper's Garden: Death and Power in the World of Atlantic Slavery* (Cambridge, MA: Harvard University Press, 2008), 29. See also Stephanie E. Smallwood, *Saltwater Slavery: A Middle Passage from Africa to the American Diaspora* (Cambridge, MA: Harvard University Press, 2007).

[9] See, e.g., Robert Harms, *The Diligent: A Voyage through the Worlds of the Slave Trade* (New York: Basic Books, 2002); Marcus Rediker, *The Slave Ship: A Human History* (New York: Penguin, 2007); Lisa A. Lindsay and John Wood Sweet (eds.), *Biography and the Black Atlantic* (Philadelphia: University of Pennsylvania Press, 2014).

[10] For a discussion of these sources, see Richard Anderson, "Uncovering Testimonies of Slavery and the Slave Trade in Missionary Sources: The SHADD Biographies Project and the CMS and MMS Archives for Sierra Leone, Nigeria, and the Gambia," *Slavery & Abolition*, 38.3 (September 2017): 620–644.

century. Several of these sources have helped historians determine the basic chronology of particular battles and campaigns outlined in the previous chapter. Beyond their obvious emotive quality in conveying the lived experience of enslavement is what they reveal about how these conditions and this journey necessitated a reappraisal of self-identity and belonging, as enslaved Africans moved from their societies of birth to increasingly alien surroundings. Moreover, the context of enslavement – who one's enslavers were, what became of their family and kin, and what vestiges of community were left behind – had implications for how recaptives defined themselves and interacted with others once in Sierra Leone.

Enslavement

Testimonies from Liberated Africans indicate that most were captured in war. Among Koelle's informants, 141 specified the nature of their enslavement. Though it is important not to extrapolate from these 141 biographical records to make conclusions regarding 100,000 recaptives, certain commonalities emerge from the accounts of Koelle's informants. Forty-eight (34 percent) had been taken in war, while forty-three stated they had been kidnapped. Thirty-two recaptive informants stated they had been enslaved for a year or more prior to being sold into the Atlantic trade. Among those who had spent the longest period enslaved was Isambakon, also known as George File, Koelle's "Fulop" (Diola) informant. Isambakon was five years a slave to his kidnappers, "three years in the hand of a Portuguese; and after this he was about five years at Bisao [Bissau]." Adibe, otherwise known as George Rose, similarly spent many years as a slave, having been "born in the Isoama country, whence he was stolen and brought to Aro when a little boy. He was brought up in the village of Asaga of the Aro country, and lived there until about his twenty-fourth year, when he was sold to the Portuguese at Obane."[11] As Adibe's ordeal suggests, many of those held for years as slaves had been enslaved as children. By contrast, many adult males, particularly those taken in battle, were less easy to control and so were "at once carried to the sea."[12]

---

[11] Koelle, *Polyglotta Africana*, 1, 8.
[12] For example, Koelle's Hausa informant from Kano "was made prisoner on a war-expedition against Go bur, where he was bought by slave-dealers, and at

Enslavement

The most detailed accounts of enslavement come from individuals whose captures were the result of the religious revolutions of the central Sudan and the demise of Oyo. Ali Eisami was witness to and victim of the jihad of Uthmān dan Fodio in Borno. Ali recalled how, when traveling to visit a friend in another town, "seven Fulbe waylaid us, seized us, tied our hands upon our backs, fettered us, out us in the way, and then we went till it became day."[13] Eisami was carried through the nascent Sokoto Caliphate via Katsina, being purchased by a member of the Oyo aristocracy and taken to Oyo Ile. He was held in the Yoruba capital for four years, until Afonja's revolt spurred the enslaved Hausa soldiers of the city to rise up. Eisami's owner was told by a friend, "If you do not sell this slave of yours, he will run away, and go to the war, so that your cowries will be lost." In order not to lose his investment, his owner took Eisami to the coast at Porto Novo "where white men had landed."

Samuel Crowther, born as Ajayi at Osogun in the south of Oyo, was similarly impacted by these revolutionary changes. Following the Hausa uprising, violence spread southward from the imperial capital to Ajayi's homeland in early 1821. Crowther recalled the day "in which I was violently turned out of my father's house, and separated from relations; and in which I was made to experience what is called to be in slavery." In two versions of his narrative, Crowther variously identified those who destroyed his village and took him and his family as slaves. In one account, he identified the perpetrators as "principally the Oyo Mahomedans, with whom my country abounds – with the Foulahs [Fulbe], and such foreign slaves as had escaped from their owners." Later, he placed the Fulbe before the Oyo Muslims, describing the "enemies" as an army "composed of Foulahs, Yorriba Mahommedans and slaves of every description." In the latter account, Crowther described how "[i]n attempting to escape in the crowd with my mother, two sisters and a cousin, we were taken by two Yorriba Mahomedans who immediately threw nooses of cords around our necks and led us away as their prey." The captured family had not even been taken from the ransacked town "when two Foulah men attacked our captors and contended with them about dividing their

---

once carried to the sea by way of Kadzina, Zalia, Nupe, Ilori [Ilorin], Dsebu [Ijebu], and Eko [Lagos]." Koelle, *Polyglotta Africana*, 17.

[13] Eisami in Curtin (ed.), *Africa Remembered*, 211.

prey as they had not got in time to get any."[14] Crowther was first taken north to Iseyin, allotted to the chief of the captors, before being traded for a horse. He was a slave first to the horse merchant at Iseyin and later an Oyo market woman. Through this transaction Crowther was "separated from my mother and sister, my then only comforts, to meet no more in this world of misery."

Over a period of fourteen months, Crowther was sold multiple times. During this ordeal, Ajayi "was sold to a Mahomedan woman, with whom I travelled to many towns on our way to the Popo country on the coast." As Crowther moved away from Osogun, he met an increasingly unfamiliar environment. The man who would later take the formative steps in standardizing a written "Yoruba" language self-identified at this time more narrowly with "my Eyo [Oyo] country." In his forced travels, Crowther noted how, "[f]rom Ijaye to Itoko all spoke the Ebwah [Egba] dialect, but my mistress, my own dialect. Here I was a perfect stranger, having left the Oyo country far behind." From the unfamiliar Egba territory, Crowther was again "bartered for tobacco, rum, and other articles" to an Ijebu slave trader who held him for two months before taking him to the coast at Lagos. At the coast, Ajayi "got once more into another dialect, the fourth from mine; if I may not call it altogether another language, on account of now and then, in some words, there being a faint shadow of my own."

Eisami and Crowther's journeys to Sierra Leone, through Porto Novo and Lagos, respectively, were outcomes of an expanding radius of violence and instability. The accounts of recaptives beyond Oyo and the frontiers of jihad, who generally reached Sierra Leone in subsequent years, present an image of comparative stability but also foreboding. Joseph Wright, whose birth name is not known, was born of the Egba Alake, though he later titled his narrative more broadly as "a native of Ackoo." Wright, whose enslavement came some six years after Crowther, recounted how "all the time we heard of that war in a far distant land, we confidently thought they will not come to us. Alas, in the space of about seven years after [the wars began] they came to us unexpectedly."[15] Unlike Eisami and Crowther, who noted the ethnic or religious foreignness of their captors, Wright recounted that his captors were not foreigners, but that they were "all one nation

---

[14] Crowther in Curtin (ed.), *Africa Remembered*, 299.
[15] Wright in Curtin (ed.), *Africa Remembered*, 323.

Enslavement

speaking one language." Wright did not reflect on how this made him feel toward other Yoruba speakers or how this might have affected relations between those in Sierra Leone who had been on opposing sides of these conflicts. He did write that "[t]he inhabitants of Ikko [Lagos] are very cruel people. They would even sell the children of their own bosom." Like Crowther, linguistic similarity fell far short of feelings of affinity toward those who sold him.

The reality of being captured and sold by others of "one nation" shaped feelings of distrust and resentment. James Will was, like Joseph Wright, a Methodist recaptive preacher who left an account of his enslavement. Like Wright, Will stated that he was "born in the land of Akue," and that "the place where I was born undoubtedly is about seven days journey to the sea shore." Will does not specify his place of birth within the Yoruba-speaking territory, but notes that war had not reached his particular town until around the time of his enslavement (c. 1829–1830), when he was captured by raiders carrying firearms. Here, Will lived

> until it has pleased the almighty God to pour upon us a very great confusion, and they began to war one city against other they that win the battle will then kill so many in that day the rest they took and bound them all and made them slaves .... So this confusion and inrespites proceeds on until, and last of all the war came in to our native place where I was born we use to run from place to place that we may not become their pray ... and every time when they come against us they will go and surround about one city first and when they broken that city they come another by so doing they have destroyed all our lands and the places were then left desolates and we fled into a large body of army in another part.[16]

Unlike Crowther, Will was not enslaved at the time of his town's destruction. Instead, like many Yoruba speakers in this "great confusion," Will and his family sought security with others who spoke the same language, but found their trust betrayed. Will remembered how

> we found some men of the same place where we going we begged them to lead us home and they willing immediately they told us to trust on them, but alas they did not lead us home alone but they led us to their own house and separated us into a different places.

---

[16] James Will narrative, part 1 MMS/SpecialSeries/VariousPapers/FBN44 (mms/ 17/03/01/58); James Will narrative Part 2 – MMS/17/02/03 [H-2723 Box 593].

Having been made a slave by "our country men" with whom he sought refuge, Will arrived in Sierra Leone, most likely via Ouidah. At Freetown, Will and his shipmates "were landed on shore and we were very glad for what we have once again permitted again to tread on the face of the earth." But Will's distrust lingered. Though "the white people have compassion on us and delivered us from men dealers and make us free from slave," Will could not forget that when "we fled to our country men for refuge, they did us no good ... because they are tyrant and barbarous creature." For James Will, like Joseph Wright, identifying as "Aku" in the diaspora meant looking past being enslaved by their "country men" and those "of one nation."

The narratives presented above are concentrated from what is today Nigeria. Many recaptives lived in regions far from these narrators and their enslavement was not the result of seismic historical processes. Yet these stories illuminate commonalities that all recaptives endured: alienation from home and family, and often a sense of anger and betrayal. Prior to their enslavement, these narrators identified primarily in terms of family and their local community. Slavery and forced migration necessitated a reimaging of self-identity.

Once enslaved, Crowther and Eisami, like many of Koelle's informants, did not experience a linear march to the coast, and their sale into the transatlantic trade was never a foregone conclusion. As Koelle's informants attest, many recaptives spent months and years as captives before entering the Atlantic commercial system, often by a turn of fate. This protracted land journey often took far longer than the Middle Passage. Herbert Klein has estimated that most slaves spent at a minimum six months to a year from capture until they boarded European ships, averaging three months on the coast waiting to board.[17] The biographical accounts from Sierra Leone substantiate these estimates. James "Kaweli" Covey, a Liberated African who later served as interpreter in the famous *Amistad* case, was kidnapped before his tenth birthday and "was carried to the Bullom country, and sold as a slave to Ba-yi-mi, the king of the Bul-loms, who resided at Mani." He then "lived there for three years, and was employed to

---

[17] Herbert S. Klein, *The Atlantic Slave Trade* (Cambridge: Cambridge University Press, 1999), 130.

plant rice for the wife of Ba-yi-mi, who treated him with great kindness."[18] The kindness ended when he was sold to the coast in 1833. Ali Eisami spent eight years as a bondsman in Kano, Katsina, and Oyo Ile between his capture c. 1810 and his Atlantic passage in 1818. Similarly, by the time Crowther got to the coast he could describe himself as "a veteran in slavery." Clearly, the British were not intercepting Africans at the outset of their journey to New World slavery. Whether judged by time or distance, much of their journey as slaves had already past when it was aborted by naval intervention.

Embarkation and Interception

The entry of recaptives into the Atlantic trade commonly began in coastal barracoons – walled, prison-like compounds – where slaves awaited purchase and transferral to the slave ship. John Attarra, who reached Sierra Leone between 1816 and 1819, recounted conditions on the coast. In the barracoons, the enslaved boy "found here, many Africans, who were already bought before me. But, here, I could not find any with whom I might converse." Attarra "remained here, only for a couple of weeks, and then we were conveyed into the open sea, where I had with trembling, to behold the faces of many of the Portuguese."[19] Another Liberated African, Josiah Yamsey, shared Attarra's shock on encountering Europeans for the first time. Yamsey told the German missionary W. A. B. Johnson how he "had never seen white people before & I was [a]fraid too much; now I have come to the people who will surley eat me."[20]

In the nineteenth century, enslaved Africans could be imprisoned in barracoons for weeks and even months. With British ships patrolling the West African coast, slave traders adopted new tactics in order to elude detection. Slave ship captains were now disinclined to wait

---

[18] John Warner Barber, *A History of the* Amistad *Captives* (New Haven, CT: E. L. & J. W. Barber, 1840), 47. See also Benjamin N. Lawrance, "La Amistad's 'Interpreter' Reinterpreted: James 'Kaweli' Covey's Distressed Atlantic Childhood and the Production of Knowledge about Nineteenth-Century Sierra Leone," in Lovejoy and Schwarz (eds.), *Slavery, Abolition, and the Transition to Colonialism in Sierra Leone*, 217–255.
[19] Attarra, Letter, March 3, 1837, CMS/CA1/O33/5; "A Liberated African's Account of His Slavery, and Subsequent Course," *Church Missionary Gleaner*, vol. 6, no. 2, February 1846, 16–18, and no. 3, March 1846, 27–28.
[20] Johnson, March 24, 1820, CMS/CA1/O126/121.

offshore with a partially filled complement of slaves or to visit multiple ports to secure the best prices. This was a prudent move on the slavers' part, as the presence of slaves on board was the only irrefutable evidence accepted by the courts of Sierra Leone in order to confiscate the vessel. The enslaved therefore spent a greater amount of time in barracoons until enough of them were gathered to fill an entire slave cargo and immediately depart.

At the Gallinhas, there was a practice in place by 1825 to "never embark slaves until the vessels are quite ready for sea."[21] In the 1840s, Captain Tucker of HMS *Wolverine* reported that slave traders at the Rio Nun had adopted a system that allowed a slave vessel to load its cargo and sail within four hours. Slave traders would use a white flag with a black border to signal to shore, at which point large canoes carrying as many as 90–100 slaves each were quickly deployed.[22] At Lagos, a similar system of expedited loading times emerged. The Brazilian slaver *Relâmpago* anchored at Lagos for barely twenty-four hours in September 1851. In that time, it discharged its outbound cargo and loaded 820 slaves assembled on shore.[23] British patrols may have thus led to overcrowding, long confinement to coastal barracoons with poor food and water provisions, and the shipping of slaves at high-risk periods of the day and year.[24] Eltis has argued that these changes in the nature of the slave trade did not have a detrimental effect on the mortality experienced at sea. Nonetheless, the extended stay in these cramped, diseased barracoons was but another facet of the ambiguous human consequences of British naval suppression.

The navy could capture a vessel with only part of its human cargo loaded or, in the era of the equipment clause, with the entirety of its purchases still imprisoned on shore.[25] In such incidences, the slaves remained in the hands of coastal slave dealers, their fates largely

---

[21] Hamilton and Refell to Foreign Office, April 10, 1825, FO 84/38.
[22] Lt. Norcott to Tucker, letter extract in Tucker to R. More O'Ferrall, Admiralty, February 15, 1841, CO 267/177.
[23] Ojo, "Organization of the Atlantic Slave Trade in Yorubaland," 84.
[24] David Eltis, "Fluctuations in Mortality in the Last Half Century of the Transatlantic Slave Trade," *Social Science History*, 13.3 (Fall 1989): 330.
[25] The equipment clause allowed for slave vessels to be captured without slaves on board. These clauses were inserted into treaties with the Netherlands in 1823 and Spain in 1835. Lord Palmerston's Act of August 24, 1839, unilaterally authorized the capture of Brazilian and Portuguese vessels equipped for slaving. Bethell, "The Mixed Commissions," 79–93.

unaffected, held to be resold to the next arriving slaver or until the original purchaser could commandeer a new vessel and return to claim their cargo. One strategy used by the navy was to coerce coastal slave traders to hand over their captives. The crew of HMS *Owen Glendower* boarded the Spanish *Maria la Luz*, only to find that they had been spotted on approach and the slaves landed. One midshipman from the *Owen Glendower* wrote that their boats "anchored off the town [and] sent a flag of truce in to know whether they would give us up the schooner and slaves – if not we should land and burn the town." According to this account, the threat "so alarmed the poor wretches that our request was complied with and in less than two hours 181 slaves were brought off most of them women and children from 3 to 15 years old."[26]

While many slave vessels were captured at anchor or had their slaves forcibly embarked from shore, others were intercepted in the Atlantic, often after harrowing chases. The Spanish ship *Veloz Pasajera* was captured in 1830 after a twenty-minute gun battle in which five slaves and three crewmen were killed and many more injured.[27] Facing interception, some slave crews took drastic action. Knowing that vessels could only be condemned with slaves found on board, they jettisoned their captives overboard to their deaths. A naval officer reported in 1814 that while chasing the Spanish ship *Carlos* "eighty were thrown overboard before we captured her."[28] In another incident, it was suspected that the slavers on board *La Jeune Estelle* had placed twelve slaves in casks that were thrown overboard during the navy's pursuit.[29] Interception, then, was at once a moment of rescue from New World slavery, but also at times the unintended catalyst of mass killings at sea.

Whether intercepted at anchor, along the coast, or in the Atlantic, the immediate response of captives on board was likely bemusement rather than celebration. Many Africans would have been astounded by the idea of combat on water, let alone having to suffer through it. Ali Eisami recounted that he and his shipmates were being exercised above

---

[26] Cheesman Henry Binstead, *Memorandum of Remarks on Board HM Ship Owen Glendower Commodore Sir Robert Mends, from England, and along the Western Coast of Africa*. 2005.76/1, January 21–May 9, 1823, Royal Naval Museum Library, Portsmouth.
[27] Findlay to George Murray, October 8, 1830, CO 267/105.
[28] Buxton, *African Slave Trade and Its Remedy*, 109.   [29] Ibid., 140.

decks when the British were spotted in the distance. Eisami was amazed to see the British preparing their guns as "we had never seen any one make war in the midst of water."[30] Samuel Crowther similarly felt "no safety in the land nor on the sea, particularly at sea where we thought war was totally impracticable."[31] British naval men thus faced the task of convincing those on board that they were different from other white men, whom they likely knew only as slave traders. Without a common language, the first step to convince the Africans on board of their intentions was a symbolic one: the removal of chains. Eisami recalled that the British men "took off all the fetters from our feet, and threw them into the water ... they opened the water-casks, that we might drink water to the full, and we also ate food ... we said, 'Now our Lord has taken us out of slavery,' and thanked him."[32]

Other recaptives were not so immediately convinced of British intentions. Crowther recalled that when the British stormed the *Esperanza Feliz*, he felt as though he was "in the hands of new conquerors, whom we at first much dreaded, they being armed with long swords." Before interception, the *Esperanza Feliz*'s crew fueled Crowther's fears by claiming the British were sea robbers. It was only when Crowther found himself able to explore the ship freely in search of food that he "began to entertain a good opinion of our conquerors."[33] Joseph Wright's captors played upon African fears of European cannibalism, telling him that "these [the British] were the people which will eat us, if we suffered them to prize us."[34] These thoughts must have run through the minds of many recaptives, whether captured at sea, at anchor, or coerced from shore onto sailing ships.

To what degree could British sailors communicate with Africans? Could the British effectively convey the message that they were liberators? Was this message believed? How were obedience and order ensured? The historical record – as written by both Africans and Navy men – provides only partial answers to these questions. For one, evidence of violent disputes and insurrections are few. When females rebelled below the decks of the captured slaver *Veloz* in 1836, Lieutenant James Stoddart and his crew allied with the slave ship captain to

---

[30] Eisami in Curtin (ed.), *Africa Remembered*, 214.
[31] Crowther in Curtin (ed.), *Africa Remembered*, 312.
[32] Eisami in Curtin (ed.), *Africa Remembered*, 214–215.
[33] Crowther in Curtin (ed.), *Africa Remembered*, 312–313.
[34] Wright in Curtin (ed.), *Africa Remembered*, 331–332.

suppress the revolt. According to Stoddart, "cats and cutlasses ... had to be used freely."[35] Yet the *Veloz* appears to be a rare occurrence of violence. Given that the Africans always greatly outnumbered the British, were unchained, and were often in sight of the African coastline, the absence of revolt suggests a measure of trust. Perhaps the act of releasing the chains was enough to convey British intentions.

Trust was essential as voyages to Sierra Leone could last weeks or even months. As a pre-existing colony for free slaves, Freetown had been a natural choice as the navy's base for patrolling West Africa. Yet it was in many ways also a poor choice. The colony lay far northwest of the major ports of the nineteenth-century slave trade in West Africa. Traveling westward along the African littoral meant sailing against the prevailing winds and currents, or sailing far into the Atlantic and catching the northern current to loop back toward Freetown. An 1827 Colonial Office report calculated that of sixty-four vessels captured to the south of the colony between 1819 and 1826, their coordinates at the time of seizure gave an average distance of 790 miles from Sierra Leone.[36] Seventeen of these vessels were captured upward of 1,200 miles to the leeward of the colony. Of fifty-seven vessels with enslaved Africans on board, the average voyage was sixty-two days between capture and adjudication, with two vessels exceeding two hundred days.

These journeys often took place in the company of some of the Navy's slowest and oldest ships, as the Admiralty felt the unpopular West African station unworthy of their best vessels. The combination of long distances, contrary winds and currents, and slow vessels meant that recaptives experienced a voyage of comparable length with slaves transported to the New World from the same regions (Table 2.1).

Liberated African voyages to Sierra Leone were comparable to the Middle Passage in another crucial respect: the high level of mortality on board. David Northrup was the first to show that mortality rates on 100 slave ships intercepted from the Bight of Biafra between 1821 and

---

[35] Quoted in Rob Burroughs, "Eyes on the Prize: Journeys in Slave Ships Taken as Prizes by the Royal Navy," *Slavery & Abolition*, 31.1 (2010): 102.

[36] This calculation excluded one unnamed vessel, caught at 2° 23′ North and 9° 50′ East, nearly 1,500 miles from the colony. The commissioners compiling the report suggested that the longitude may have been recorded in error, but the period of 209 days between capture and condemnation suggests a uniquely long voyage distance, CO 267/91. Peterson, *Province of Freedom*, 182–183.

Table 2.1 *Average voyage length to Sierra Leone versus slave ship voyages to the Americas, 1808–1863*[a]

Region of embarkation	Recaptives landed at Freetown	Slave voyages to the Americas
Senegambia	42.0	40.8
Upper Guinea	26.7	33.5
Windward Coast	31.5	36.3
Gold Coast	45.9	47.6
Bight of Benin	41.0	41.2
Bight of Biafra	42.2	45.2
West Central Africa	36.2	37.0
Southeast Africa	73.0	66.4
Other Africa	N/A	36.2
Totals	40.4	42.5

[a] Data are derived from the *Voyages* database and include only recaptives taken from transatlantic voyages. Voyage length to Sierra Leone is from date of interception; time from embarkation to disembarkation would have been somewhat longer.

1833 equaled and even exceeded the mortality rates on slave vessels traveling to the Americas in the same period.[37] Expanding Northrup's data to include all vessels adjudicated at Freetown from all major embarkation regions between 1808 and 1863 (for which embarkation and disembarkation data are known) confirms his initial conclusions. An estimated 11 percent of recaptives lost their lives between interception and emancipation in Freetown. This figure is almost identical to the mortality rate of slave vessels crossing the Atlantic during the nineteenth century (Table 2.2).

High mortality rates were often the result of gastrointestinal ailments and fevers contracted on the march to the coast, while waiting in coastal barracoons, or once on board.[38] Dysentery was the most common affliction on slave voyages, and could break out in epidemic proportions. Fevers, chiefly malaria and yellow fever, were the next

[37] David Northrup, "African Mortality in the Suppression of the Slave Trade: The Case of the Bight of Biafra," *Journal of Interdisciplinary History*, 9.1 (1978): 47–64.

[38] Joseph C. Miller, "Mortality in the Atlantic Slave Trade: Statistical Evidence on Causality," *Journal of Interdisciplinary History*, 11.3 (1981): 385–423; Herbert S. Klein and Stanley L. Engerman, "Long-Term Trends in African Mortality in the Transatlantic Slave Trade," *Slavery & Abolition*, 18.1 (1997): 36–48.

Embarkation and Interception

Table 2.2 *Mortality between interception and emancipation, 1819–1863[a]*

Region of embarkation	Embarked	Disembarked	Average mortality (percent)
Senegambia	1,072	1,002	3.9
Upper Guinea	10,391	9,737	5.9
Windward Coast	2,111	1,953	2
Gold Coast	1,183	1,087	4.9
Bight of Benin	41,856	38,360	7.7
Bight of Biafra	37,828	30,982	17
West Central Africa	8,970	7,559	15.7
Southeast Africa	785	596	24.1
Unknown	521	429	17.7
Totals	104,717	91,705	11.1

[a] These data are based on the *Voyages* dataset, augmented by data on non-transoceanic vessels. Data are only for cases when the numbers of intercepted and disembarked are documented.

most common causes of death. These were similarly attributable to both coastal and shipboard conditions. There was often little the British could do to treat recaptives and keep them in good health. Overcrowding or so-called tight packing on slave ships was not the main cause of mortality and sickness as abolitionists at the time thought it to be. Slave ships captured by the British between 1839 and 1852 had an average of four square feet for each slave, making it difficult to either lay full length or stand upright.[39] While mitigating the claustrophobic conditions of the slave ship may have provided some relief and comfort on the long journey to Freetown, this alone was no barrier to the spread of disease.

Recaptives faced other threats at sea. Violent storms could run vessels aground or sink them entirely. Of 197 Africans on board the slaver *Teresa* in late 1825, only 6 survived a storm that consumed the ship in the Bight of Benin. Similarly, only 12 of the 380 captives on the *Icanam* lived through a storm that overtook the ship on a voyage

---

[39] David Eltis, *Economic Growth and the Ending of the Transatlantic Slave Trade* (Oxford: Oxford University Press), 136.

from Bonny in 1822.[40] Such long voyages also brought with them the issues of food and water provisions. The crew of HMS *Owen Glendower* saw their rations cut to halves and then quarters, in a desperate attempt to feed the 246 captured Africans under their charge.[41] The combined threats of disease, natural disaster, and malnourishment meant that while interception altered the course of slave ships, it did little to alleviate shipboard conditions.

Adjudication, Liberation?

Anchoring at Freetown marked the end of a forced oceanic voyage, but not freedom from slavery or the conditions of the slave ship. While naval men could disembark to inform the authorities of their arrival, Africans were forced to remain on board. The humanitarian imperative of immediately landing captives was trumped by the legal reality that vessels and their human cargoes could be restored to their owner, based on the ship's national flag and the place of embarkation. As one observer put it, "with the green hills and valleys of the colony close to them, they must not leave their prison."[42]

The instructions for commissioners of the Mixed Courts were that sentences should be passed "as summarily as possible," preferably within twenty days of a ship's arrival and certainly within two months.[43] While some cases could be adjudicated quickly with little additional loss of life, others could drag on for several weeks. Delays could result from a backlog of vessels in the harbor or the absence of key court officials. The trial of the Spanish schooner *Nuestra Señora de Reglas* in 1819 was delayed due to the sickness of the Spanish judge. The Portuguese *Nova Felicidade*, at anchor alongside it, was delayed by the failure of the Portuguese judge to arrive from Rio de Janeiro. An 1827 report on the Colony wrote that the practice of the Vice Admiralty court before 1819 was "to land the negroes the day after their arrival ... but since the establishment of the Courts of Mixed

---

[40] "List of vessels adjudicated in the court of the British and Spanish Mixed Commission showing the number of slaves captured, emancipated, and registered from its establishment to the 6th February 1826," CO 267/91.
[41] Binstead, *Memorandum of Remarks on Board HM Ship Owen Glendower.*
[42] F. Harrison Rankin, *White Man's Grave; A Visit to Sierra Leone in 1834*, vol. 2 (London: R. Bentley, 1836), 98.
[43] Bethell, "The Mixed Commissions," 87.

Commission, they are not brought on shore (unless sick) until adjudicated, which generally causes a delay from 12 to 15 days, or more."[44]

Officials made some attempts in the 1820s to allow recaptives to land prior to adjudication. Charles MacCarthy – governor for the first five years of the Mixed Courts existence – took personal measures to land sick recaptives prior to adjudication. This was done in the cases of the abovementioned *Nuestra Señora de Reglas* and the *Nova Felicidade*, with the governor placing the captives under his protection. When MacCarthy repeated this action to land the sick slaves of the slave ships *Anna Maria* and *Eugenia* in 1822, Lord Bathurst reprimanded him for doing so without the consent of the Mixed Courts.[45]

One jaded Royal Navy surgeon was left to remark that "the slaves continue cooped up in their filthy and wretched abode, until all the tedious paltry ceremonies of the law are punctiliously attended to."[46] In some cases, these "tedious paltry ceremonies" proved disastrous. The Dutch slave ship *La Fortunée* arrived in Freetown on June 7, 1826, twenty-one days after being intercepted by HMS *Brazen* near Príncipe.[47] On route, 46 of the vessel's 245 incarcerated Africans died. But the anchorage at Freetown proved more protracted and deadlier than the voyage. Deliberations on shore at the Anglo-Dutch Mixed Commission Court stretched to July 17, during which time seven more died on board. The ship became so sickly that by the time *La Fortunée*'s captives were finally released, a further twenty-five had passed away. In total, the victims of *La Fortunée* spent two months on a vessel from which only 100 of the initial 245 Africans survived to begin new lives in Sierra Leone.[48]

It is perhaps not surprising, then, that in 1826 the Africans confined to the ship *Activo* chose to escape their British overseers while their case was being decided.[49] Anchored off Freetown, land was in sight, and some of the *Activo*'s captives made their way to shore. Uncertain of how to handle this bold act, colonial officials turned to the precedent

---

[44] Report of the Commissioners of Inquiry into the State of the Colony of Sierra Leone, May 7, 1827, CO 267/91.
[45] Secretary of State Despatches 1816–1821, SLPA.
[46] Peter Leonard, *Records of a Voyage to the Western Coast of Africa in H.M.S. Dryad* (Edinburgh: William Tait, 1833), 85–86.
[47] Case of *La Fortunée*, July 17, 1826, FO 315/20.
[48] This case is recorded in FO 315/2. Figures are presented as recorded in the source material, despite the mathematical error.
[49] Dudley to Commissioners, December 13, 1827, FO 315/2.

provided by the 1772 case of James Somerset, and ruled the slaves emancipated by virtue of their stepping foot on British soil.[50] Reaction from the metropole disapproved of this interpretation of the Somerset case as an "abstract or universal principle." Instead, London warned that principle of free soil was "wholly inapplicable to the case of slaves landing upon the territory of the Colony of Sierra Leone."[51]

The case of disease on *La Fortunée*, discontent on the *Activo*, and similar stories of protracted human misery in Freetown harbor prompted acting Governor Kenneth Macaulay to plead with Secretary of State Bathurst for "more efficient regulations by which this horrible waste of human life may be prevented in the future."[52] The legalistic response from Whitehall stated that "such slaves may, on account of sickness or other sufficient cause, be lawfully disembarked and put on shore, pending adjudication: but being so landed, the slaves be kept and detained *in their character of slaves* until the sentence be pronounced whether they shall be restored, or not."[53] This was despite the fact that after 1815 Africans were never re-embarked on a slave vessel even if the Freetown court concluded its proceedings by restoring the slave vessel to its owners.[54] In cases where the capture was deemed illegal, "restoration" took the form of monetary compensation, but the Africans remained on board as property of the slave traders until the legality of the interception was determined.

By the late 1820s the necessity of landing the most at-risk slaves was finally recognized. In 1827 the Liberated African Department took over a series of dilapidated buildings at Kissy for "the sick distressed

---

[50] The famous 1772 Somerset judgment of the English Court of the King's Bench held that slavery was unsupported by existing law in England and Wales (though not elsewhere in the British Empire). Public opinion at the time and many subsequent historians have taken the ruling to represent the end of slavery in England and Wales, whereas in reality the case dealt with the narrower question of whether a slave could be forcibly removed from England against the slave's will. The abovementioned colonial officials seem to have subscribed to the popular misconception that the ruling decreed that no person was a slave on British soil even though slavery remained legal in the British Empire.

[51] Court case of the *Activo*, FO 315/2.

[52] Macaulay to Earl Bathurst, July 9, 1826, FO 315/2.

[53] Canning to Commissioners of the Mixed Commission Courts, February 26, 1827, FO 315/2.

[54] Such was the case for vessels apprehended south of the equator (in the case of Portuguese vessels), or those of nations with whom the British had not signed an antislavery treaty (such as the United States and France).

Liberated Africans from the villages and for such newly arrived people from slave vessels."[55] The Kissy hospital expanded to meet the acute crisis of large numbers of Africans disembarking from the slave ships. In 1830 Governor Findlay planned for a "lazaretto" which would be "surrounded with a stone wall seven feet high to prevent them having any communication with the inhabitants of the village of Kissey."[56] In 1832, the Colonial Secretary amended regulations to allow the colonial surgeon to appeal to the court for slaves to be landed prior to adjudication should their condition warrant it.[57] From then on, the surgeon and marshal to the Mixed Commission Court visited anchored ships immediately after their arrival. The surgeon assessed their health and often recommended they be landed immediately.[58]

F. Harrison Rankin accompanied officials visiting an arriving slave ship, providing a rare first-person account of the conditions on vessels in Freetown harbor. On board the ship – the Spanish *La Pantica* – were the 274 survivors of the 315 embarked at Old Calabar. The boarding party saw that "before [them], lying in a heap, huddled together at the foremast, on the bare and filthy deck, lay several human beings in the last stage of emaciation – dying." Rankin estimated that one-third of the Africans were above deck, while the majority stared through the locked hatches from below, seated and divided between men and women. The officials counted the captives, recorded their sex, and "in a glance decided the age, whether above or under fourteen."[59] Boatswains wielding whips and sticks ensured an orderly process.

The Watchman, a nineteenth-century Freetown newspaper, described disembarkation from the slave ship *Paquetta de Rio* in 1846 as a moment of jubilation. The paper noted that, "after the various colonial officials and law-court officers had visited them, and the slaves had been made to understand that they were free – the scene on deck changed. Shouting, leaping, frenzied crowds swarmed on every upper part of the ship, their fears, even their weakness and disease

---

[55] Cole, October 20, 1828, LADLB, 1828–1830.
[56] A lazaretto or lazaret is a quarantine station for military travelers. Findlay to Murray, October 28, 1830, CO 267/105.
[57] Rishton to James Boyle, colonial surgeon, March 13, 1832, Colonial Secretary's Letterbook 1831–1833, SLPA.
[58] William Hamilton, "Sierra Leone and the Liberated Africans," *Colonial Magazine and Commercial-Maritime Journal*, 6 (1841): 327.
[59] Rankin, *White Man's Grave*, vol. 2, 118–122.

forgotten."[60] The captives were said to knock off their shackles using the billets of wood that had formed their beds, throwing them overboard in proclamation of their newfound freedom. The image that appears on this book's cover, taken from the *Church Missionary Gleaner*, similarly conveys landfall as a joyous assertion of liberation. The accompanying description, intended for mission subscribers in Britain, wrote apocryphally of how "the inhabitants of the villages, who had been themselves previously emancipated, were assembled in thousands, in the hope of recognizing some friend or brother, some mother or sister, from whom they had been cruelly torn in a distant land." As the boats neared the shore, "the shouts from those on the land and those in the boats became loud and incessant."[61]

Peter Leonard, serving on HMS *Dryad*, provides a more sobering account of disembarking in an alien setting. Over two hours he watched large canoes bring the Africans to shore. Leonard witnessed the initial euphoria of "singing on board the schooner, in anticipation of the boat's return, and continuing their song all the way to shore, laughing and clapping their hands." Yet the jubilation proved short lived and "the men and women, after they reached the yard, when the momentary gratification of setting foot on land once more had passed away, looked sullen and dissatisfied, but not dejected." It struck Leonard that "on landing they expected to go wherever they pleased, and were consequently disappointed and angry when they found themselves still under control."[62]

Whether jubilant or ambivalent about escaping the slave ship, many recaptives disembarked in a state of physical and mental exhaustion. Some required constables to assist them; others had to be carried from the shore to the yard.[63] Of 296 recaptives landed from the *Arcenia* in 1828, "scarcely one of them were capable of walking from the waterside."[64] Landfall itself was not the end of crowding, disease, and death. In the early years, the want of adequate buildings in the colony meant that recaptives were sent to the nearby Falconbridge barracks and

---

[60] Quoted in F. W. Butt-Thompson, *Sierra Leone in History and Tradition* (London: H. F. & G. Witherby, 1926), 160.
[61] "Recollections of the Coast of Africa," *Church Missionary Gleaner*, new series 3, no. 1 (1853): 2–3.
[62] Leonard, *Records of a Voyage*, 106.
[63] Hamilton, "Sierra Leone and the Liberated Africans," 327.
[64] Cole, December 7, 1828, LADLB 1828–1830.

Adjudication, Liberation?

placed in the lower storeroom of the dilapidated building. A corporal of the Royal African Corps guarded the storeroom until its occupants could be enlisted, apprenticed, or settled in the colony. When James Higgins arrived in the colony as the new first surgeon in 1810, he "found more than a hundred negroes captured in prize vessels afflicted with various diseases, chiefly ulcers of the worst description. They had been neglected with respect to medical treatment, and their habitation extremely offensive."[65] Over the next six months Higgins and his assistants oversaw the care of sixty to eighty recaptives housed within the barracks.

Most recaptives landed at Freetown were first taken to the King's Yard, a walled compound constructed on the waterfront in 1817. At times, the 150-by-103-foot yard would hold as many as 900 recaptives under cramped conditions.[66] Governor Findlay lamented that in 1830, "the number of slaves landed from captured vessels had accumulated in a period of nine weeks to nine hundred and thirty-seven ... and being thus congregated in a small space, the degree of misery which they had experienced during their confinement on board the vessels was scarcely lessened."[67] On February 3, 1836, the Liberated African Department received in a single day 762 Africans landed from three Spanish vessels.[68] For recaptives, the conclusion of their oceanic migration ended much as it began: confined to a crowded outdoor yard. One observer went so far as to deem the yard "a large species of prison ... encompassed by high walls and secured by well-guarded gates."[69]

Once emancipated, recaptives marched through a gate in central Freetown inscribed with the words "freed from slavery by British valour and philanthropy."[70] These newly landed shipmates still faced the challenge of acclimatizing physically and mentally to their new environment. One chief superintendent of the Liberated African Department believed that as many as one-third of all recaptives died from malnourishment and communicable diseases within three months

---

[65] James Higgins to Secretary of State, August 8, 1811, CO 267/31.
[66] J.S. and A.S. to Lieutenant Governor Campbell, March 1835, LADLB 1834–1837.
[67] Findlay to Hay, October 6, 1830, LADLB 1830–1831.
[68] Macaulay and Lewis to Campbell, February 3, 1836, FO 315/12.
[69] Rankin, *White Man's Grave*, vol. 2, 106.
[70] The gate was constructed in 1817 and still stands on the Freetown waterfront as part of the Connaught Hospital complex.

of settling in the villages.[71] As Chapter 1 showed, the lingering impact of forced migration was felt most severely by receptives from the Bight of Biafra. The CMS missionary W. A. B. Johnson recorded that of 217 receptives assigned to Regent from the *Anna Maria*, which purchased its slaves at Bonny in 1821, nearly 50 died before the first rains.[72] Throughout the nineteenth century, colonial officials cited the privations of the Middle Passage and the subsequent mortality in explaining to London why the population of the colony was far less than the number of receptives who had disembarked.[73]

There were immediate and lingering effects for survivors too. One was a continued distrust of Europeans. The Rev. Henry Düring captured the lingering uncertainty that the terror of the slave ship had instilled, recording in his journal how

> the first day they were fatigued and having more victuals than they could eat, prepared for them by their country people; they were quiet that day; the next being Sunday, they were clothed, and seeing all the old people going to church, decently clothed and cheerful; they began to imagine that now they were to be sold as many were well, and the poor, or sick ones to be killed.... I had the greatest difficulty through their own country men to persuade them that that would not be the case.[74]

Samuel Crowther later acknowledged similar feelings of insecurity, remembering that, "a few days after our arrival at Bathurst, we had the mortification of being sent for at Freetown to testify against the Portuguese owner [of the slave ship *Esperanza Feliz*]. It being hinted that we should be delivered up to him again."[75] The visceral fear of the slave ship and its crew shaped receptive experience long after their disembarkation in Sierra Leone.

Shipmates

Receptive voyages to Sierra Leone were clearly voyages of suffering. Because of this, they were also voyages of intense bonding among

---

[71] The superintendent pointed to the deaths of 54 of the 73 children sent to the village of Leopold in 1822, and the deaths of 58 of 246 children sent there in 1825. Commissioners of Enquiry to Hay, January 28, 1826, CO 267/90.
[72] Johnson to Pratt and Bickersteth, October 10, 1821, CMS/CA1/O126.
[73] 1831 Census of Population and Liberated Africans, CO 267/111.
[74] Henry Düring, October 10, 1821, CMS/CA1/O89/7.
[75] Crowther in Curtin (ed.), *Africa Remembered*, 314.

Shipmates

sufferers. Historians of Atlantic slavery have increasingly recognized that the Middle Passage was a crucible for the formation of "communities made in crossing."[76] Philip Curtin's 1955 *Two Jamaicas* was the first study to note the "strange bond between shipmates" who had endured the Middle Passage together.[77] Roger Bastide noted similar bonds existing in nineteenth-century Brazil, where people of African descent used the term *malungo* to designate those who had traveled on the same ship.[78] Terms for shipmates were prevalent in most New World slave societies, referred to as *malungo* in Brazil, *sippi* and *máti* in Surinam, *malongue* in Trinidad, *batiment* in Haiti, and *Calabera* in Cuba.[79]

Mintz and Price's influential 1976 essay *The Birth of African-American Culture* presented the significance of shipmate bonds in bolder terms. Mintz and Price argued that slave cargoes were "crowds" of heterogeneous origins, and that shipmate bonds became a major principle of those separated from kin and those speaking the same language.[80] This conceptualization of slave ship cargoes as "crowds" has been countered by statistical evidence that a single slave ship cargo was likely comprised of a few ethnic groups. This has led scholars to consider how the Middle Passage could reinforce pre-existing identities. Paul Lovejoy has noted that the participants of the 1835 slave rebellion in Bahia arrived on the same Portuguese-Brazilian ships and, therefore, "formed allegiances that were further consolidated by similar ethnic backgrounds."[81]

Many studies have thus asserted the importance of shipmate bonds in the diaspora. Yet the challenge in testing the concept of shipmates

---

[76] Byrd, *Captives and Voyagers*, 154.
[77] Philip D. Curtin, *Two Jamaicas: The Role of Ideas in a Tropical Colony, 1830–1865* (Cambridge, MA: Harvard University Press, 1955), 26.
[78] Roger Bastide, *The African Religions of Brazil: Toward a Sociology of the Interpretation of Civilizations* (Baltimore: Johns Hopkins University Press, 1978), 45. Hawthorne adds that Mulungo was derived from the Mbundo word "malunga," which were ancient authority symbols brought by ancestors from the sea. Walter Hawthorne, "'Being now, as it were, one family: Shipmate Bonding on the Slave Vessel *Emilia*, Rio de Janeiro and throughout the Atlantic World," *Luso-Brazilian Review*, 45.1 (2008): 53–77.
[79] Manuel Barcia, *West African Warfare in Bahia and Cuba: Soldier Slaves in the Atlantic World, 1807–1844* (Oxford: Oxford University Press, 2014), 66.
[80] Sidney Mintz and Richard Price, *The Birth of African-American Culture: An Anthropological Perspective* (Boston: Beacon Press, 1992), 18, 42.
[81] Lovejoy, "Background to Rebellion," 155.

has been the limited ability to trace the subsequent lives of captives disembarked from the same ship through extant records. Walter Hawthorne is the first to track shipmates from a single voyage over time; incidentally on a vessel intercepted by the British Navy in 1821 and brought before the Mixed Commission at Rio de Janeiro.[82] Hawthorne shows that these 354 Liberated Africans, who survived a 149-day voyage from Lagos on the slave ship *Emilia*, forged enduring bonds during their Middle Passage and the time they subsequently spent waiting in Rio warehouses to be apprenticed. So strong were these connections that many later congregated for a return voyage to Lagos under the leadership of a former *Emilia* captive who had found economic success in Rio de Janeiro.

The archival record on Liberated Africans affords unique comparative insights given the ability to trace groups of shipmates over time.[83] Shipmate bonds – whether on voyages to Sierra Leone or the Americas – were forged in a context of uncertainty and duress. What differed was that intercepted recaptives were unshackled and often split between the captured slave ship and the apprehending British cruiser (or cruisers). These arrangements were likely conducive to shipmate interactions, as recaptives could more freely interact with those who spoke their language. It was also the case that men, women, and children could interact, whereas on slave ships barriers often separated adult males from the rest of the cargo.

British naval tactics likely led to the formation of bonds before boarding the ship, as many slaves sold to the same ship would have spent periods confined together in barracoons. Crowther's narrative recalls that not long after the embarkation and interception of the *Esperanza Feliz*, the British attempted to ease crowding by moving captives between the slaver and the navy cruiser. For Crowther, "this was now cause of new fears, not knowing where our misery would end. Being now, as it were, one family, we began to take leave of those who were first transshipped, not knowing what would become of them and ourselves."[84] The relationship Crowther described between what he called his "friends in affliction" suggests the need to extend the concept of shipmates to both ship and shore.

---

[82] Hawthorne, "Being now, as it were, one family," 53–77.
[83] For shipmate bonds among Liberated Africans in Guyana, see Schuler, "Liberated Central Africans in Nineteenth-Century Guyana," 326.
[84] Crowther in Curtin (ed.), *Africa Remembered*, 313.

The relationships forged on these journeys could last a lifetime. Among the five shipmates with whom Crowther congregated on HMS *Myrmidon* was "my brother Joseph Bartholomew," both of whom would have subsequent missionary careers. F. Harrison Rankin visited the Colony in 1834 and noted these bonds even among those of a young age. While traveling through the Liberated African village of York with the village manager, he spotted two girls in the schoolyard eating rice from the same bowl, showing "much attachment to one another." The manager told Rankin that "they had been ship friends; that is, had contracted a friendship whilst fellows in misfortune in the slave-ship, torn from all they once knew and loved." Rankin added that "this tie having its origin in misery, is one not easily loosened. The ship-friends may be afterwards separated, but the feeling survives; and one will walk many a weary mile to attend the funeral of the other."[85] Robert Clarke similarly observed:

[I]t not infrequently happens, that such Liberated Africans as have arrived together at Sierra Leone as Slaves, contract an eternal friendship, which is beautifully displayed in their coming from great distances to attend one another's funerals. This noble sentiment, developed under circumstances of the most intense misery, may be aptly illustrated, by comparing its growth to the oak, which strikes its roots more firmly into the soil, the more intense the shocks which it sustains.[86]

Rev. Christian Theophilus Frey recorded such a case after he was summoned to the house of a dying recaptive in the village of Waterloo in 1848. Frey observed that the man "pointed out R.B. (one of his country people, they are Popoes) who is also a member of the Church, saying to him 'my brother, we have been brought in one ship to this colony, by God's good will, we have since that been walking together for 19 years.'"[87] R.B. was asked to care for his shipmate's wife and to ensure that if she should remarry, that it would be in the church they had attended together for many years.

Shipmate bonds were forged at both the dyadic and communal level. Jacob Boston Hazeley, a superintendent of the Liberated African

---

[85] Rankin, *White Man's Grave*, vol. 2, 20–21.
[86] Robert Clarke, *A Description of the Manners and Customs of the Liberated Africans, with Observations upon the Natural History of the Colony, and a Notice of the Native Tribes* (London: J. Ridgway, 1843), 69.
[87] Frey, Journal extracts for the quarter ending March 25, 1848, CMS/CA1/O94.

village of Wellington in the 1840s, observed, "If a slave-vessel arrives with people of different tribes or nations, as soon as they are located they form themselves into clubs." These clubs included "the whole of their shipmates, without distinction of nation, for the purpose of affording mutual assistance, whether it be for procuring food, raiment, lodging, or such minor acts of kindness as are within the reach of every individual."[88] Shipmate clubs took the name of the "big company." Their mandate read much like that of slave brotherhoods in the Americas. Chief among their duties was clearing farms, caring for the sick, covering funeral expenses for members and their immediate family, and advancing money to pay for destroyed property or criminal fines. With mutual benefits came mutual responsibilities; members could be fined or ostracized for crimes such as theft or infidelity.[89]

While much of the recent research on shipmates has focused on ethnogenesis among slaves of similar language and culture, what we see among recaptives in Sierra Leone are communities forged "without distinction of nation." At the same time, many recaptives did opt to join a "little company" arranged on ethnic identification. John Gerber, Koelle's linguistic informant for the Ebe language, attested that "he has been in Sierra Leone twenty-nine years, with eleven countrymen, all of whom were brought here in one ship, no other 'Ebēans having come to Sierra Leone before or after."[90] Sometimes these shipmate bonds transcended ethnicity; at other times they reinforced identities based on shared language.

Nineteenth-century Sierra Leone was populated first and foremost by the arrival of some five hundred cohorts of shipmates. On landing, recaptives were settled in various parts of the small colony, based on the labor needs of districts and the demand for apprentices. Though a particular shipload of recaptives was scattered around the colony, many from a particular ship were assigned to the same Liberated African village. Of 579 recaptives landed from the *Princepe de Guinea* in 1826, 194 were sent to Leopold, 108 to Kent, and 106 to York.[91] In one exceptional case, all 152 survivors from the Brazilian slaver *Zepherina* were located at Wellington.[92] It is probable, then, that the

---

[88] Hamilton, "Sierra Leone and the Liberated Africans," 34–35.
[89] Fyfe, *History of Sierra Leone*, 171–172.   [90] Koelle, *Polyglotta Africana*, 9.
[91] Liberated African Department Statement of Disposals, 1821–1833, SLPA.
[92] LADLB 1828–1830; Liberated African Department Statement of Disposals, 1821–1833, SLPA.

inhabitants of a particular village were comprised of Africans from a small number of vessels, given that the population of these villages rarely exceeded a few thousand. For example, of 1,493 recaptives sent to Regent between 1821 and 1828, 836 were drawn from only five ships.[93]

The process of shipmates becoming co-inhabitants of a particular district of the colony is most apparent in the remarkable case of the American slave ship *Amelia*. The vessel departed Cabinda, north of the Congo River estuary, on January 1, 1811, with 275 captives destined for Havana. After twenty days at sea, the Africans on board rebelled and took command of the ship in the mid-Atlantic. Jack White, a slave of the captain who had traveled with the vessel from Charleston, fomented the rebellion. White showed the scars on his back and warned the captives of a future of physical abuse. Soon after, White orchestrated a morning uprising, opening the hatches while the unchained slaves below deck shouted his name. Outnumbered and with few weapons, the ship's crew were spared their lives. Nine of the crew, including the captain, sailed away in a small boat; four others were detained to guide the vessel, likely back to where they had sailed from.[94] The vessel instead sailed around the African coast for four months until, malnourished and dying, they landed at Cape Mount (present-day Liberia) to beg for water. The landing party was instead taken captive. John Roach, an old Liverpool slave trader who became a self-stylized abolitionist on the West African coast, intervened. He retook the *Amelia* and escorted it to Freetown, claiming to have emancipated those who had already freed themselves.[95] The *Amelia* reached Freetown harbor on May 11; only eighty-five had survived the 143-day passage.

On their arrival, forty-two survivors from the *Amelia* were assigned to a new settlement on the site of an abandoned Temne town. British officials named the settlement New Cabenda, "because the persons pitched upon for the town are natives of Cabenda who were found in

---

[93] Liberated African Department Statement of Disposals, 1821–1833, SLPA.
[94] Council, June 11, 1811, CO 270/12; HCA49/97.
[95] Emma Christopher, *Freedom in Black and White: A Lost Story of the Illegal Slave Trade and Its Global Legacy* (Madison: University of Wisconsin Press, 2018), 82–83; "Case of the *Amelia*," *Sixth Report of the Directors of the African Institution*, 36, 40–41.

the brig Amelia."[96] The settlement was located on a ridge above Cape Sierra Leone, known as Devil's Hill or Signal Hill. The villagers resettled in 1816 at Whiteman's Bay, supposedly due to the preference of the "Congolese" to live near the waterside.[97] The settlement was named "Congo Town" and the nearby creek was dubbed the "Congo River"; the names of both town and river have remained in use for two centuries. New Cabenda and Congo Town were thus founded by a single vessel of captives who conspired to forcibly claim their freedom and endure a journey from which only a minority survived. Individuals who had undergone a shared experience of many thousands of miles turned their bonds on board the slave ship into a lasting community in Sierra Leone.

Conclusion

The abolitionist Thomas Fowell Buxton wrote in 1839 that the Atlantic slave trade and the mortality inherent in it could be divided chronologically into five stages:

1. The original seizure of the slaves.
2. The march to the coast, and detention there.
3. The middle passage.
4. The sufferings after capture and after landing.
5. The initiation into slavery, or the "seasoning," as it was termed by the planters.[98]

In the first two stages, the experience of recaptives was identical to Africans taken as slaves to the Americas; for the latter three stages, the experience was in many ways similar. From the perspective of lived experience, British abolition and suppression produced ambiguous results. Often, misery could not be alleviated; at times it was greatly exacerbated. Sierra Leone's Liberated Africans showed the limitations of early humanitarian intervention and the ability to ameliorate human suffering through the deployment of military force. But Liberated African experiences also reflect how forced migrations – whether

---

[96] Council, June 11, 1811, CO 270/12.
[97] A. B. C. Sibthorpe, *The History of Sierra Leone (1868)*, 4th edition (London: Cass, 1970), 30.
[98] Buxton, *African Slave Trade and Its Remedy*, 73.

toward slavery or liberation – were crucibles that shaped the societies into which these migrants were settled. The Middle Passage experienced by recaptives was both an ending – to family, to friends, to familiar sights and sounds – but also a beginning, to new communities, families, and affinities that helped define colonial society in Sierra Leone.

3 "Particulars of disposal"
Life and Labor after "Liberation"

In April 1810 the American slave vessel *Lucia* entered Freetown harbor under the guidance of HMS *Tigress*. On board were sixty men, eighteen women, and fifty-one children who had been purchased by the Charleston-based vessel's crew at the Rio Pongo. The case was heard before Freetown's Vice-Admiralty Court. The vessel was declared a legal prize and its human cargo forfeited to the Crown. The Navy Board dispensed £3,450 as bounty to the officers and crew of the *Tigress*.[1] The naval men were awarded for their exertions in the name of British abolition; the enslaved were disembarked and registered in a large leather-bound book, which recorded the form that their "liberation" would take.

Thirty-eight of the men who emerged from the *Lucia* with sufficient strength were immediately enlisted into the Royal African Corps as defenders of British West Africa against the threat of Napoleon's France. Five boys, aged nine and ten, were enlisted on HMS *Crocodile*. Most of the others were bound out as apprentices to Freetown's earlier settlers. Within a few years, eight of the sixty-two apprenticed Africans from the *Lucia* had fled their masters, their whereabouts unknown to colonial officials.[2]

Eleven years after the case of the *Lucia*, the crew of HMS *Tartar* brought the Cuban slaver *Anna Maria* to Freetown's waterfront. George Collier, the commodore of the squadron, described the conditions on board the *Anna Maria* after finding the vessel at anchor off Bonny. Below decks were five hundred Africans separated by floors only three feet apart. In the suffocating conditions Collier saw the imprisoned "clinging to the gratings to inhale a mouthful of fresh or

---

[1] Condemnation of the *Lucia*, HCA 49/97. Thanks to Padraic Scanlan for assistance with these records.
[2] Alterations to the Registers of Liberated Negroes, CO 267/35 and CO 267/38.

pure air."[3] The commodore placed 112 of the *Anna Maria*'s captives on board his flagship and the vessels proceeded to Freetown. Some 391 survived their forty-nine-day Middle Passage.

Clerks in Sierra Leone's Liberated African Department made some attempt to disaggregate the "country of origin" of those on board. In their registers they listed 309 as "Heboo" (Igbo) and 61 as "Calabar." The department's officials then notified W. A. B. Johnson, the resident missionary at Regent village, that 238 of the *Anna Maria*'s captives had been assigned to Regent. The German-born missionary Johnson, who commonly recorded in his journals the arrivals of new villagers, wrote of the arrival of the *Anna Maria*'s captives that

> as soon as we came in sight all the people came out their houses towards the road to meet us & that with loud acclimation; when they beheld the new people weak & faint; they caught hold of them carried them & led them up towards my house: after they laid exhausted on the ground many of our people recognized their friends & relatives, & there was a general cry "my brother" "my country man! He live in the same town!"[4]

Johnson's apocryphal account of reunions was in keeping with the earnest writing that made his journals popular in Britain.[5] But his embellished retelling should not diminish how such greetings represented the true ending to recaptives' Middle Passage.

For recaptives, their voyage ended in a place that would not have seemed entirely alien to them. The Africans taken to Regent would have encountered a similar climate, vegetation, and seasonal patterns to their places of birth and numerous people with whom they could converse. The "Igbo" and "Calabar" people on board the *Anna Maria* would have found at Regent many others taken off slave vessels from the Bight of Biafra. Indeed, more Liberated Africans traded at the port of Bonny were sent to Regent than any other Liberated African village.

---

[3] Collier to Registrar of the British and Spanish Mixed Commission, June 7, 1821, FO 84/11.
[4] Johnson, Journal, April 4–June 6, CMS/CA1/O126/114.
[5] Johnson's career at Regent reached British audiences through accounts published after his death in 1823. See [Robert Benton Seeley, comp.], *A Memoir of the Rev. W. A. B. Johnson, Missionary of the Church Missionary Society, in Regent's Town, Sierra Leone, Africa* (New York, 1853); W. A. B. Johnson, *The Gospel in Africa: An Account of the Labors and Success of the Rev. W. A. B. Johnson, Missionary of the Church Missionary Society in Regent's Town, Sierra Leone, Africa* (New York, 1858); Maria Louisa Charlesworth, *Africa's Mountain Valley; or, The Church in Regent's Town, West Africa* (London, 1856).

Years later, one of Johnson's successors at Regent described how "chief of the inhabitants of Regent [were] of the Ebo tribe."[6] The formerly enslaved of the *Anna Maria* helped form a diasporic Igbo village in the mountains of the Sierra Leone peninsula.

The divergent fortunes of the Africans on board the *Lucia* and *Anna Maria* exemplify the multifarious experiences that life after "liberation" could bring. Emancipation in one of Freetown's antislave trade courts could mean being scattered around Britain's Atlantic Empire as soldiers, sailors or "labourers" or resettlement into a prototypical Evangelical post-slavery colony. Much depended on when a would-be Liberated African reached the colony; a captive African's age and gender were also important in dictating what liberation actually meant. This chapter traces life after liberation, focusing on settlement policies that shaped the demographic contours of recaptive society, and the social and cultural implications of colonial policies. Settlement patterns had profound social consequences, including the nature of the missionary encounter and the development of the Krio language. Focusing on different settlement policies over time, this chapter allows a discussion of how settlement affected social interactions, the persistence of customs, and the everyday usage of language.

For half a century after 1807, a primary occupation of Sierra Leone's colonial government was the settlement of recaptives disembarking from 500 slave vessels. At the time of the Abolition Act, the colony was a small trading entrepôt of some 2,000 inhabitants. The arrival of 99,752 recaptives altered the colony's demographics, and expanded its population and borders. However, not all who disembarked were settled within the Colony. Approximately one in four recaptives were dispatched to serve the labor and defense needs of other parts of Britain's Atlantic Empire.[7] In addition, some from the vicinity of the colony returned home, while others died soon after their arrival. These out-migrations in addition to those Liberated Africans who died before leaving the King's Yard suggest that approximately 72,284 liberated slaves were settled within the Sierra Leone peninsula between 1808 and 1863. Beginning new lives atop a narrow laterite peninsula

---

[6] Denton, Journal extracts for quarter ending June 25, 1845, CMS/CA1/O87/22.
[7] This included an estimated 5,169 recaptives enlisted into the army, 306 to the navy, 3,478 to the Gambia, and 15,230 sent to the British Caribbean. See Anderson, "Diaspora of Sierra Leone's Liberated Africans," 105.

some thirty kilometers long by ten kilometres wide, receptives formed one of the most geographically concentrated populations of people forcibly moved by the nineteenth-century slave trade.

For most of its existence the Liberated African Department recorded, with varying degrees of detail, what it termed the "particulars of disposal" or simply "disposal" of recaptives in the Liberated African registers. As the euphemisms of "disposal" suggests, there was little volition in this process. "Disposal" could refer to a particular colonial village where recaptives were sent; the apprenticeship of recaptives fourteen years and younger; the "marriage" of adult women and the enlistment or "recruitment" of recaptives into the army, navy, or migration to the West Indies. Through these data we can trace the trajectories of individuals settled within the colony, or those sent elsewhere in the British Empire. This information provides a record of settlement that is unique in the African diaspora.

A central question in African diaspora studies has been the extent to which Africans of different ethnolinguistic groups interacted on a daily basis, or were settled among those of similar language, culture, and cosmologies. Scholars of the diaspora have argued that the numerical dominance or even prevalence of certain ethnic groups is not in itself a good indicator for the possibilities and processes of cultural continuity and change.[8] Equally important to cultural vitality and ethnic identification is the structural continuity of social patterns, proximity, and marriage.[9] The question of whether people of certain regions or ethnic groups were concentrated or "randomized" within diasporas is therefore of central importance.[10]

Most recaptives were assigned to Liberated African villages founded in the 1810s and 1820s across the Sierra Leone peninsula (Map 3.1). Recaptive life was thus overwhelmingly a rural or peri-urban, agrarian life. By 1820, a population of 6,104 in thirteen Liberated African

---

[8] David V. Trotman, "Africanizing and Creolizing the Plantation Frontier of Trinidad, 1787–1838," in Lovejoy and Trotman (eds.), *Trans-Atlantic Dimensions*, 235.
[9] Morgan, "Cultural Implications," 133.
[10] For differing interpretations of whether Africans in the diaspora were "randomized," see Klein, *Atlantic Slave Trade*, 173; Hall, *Slavery and African Ethnicities*, 56; John Thornton, *Africa and Africans in the Making of the Atlantic World, 1400–1800*, 2nd edition (Cambridge: Cambridge University Press, 1998), 195–197.

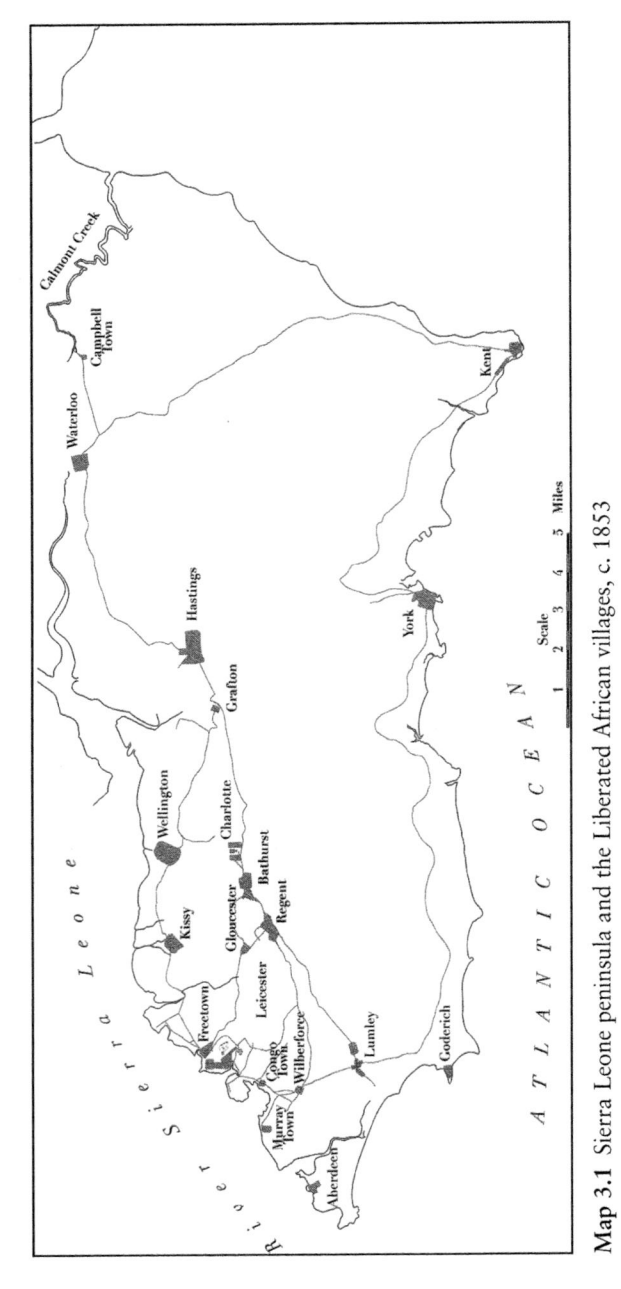

Map 3.1 Sierra Leone peninsula and the Liberated African villages, c. 1853 (map by author, based on map in CO 267/234)

villages exceeded Freetown's estimated population of 4,785.[11] Much of the analysis will therefore focus on the composition of these villages. I argue that these communities, in their formative stages, were comprised of recaptives taken from a few slave ships, strengthening bonds made on board. Often, new villages were formed by a single group of shipmates. In short, the fictive community formed on the Atlantic voyage was made reality in the various villages of the Sierra Leone peninsula.

1807 and Its Aftermath

"Liberating" Africans was an afterthought for the framers of Britain's Abolition Act. Despite two decades of campaigning to outlaw the slave trade and the deployment of a small contingent of the world's most powerful navy to suppress it, very little consideration was given to the victims of the trade. The Act itself focused on the interdiction of slave ships in the context of European maritime warfare and the prize money to be allotted to captors. Of the twenty-seven original clauses in the 1807 Act, only one directly addressed the human consequences of the law. While twenty-six of the legal clauses dealt with the capture and prosecution of slave vessels, the seventh clause instructed how to "receive, protect and provide for such Natives of Africa" on board confiscated ships.[12] The Act required that recaptives either enlist in the armed forces or be bound "whether of full Age or not, as Apprentices, for any Term not exceeding Fourteen Years." During the Napoleonic Wars enlistment took priority. For those unsuited for enlistment, the Act empowered the government to establish "Regulations for the future Disposal and Support of such Negroes as shall have been bound Apprentices ... after the term of their Apprenticeship shall have expired ... as may prevent such Negroes from becoming at any Time chargeable" to the public purse.[13]

The irony of the earliest Liberated African policies was that Britain – the most active European participant in the transatlantic slave trade in

---

[11] Robert R. Kuczynski, *Demographic Survey of the British Colonial Empire, West Africa*, vol. 1 (London: Oxford University Press, 1948), 158.
[12] "An Act for the Abolition of the Slave Trade," 47 Geo. III. c. 36, Session 1, March 25, 1807, *The Statutes of the United Kingdom of Great Britain and Ireland: 1807–1869* (London, 1807–1869).
[13] CO267/24; *Sierra Leone Gazette*, August 20, 1808.

the century before 1807 – was seemingly incognizant of how many enslaved Africans might arrive in Freetown. Abolitionist Zachary Macaulay's May 1808 letter to Governor Thomas Ludlam typified Britain's unpreparedness to accommodate this mass migration, predicting that "some increase of the native population may doubtless be expected at the colony, from the confiscation of slave ships, under the Act abolishing the slave trade. It may prove considerable, but at the same time it may, and it is to be hoped will, prove very insignificant."[14] Parliament was equally oblivious to the potential success of a naval squadron, however small, to intercept slave vessels. Sierra Leonean governors were thus left with a law entirely inadequate to dictate how this large influx of people should be treated.

The first recaptives were 167 individuals taken from the *Eliza* and the *Baltimore*, American slave ships captured by HMS *Derwent* in March 1808. The ships arrived before the establishment of the Vice-Admiralty court on March 16, 1808, and before the Orders in Council respecting "Captured Negroes" reached the Colony.[15] Governor Ludlam proceeded according to his own interpretation of the Abolition Act and its narrow stipulations. Forty of the ablest men were placed in government service for a period of three years. The remainder – eighteen men, fourteen women, and ninety-five children – were bound out as apprentices for varying periods.

Ludlam's treatment of the earliest recaptives immediately caught the ire of his successor, Thomas Perronet Thompson, who arrived in Freetown on July 21, 1808, as the first Crown-appointed governor. The twenty-five-year-old army and navy veteran, son of a Hull banker, and friend of William Wilberforce, was appalled at what he saw as an egregious, unprincipled settlement policy. In particular, Thompson vehemently objected to the means by which the apprenticeships had been made. He "found that a number of natives of Africa brought into the Colony by HMS *Derwent* in March last had been sold within the Colony" from a cattle pen at the back of Fort Thornton.[16] Moreover, "other natives of Africa brought in the same vessel had been given away to the inhabitants of Sierra Leone for no other reason but

---

[14] Zachary Macaulay, *Letter to the Duke of Gloucester*, appendix, 5, quoted in Kuczynski, *Demographic Survey*, 96.
[15] John Joseph Crooks, *A History of the Colony of Sierra Leone, Western Africa; with Maps and Appendices* (Dublin: Browne & Nolan, 1903), 75.
[16] Testimony of Frederick Forbes, February 4, 1810, CO 267/27.

because no one would give any thing for them."[17] Worse still, when twenty-one of those apprentices had subsequently fled their masters, they were captured and thrown into irons in the town's jail.[18] In August 1808, Thompson passed an ordinance declaring the system of apprentices within the colony to be illegal, null, and void.[19] Despite this, the Liberated African registers show that Thompson was obliged by the 1807 Abolition Act to keep on apprenticing in order to accommodate the continued influx of Africans into the small colony. For all of Thompson's objections, this was not a watershed moment in the colony's labor history, and apprenticeship remained a primary means of "disposing" children.

As with apprenticeship, Thompson similarly discouraged recruitment to "His Majesty's Black Regiments." He disdained apprenticeship and enlistment while advocating that Sierra Leone was "favorable to agriculture" and would reveal the validity of free cultivation in Africa.[20] Thompson perceived the arrival of recaptives as not just a challenge but an opportunity. A Governor's Council resolution condemning the *Derwent* case declared that "the cultivation of the land is the grand object to which the government of this colony should be directed."[21] Recaptives afforded a chance to restore the earlier agricultural aspirations for the colony, goals that the first settlers as freed plantation slaves had little desire to help into fruition.

Thompson's plans for recaptives are discernible through the Liberated African registers for the period of his governorship between 1808 and 1810. They record the settlement for most of the first 761 recaptives landed. Many are registered simply as "living in the colony" or "living with country people," reflecting the lax oversight and meager expenditure government was providing. But until 1813 clerks also kept an annual list headed "Alterations to the Register of Liberated Negroes."[22] These first recaptives are thus unique as their

---

[17] Thompson to Castlereagh, August 1, 1808, CO 267/24.
[18] Peterson, *Province of Freedom*, 52. This initial controversy over apprenticeship between Thompson and the African Institution has received considerable scholarly attention from Christopher Fyfe, Michael J. Turner, and Suzanne Schwarz, among others. See Turner, "The Limits of Abolition," 319–357.
[19] Crooks, *A History of the Colony of Sierra Leone*, 75.
[20] Thompson to Secretary of State, July 27, 1808, CO 267/24.
[21] Council, November 11, 1808, CO 270/11.
[22] CO 267/35 and CO 267/38. It is unclear why such fastidious documents were kept during this time. This scrutiny may have arisen from the initial controversy

occupation and whereabouts within the Colony were monitored over a period of several years. Those landed in early 1808 are re-recorded in December 1809, by which time many had been given anglicized names and taken on new professions.[23] What is notable among these earliest recaptives is the change of their status and roles within a short period after their arrival. For example, Masamba, a young male taken from the slave ship *Marie Paul*, was immediately placed on public works. By 1811 he was working as a mason in the colony, though the following year he was listed as "gone to Gorée," the island taken from the French in 1800.[24]

The registers also provide some account of the number of Mende, Sherbro, Temne, and Susu who absconded from Sierra Leone once they had left their slave ships in order to return to their home countries. Within the "Alterations to the Register of Liberated Negroes," seventy-seven individuals are recorded as having "left the colony" or "returned to his [or her] country," and for a further seventy-eight the entry is "runaway." All but three of the first group and twenty of the runaways were native to Sierra Leone and the surrounding areas. For example, Ansimanee, an eighteen-year-old who arrived in the Colony in the *Santiago* in 1810, subsequently "returned to his home in the Foula country."[25] The "Alterations" lists also omit a large number of individuals who could not be accounted for. A note at the end of the document explained: "Those captured negroes that are not accounted for have deserted to native towns in the back parts of the country."[26] Most absconders were adults who had arrived on vessels captured as they left Gallinhas, the Rio Pongo, and other embarkation points along the Sierra Leone coast.[27] Many of those listed as returning home were

---

surrounding the sale of apprentices or fear of the re-enslavement of freed Africans. Suzanne Schwarz notes that this registration also reflected broader developments of administrative practices in Britain, most notably the national census of 1801. Suzanne Schwarz, "Reconstructing the Life Histories of Liberated Africans: Sierra Leone in the Early Nineteenth Century," *History in Africa*, 39 (2012): 184.

[23] Annual Report of the Natives of Africa, December 31, 1809, CO 267/27.
[24] Masamba, Liberated African no. 16, Sierra Leone Liberated African Register vol. 1; CO 267/31; CO 267/35.
[25] Liberated African Department Registers vol. 1, SL ID 1029, CO 267/31.
[26] "Alterations to the Registers of Liberated Negroes," CO 267/35 and CO267/38.
[27] Domingues da Silva et al., "The Diaspora of Africans Liberated from Slave Ships," 353.

brought to the Colony on the same vessel, and may have decided to make the trek back together.

The original registers list 116 recaptives who immediately opted to return to their homelands, almost all of whom were from near the colony. J. McCormack reported: "Those liberated Africans who have been taken in the wars between the Timmaness, Sherbros, Bulloms, Soosoos, Cussoos, Loccos Annullas and Korankas, (i.e.) in the neighbourhood of the Colony, and who have not been sold for slaves for any crime, on their emancipation, universally voluntarily return to their native country."[28] The earliest recaptives established a pattern of flight and return to homelands that later Liberated Africans from Upper Guinea would replicate.

The Early Recaptive Villages

While this early period was marked by mobility and lax oversight, Governor Thompson also developed an inchoate plan with far-reaching consequences for recaptive settlement over the ensuing decades. Thompson thought it best to settle recaptives as "independent cultivators" who would form a "free and hardy peasantry."[29] The young governor suggested a scheme of agricultural villages in the mountains fringing Freetown. The colony's original settlements stood on low-lying land on the south shores of the Sierra Leone estuary. Behind this coastal strip, barely two miles wide, rose wooded hills whose peaks reach between 1,800 and 3,000 feet. Thompson sent a group of recaptives – supposedly of Bambara and Wolof origin – to farm Leicester Mountain, the peak rising behind Freetown that his predecessor Ludlam had likely named after his hometown of Leicester. The 1816 Proceedings of the CMS described Sierra Leone's Leicester as a settlement of "150 inhabitants, who are a mixed people – Jaloofs, Bambarras, and Yeolas."[30] If so, they would have been among the few Bambara to settle in the colony, as the ethnonym rarely appears in colonial and missionary documents.[31] Yet the source speaks of a multi-ethnic agricultural village that would be replicated across the colony.

[28] Quoted in Kuczynski, *Demographic Survey*, 134–135.
[29] Thompson to Castlereagh, August 8, 1808, CO 267/24.
[30] *1816 Proceedings of the CMS*, 174.
[31] Koelle's Bambara informant stated, "He is the only Bambaran at present in Sierra Leone." Koelle, *Polyglotta Africana*, 3.

In April 1809, the Governor's Council approved an initiative to establish an "interior settlement" in the mountains above Freetown. Thompson chose a location some five miles from Freetown known as Hogbrook for the warthogs in its stream. The location possessed "the largest stream of fresh water known to exist within the Colony" and recaptive forced laborers had already constructed a small road up the hillside from Leicester. A day after the resolution passed council, Thompson joined a party of militiamen and would-be settlers. Together they christened the new settlement Kingston-in-Africa in honor of Thompson's hometown of Kingston-upon-Hull.[32] This experiment in the mountains surrounding Freetown had been an aspiration of British officials and abolitionists from the Colony's onset. It was simultaneously a test of both free labor and of the peninsula's supposed fecundity, much touted in abolitionist tracts promoting Sierra Leone. It was also a creeping colonial frontier spreading beyond Freetown in order to accommodate the continued arrival of newly liberated Africans. On hillsides and in valleys each recaptive would receive one or two acres of land. The governor envisioned a regimented settlement in which freedmen gave their employment every alternate week for wages to procure rice, while spending the other week building their houses and clearing their land.[33] Thompson saw the settlements as sources for supplies, refuges from a potential coastal attack, and the first penetration of "civilization" into the African interior.[34]

Thompson's governorship was short-lived, recalled following his accusations against Ludlam in the apprenticeship scandal. His successor, E. H. Columbine, was instructed to cut expenditure and curtail public works. During his sixteen-month administration, Columbine largely abandoned village settlement in favor of "voluntary" enlistment and apprenticeship. Other recaptives, especially those unfit for military service, were neglected by Columbine's parsimonious administration. Many formed their own suburban settlements outside the colony's jurisdiction. New communities continued to be formed, but without government assistance.

[32] Council, April 8, 1809, CO 270/11.
[33] Leonard G. Johnson, *General T. Perronet Thompson, 1783–1868: His Military, Literary, and Political Campaigns* (London: George Allen & Unwin, 1957), 45.
[34] Manon Lily Spitzer, "The Settlement of Liberated Africans in the Mountain Villages of the Sierra Leone Colony 1808–1841," MA thesis, University of Wisconsin, 1969, 31.

Columbine left the colony due to illness in May 1811 and died at sea a month later. Lieutenant Bones, a naval officer appointed acting governor, ordered a muster of recaptives. He found many had run away, presumably those originally from the surrounding areas.[35] By contrast, Thompson's "Bambara" population at Leicester struck Bones as an industrious community to be replicated. A June 1811 order of the Governor's Council declared the "forming [of] a new town of captured negroes on the ridge of hills commonly known by the name of Signal hill." The council envisioned the settlement as a lookout against coastal attacks as well as promoting agricultural labor. They concluded that, "because the persons pitched upon for the town are natives of Cabenda who were found in the brig Amelia ... that the town have the name of New Cabenda."[36] New Cabenda was thus founded by the recaptives of the slave ship *Amelia*, discussed in Chapter 2, who rose up against the slave ship crew and redirected it back toward the African coast. While the particular act of shipboard insurrection may have been unique among recaptives, the settlement of Africans from the same ship in new communities would eventually become a regular occurrence.

At first, though, Lieutenant-Colonel C. W. Maxwell abandoned Bones's plan to settle shipmates together, placing the policy under official review. The new governor found most recaptives living in suburban communities outside the colony's legal authority and influence. Maxwell was the first governor to recognize that the recaptive population would continue to grow. Whitehall, adamant that the slave trade would not persist at its current volume, instructed him to adhere to the meager instructions of the Abolition Act.[37] Far from metropolitan oversight, and with little funds to support recaptives, Maxwell simply allowed many of them to found independent villages at predetermined locations. Of those landed in 1812, 752 were listed as "settled in the Colony in villages formed by their country people."[38]

The unauthorized, impromptu founding of these early villages means we know little about their populations. But shipmate bonds appear to have been of vital importance. The Methodist Thomas Coke noted in 1812 that since "these slaves belong to different nations, some of which lie far in the interior, they have no knowledge whatever of one

---

[35] Ibid., 32. [36] Council, June 11, 1811, CO 270/12.
[37] Spitzer, "The Settlement of Liberated Africans in the Mountain Villages," 34.
[38] Liberated African Register, CO 267/35.

another, excepting that which arose from the common misery which they mutually endured while on board the ships." Because of their lack of linguistic familiarity, they "therefore, live in distinct little towns, without the precincts of the city, but very near to it. These towns are called by the names of the people who inhabit them."[39] A May 1813 census recorded that most of the settlements outside the official boundaries of the colony had names reflecting the regional origins of the earliest recaptives: Bambara Town, Jolify Town, Cabenda, Cossoo Town, and Bassa Town.[40]

It is unclear whether these early villages were the product of unsupervised recaptives, migrants from the interior, or likely a combination of both.[41] The ethnic groups listed in many town names were groups that could travel over land as well as be rescued at sea by patrols along the Upper Guinea coast. In 1812 a group settled about four miles from Freetown on a hill above the deserted Granville Town and called their settlement Kissy Town. The name suggests they came from the Kisi region, shipped perhaps from Sherbro or Gallinhas. Village tradition, according to Fyfe, traces the first inhabitants from the Kise-Kise (then called Kissi) River north of the Melakori.[42] By 1813, an adolescent Liberated African named Tamba was listed as "settled with Kissey people."[43] Yet it was only in 1817 that the government officially sent recaptives to populate the town.

The archival record is similarly opaque on early villages founded by the government. Despite its optimistic founding, Kingston-in-Africa virtually disappears from records after 1809.[44] Recaptives appear to have continued to settle themselves at the nearly abandoned site, still generally called Hogbrook. In 1812 the colonial government officially recognized the settlement and renamed it Regent.[45] A year later, the arrival of a new cohort of recaptives resuscitated the village. In late June 1813, the crews of HMS *Thais* and the colonial schooner *Princess Charlotte* raided the slave-trading factory of Charles Mason and

---

[39] Thomas Coke, *An Interesting Narrative of a Mission Sent to Sierra Leone in Africa by the Methodists, in 1811* (London: Paris & Son, 1812), 40.
[40] Population Return for Sierra Leone, May 1, 1813, CMS/CA1/E3/76.
[41] For the founding of early immigrant villages, see Harrell-Bond et al., *Community Leadership*, 30–40.
[42] Fyfe, *History of Sierra Leone*, 119.
[43] "Disposal of Captured Negroes," CO 267/38.
[44] Scanlan, *Freedom's Debtors*, 91.
[45] Peterson, *Province of Freedom*, 93, 108.

Robert Bostock on the St. Paul River (present-day Liberia). The naval men rounded up 233 Africans – whom they took to be the prisoners of the burned-out barracoons – and proceeded to Freetown.[46] After adjudication, 108 recaptives – those not siphoned off by army and navy recruitment – were "settled in the mountains" to repopulate the fledgling settlement of Regent.[47] Their arrival was significant enough that observers soon after credited their arrival as having "formed" the village "in July 1813, chiefly by people brought by a slave ship from [Cape] Mesurado, principally Foy people, but it contains some of almost all the neighbouring nations."[48]

David Noah, a Bassa recaptive who would later serve as CMS schoolmaster, was among those taken in the St. Paul River raid. In a later account, Noah recalled how he had been enslaved while on a trading trip and "had been about three weeks a slave when it blessed God to send English men to deliver me & many more." In the early morning "5 boats full of soldiers and sailors were landed" and Noah, whose birth name is unknown, was among those that the British landing party confiscated. They then

> sailed for Sierra Leone where we were landed immediately. After we had stayed about one month in Freetown, we were send to Regent's then called Hog Brook. At the first, when we were at Regent's, which was then a desert, Mr. Macaulay and one Capt. William were there, we were surrounded with nothing but bushes and we did not like to stop there but we were forced to do so. I believe we were at Regent's a whole year without a white man, and we lived in a most wretched way.[49]

Like many recaptives in this era, Noah would have been an early settler in a rural village of little to no European oversight.

The Parish Plan

The appointment of Charles MacCarthy as governor of Sierra Leone had profound implications for recaptive policy over the ensuing

---

[46] Christopher, *Freedom in Black and White*, 91–94.
[47] "Disposal of Captured Negroes," CO 267/38, Liberated Africans numbered 4338–4570.
[48] *Proceedings of the CMS 1816–1817*, 175.
[49] Noah, Speech at Anniversary of Kissy Church Missionary Association 1824, CMS/CA1/O165/3.

half-century. MacCarthy, whose governorship (1814–1824) was the longest of the nineteenth century, formulated an idyllic vision of ordered Christian villages, each grouped around its own church tower. His parish plan drew on the ad hoc policies of his predecessors, but presented a more systematized settlement policy. MacCarthy shared the vision of agricultural villages, but objected to settlements where recaptives were left without paternalistic oversight. Along with cultivation, Christianization was central to this vision of village life. The Rev. Edward Bickersteth, sent in 1816 to inspect the CMS mission, shared MacCarthy's assessment of recaptives as a promising mission field. The CMS had heretofore used the colony as a base to proselytize to the surrounding indigenous peoples, but had found little success among the Susu, who lived one hundred miles north of the colony.[50] With the prospect of a more malleable population, the colony was divided into parishes, each to be superintended by a CMS clergyman.

MacCarthy's appeal to Lord Bathurst to endorse the plan noted the arrival of 2,546 recaptives from July 1815 through May 1816. The end of the Napoleonic Wars had not slowed the arrival of captured ships, despite the dubious legality of their interception in peacetime. MacCarthy's governorship coincided with the implementation of the bilateral treaty system and the deployment of a permanent naval squadron, meaning that MacCarthy's parishes would have a steady stream of new inhabitants from slave ships. These plans also coincided with the establishment of the Liberated African Department (called the Captured Negro Department until 1822) and the Mixed Commission courts, meaning that the documentation for these villages after 1816 is particularly detailed.

MacCarthy's experiment greatly expanded the village system. Prior to 1815, the colonial government recognized only three villages: Leicester (founded 1809), Wilberforce (founded 1810), and Regent (founded 1812). Between 1815 and 1820, MacCarthy founded a further ten villages. In 1819, MacCarthy entered negotiations with Ka Kouka and his deputy Pa Souba to obtain the southern portion of the Sierra Leone peninsula in order to settle the ever-expanding recaptive population.[51] A year later, the Sherbro chiefs George and Thomas

---

[50] See Bruce Mouser, "Origins of the Church Missionary Society Accommodation to Imperial Policy: The Sierra Leone Quagmire and the Closing of the Susu Mission, 1804–17," *Journal of Religion in Africa*, 39 (2009): 1–28.

[51] Sibthorpe, *The History of Sierra Leone*, 30.

Caulker ceded the Banana Islands, off the southern tip of the peninsula, to the British. By 1822, nearly 8,000 people lived in villages across the peninsula, compared with about 5,600 in Freetown itself.[52]

While historians such as John Peterson have characterized these villages as spaces in which Liberated Africans could create their own "province of freedom," more recent interpretations by Padraic Scanlan have stressed the strict regime of surveillance and control.[53] These villages were, by definition, theocracies. The resident missionary was in charge of all religious and secular aspects of village life. He, invariably, wielded a degree of power far greater than Protestant missionaries around Britain's Atlantic Empire. At times, missionaries complained about how much power was devolved to them. Gustavus Nylander wrote candidly to the CMS in London in 1819, confessing that "we are encumbered with everything connected with our situation, *as superintendents of public works, clearing and repairing roads, and punishing & settling disputes & quarrels* between people and so forth; which indeed must be done, but I think it should be the business of some other persons."[54]

MacCarthy's villages grew and multiplied. The registers record 29,287 recaptives sent to twenty-six different villages between 1811 and 1848. The villages were thus the center of Liberated African settlement for more than three decades. Broadly, these settlements can be distinguished between large, diverse villages of thousands of inhabitants, and smaller settlements often comprised of one or two groups of shipmates. The villages can also be distinguished between the more compact mountain villages of Leicester, Regent, Gloucester, Bathurst/Leopold, and Charlotte; and the sprawling littoral settlements of Kissy, Wellington, Hastings, Waterloo, Kent, and Aberdeen (Map 3.1).

Table 3.1 presents the thirteen largest villages based on the number of recaptives sent to each, as recorded in the Liberated African registers. These data are not a full account of all recaptives sent to each village, but provide a large sample that reflects the size and composition of each village by the inhabitants' coastlines and ports of origin. All of the villages were founded or refounded for the purpose

---

[52] *The Royal Gazette and Sierra Leone Advertiser*, August 10, 1822.
[53] Padraic X. Scanlan, "The Colonial Rebirth of British Anti-Slavery: The Liberated African Villages of Sierra Leone, 1815–1824," *American Historical Review*, 121.4 (October 2016): 1097.
[54] Nylander to Bickersteth, March 3, 1819, Kissy, CMS/CA1/E7A/30.

Table 3.1 *Recaptives sent to major villages, 1811–1848*[a]

Village (founding date)	Recaptives sent
Wellington (1819)	3,760
Waterloo (1819)	3,495
York (1819)	3,317
Hastings (1819)	2,825
Regent (1812)	2,645
Kissy (1812, reorganized 1817)	2,122
Bathurst (1818)[b]	1,612
Charlotte (1818)	1,556
Banana Islands (1820)	1,540
Kent (1819)	1,279
Wilberforce (1810, reorganized 1818)	1,228
Leopold (1817)	1,027
Gloucester (1816)	972
Aberdeen (c. 1828)[c]	675

[a] Totals calculated from Liberated African registers. Founding dates of villages taken from Report of the Commissioners of Inquiry, CO 267/91.
[b] Leopold and Bathurst were amalgamated in 1825 on the site of the former, but given the name of the latter. The analysis in the text combines the figures for their population.
[c] Fyfe, *History of Sierra Leone*, 173.

of settling recaptives. The only exceptions were Wellington, Hastings, and Waterloo, which were established in 1819 for disbanded soldiers returning from service in the Royal African Corps or West India Regiments. However, even these settlements quickly acquired a recaptive majority.

On their arrival, new villagers were provided with daily rations of rice, salt, and palm oil, with fresh beef and vegetables for "those who are greatly emaciated."[55] Women were expected to marry – ostensibly of their own volition – and men to clear a plot, build a house, and raise crops.[56] Villages were consciously modeled on English hamlets; notions of order and progress were projected through streets, numbered houses, and demarcated property, all built around the local

[55] 1827 Report of the Commissioners of Inquiry, CO 267/90, 27.
[56] Reffell to village superintendents, August 15, 1822, LADLB 1820–1826.

church. Land was often allocated according to how building would appear within the village, rather than on the basis of its fertility.[57]

Beyond these broad aspirations, no specific instructions exist for how a particular contingent of captives should be settled or how villages were to be populated. Joseph Reffell of the Liberated African Department stated in 1827, "In distributing them to the villages care has always been taken not to separate relatives or friends and generally when the numbers on board a vessel was not too great to send the whole of them to one town or to locate them as near to each other as circumstances would admit."[58] The populating of these villages, especially in their formative years, thus lent itself to the persistence of shipmate bonds. Many villages were comprised of Africans taken from the same few vessels; in certain cases, a large segment of the population was settled from a single vessel.

As new villages were founded, recently arrived recaptives became their charter residents, tasked with cultivating swathes of land. Rev. Henry Düring, recently arrived from Hanover, recorded in his journal that he "left Leicester Mountain the 18th of December 1816 in order to superintend about 130 recaptured negroes in a new town, which is to be called Gloucester Town," adding that "the people here are of five different tribes."[59] Düring recounted how he "had to cut my way through in many places before I arrived on the spot fixed upon where I found 107 individuals lately rescued from the chains of the slave trader."[60] Ali Eisami similarly described how "we went and settled in the forest at Bathurst," in April 1818, within a year of Bathurst's founding.[61] Eisami added that he and his wife (another recaptive to whom he was married immediately after his arrival) "went and remained in the house of our people."

In certain cases, a single group who had experienced the Middle Passage together settled new villages. In March 1827, the assistant superintendent of the Liberated African Department ordered that

---

[57] Maeve Ryan, "'A Most Promising Field for Future Usefulness': The Church Missionary Society and the Liberated Africans of Sierra Leone," in William Mulligan and Maurice Bric (eds.), *A Global History of Anti-Slavery in the Nineteenth Century* (New York: Palgrave Macmillan, 2013), 46.
[58] Sierra Leone Commissioners of Enquiry, vol. 2, appendix b, CO 267/92.
[59] Düring to Pratt, February 5, 1817, CMS/CA1/E5A/51.
[60] "Memoir of the Rev. Henry Düring," November 1822, CMS/CA1/O89/9.
[61] Eisami in Curtin (ed.), *Africa Remembered*, 215.

forty-seven men liberated from the slave ship *Dos Amigos*, after a journey from Badagry, "be settled at the small village situated between Wellington and Charlotte which is to be called 'Newlands.'" When George William Emmanuel Metzger visited the settlement later that year, he noted 78 inhabitants "have but short time ago arrived in a slave vessel ... [T]he people themselves have not yet built their own houses. They live in two large houses. One is occupied by the females and the other by the males."[62] In 1828, fifty-eight men from the slave ship *Santa Effigenia* were sent to form a new settlement named Murray Town. Most of the first inhabitants were taken as slaves during the destruction of the Egba settlements.[63] In total, Murray Town received freed captives from nine slave vessels between 1828 and 1839. Of the 377 recaptives sent there, 337 were embarked at the Bight of Benin ports of Badagry (58), Ouidah (7), and Lagos (272), primarily in the period of 1828–1830 in the wake of the Egba wars. At Murray Town they were placed under the superintendence of John Ashley, a former sergeant of the West India Regiments. Ashley was known for wearing a broad-brimmed hat (in Yoruba, *Alaté*), so the Yoruba population of Murray called the village "Oko Alaté."[64] In 1873, the Oyo-born Methodist minister Joseph May recounted that Murray was "the only town originally inhabited by a single tribe of Liberated Africans; hence to this day the whole inhabitants, not excepted other tribes who might choose to dwell with them, speak all one language, the Yoruba, and subsequently English by their descendants."[65]

Over time, multiple groups of shipmates increased the size and diversity of these villages. Yet much of the historiography on Sierra Leone suggests that certain ethnic groups congregated in certain villages as a result of conscious British policy. The perception of ethnically homogenous villages is usually attributed to John Peterson and his discussion of "settlement by tribe."[66] The main evidence for this conclusion is an 1822 circular from Joseph Reffell of the Liberated

---

[62] Metzger, Report on Eastern District, October 3, 1827, CMS/CA1/O150/49.
[63] Among them was William Lewis, father of Sir Samuel Lewis, the future mayor of Freetown and first West African to be knighted. John Hargreaves, *A Life of Sir Samuel Lewis* (London: Oxford University Press, 1958), 2.
[64] Fyfe, *History of Sierra Leone*, 173.
[65] May to MMS, November 8, 1873, MMS, Sierra Leone Correspondence, fiche box 26, box no. 283.
[66] Peterson, *Province of Freedom*, 161–174.

African Department stating Governor MacCarthy's opinion that Liberated Africans "will more rapidly recover their health and at the same time be rendered more happy by being settled with their country people." MacCarthy directed the Liberated African Department that the most recently landed recaptives were to "be divided among the houses of the best conducted persons of their own country in the villages who it is hoped will feel a pleasure in instructing them in our language and the habits of civilized life."[67]

Gibril Cole has argued that the implication of this was that "with the newly arriving batch of rescued captives being placed in the rural villages according to their ethnicity and left largely unsupervised, the immigrants were able to reproduce their way of living." Cole adds that "Waterloo and Hastings, in particular, were dominated by people speaking dialects of Yoruba, many of whom were Muslims or orisha worshippers."[68] However, Cole and most other historians have misconstrued Peterson's analysis and the original statements from MacCarthy. Many have taken Peterson's interpretation of "settlement by tribe" to suggest that certain ethnic groups dominated certain villages, and that this occurred through conscious settlement policies. In fact, Peterson was arguing that *within* a particular village, those of the same language and culture – "countrymen" – congregated in particular neighborhoods and that "each village in the rural areas developed definable sections within its limits."[69]

There is little quantitative evidence to suggest any conscious effort on the part of the colonial state to settle captives based on ethnicity. Rather, a comprehensive examination of the Liberated African registers indicates that landed captives were scattered randomly around the colony, with no regard for their geographic origin. Table 3.2 shows data for Wellington, Waterloo, York, and Hastings. Arriving recaptives populated these villages throughout the 1820s and 1830s, ultimately becoming the largest settlements outside Freetown. Wellington had a population of peoples sold into the transatlantic trade from at least twenty-two different locations on the African coast and brought to the colony on at least ninety-eight different slave ships. Likewise, the village of Hastings had recaptives from at least seventy-seven different

---

[67] Reffel to village superintendents, August 15, 1822, LADLB 1820–1826.
[68] Cole, *Krio of West Africa*, 76.   [69] Peterson, *Province of Freedom*, 163.

Table 3.2 *Port and coastal origins of recaptives sent to largest Liberated African villages, November 1816–June 1848*

		Wellington	Waterloo	York	Hastings
Senegambia	Bissau	14		45	61
	Cacheu				4
Sierra Leone	Freetown	13	2	2	
	Gallinhas	101	308	240	233
	Rio Pongo	111	7	233	5
	Sherbro	42	14	100	18
	Sierra Leone Unspecified	1	17	74	11
Windward Coast	Grand Bassa	22			85
	Little Bassa				28
	Sestos		36		
Gold Coast	Anomabu	31		149	124
	Gold Coast Unspecified				13
Bight of Benin	Badagry	520	224	65	261
	Jacquin		14	35	46
	Ouidah	525	370	234	230
	Keta	40	1		
	Lagos	705	941	795	664
	Rio Nun	18	1	107	
	Bight of Benin Unspecified	32	33	36	107
Bight of Biafra	Bimbia		2	4	1
	Bonny	569	728	529	280
	Old Calabar	339	260	297	208
	Cameroons, unspecified			53	
	Cameroons River	185	137	73	131
	Cap Lopez		12	1	10
	Gabon	37	64		6
	New Calabar		78	72	10
	Rio Brass	296	172	38	181
	Bight of Biafra Unspecified		25	25	88
West Central Africa	Cabinda	6	1		
	Congo North	4			
	Malembo			6	6

The Parish Plan 117

Table 3.2 (*cont.*)

		Wellington	Waterloo	York	Hastings
	Nova Redonda	49	1		10
Southeast Africa	Mozambique	2	8		3
Total		3,706	3,456	3,213	2,824

slave ships who purchased their slaves at twenty-three or more locations on the African coast.

Most villages were multiethnic, reflecting the coastal origins of recaptives landed during their periods of settlement and growth. But the large number of Yoruba and Igbo-speaking recaptives meant that they formed a sizable proportion of each village. The large Yoruba presence, and particularly that of Yoruba Muslims, at Waterloo and Hastings was less by design than the coincidence of mass arrivals from the Bight of Benin in the years when these villages expanded. The Bight of Benin was the primary region of embarkation for recaptives sent to every one of the larger villages except Regent and Gloucester (Table 3.3). More specifically, Lagos was the greatest port of embarkation for populations of ten of the eleven villages to which more than one thousand recaptives were sent (Regent being the one exception). Yoruba speakers, traded in large numbers as slaves at Lagos, therefore had a significant presence in all of the major villages in the Sierra Leone peninsula.

The multiethnic character of villages apparent in the statistical record is corroborated by missionary reports, travel narratives, and other colonial documents. The Rev. Charles Decker wrote in 1821 that "the town of which I have the superintendency [Wilberforce] is composed of various nations and characters and many difficulties occur to reconcile them together."[70] In 1827 the Quaker missionary Hannah Kilham visited the villages of Wellington, Allen Town, Leopold, Regent, and Gloucester, accompanied by the Rev. John Weeks. Their shared linguistic curiosity and desire to know "how many tribes were resident" in each village led to a preliminary compilation of

---

[70] Decker, Report for quarter ending December 24, 1821, CMS/CA1/O86/10.

Table 3.3 *Recaptives from Bight of Benin sent to Liberated African villages, November 1816–June 1848*[a]

Village	Total recaptives sent	Recaptives from Bight of Benin (%)	Recaptives sold at Lagos (%)
Wellington	3,706	1,884 (50.9)	705 (19.0)
Waterloo	3,456	1,584 (45.8)	941 (27.2)
York	3,213	1,272 (39.6)	795 (24.7)
Hastings	2,824	1,308 (46.3)	664 (23.5)
Regent	2,596	923 (35.6)	434 (16.7)
Bathurst/ Leopold	2,546	1,291 (50.1)	561 (22.0)
Kissy	1,966	1,002 (50.9)	374 (19.0)
Banana Islands	1,531	796 (52.0)	429 (28.0)
Charlotte	1,517	777 (51.3)	458 (30.2)
Wilberforce	1,228	452 (36.8)	330 (26.9)
Kent	1,223	536 (43.8)	274 (22.4)
Gloucester	798	265 (33.2)	24 (3.0)
Aberdeen	674	412 (61.1)	383 (56.8)
Murray	377	339 (89.9)	272 (72.1)
Leicester	95	28 (29.5)	1 (1.1)
Calmont	73	63 (86.3)	25 (34.2)
Newlands	26	26 (100)	26 (100)
Allen Town	20	20 (100)	20 (100)
Total	27,869	12,978 (46.6)	6,716 (24.1)

[a] Calculated from Liberated African registers. Totals exclude individuals for whom port and region of embarkation are currently unknown.

twenty-three languages or dialects spoken in the five villages.[71] Rev. Nathaniel Denton wrote of Regent's Aku Town in 1845, noting, "Some years ago a large number of that nation were located across a little hill branching out of the south west of the town. The chief of the inhabitants of Regent being of the Ebo tribe there has been but little intercourse between the two. The Yorubeans kept to themselves & lived much the same as in their own country."[72]

[71] Kilham, *Report on a Recent Visit*, 7–8.
[72] Denton, Journal extracts for quarter ending June 25, 1845, CMS/CA1/O87/22.

The Parish Plan

Within particular villages, those of similar language settled into visible neighborhoods. Robert Clarke observed how "the desire to live separately is strongly manifested by the liberated Africans; thus we have Moco, Bassah Town or Hamlets, Congo, Bambarrah, Kroo, Kossoh, throughout the Colony where are located these various nations."[73] Life in the villages would obviously have been very different for individuals who found a contingent of people speaking a familiar language versus those who encountered a linguistically alien population. By the time the young Ajayi – soon to be renamed Samuel Crowther – arrived at the village of Bathurst on June 17, 1822, he was one of fifty recaptives from Lagos who had been settled there in that year.[74] Ajayi was comforted that "here we had the pleasure of meeting many of our country people, but none were known before. They assured us of our liberty and freedom; and we very soon believed them."[75]

The 1827 Commission of Enquiry on Sierra Leone described how, "upon first arrival at the villages where they are to be located, the new negroes, as far as it is practicable, are placed in the houses belonging to the older settlers of their own country or tribe, where they remain till they have erected houses for themselves. In this labour they are usually assisted by their country people."[76] Such connections were of vital importance, as government provisions for the newly landed wavered over time. Recaptives were supported in the villages for three months, less time than it took to plant and grow crops. New villagers were forced to labor for others in return for support. Some went back to their homes once their crops had grown. Others rebuilt their dwellings elsewhere, since their original allotments were laid out based on an aesthetic criteria of filling empty roadsides and rounding off village streets. Those who arrived around the rainy season faced particular difficulties in building dwellings or clearing plots on the peninsula's steep slopes.

Many recaptives preferred to dwell with their "country people" rather than conform to British norms of a male-led family household. A contemporary observed that "it appears to be useless to persist in

---

[73] Clarke, *Manners and Customs*, 28–29.
[74] Calculated from Liberated African Register 11909–15967, SLPA.
[75] Crowther in Curtin (ed.), *Africa Remembered*, 314.
[76] Commissioners of Enquiry, citing report of Chief Superintendent Reffell, CO 267/91.

making them erect a line of huts, which it is certain they will *not* continue to inhabit, as well as cruel to make them remain in a location." The writer concluded that recaptives "settled in a strange land, without a friend, or a relative ... is driven, *absolutely driven*, by the want of society and friends, to domicile with his neighbours or country people."[77]

Two forms of bonds developed in the villages: those among shipmates and those between the established and the newly landed of the same ethnic group. Shipmate bonds would have been particularly important when a group of freed slaves were the only ones from their particular regions of origin. Tom Pierce, a recaptive living in Hastings, told Koelle that he had "been in Sierra Leone for fourteen years, with ten of his countrymen, all of whom live in Hastings."[78] Pierce, whose birth name was recorded by Koelle as Ndsondo, was from the town of Madukumangun, along the banks of the Muni River in present-day Guinea-Bissau. As Koelle noted, he was part of a small group who spoke the Seki language and lived close to one another.

Those with few "countrymen" in the colony formed bonds between villages. Shipmates in particular maintained networks of communication and support. Kolo John Gerba, an Ebe from northwest Nupe, who was put aboard a slave ship via the Niger, informed Koelle that he was one of "eleven country men, all of whom were brought here in one ship." Likewise, Ali Eisami recounted how he "was brought to Sierra Leone on the 12th of April 1818, where he resided ever since with his countrymen, whose number, when greatest, amounted to about 200, but is now reduced to thirty."[79] Eisami noted that he "lived amongst a good many of his countrypeople, and had abundant opportunity for speaking his native tongue."[80]

Recaptives did not simply live and work in those locations to which they were assigned, as the movement of "shipmates" and "countrymen" around the colony makes clear. The settlement data presented above are not meant to convey a static image of where recaptives resided, or that they universally accepted their forced settlement. As we have seen, many of the first recaptives returned home while others ran away. In 1811 Kenneth Macaulay wrote to George Stephen

---

[77] Hamilton, *Sierra Leone and the Liberated Africans*, 33.
[78] Koelle, *Polyglotta Africana*, 13.   [79] Ibid., 9–10.
[80] Sigismund Wilhelm Koelle, *Grammar of the Bornu or Kanuri Language* (London: Church Missionary House, 1854), viii.

Caulker, the chief of the Plantain Islands, that "several persons Captured Negroes have run away from this place and gone to a town named Bombotook said to be and in your jurisdiction." Bompetuk lay on the mainland to the south of the colony, adjacent to the Plantain Islands. Governor Maxwell demanded that Caulker assist in the immediate return of the recaptives (all of whom were apprentices), threatening "the unpleasant necessity of appealing to force."[81] One report from 1838 suggested that as many as three thousand recaptives had vacated the colony to the nearby Koya country.[82]

Some Liberated Africans immediately rejected their forced settlement. In March 1829, fourteen Liberated Africans being escorted to York escaped from their overseers and disappeared into the forest.[83] That these Africans were not free to choose their own future was underscored by official instructions that anyone harboring them faced imprisonment. In 1843, Wilkins George Terry, the assistant superintendent of the Liberated African Department, reacted forcefully to news that ninety-five newly arrived men refused to be settled at the outlying villages of Tombo and Russell. Terry stated that "they are certainly their own masters as to the spot they may choose to locate themselves but in the event of their not obeying the orders of the Government ... you will cease to pay them their coppers and withhold all their implements and other indulgencies provided for them by our benevolent Government."[84]

As the recaptive population expanded, people gravitated toward those linguistically and culturally similar, while also moving away from imperial authority. The theocratic character of the villages and their multilingual populaces strengthened the imperative for unsanctioned breakaway settlements. Paths between villages and intersections in the forest became sites of new communities formed by common language speakers from nearby villages. A group of Bassa recaptives set up a village between Leicester and Wilberforce, described by the Rev. Johnson in 1818 as "happy when they can live without society."[85]

---

[81] Macaulay to Caulker, June 15, 1811, Governor's Letterbook, 1808–1811, SLPA.
[82] Parker to Thorpe, March 19, 1838, LADLB 1837–1842.
[83] Cole to Brown, McFoy, Pierce, and Coker, March 28, 1829, LADLB 1828–1830.
[84] Terry to Hughes, February 18, 1842, LADLB 1842–1847.
[85] Johnson, October 6, 1818, CMS/CA1/E7A/66.

The Rev. William Betts wrote in 1826 that "a large proportion of the inhabitants from Regent" had "forsaken their houses and lots in the latter town, to reside in a state of native wilderness & uncontrol and are separating into their different tribes, whereas in the government towns they are mixed, without any particular regard to tribe."[86] The missionary's account of the population recorded two "Bassa" villages of 28 and 38 people, and three "Coosoo" villages of 10, 34, and 41 people. The villages operated under their own headmen, grew their own food, and had been scattered in the bush to avoid British detection. Governor Neil Campbell bemoaned that Liberated Africans from every village had "been permitted to form detached villages, where they speak no language but their own, and always continue naked, as they were in Africa, with all their former usages; never altering from the state in which they landed from the slave ship." While Campbell did not find it appropriate to expel these groups from their unsanctioned villages, he hoped to extend their farms to the major roads between villages "where they will find it necessary, to speak the English language, to other Liberated Africans of the different tribes."[87]

The search for better agricultural land spurred movement. The Commissioners of Enquiry observed in 1826 how newly arrived recaptives would "select farms, burn down the timber, and, aided by the manure thus supplied, they support themselves, perhaps for two, or three years, upon these plots of ground, which have never been regularly granted to them." But if the land's productivity declined,

some of them move further off, and select other farms, where they go through the same process of burning, cultivating, impoverishing, and quitting them for others; thus the circle becomes wider and wider till the liberated African, returning in some measure to his earlier habits and mode of life, extricates himself from restraint, or control, and is lost to the colony as a settler.[88]

Regulations against movement and unsanctioned villages only underscored the ubiquity of the practice. In March 1821 Joseph Reffell, the

---

[86] "Return from the Revd. W. Betts of villages formed independently under their own headmen between Freetown and Regent," December 1, 1826, CO 267/81.
[87] Campbell to Earl Bathurst, March 7, 1827, CO 267/81.
[88] Commissioners of Enquiry (James Rowan and Henry Wellington) to Robert William Hay, undersecretary of state for war and colonies, January 28, 1826, CO 267/90.

head of the Liberated African Department, distributed a circular to the village superintendents declaring that "in future whenever any stranger (Captured Negro) is known to be in a village that the supt. send for him or her and unless it appear that they have come on a visit to any of their friends that he immediately send them to my office for the purpose of being sent back to their place of residence."[89]

Thomas Cole of the Liberated African Department wrote to village managers in 1829 declaring that "no Liberated African shall be allowed to remove from the village where he was first located to settle in any part of the colony without permission from the assistant superintendent in writing approved of by the Governor. Persons found offending against this order are to be treated as rogues and vagabonds."[90] Three years later, a proclamation from Lieutenant-Governor Alexander Findlay declared that Liberated Africans could not leave the settlements in which they were located, except for those with permission to return to their "Native Country."[91] Despite these proclamations, the availability of land, the minimal European presence, and the lack of a substantial export economy allowed recaptives to exercise their mobility.

Settlement after MacCarthy

By the end of MacCarthy's governorship there were, in effect, two Sierra Leones: the colonial capital inhabited by the older settler population, and rural agricultural villages under missionary superintendence.[92] Cynicism over the prospects for these villages grew in the years following 1824, the year that MacCarthy – governor of not only Sierra Leone but all Britain's West African possessions – was killed in conflict with the Asante at the Gold Coast. Even prior to this, the CMS felt the reality of high mortality, while the sanguine hopes of agricultural abundance subsided. These concerns became more acute as the number of recaptives continued to grow.

Charles Turner, who succeeded MacCarthy, wrote to Lord Bathurst in early 1826, noting that 2,400 recaptives had arrived over the

[89] Reffell circular, March 1821, LADLB 1820–1826.
[90] Circular, Cole to managers of mountain districts, October 5, 1829, LADLB 1828–1830.
[91] Council Chamber, October 24, 1832, CO 267/119.
[92] This observation is cogently made in Scanlan, "MacCarthy's Skull," 301.

previous year and that "there is no doubt, from the activity of our cruisers, but the number brought in here will increase also." Turner warned that the "villages and the poor land of the mountains where they are situated already begin to refuse to them a scanty subsistence and they have begun to wander in search of better soil and easier sustenance."[93] Turner and his successor, Sir Neil Campbell, saw the budget for arriving recaptives repeatedly slashed. After 1825, only the elderly and young were given government support.[94] Rations and supplies for newcomers were replaced with a daily allowance for six months. Government austerity combined with tensions with the CMS and high levels of European mortality to stifle MacCarthy's idyllic, if theocratic, villages. Four months after MacCarthy's death, the CMS asked to be relieved from superintending the villages. Their clergymen remained in the colony, overseeing Freetown's schools; the villages were taken over by government managers.

Recaptives felt the change. Many moved to Freetown and sought employment in petty trade; others relocated their farms to seek more fertile or flatter land. The population of Regent declined from 2,000 in 1824 to 1,300 in 1825. Turner's attitude toward landing recaptives reflected this broad cynicism. Turner believed the village inhabitants had been "for years supported in idleness by the government."[95] He held recaptives in Freetown for three months on public works, supposedly to encourage "industry," before sending them to the villages. The older, cheaper policies of enlistment and apprenticeship were reverted to.

Twenty-eight different administrators governed the colony in the twenty-seven years after MacCarthy's death. Recaptives were still sent to villages but without the same provisions or lofty aspirations attached. The villages populated in this era were low-lying tracts of land farther from Freetown: Hastings, Wellington, York, and Kent. Unlike the first villages, they were not situated on hillsides and valleys, but were adjacent to the Sierra Leone estuary and the Atlantic coast. While the earliest mountain villages lay some three or four miles behind Freetown, many of the new settlements were up to eighteen miles away.

[93] Turner to Bathurst, January 20, 1826, CO267/71.
[94] Ryan, "'A Most Promising Field for Future Usefulness,'" 50.
[95] Spitzer, "The Settlement of Liberated Africans in the Mountain Villages," 61–68.

Details on settlement are sparse for the late 1830s, when the Liberated African Department was cut in size due to the Foreign Office's overly optimistic prediction that the slave trade's demise was imminent. The Liberated African registers cease altogether in 1848, meaning there is no record for the 7,630 Africans who arrived between 1849 and 1863. Tracing their subsequent fate requires other documentation, which lacks the comprehensiveness of the registers. In later records, the names of particular villages were often replaced with larger administrative units such as "mountain district" or "western district," areas that contained several villages. It is unfortunate that we cannot see how West Central Africans who arrived from 1839 onward were incorporated into Liberated African society.

The majority of recaptives emancipated at Freetown after 1840 were, however, not settled within the colony. In that year, the Colonial Office approved labor migration from Sierra Leone to Jamaica, British Guiana, and Trinidad. An estimated 15,230 Liberated Africans migrated to the West Indies between 1841 and 1863.[96] This included some Liberated Africans previously settled in the colony, who opted to voluntarily migrate. But the vast majority of those transported to the West Indies had only recently arrived and were "recruited" from the Liberated African yard. Given that 24,485 Liberated Africans landed at Freetown between 1841 and 1863, and that the vast majority of the 15,230 Africans transported to the West Indies in these years had only recently arrived, probably one out of every two recaptives brought to Sierra Leone after 1840 were sent to Jamaica, Trinidad, or British Guiana (see Chapter 1, Table 1.2).

Were it not for this forced out-migration, the demographic profile on Sierra Leone's Liberated African population in the mid-nineteenth century would have looked quite different. West Indian migration greatly diminished the number of recaptives landed in a given year. Sierra Leone's recaptive community was a diaspora formed primarily through a mass influx of people over three decades before 1841. Migration also shaped the ethnolinguistic composition of Sierra Leone's population. This out-migration likely reduced the cultural impact of West Central Africans on Sierra Leone, since they only arrived in large numbers from 1839 onward. An estimated 6,324 West

---

[96] Anderson, "Diaspora of Sierra Leone's Liberated Africans," 101–138.

Central Africans were emancipated in Freetown between 1839 and 1863, though it is probable that roughly half were sent to the British Caribbean.

Conclusion

"Liberation" in Sierra Leone brought with it a range of experiences. Some trajectories were in keeping with the lofty aspirations of the abolitionists who championed the colony and the suppression of the slave trade; others' lives were marked by involuntary migration and forced labor or impressment. The date when recaptives landed in the colony shaped their subsequent lives, as the whims of particular governors and a parsimonious metropole brought different settlement strategies over time. This in turn dictated the level of support provided immediately after their arrival, the education they received, and the type of labor they were assigned to undertake.

For those who were settled within the Sierra Leone peninsula, recaptive life was largely rural and agrarian. The Liberated African villages were each an African diaspora in microcosm. Africa's linguistic heterogeneity was evident in individual villages, church congregations, and schoolrooms. These communities were the culmination of forced migrations from recaptives' societies of birth to a foreign colonial setting. The remainder of this book is devoted to the communities they forged and the new bonds they made in this African diaspora in West Africa.

4 | *Liberated African Nations*
Ethnogenesis in an African Diaspora

Visitors to nineteenth-century Freetown and its surrounding villages were struck by the multitude of language and dialects spoken among the Liberated Africans. F. Harrison Rankin, visiting the colony in 1834, concluded that "representatives of between twenty and thirty distinct nations, of perfectly different language and costume, form the population of Freetown, few of whom have as of yet given up their native dress and habits." He added that "amongst the principal citizens peopling the 'Mountain of Lions,' are the Akoo, the Ibbo, the Bassa, the Papaw, the Congo, the Calabar, the Coromantin, and the Bonny."[1] A decade later, the Methodist missionary Thomas Raston was taken by how "this mass of people, these 50,000, compose not an individual nation ... but extend to many nations and many tribes, not fewer than thirty different nations are thrown together." Among those "released from those 'floating dungeons' the slave ships" Raston saw "natives of almost every part of Africa, Akus, Iboes, Mokos, Housas, Boumous, Popos, Calabars, Congos, Mozambiques, Sherbros, Sussus, Mandingos, Kossos, etc." The Methodist concluded that he was a missionary to not one, but thirty, "nations of Africa."[2]

Raston and Rankin, like European observers around the Atlantic, recognized that Africans in the diaspora were divided into manifold "nations" or "countries."[3] *Nación* (*nação* in Portuguese) or *castas* were common terms in Spanish and Portuguese slave societies. French-speaking areas commonly used *terre* (land), while English colonies often employed the term "country." In Sierra Leone, these "national" categories were common currency not just because they designated where people came from, but also because they delineated who people

---

[1] Rankin, *White Man's Grave*, vol. 1, 76, 210.
[2] Raston, MMS/Special Series/Biographical/West Africa/FBN 4 (fiche 122), undated, c. 1845–1847.
[3] Thornton, *Africa and Africans*, 184; Roger Bastide, *African Civilisations in the New World* (New York: Harper & Row, 1971), 9–10.

127

claimed to be. Group identities were defined and redefined through the process of forced migration, settlement, quotidian interactions among recaptives, and the relationship with missionaries and the colonial state. Such national groups became a locus of community interaction and communal action.

Much of the scholarship on the Atlantic slave trade and the African diaspora has focused on documents containing "national" descriptions of enslaved Africans. Gwendolyn Midlo Hall has argued that such documents are the best evidence for the distribution of Africans in the Americas, even though these ethnic designations are often unclear or equivocal.[4] Other scholars have refuted the very notion of the diasporic "nation." Kwasi Konadu notes that the recorded "nation" and "country" of Africans inventoried in neo-European documents were based on language with little consideration of African polities. Konadu concludes that "these 'nations' and 'countries' were early inventions that anticipated the concept of 'ethnicity,' a colonial creation based largely upon the European idea of a nation" and built on the linguistic and ethnographic categorizing of missionaries.[5] Philip Morgan has similarly criticized scholars of the African diaspora for uncritically employing the terms "countries," "nations," and "national loyalties" as imposed, anachronistic taxonomies.[6] Such terminology was obviously foreign to Africa, and can easily misconstrue the form and variety of pre-colonial African political structures and political identities.

Yet as Matory points out, the imagined communities of the African diaspora referred to themselves and others as "nations."[7] "Nation" is employed here since this was the very language recaptives used, and to dismiss the nation as imposed European inventions is to deny the terms

---

[4] Hall, *Slavery and African Ethnicities*, 23, 26, 38. Hall's work draws on American documents that she argues contain "strong evidence that Africans often identified their own ethnicities" and that "the knowledge and perceptions of slave traders had much less to do with this process than scholars have assumed."

[5] Kwasi Konadu, *The Akan Diaspora in the Americas* (New York: Oxford University Press, 2010), 14. Konadu's argument assumes that enslaved Africans maintained loyalty or identification with particular African polities. This is not self-evident, especially for polities that were destroyed or reconstituted in warfare. Moreover, as Thornton points out, "nations" in the diaspora could be recognized by nonlinguistic features such as scarification. Thornton, *Africa and Africans*, 184–185.

[6] Morgan, "Cultural Implications," 135.

[7] Matory, *Black Atlantic Religion*, 73.

in which recaptives self-identified. This chapter builds on Walter Rucker's contention that specific ethnic or national labels in the diaspora, however problematic and inaccurate, held meaning for those who identified with those labels and who redefined them over time.[8] The point here is certainly not to reify what V. Y. Mudimbe calls the "colonial library," the European knowledge of Africa found in the writings of colonial administrators, missionaries, and ethnologists.[9] It is rather to critically unpack how and why people claimed and invoked certain appellations of group membership, and how they appropriated and continually redefined a range of ethnic labels.

Nation, Language, and the Christian Mission

Lovejoy has argued that in both pre-colonial Africa and the African diaspora the charter principle in determining ethnicity was common language.[10] In the diaspora the "umbrella of common language" proved the foundation for group identities, as localized identities were put aside for an emergent linguistic loyalty. The development of this linguistic loyalty was not an easy or forgone process, as Byrd points out, as many would have had to question and alter important aspects of their native tongues.[11] Ethnic identity in the diaspora was never a replication of home, even when certain ethnonyms or national designations seemingly correspond with recognizable linguistic groupings in Africa. Location and social environment in the diaspora shaped how Africans of the same language group, but from different lineages and/or subdivisions of an ethnic group, associated with one another, often under the label of an African nation.[12]

Diasporic nations were the result of linguistic affinity, shared experience in forced oceanic migration, and new alien settings. But the nations of the Sierra Leone peninsula were also shaped by colonial

---

[8] Rucker, *Gold Coast Diasporas*, 7.
[9] V. Y. Mudimbe, *The Invention of Africa: Gnosis, Philosophy, and the Order of Knowledge* (Bloomington: Indiana University Press, 1988).
[10] Paul E. Lovejoy, "Trans-Atlantic Transformations: The Origins and Identity of Africans in the Americas," in Willem Klooster and Alfred Padula (eds.), *The Atlantic World: Essays on Slavery, Migration, and Imagination* (Upper Saddle River, NJ: Pearson/Prentice Hall, 2005), 128.
[11] Byrd, *Captives and Voyagers*, 250.
[12] Mieko Nishida, *Slavery and Identity: Ethnicity, Gender, and Race in Salvador, Brazil* (Bloomington: Indiana University Press, 2003), 38.

and missionary input, though far from simply colonial creations. The missionary study and classification of language among the receptive population became a contributing factor to both the identification of nations by outsiders and to self-ascriptions. Implicit in the act of translating the Gospel was the acceptance of "nations" as units to which the Church must speak.[13] Over time, CMS missionaries in Sierra Leone came to see the receptive population as a resource to unlocking the linguistic complexities of the continent, as they represented so many potential mission fields. Sierra Leone became a linguistic laboratory where missionaries undertook pioneering work in the study of many West African languages. Their assumption that language, territory, and "national" identity were coterminous informed their work, and the tentative names they gave to many languages were those of receptive nations within the colony.

The colonial and missionary documents that list the "national" categories of receptives are artifacts of a particular type of colonial knowledge that attempted to rigidly fix ethnolinguistic categories. In an attempt to understand, categorize, and control this population, the CMS recorded the nation of the children within their schools, while the 1848 census of Liberated Africans and their descendants grouped the population into nineteen nations. No matter the number or variety of ethnonyms present, such documents created a simplified world of discernible categories. Taking colonial and mission agents as unproblematic proto-ethnographers of these "nations" risks uncritically adopting the hermeneutics of the European observer. It is clear that certain "national" names had no saliency in receptives' places of origin. In instances where they did, their meaning was often greatly changed in this new diasporic setting. Missionaries had only the faintest idea of where these territories actually were and whether the terms they were recording referred to a language, a polity, or a people. Indeed, when missionaries eventually reached many of these "nations" – as they did through ventures such as the Niger Expedition – they found the reality at odds with their previous assumptions. Yet their inquiries in Sierra Leone reveal a great deal about how receptives were identifying based on common language, and missionary attempts to reduce a standardized version of these languages to writing only reinforced this process.

---

[13] Peel, *Religious Encounter*, 281.

CMS missionaries began analyzing the languages of West Africa before the arrival of the first recaptives.[14] Their earliest efforts at the turn of the nineteenth century focused on Temne, Bullom, and Susu, languages of Upper Guinea. Within the colony, the process of linguistic study and classification began tentatively, and perhaps unintentionally, as school instructors sought to categorize the numerous languages among recaptive children placed under their care in the 1810s. A half-century later, these inquiries culminated with Koelle's monumental *Polyglotta Africana*. In the intervening decades, European and African-born agents of the church published numerous vocabularies and grammars of the "national" languages within the colony.

In 1828, the Quaker missionary and linguist Hannah Kilham produced the first noteworthy vocabulary of West African languages.[15] She drew on the knowledge of the recaptive population whose numbers and linguistic heterogeneity were growing throughout these years. Kilham was followed in her efforts by the Rev. John Raban, who joined the Freetown mission in 1825 with explicit instructions to "collect information relative to tongues," while stressing that "the most promising Natives not only retain, but grammatically learn, their own tongues."[16] The establishment of Fourah Bay College in Freetown in 1827 as a seminary for training priests, catechists, and teachers greatly expanded these linguistic investigations. Situated on the eastern edges of Freetown, the college lay in close proximity to the peninsula's recaptive nations.

With the exception of Yoruba, mission agents did not preach in these languages.[17] Yet the act of translation served to define these nations linguistically, based on inquiries with recaptive informants.

---

[14] See volumes 1–5 of the *Sierra Leone Language Review* (1962–1966), in particular the essays of P. E. H. Hair, including "The Contribution of Freetown and Fourah Bay College to the Study of West African Languages," *SLLR*, 1 (1962): 7–18; "The Sierra Leone Settlement – The Earliest Attempts to Study African Languages," *SLLR*, 2 (1963): 5–10; and *The Early Study of Nigerian Languages: Essays and Bibliographies* (Cambridge: Cambridge University Press, in association with the West African Language Survey and the Institute of African Studies, Ibadan, 1967).

[15] Hannah Kilham, *Specimens of African Languages Spoken in the Colony of Sierra Leone* (London: 1828).

[16] Hair, "The Contribution of Freetown and Fourah Bay College to the Study of West African Languages," 9.

[17] Kilham, a pioneering advocate for instruction in African vernaculars, started a girl's school at Charlotte in 1831. That year she gave the first instruction in

By the 1840s, this culminated in publications on Yoruba, Igbo, and Hausa, while roughly mapping the languages of the lower Niger. Codifying these linguistic nations took on a new importance as clergymen in the 1830s and 1840s began envisioning the conversion of recaptives' homelands. James Frederick Schön articulated this strategy prior to the Niger Expedition, the failed 1841 missionary expedition to the confluence of the Niger and Benue Rivers. As chaplain of the expeditionary ship *Wilberforce*, he selected thirteen volunteers as interpreters and agents, including "Ibu [Igbo], Kakanda, Yarriba [Yoruba], Bornu, Eggarah [Igala], Haussa, Nufi [Nupe], Benin [Edo], and Filatah [Fulani, Fulbe]."[18] Since recaptive converts did much of this work – first as informants for European mission agents and then taking the lead in compiling vocabularies and grammars – it was also a process of self-reflection. For converts, the act of translation brought with it ruminations on the links between language and self-identity.

Missionary efforts to delineate the linguistic boundaries of "nations" in the Sierra Leone peninsula involved an interaction between classification and recaptive self-identification. Recaptive nations were communities that defined themselves in relation to others, and reflected in part how outsiders defined them. Through his interviews, Koelle observed this dynamic. Along with classifying 194 "countries," Koelle noted other names for these groups, often "nicknames" or how outsiders referred to these populations. Of these 194 groups, 37 had at least one alternate term used by "foreigners" to identify them; in 13 cases there were multiple alternative names. Koelle noted that the Ekiti were referred to as "'Akuya' by the Basas, 'Bunu' by the Nupes, and 'Kakandsa' by the Ibos."[19] The Boritsu were alternatively called "'Afiten' by the Burubos and Mbarikes, and 'Difu' by the Urapan or Gbagban, as the Boritsus call the Dsukus or Kurorofas." In many cases, these terms were derogatory. The Jarawa (written by Koelle as Dsarawa) were noted to be referred to "by the Bornuese and others called 'Nyamnyam' i.e. cannibals." Many of these nicknames were

---

African languages in the colony, choosing "Kossa" and "Aku." However, Yoruba was the only language regularly used within the mission.

[18] William Allen and T. R. H. Thompson, *A Narrative of the Expedition Sent by Her Majesty's Government to the River Niger in 1841*, vol. 1 (London: Richard Bentley, 1848), 78–79.

[19] Koelle, *Polyglotta Africana*, 6.

nevertheless embraced, Aku being the most obvious but far from only example.

This large array of terms remained in currency in mid-century Freetown as individuals asserted group identities and defined themselves in relation to others. Yet despite the plurality of ethnonyms appearing in Koelle's volume, a select range of "national" designations dominated colonial and missionary sources, especially those in which recaptives self-identified. Colonial officials, missionaries, and recaptives recognized these as the largest nations within the Sierra Leone peninsula. The terms that dominated the school rosters of the 1810s and 1820s (Appendix A) were also the largest nations enumerated in the 1848 census (Appendix B). All these terms represented broader, linguistically defined identities than recaptives possessed in their homeland. But the defining features of each nation were shaped by the scale of migration, as well as by proximity to homelands and the prospects for return. Exploring the largest of these nations – Akoos, Eboos, Paupahs, Housas, Koosoos, Mokos, Congos, and Calabahs – as recorded in the 1848 census highlights the process of ethnogenesis through which the receptive nations of Sierra Leone were formed.

From "Cosso" to Mende

"Where were you born?" asked the chairman of a British Select Committee on the Slave Trade. "In the Cossoo country," replied James Campbell. "How did you leave your country?" the chairman asked. "I was captured by war," said Campbell. The chairman continued: "Where were you taken to from your own country?" "The Gallinas River," was the reply.[20] By 1848 when this deposition took place, the British and Africans in the region of the Sierra Leone colony had developed a working misunderstanding of the term "Cossoo" and the population it described. The same year that the James Campbell appeared before the Select Committee, the colonial census would report that Campbell was one of 609 "Koosoos" among the recaptives. But what, if anything, did the name mean to census takers or Liberated Africans like James Campbell?

---

[20] First Second and Fourth Reports from the Select Committee on the Slave Trade with Minutes of Evidence Appendix and Index, vol. 4, 78–80.

Cossoo, or the variations Cosso, Kosso, Kussoh, or Kossa, developed as a referent to Mende speakers to the southeast of Freetown. Written references to "Cursa" date back to at least 1713, though it is unclear where the term originates.[21] The terms used after 1807 to describe recaptives from nearby regions were informed by earlier interactions since 1787 and by the CMS mission and its accompanying study of languages outside the colony. Recaptives from these societies were among the first to reach Freetown, as the Navy patrolled the nearby coastlines in the 1810s. In the colony, the term appears in reference to recaptives in the earliest CMS school rosters. The 1816 roster lists 57 of the 250 children attending Leicester Mountain School as "Cosso." Between 1816 and 1824, Cosso was the second most recorded "nation" after "Eboo" among school children. "Cosso" recaptives – both children and adults – were settled in the Freetown area as early as 1813. Many resided in Kossoh Town in east Freetown, established about 1818.[22] Those located in the colonial villages often made contacts with Mende speakers a few days' journey away and many moved into the nearby Koya country.[23] "Cosoo" could thus refer to both recaptive groups of landed slaves and migrants who voluntarily entered the colony over land.

The term "Cosso" persisted even as missionaries traveled and became better acquainted with Mende territory. Thus when the former *Amistad* captives returned to Africa via Freetown, local officials described them as "30 Kussoo people" despite the fact that they were returning as part of the Mendi Mission. The CMS missionary Alfred Menzies visited what he referred to as "the Mende Country," describing the region as "a very *great* country." Rather than a singular "country," Menzies described what was, in reality, a large

---

[21] "York, 8 June 1713, an inland people called Fula, who live as far as Gambia and have often attempted to trade to Sherbro but hindered by the natives, have this year taken the country of Cursa, 3 days journey from Sherbro, and if they force their way there the trade will be very considerable to what has been." T70/5, the National Archives. Thanks to Philip Misevich for providing this source. Michael Banton wrote in 1957 that "Kosso" was "the Temne name for the Mende," though he provided no evidence to support this. Michael Banton, *West African City: A Study of Tribal Life in Freetown* (London: Oxford University Press, 1957), 4.

[22] R. J. Olu-Wright, "The Physical Growth of Freetown," in Christopher Fyfe and Eldred Jones (eds.), *Freetown: A Symposium* (Freetown: Sierra Leone University Press; London: Oxford University Press, 1968), 27.

[23] Fyfe, *History of Sierra Leone*, 209.

agglomeration of localized societies connected by language.[24] The Mende formed no large political state, despite the presence of a common language and culture over a wide geographic expanse. The acquisition of such a common identity likely therefore emerged among those that Menzies referred to as "the Liberated Mendians," who most of his contemporaries (and Mende speakers themselves) in the colony referred to as Cosso. British officials and missionaries knew little about the meaning of the term "Cosso," or about these peoples and their homelands, yet Mende-speakers adopted the term, especially in petitioning the government, to denote themselves as a large linguistically defined constituency.

Congo: West Central Africans in a West African Diaspora

In contrast to Mende speakers and other Liberated Africans of Upper Guinea, recaptives from West Central Africa were far from their communities of birth and had little prospect of return. While West Central Africa was the most important region of embarkation in the history of transatlantic slavery, recaptives from this region were a distinct minority in Sierra Leone owing to the vagaries of antislave trade treaties and intermittent British naval patrolling south of the equator. Perhaps no other society of captives from the Atlantic slave trade contained such a small percentage of Central Africans. Being so greatly outnumbered by West Africans who were culturally and linguistically different may have strengthened their solidarity and allowed them to incorporate those who would be considered outsiders in their homelands.

Koelle noted that all speakers of what he termed "Kongo-Ngola languages" were "called Kongo people in Sierra Leone."[25] At the most superficial level, "Kongo" became a colonial shorthand for all Africans arriving from south of the equator. When the slave ship *Arrogante Mayagüesana* arrived following a thwarted journey from Loango to Puerto Rico, William Benjamin Pratt of the Liberated African

---

[24] Marcus Rediker, *The Amistad Rebellion: An Atlantic Odyssey of Slavery and Freedom* (New York: Viking Penguin, 2012), 25, 249, citing A. Menzies, "Exploratory Expedition to the Mende Country," *Church Missionary Intelligencer*, vol. 15, 115; "The Liberated Mendians," *Pennsylvania Freeman*, August 18, 1841.
[25] Koelle, *Polyglotta Africana*, 13.

Department referred to the 309 "newly arrived Congo people."[26] Yet many recaptives also self-identified as "Congo" and had their own ideas of what this meant.

The earliest reference to "Congo" comes in two documents produced by the CMS in 1816. The mission's yearly report for that year recorded that "Cabenda or Congo Town ... may contain about 400 inhabitants, almost entirely Congo."[27] As Chapter 2 showed, former captives of the slave ship *Amelia* founded New Cabenda in 1811. The community later moved to the waterfront near Freetown and renamed itself Congo Town. Also in 1816, the CMS school roster for students at Leicester Mountain recorded 15 of 250 students as "Congo." By 1848, the colonial census listed "Congos" as the seventh largest recaptive nation and the only one of Central African origin.

"Congo" held multiple meanings across the African diaspora. Even within Africa, the term had various meanings, being initially used for the Christian monarchy of the *mani kongo* lords who struggled to consolidate their rule over one part of the region in the sixteenth century.[28] Over time, European merchants operating below the equator generically designated as "Congo" speakers of Kikongo who came from locations distant from the Kongo kingdom and remote from one another. European documents from the slave trade often categorized Africans from the region under the broad terms of "Angola" or "Kongo."

Whether slaves were listed "Anogla" or "Kongo" often had more to do with the nationality of the European recorder than specific point of embarkation in relation to either kingdom. English slave traders tended to designate all of West Central Africa as Angola. Among the 933 English voyages to West Central Africa recorded in *The Trans-Atlantic Slave Trade Database*, 641 (68.7 percent) list the principal port of slave purchase simply as Angola. By contrast, French- and Spanish-language documents tend to list all West Africans as Kongo.[29] However the West Indian slave registries which list African birthplace – St. Kitts (1817), St. Lucia (1815), Trinidad (1813), Berbice (1819), and

---

[26] Pratt, November 11, 1834, LADLB 1834–1837.
[27] *Proceedings of the CMS 1816–1817*, 174.
[28] Miller, "Retention, Reinvention, and Remembering," 87.
[29] Hall, *Slavery and African Ethnicities*, 47.

Anguilla (1827) – record large numbers of West Central Africans as "Congo."[30] Moreover, although all West Central Africans were normally recorded as Angolans in British colonies, the term "Kongo" did appear in runaway slave ads in Jamaican newspapers after 1775.[31]

If colonial officials and missionaries in Sierra Leone simply adopted the terminology of the British slave trade before 1807, it is unclear why "Congo" appeared regularly while "Angola" did not. Part of the answer may lie in where recaptives embarked. Twenty-eight vessels adjudicated at Freetown between 1811 and 1863 embarked their slaves in West Central Africa. From these vessels, a total of 7,559 slaves were emancipated. Most of these vessels purchased their slaves north of the Congo River, rather than from the Angolan ports of Luanda and Benguela: Cabinda (9), "Congo North" (7), Ambriz (3), Loango (2), Luanda (2), Benguela (1), Coanza River (1), Malembo (1), Nova Redonda (1), and Quicombo (1).[32] The preference for "Congo" by observers in Sierra Leone was perhaps because the earliest arrivals were from north of the Congo estuary.

Like larger documentary patterns across the Black Atlantic, Sierra Leone lacked a significant number or variety of distinctive West Central African ethnic designations. The generalized terms of Congo/Kongo and Angola are at odds with patterns of self-identification in West Central Africa, where the general absence of stratified state systems resulted in people identifying in terms of their immediate vicinity. Koelle discerned some of these dynamics in collecting his "Kongo-Ngola" linguistic samples. His informants included an Ambundu man from the hinterland of Luanda, who had "many" countrymen in Sierra Leone, as well as Vili, Yombe, Boma, Nsundi, and Kongo from the vicinity of ports north of the Congo River. All but one of his West Central African informants had arrived from the 1830s onward, as British ships began patrolling south of the equator. The

---

[30] "Congo" was often the most or second-most common designation in these colonies, representing 45.9 percent (1,337) of Africans with listed birthplaces from St. Kitts, 20.7 percent (574) in St. Lucia, 17.8 percent (2,450) in Trinidad, 17.7 percent (212) in Berbice, and 37 percent (20) in Anguilla. In total, some 4,593 (22.2 percent) out of 20,692 slaves registered in these colonies were recorded as "Congo," making it the most common designation in the slave registries. Barry W. Higman, *Slave Populations of the British Caribbean* (Baltimore: Johns Hopkins University Press, 1984).
[31] Hall, *Slavery and African Ethnicities*, 47.
[32] *Voyages* database, http://slavevoyages.org/voyages/kYkoWxNW.

only exception was Thomas Tob, an Mboma man who had been in Freetown some forty years (since c. 1809–1810) and was now the "Kongo headman."[33]

Discerning who identified as "Congo" in Sierra Leone suffers from a comparative lack of documentary evidence. Missionary neglect and the lack of prominent recaptives of West Central African origin accounts for this lacuna. Missionaries saw comparatively few West Central Africans within the colony, and did not envision the Kongo or Angola – places of long-established Catholic influence – as potential mission fields. West Central Africans were thus overlooked in the linguistic studies through which we can glimpse how recaptives self-identified. No West Central African came to prominence within the CMS or MMS missions and none left first-hand accounts of their experiences of enslavement. Many of the earliest Liberated Africans did, however, self-identify as Congo, as they did when they went before the Governor's Council to appeal for land allotments and other assistance. Joseph Macaulay, a recaptive stone mason, came before the council in 1819, identifying himself as "a native of the Congo country, and had resided in the colony ten years."[34] Two years prior, Tom Brown and Peter Brown identified themselves before the council as "natives of the Congo River."[35]

"Congo" in Sierra Leone certainly came to mean more than those who identified as KiKongo in the early to mid-nineteenth century, likely becoming a blanket term for the minority of West Central Africans in the colony who would have spoken mutually comprehensible languages. In Sierra Leone, much like in the New World, the label "Congo" lumped together people whose relations within Central Africa may have been minimal or even hostile. But it also reflected a process in which a West Central African minority, faced with a West African majority, sought out others. In Sierra Leone, they also remained a literal community, and the Freetown neighborhood of "Congo Town" persists, if in name only, more than two centuries later.

---

[33] Koelle, *Polyglotta Africana*, 13.
[34] Council minutes, June 19, 1819, CO 270/15.
[35] Council minutes, July 11, 1817, CO 270/14.

Igbo

Processes of community and identity formation were far different among the large number of recaptives from the Bight of Biafra than for those from West Central Africa. As Chapter 1 showed, perhaps one in four recaptives landing in Freetown spoke dialects of what missionaries in the colony classified as the "Ibo" or "Eboo" language, and both contemporary observers and historians have generally recognized the Igbo as the second largest recaptive "nation." But who were the "Eboo" of Sierra Leone? The meaning of "Igbo" and the notion of an "Igbo nation" in the African diaspora has become a contested debate.[36] It is a debate that has drawn on comparative evidence from Sierra Leonean sources in order to substantiate or refute the existence of a "diasporic Igbo" identity. The region today referred to as Igboland was in pre-colonial times marked by high population densities, political decentralization, and an agrarian economy. Northrup notes that for most inhabitants of southeastern Nigeria the largest unit of identity was not the primary ethnic unit such as Igbo or Ibibio, but rather the smaller dialect or cultural group.[37] The basic political unit was the localized patrilineage; the smallest social unit the extended family, or *umunna*.[38] The Igbo describe themselves as a kingless people, exemplified in their saying *Igbo enwe eze* (Igbo has no king).[39]

Much like the case of "Congo," the term "Igbo" in Sierra Leone may have been simply a holdover from Britain's involvement in the slave trade. Prior to 1807, the British dominated the slave trade from Biafran ports through which large numbers of Igbo-speaking peoples were funneled. For many, their destination was the Anglophone Caribbean or mainland North America. "Ibo/Eboe" had a long history of usage in British colonies. Variants of Igbo (Ibo, Ebo, Eboe, Ebbo, Ebooh), along

---

[36] See Douglas B. Chambers, "'My Own Nation': Igbo Exiles in the Diaspora," *Slavery and Abolition*, 18.1 (1997): 72–97; Northrup, "Igbo and Myth Igbo," 1–20; Chambers, "The Significance of Igbo in the Bight of Biafra Slave-Trade: A Rejoinder to Northrup's 'Myth Igbo,'" *Slavery and Abolition*, 23.1 (2002): 101–120; Femi J. Kolapo, "The Igbo and Their Neighbors during the Era of the Atlantic Slave-Trade," *Slavery & Abolition*, 25.1 (April 2004): 114–133.
[37] Northrup, *Trade without Rulers*, 15.
[38] Gomez, *Exchanging Our Country Marks*, 126.
[39] Hannah Chuckwu, "The Kingless People: The Speech Act as Shield and Sword," in Falola and Njoku (eds.), *Igbo in the Atlantic World*, 17.

with "Congo," were the most prevalent ethnonym in the British Caribbean slave registers after 1807.[40]

Who then, if anybody, self-identified or were identified as Igbo in pre-colonial West Africa? Hall has suggested that the term became associated in the Biafran interior with "slave," while Byrd notes that "Igbo" was an insult or expression of contempt in the region. In other words, it was a designation of otherness. However, in the process of multiple sales and transferral to the coast, captives may have been ascribed as Igbo and eventually internalized an Igbo identity. Byrd suggests that this resulted from slaves' experience of alienation combined with well-developed associations between "Igbo" and otherness in Atlantic ports such as Bonny, New Calabar, and Old Calabar.[41] Here, as in the interior, Igbo was a term for strangers or foreigners. But there is evidence that the term held specific meaning on the coast as those beyond the littoral, as residents of these Biafran ports labeled as Igbo the enslaved from the interior.[42]

In Sierra Leone, the earliest references to "Ebo" or "Eboe" appears to be the 1816 register of children at the Christian Institution on Leicester Mountain. The register lists 95 of the 250 children Ebo, and a further 21 as "Calabar." Despite its common usage in the British Caribbean context, it was German-born and -educated missionaries who would likely have known little of the nomenclature of British slavery who wrote the first mention of "Eboo" in Sierra Leone. This suggests that they might have learned these terms from recaptives themselves. But while early missionary and colonial documents from Sierra Leone show the prevalence of "Eboo" among recaptives in the decade after 1808, they say little on what Igbo identity meant in the colony.

Just as scholars have different interpretations of the origins of the term itself, they disagree about if and when people of a common language saw themselves as a singular people: *the* Igbo. Michael Gomez has stated of pre-colonial Igbo speakers that "it is by no means incontrovertible that they saw themselves as a distinct ethnicity." But he concludes based on travel narratives and Igbo traditions that,

---

[40] Higman, *Slave Populations of the British Caribbean*, 128.
[41] Byrd, *Captives and Voyagers*, 27.
[42] Ibid., 29–30. The adoption of a derogatory term in the diaspora has many parallels. This interpretation does not, however, explain why the term emerged within Nigeria, even if it was only grudgingly accepted.

despite the primacy of local village group identities, "many were very much aware of their shared qualities" and felt that they belonged to an Igbo ethnic group before the advent of Europeans. Moreover, Gomez claims that the "latent potential of Igbo ethnicity matured very rapidly under the pressures of North American slavery."[43] Chambers is more assertive than Gomez in arguing that "the Igbo peoples were a distinct ethno-historical group" with a distinctive set of ancestral traditions, concluding that "they were a people whom modern scholars can study as a separate 'nation' in the transatlantic diaspora." The reason for this was that "Although fiercely localistic in their home areas, Igbo-speaking peoples, once thrown into the diaspora, embraced a collective identity derived from being a member of 'my own nation'" in the words of Olaudah Equiano.[44]

Northrup has taken exception to the similar conclusions of Gomez and Chambers. Among Northrup's objections are Gomez's generic referrals to "Igbo/Biafrans." This interpretation assumes that Igbo speakers were preponderant among slave cargoes leaving the Bight of Biafra.[45] It also assumes that the contemporary term "Calabar" was simply a synonym for Igbo. As this chapter will show, the terms "Igbo," "Calabar," and "Moko" in Sierra Leone – the three main ethnonyms attributable to the Bight of Biafra – had distinct meanings and group memberships. Gomez and Chambers open themselves up to further criticism over their ambiguity regarding identity prior to enslavement. Was the potential for a pan-Igbo identity latent, inchoate, or fully realized prior to European contact? Was it one form of identification among many? Alexander Byrd points out that while Chambers and Gomez rightly see becoming Igbo as a social process, they do not fully interrogate this process. Rather, both authors describe the Igbo as

---

[43] Gomez, *Exchanging Our Country Marks*, 125–126.
[44] Chambers, "My Own Nation," 73.
[45] Northrup's critique misconstrued Gomez and Chambers's arguments as attempting to rectify an outmoded conception of a precolonial Igbo "tribe." Northrup states that Chambers and Gomez "exemplif[y] the tribal approach" by arguing that "something closely resembling the ethnolinguistic 'tribes' of the twentieth-century nationalist politics emerged in the Americas and made important contributions to the development of African-American cultures" (Northrup, "Igbo and Myth Igbo," 3–4). In reality, both authors were arguing for the dynamic aspect of identification between Igbo speakers thrown into the transatlantic slave trade and New World slavery. Northrup is on much firmer ground in his critique of Chambers's conception of "Igboization," i.e., the cultural integration of non-Igbo groups.

possessing certain traits, performing certain actions, and practicing certain behaviors.[46]

Gwendolyn Midlo Hall has suggested that there was some sense of pan-Igbo consciousness and has objected to historians who conclude that the Igbo "identified only with their regions and villages and had no broader identity before they were brought to the Americas, where the Igbo ethnic identity arose." She adds that "the Igbo were not as isolated as many historians claim," while acknowledging that the region displayed a "segmented" system of social organization that does not conform with western concepts of "states."[47] Yet at the same time, Hall insists that these segments must have had some broader shared identity. Hall points to ancient trade routes to suggest that the Igbo were not "isolated or immobilized," though it is not clear that any historian has claimed they were. Hall contends that such interaction led to a process of "creolization" in Africa, though it is unclear that this creolization resulted in a people self-identifying as *the* Igbo. John N. Oriji has similarly asserted the antiquity of Igbo identity, particularly among the Isuama who trace their origins to a common mythical ancestor called "Igbo," who lived at Amaigbo (lit. the abode of Igbo). Oriji concludes that based on a comparative analysis of oral traditions "the Isuama, who are the largest autochthonous settlers of Igboland, shared a common culture" and that "there is little doubt that before colonialism, some Isuama and other groups associated themselves with their common Igbo name."[48]

Much of this debate on Igbo identity in the Biafran interior and the diaspora has been informed by the observations made by Koelle in his *Polyglotta Africana*.[49] Koelle identified five Igbo dialects in Sierra Leone: "Isoama" (Isuama), "Isiele" (Ishielu), "Abadsa" (Abaja), "Aro" (Aro), and "Mbofia" (Mbofia).[50] Koelle noted that "in Sierra Leone certain natives who have come from the Bight [of Biafra] are called Ibos," though "in speaking to some of them respecting this

---

[46] Byrd, *Captives and Voyagers*, 18, and 256 note 3.
[47] Hall, *Slavery and African Ethnicities*, 135. In neither case does Hall state which historians she is referring to, and few historians of this region have made such concrete claims.
[48] John N. Oriji, *Political Organization in Nigeria since the Late Stone Age: A History of the Igbo People* (New York: Palgrave Macmillan, 2011), 5–6.
[49] Northrup, *Trade without Rulers*, 15; Chambers, "My Own Igbo Nation," 74
[50] Curtin, *Atlantic Slave Trade*, 293; Dalby, "Provisional Identification of Languages in the Polyglotta Africana," 85–86.

name, I learned that they never heard it till they came to Sierra Leone."[51] The *Polyglotta* enumerated fifteen "countries" that were "called Ibo in Sierra Leone, whereas this name is not used by any one of these tribes: 1. Mbofia or Mbohia 2. Elugu 3. Ungua 4. Ozozu 5. Okua or Ndoki 6. Iselu 7. Ohuasora 8. Abadsa 9. Bom 10. Mudioka 11. Isoama 12. Oru 13. Mboli 14. Upani or Obani 15. Amoni." All of these can be identified as Igbo-speaking communities, with the exception of "Bom." Bom was the Ozuzu Igbo name for New Calabar (Elem Calabari), though this was a port community that had absorbed many Igbo speakers by the nineteenth century.[52]

William Balfour Baikie, who journeyed up the Niger in 1854, disagreed with Koelle's conclusion that "Igbo" was an unknown or unfamiliar term, stating that "the name Ibo or Igbo is familiarly employed amongst the natives as London is among us."[53] However he was more circumspect regarding *how* Igbo was used, and conceded Koelle's points on the primacy of local identification and on the ambiguity of Igbo as a term of self-identification.[54] If Koelle was correct that "they never heard it till they came to Sierra Leone," it remains to be explained why Yoruba speakers (who Koelle similarly claimed possessed no national name) in the diaspora invariably described themselves by a moniker other than Yoruba (Aku, Lucumí, Nagô), while Igbo speakers in Sierra Leone and across the diaspora seem to have readily accepted the name Igbo abroad.

Whether or not recaptives were previously familiar with the term "Igbo," in Sierra Leone it came to refer to a population speaking a range of related dialects. Crowther and James Frederick Schön commenced the systematic study of the Igbo language in preparation for the 1841 Niger Expedition.[55] Schön only came to appreciate the variety of "Ibo" dialects while sailing up the Niger through Igbo territory. He lamented that "the dialect of the Ibo language on which I had bestowed so much labour in Sierra Leone, differs widely from

---

[51] Koelle, *Polyglotta Africana*, 7. [52] Northrup, "Igbo and Myth Igbo," 13.
[53] William Balfour Baikie, "Summary of an Exploring Trip up the Rivers Kwora and Chadda," *Journal of the Royal Geographical Society*, 25 (1855): 111. Baikie misconstrued Koelle's argument as stating that "I'bo is a name unknown to the natives, until they learn it from the white man."
[54] Byrd, *Captives and Voyagers*, 258–259, note 14.
[55] See Dmitri van den Bersselaar, "Creating 'Union Ibo': Missionaries and the Igbo Language," *Africa: Journal of the International African Institute*, 67.2 (1997): 273–295.

that spoken and understood in this part of the country." It had not escaped Schön "that a great diversity of dialects existed: but I blame myself much for not making stricter inquiries about that which would be most useful for the present occasion."[56] Context and audience shaped whether people in Sierra Leone identified themselves in local terms or in terms of a larger language group. In reality, many people saw themselves as members of both simultaneously. One recaptive named herself Nancy Bishop Eboe and identified herself as "of the Isworma tribe" (Isuama), suggesting that the emergence of a pan-Igbo identity did not subsume more local affiliations (see figure in Appendix D).

James Africanus Beale Horton (1835–1883), born in Gloucester village to Igbo parents, was both the progeny of the diasporic Igbo nation and a contemporary commentator on it. Born James Beale Horton, he added "Africanus" to his name as a point of pride after the British chose him to study as an army medical officer at King's College London and the University of Edinburgh. Returning to West Africa after his studies, he published his *West African Countries and Peoples* in 1868. The book – an impassioned refutation of derogatory Victorian racial theories – devoted much of its discussion to "African nationality." While other chapters were devoted to several "kingdoms" from the Gambia to the Niger, Horton titled his eighth chapter grandly as the "Empire of the Eboes (Iboes, Igboes, Egboes)." The son of Igbo recaptives noted that this "empire" was "divided into several districts or countries, each speaking different dialects, although derived from one root." However, Horton concluded:

Although there are considerable dialectic differences among the Egboes in the different parts of this extensive country, such as those between Elugu on the north and Ebane or Bonny on the south, yet still in their country or Egboeland "each person hails, as a sailor would say, from the particular district where he was born"; but when in a foreign country or when away from their home all are Egboes.[57]

---

[56] James Frederick Schön and Samuel Crowther, *Journals of the Rev. James Frederick Schön and Mr. Samuel Crowther Who, with the Sanction of Her Majesty's Government, Accompanied the Expedition Up the Niger, in 1841, in Behalf of the Church Missionary Society* (London: Hatchard & Son, 1842), 47.
[57] James Africanus Horton, *West African Countries and Peoples* (Edinburgh: Edinburgh University Press, 1969 [1868]), 171, 182.

The latter half of this quotation was taken verbatim from William Baikie's travel narrative, though the phenomenon of simultaneous local and broader linguistic identification was likely something Horton saw firsthand through his parents and his upbringing in Gloucester.

Calabar and Moko

Within recaptive society Moko and Calabar were the other nations of Biafran origin, listed, respectively, as the sixth and eighth largest national groups in the 1848 census. As Chapter 1 noted, there is considerable historical ambiguity over the meaning of "Calabar," and to a lesser extent "Moko," around the Atlantic. Analyzing the Bight of Biafra's diaspora has meant unpacking the terms "Igbo," "Calabar," and "Moko," and the relationship between the three in various contexts. As Chapter 1 showed, in Sierra Leone "Calabar" referred to a portion of the large number of captives sold through Old Calabar (7,077) or Bonny, rather than the smaller number of captives embarked at Elem Kalabari (1,524).

Old Calabar grew from an original settlement of Ibibio-speaking people at Creek Town (Obio Oko) into a number of settlements, or "wards," by the mid-eighteenth century. In this process, these Ibibio speakers adopted a new ethnic label, Efik. Wards were founded and headed by single families, often becoming identified with particular Efik families and their lineage that had migrated from Obio Oko. Here, distinctions based on language or dialect reinforced kinship in separating insiders from outsiders. These kinship structures were fundamental to the creation of distinctions between those who could and could not be legally enslaved at Calabar.[58]

Did "Calabar" in Sierra Leone refer to those who had lived in the vicinity of the port? Or was "Calabar" simply a catchall term for enslaved who traveled through the port? In Sierra Leone, Calabar referred to a separate nation from the Igbo, even if the two groups came from nearby regions and traversed the same ports. Koelle placed "Kalabá" separately within the *Polyglotta Africana*'s linguistic

---

[58] Paul E. Lovejoy and David Richardson, "Anglo–Efik Relations and Protection against Illegal Enslavement at Old Calabar, 1740–1807," in Sylvaine Diouf (ed.), *Fighting the Slave Trade: West African Strategies* (Athens: Ohio University Press, 2003), 103–104.

classifications, recognizing the mutual unintelligibility of Igbo, Ijo, and Efik.[59] Koelle noted that "the people who are called Kalaba in Sierra Leone and all of whom speak nearly the same language, came from the following districts or countries: Anan, Bie or Bibie, Nkuo, Okua, Ekoe, and Efik." Three of the "districts" Koelle mentions are readily identifiable with the major divisions of the Ibibio-speaking peoples: Annang, Bibie (Ibibio), Efik. The other three (Ngkwo, Okua, Ekoe) are obscure.[60] Given Koelle's evidence, it is too simple to claim that recaptives were slaves who had "become Calabars" when exported.

Koelle's Annang informant was Egbeno, otherwise known as W. Johnson, of Waterloo. Somewhat ironically, he had never been to either Calabar, having been sold to the Portuguese at Bonny. Egbeno noted that he knew of "at least two hundred other Kalaba people" in the colony. As Egbeno's account makes clear, being "Calabar" in Sierra Leone did not simply – or even necessarily – refer to recaptives who entered the transatlantic trade at Old Calabar. Moreover, those sold at Old Calabar did not necessarily identify with the term. Twelve of Koelle's informants specifically mentioned being "brought to Kalaba" (presumably Old Calabar), and many noted that they spent significant periods of time there as slaves. Yet none of these informants defined themselves or the language they spoke as "Calabar"; most spoke languages of present-day Cameroon.[61] William Macfoi, a recaptive born in present-day eastern Cameroon, spent three and a half years at "Afek or Kalaba" yet identified himself primarily in terms of his hometown.[62]

Koelle's inquiries show that "Calabar" was a linguistically defined recaptive nation. Yet their lack of a common name for themselves to this day on the Biafran coast suggests how weak their sense of common identity was in their homeland two hundred years ago, and how "Calabar" was a form of unity that existed only in the diaspora. Even if the term itself derived from a port through which many were sold as

---

[59] Northrup, "Igbo and Myth Igbo," 10.
[60] David Northrup, "New Light from Old Sources: Pre-colonial References to the Anang Ibibio," *Ikenga Journal of African Studies*, 2.1 (January 1973): 2.
[61] Koelle did not generally record places of embarkation. That "Kalaba" appears more than any other port in the *Polyglotta* suggests that Koelle was perhaps attempting to discern whether those sold through the port identified as "Calabar" or spoke the dialects he referred to as Anang.
[62] Koelle, *Polyglotta Africana*, 11.

slaves, it was a term embraced within Sierra Leone. There are numerous instances of individuals and groups identifying as "Calabar" in the colony. As the next chapter will show, Calabar recaptives often petitioned the government as *the* Calabar. At Wellington, "Calabar Town" developed as an ethnic enclave within the village. Despite the ambiguity surrounding the term as an ethnonym in West Africa and around the diaspora, it is clear that many recaptives self-identified as Calabar.

Much like "Calabar," the term "Moko" had various meanings throughout the era of the slave trade. Alonso de Sandoval first recorded the term in seventeenth-century Peru. He grouped it as one of a group that he termed *caravalies particulares* trading at Elem Kalabari. A century later, C. G. A. Oldendorp, a missionary in the West Indies, placed the "Mokko" near the Ijaw of Elem Kalabari and distinguished them from both the Igbo and "Bibi" (Ibibio).[63] Among present-day scholars, Michael Mullin concluded that in British America, "Moco" referred broadly to people from the Bight of Biafra hinterland, particularly the Yako and Ekoi of the Cross River.[64] Northrup, building on Mullin, argues that in the seventeenth and eighteenth centuries the people known as Moko were Ibibio speakers who were wholly or partially associated with the Anang.[65]

In various Atlantic contexts, Moko was used interchangeably with Calabar and at times Igbo. The ability of recaptives to assert their own identity, and the steps taken by missionaries in the colony to classify and study language, mean we have a more nuanced understanding of what Moko meant in Sierra Leone. The term was frequently used for various small groups from present-day Cameroon. Koelle stated that the people known as Moko in Sierra Leone were "natives" of sixteen "tribes" belonging to two linguistic subgroups.[66] His Moko informants came from various communities from across present-day Cameroon and Gabon and identified themselves in terms of smaller, kinship-based units. Hugh Goldie, a Scottish Presbyterian missionary based at Old Calabar from 1847, assigned a much broader definition, as "a

[63] Northrup, "New Light from Old Sources," 3.
[64] Michael Mullin, *Africa in America: Slave Acculturation and Resistance in the American South and the British Caribbean, 1736–1831* (Urbana: University of Illinois Press, 1992), 30–31, 287.
[65] Northrup, "New Light from Old Sources," 4.
[66] Koelle, *Polyglotta Africana*, 11–13.

name given in Sierra Leone to all people coming from the region of Calabar and Cameroons Rivers."[67]

Like many other examples in Sierra Leone, "Moko" was not a term anyone used for themselves before they were taken from their homelands. A 1915 edition of the *Sierra Leone Weekly News* featured an article on "The Cameroons" by an author described merely as J.G.W., who had spent several years in what was then the German colony of Kamerun. The author noted, "The Mocoes or Cameroon people are like the rest of their West African brethren divided into a variety of tribes and dialects," and added, "Sierra Leoneans will be surprised to learn that the term Mocoes or Mokkohs by which the people of that place are commonly known in this country, means *warri players*, so far as we have been able to ascertain after painstaking and diligent research."[68] The term itself might therefore derive from the Warri/Oware board game popular throughout West Africa.

In Sierra Leone there was no confusion or conflation between Igbo, Calabar, and Moko. The three nations were seen as coming from different locations, even if sold as slaves at the same coastline and ports. Moreover, they were seen as linguistically distinguishable. This act of differentiation likely occurred specifically because these people came from geographically proximate locations. Byrd notes that the peoples of the Biafran interior have tended to divide the world "dichotomously" into categories of "we" and "they" – with "we" referring either to relations or to their village groups and its components, and "they" serving to denote everybody else.[69] Certainly notions of "we" and "they" were recalibrated in a new setting, yet these groups retained a sense of self-identity, regardless of whether their national name was known in their homelands.

Popo

The discussion of who self-identified as a Calabar in the African diaspora fits within a larger debate over how historians should handle port designations listed in European sources as nations or countries of

---

[67] Hugh Goldie, *Dictionary of the Efik Language* (Glasgow: Dunn & Wright, 1874), 260.
[68] J. G. W., "The Cameroons: A Bone of Contention," *Sierra Leone Weekly News*, October 9, 1915.
[69] Byrd, *Captives and Voyagers*, 19–20.

origin. Many of the most pervasive ethnonyms of the slave trade era, including "Mina," "Coromantee," "Benguela," and "Calabar," were embarkation points on the African coast. Konadu has referred to such terms as "European slaving trademarks" that need to be unpacked as historically and geopolitically situated terms.[70] Historians rightly look on these labels of provenance skeptically as little more than reflections of the "planter's preference" for slaves from certain regions based on behavioral stereotypes regarding strength and obedience. This is certainly the case with "Popo," listed in the 1848 census as the third largest of the receptive nations. Much like Calabar, the term "Popo" is associated with two ports, Little Popo (Aného) and Grand Popo (Hula), both in the Bight of Benin. The earliest record of the term "Popo," under the form of *Papouès*, dates from 1553.[71] Robin Law notes that "Popo" is sometimes applied specifically to the coastal peoples who inhabit the Badagry–Porto Novo area, who call themselves Egun. But the name seems to have originally had a much wider application, since Europeans applied it to both Grand Popo and Little Popo to the west.[72]

This region, known during the era of the slave trade as the western Slave Coast, was originally settled by the Hula people, Gbe speakers who trace their origins to the ancestral city of Tado, some sixty miles from the coast. The documentation that exists for the pre-colonial period usually divides the region between two states: the kingdom of the Hula, known to Europeans by the name of its port at Great or

---

[70] Konadu, *Akan Diaspora*, 6. For comparative discussions on the relationship between ports and ethnic designations, see Mary C. Karasch, "Guiné, Mina, Angola, and Benguela: Africans and Crioulo Nations in Central Brazil, 1780–1835," in Curto and Lovejoy (eds.), *Enslaving Connections*, 163–186. Robin Law and Gwendolyn Midlo Hall have debated the meaning of "Mina" as reference to a particular people or simply to the port of El Mina or the so-called Costa Mina of Portuguese documents. Mariana Candido has looked at the complex meanings of "Benguela" in reference to Africans in the diaspora. Gwendolyn Midlo Hall, "African Ethnicities and the Meanings of 'Mina,'" in Lovejoy and Trotman (eds.), *Trans-Atlantic Dimensions*, 65–81; Robin Law, "Ethnicities of Enslaved Africans in the Diaspora: On the Meanings of 'Mina' (Again)," *History in Africa*, 32 (January 2005): 247–267; Mariana P. Candido, "Tracing Benguela Identity to the Homeland," in Ana Lucia Araujo, Mariana P. Candido, and Paul E. Lovejoy (eds.), *Crossing Memories: Slavery and African Diaspora*, 183–207.

[71] Parés, "The Hula 'Problem,'" 326–28.

[72] Law, *Oyo Empire*, note 152. See also J. Berhto, "La Parenté des Yoruba aux peuplades de Dahomey et Togo," *Africa*, 19 (1949): 123–124.

Grand Popo, and the kingdom of Ge (Gen/Genyi/Guin) known after its port of Little Popo.[73] As Strickrodt explains, prior to the 1680s, Popo referred to the port subsequently known as Grand Popo. Little Popo entered the slave trade in 1683, when it was variously known as "Abree"/"Abrow" and "Poccahonna"/"Paokahnee" as well as "Little Paw Paw"/"Little Po Po." From the 1690s, when Grand Popo temporarily dropped from the trade, Little Popo was often referred to simply as Popo, which became regular usage by the latter eighteenth century. European visitors at this time were aware that Popo was not what the indigenous people called the place or themselves.[74] The origin of the name "Popo" is uncertain. Law suggests the Portuguese may have adopted the term from Yoruba-speaking people, particularly the Ijebu, who are known in recent times to use this term to refer to their Gbe-speaking neighbors.[75]

These ambiguities complicate any discussion of what Popo identity meant in the diaspora. This is all the more so, as Little Popo became a multiethnic urban community in the era of the slave trade, drawing immigrants to its thriving trade. By the nineteenth century, Little Popo consisted of several separate settlements along the coastal lagoon and nearby rivers. Immigrants included Akan-speaking canoe men from the Gold Coast and Ga and Adangme refugees who fled the expanding Akwamu Empire.[76] Though there are very few contemporary sources describing Little Popo in the early nineteenth century, it is clear that it was divided into a number of quarters, reflecting the diverse origins of its inhabitants.[77] One eighteenth-century visitor described Little Popo as a "considerable Black settlement formed of five separate towns, each of which has its own *kabossie* [caboceer]." Of the five towns, only one was "composed wholly of Krepees, the original inhabitants of the land," while "the other towns have been peopled by Akras [Accra]

---

[73] Silke Strickrodt, *Afro-European Trade in the Atlantic World: The Western Slave Coast c. 1550 – c. 1885* (Woodbridge: James Currey, 2015), 2–11.

[74] Ibid., 41; Robin Law, *The Slave Coast of West Africa, 1550–1750: The Impact of the Atlantic Trade on an African Society* (Oxford: Clarendon Press, 1991), 15–16.

[75] Law, *Oyo Empire*, 152.

[76] Robin Law and Silke Strickrodt, "Introduction," in Law and Strickrodt (eds.), *Ports of the Slave Trade (Bights of Benin and Biafra)* (Stirling: Centre of Commonwealth Studies, University of Sterling, 1999), 4–5.

[77] Adam Jones, "Little Popo and Agoué at the End of the Atlantic Slave Trade," in Law and Strickrodt (eds.), *Ports of the Slave Trade*, 123–125.

who, in the last century, when their king had been defeated by the Aquambos [Akwamu], sought refuge here; and who, since they understood the use of weapons better than the simple Krepees, made themselves masters over the latter."[78]

Popo was commonly written as "Pau Pau" in British colonies, and often recorded as "Mina-Popo" in Brazil and Cuba.[79] In Sierra Leone, "Popo" first appears in the 1816 CMS school roster for Leicester Mountain, in reference to fourteen children. Though the designation appears only thirty-three times across the school registers between 1816 and 1824, the 1848 census of the colony recorded "Paupah" as the third largest recaptive nation (8.1 percent of the recorded population). Much like the case of Calabar, Popo in the diaspora did not refer only to people who lived in and around the port(s), nor even necessarily those sold through them. The records of British courts listed 1,101 recaptives embarked at Grand Popo, and only three recaptives in the case of Little Popo. Both Popos were relatively minor ports among recaptives and within the transatlantic trade generally.

If Little Popo was a plural community, it is not surprising that the term "Popo" in Sierra Leone had a plurality of meanings. "Popo" within the colony did not refer simply to those born in and around Grand and Little Popo, speakers of a particular language (Ewe), or only those sold through either of these ports. Koelle noted that "Dahome" was "by foreigners called Popo."[80] This may seem a peculiar conflation of the Hula residents of Popo with their (often adversarial) Fon-speaking neighbors to the east in Dahomey.[81] Yet Hannah Kilham, a Quaker who also did linguistic work among Sierra Leone's Liberated Africans, similarly collected specimens of the "Popo" language. The 1847 annual meeting of the British Association for the Advancement of Science included a discussion by R. G. Latham titled "On the Present State and Recent Progress of Ethnographical

---

[78] Selena Axelrod Winsnes (ed.), *Letters on West Africa and the Slave Trade: Paul Erdmann Isert's Journey to Guinea and the Caribbean Islands in Columbia (1788)* (Oxford: Oxford University Press, 1992), 89.
[79] Hall, *Slavery and African Ethnicities*, 47. For "Papaw" in the American South and British Caribbean, see Mullin, *Africa in America*, 285–286.
[80] Koelle, *Polyglotta Africana*, 4.
[81] Mullin points out that "Papaw" in Jamaica and elsewhere in British America was often used in reference to Dahomey, though people often spoke of the "Fon" Kingdom or generically of "Arada." Mullin, *Africa in America*, 285.

Philology." The meeting concluded that "the Popo vocabulary of Mrs. Kilham represents a Dahomey dialect."[82] This would suggest that in the context of Sierra Leone, Popo referred linguistically to the Fon people of Dahomey. Yet Fon was a part of a related cluster of languages of the Ewe–Aja–Fon, of whom speakers of these languages are today referred to as "Gbe."[83] Despite the linguistic overlap identified in more recent decades, these similarities within the Ewe–Aja–Fon cluster of languages did not result in an overarching identity based on similarity of dialect. This fact and the lack of alternative terms to describe receptives from the various polities of the Western Slave Coast suggest that Popo in the colony took on a broader regional meaning defined by neither political unity in their homeland nor common language.

Robert Clarke, an assistant colonial surgeon in Freetown, noted that the Popo were distinguishable in the colony by their scarification or "national marks." Clarke described these as "a line drawn from the angle of the eye-brows, with raised cicatrices stained, about one inch in length, of a blue colour, on the left side of the cheek, six horizontal lines similarly stained, proceeding from the angle of the ear, to that of the mouth." Additionally, "three short cuts begin at the superior angle of the mouth, terminating beneath the lower lip. On the right cheek are eleven cicatrices just below the eye."[84]

"Popo" was a term that referred to people with no common language or prior political unity in their homelands. The name in Sierra Leone seems then to refer to slaves sold through the ports of Grand Popo and Little Popo and/or to Fon speakers from Dahomey, who in the diaspora took on a Yoruba term for those to the west, including but perhaps not limited to the Kingdom of Dahomey. The name may therefore be similar to "Jeje," a term in northeastern Brazil for people primarily of Fon, Mahi, Allada, or Ewe origin.[85]

---

[82] *Report of the Annual Meeting, British Association for the Advancement of Science*, 17 (1847): 170.
[83] Law, "Ethnicities of Enslaved Africans," 247.
[84] Clarke, *Manners and Customs*, 46–47.
[85] João José Reis, "African Nations in Nineteenth-Century Salvador, Bahia," in Cañizares-Esguerra, Childs, and Sidbury (eds.), *The Black Urban Atlantic*, 67.

Hausa

The 1848 census enumerated the Hausa as the fourth largest recaptive nation, representing 4.9 percent of the recorded population. Hausa recaptives arrived in Sierra Leone at a time when Hausa-speaking territories were experiencing profound changes in the wake of Uthmān dan Fodio's declaration of a jihad in 1804. Many Hausa recaptives may have been soldiers captured in war, including Koelle's Kano-born informant who was taken as a prisoner of war during an attack on Gobir. Compared with Popo, Calabar, Moko, Congo, and Cosso, "Hausa" – recorded variously in Sierra Leone as Haussah/Housa/Houssah/Housah – is a seemingly less ambiguous term. Hausa is one of the few instances where the same designation appears within both Africa and the diaspora. Hausa appears across many regions of the African diaspora, particularly in regions such as northeast Brazil.[86] The Hausa states were, along with the kingdom of Borno, the major political units of the central Sudan, the region west of Lake Chad and north east of the middle Niger.

Hausa was a "native" term pertaining to peoples from different city-states across the vast Central Sudan. The term therefore applied to a dispersed ethnic population. For several reasons "Hausa" cannot be treated uncritically as an ethnonym in the diaspora. First, the etymology of the term "Hausa" remains unsolved. References to the term are rare until the seventeenth century, becoming more common in eighteenth-century slave trading records. But to what or to whom did "Hausa" refer? Murray Last notes that the name "Hausa" has had at least three distinct histories: the name of one of the Chadic languages, a label that has referred to various peoples over centuries, and a region often referred to as Hausaland (or *kasar Hausa*).[87] Last postulates that because the region was a borderland between two merchant networks, it was likely merchants who standardized many of the labels found in Arabic sources, including Hausa. The label Habasha/Hausa may have been a term applied to the Muslim merchants' local trading partners, to

---

[86] João José Reis, "Ethnic Politics among the Africans in Nineteenth-Century Bahia," in Lovejoy and Trotman (eds.), *Trans-Atlantic Dimensions*, 240–264.

[87] Murray Last, "Ancient Labels and Categories: Exploring the 'Onomastics' of Kano," in Anne Haour and Benedetta Rossi (eds.), *Being and Becoming Hausa: Interdisciplinary Perspectives* (Leiden: Brill, 2010), 59.

local employees such as caravan staff or guards, and possibly to suppliers of food and livestock."[88]

Historically, many Hausa traders may have possessed some sense of a broad Hausa identity, though this is less obvious among the majority of Hausa who were sedentary farmers. Haour and Rossi's heuristic examination of "being and becoming" Hausa notes that there is "little agreement on the mechanisms by which developed complex social and settlement hierarchies, Islamic institutions, and links with the wider world, which have come to characterise 'Hausa' in the eyes of outsiders." Hausa-speaking society has been marked by regional heterogeneity in terms of lifestyles and traditions. This diversity has led to a conception of "Hausaness" as "a phenomenon looser than ethnicity."[89] At the same time, the common perception today is that to be Hausa is to be Muslim. The Hausa states between the Niger River and Lake Chad were Muslim by the thirteenth century, if not earlier, and Islam has had a huge influence on Hausa society for most of the last millennium.[90] Haour and Rossi caution that the assumption that Hausa speakers were invariably Muslim should not be assumed to have always been the case. Rather, religion formed part of a continuous renegotiation in the representation and self-representation of groups "as different ways of being Hausa found expression in different articulations of identity and religion."[91]

Despite this internal diversity, the Hausa diaspora has strongly reflected the tenacity of a Hausa identity beyond the *kasar Hausa*. This is most apparent in a series of Hausa revolts and conspiracies in Bahia in northeastern Brazil from 1807 onward, culminating in the role of "Hausa" leadership in the 1835 slave revolt.[92] In all probability, the Hausa of both Bahia and Sierra Leone were captured and enslaved during wars related to the Sokoto jihad. In the diaspora, this Hausa identity likely reflected both adherence to Islam and common language. Though regional dialects remain today, in the course of some

---

[88] Ibid., 68.
[89] Haour and Rossi, "Hausa Identity: Language, History and Religion," in Haour and Rossi (eds.), *Being and Becoming Hausa*, 1–4.
[90] Joseph McIntyre, "More Rural than Urban? The Religious Content and Functions of Hausa Proverbs and Hausa Verbal Compounds," in Haour and Rossi (eds.), *Being and Becoming Hausa*, 85.
[91] Haour and Rossi, "Hausa Identity," 4–5.
[92] Stuart B. Schwartz, *Sugar Plantations in the Formation of Brazilian Society: Bahia, 1550–1835* (Cambridge: Cambridge University Press, 1985), 468–488.

five centuries there developed the lingua franca we now call Hausa.[93] James Frederick Schön – the German CMS missionary who would produce the first combined Hausa grammar/vocabulary in 1843 – had little difficulty in finding Hausa linguistic informants in 1840s Freetown as he prepared for the Niger Expedition.[94] Yet both in Hausa territory and in the diaspora, narrower identities based on region continued to exist within this broader reference group, and both of Koelle's Hausa informants self-identified with the Hausa city-states of Kano and Katsina.

Aku

Despite the large number of recaptive nations, colonial and missionary officials in Sierra Leone commonly stated that one nation eclipsed all others in terms of their size, conspicuousness, and unity within Liberated African society. This was the Aku. Most studies of Sierra Leone have asserted that "Aku" was a colonial term for Yoruba and have echoed contemporary observations that they were the largest and most conspicuous group in the colony. Yet Aku was an ethnonym unknown to West Africa or to any other region of the African diaspora. Its etymology and meaning were products of forced migration to Sierra Leone and the context of the colonial and missionary encounter.

Pre-colonial Yorubaland was populated by peoples of shared language, cultural traits, and a regard for the town of Ile-Ife as the origin of their ancestors and their most sacred traditions. Yet as Peel points out, they did not know themselves by a common name.[95] This lack of a collective name suggests that it is doubtful whether these people had any consciousness of forming any sort of national or ethnic unit. Instead, the speakers of various Yoruba dialects knew themselves by more local identities, such as Oyo, Egba, Ìjẹ̀ṣà, Ijebu, Ekiti, Awori, or simply by the name of their *ilu*, or "town."

---

[93] Last, "Ancient Labels and Categories," 59.
[94] Hair, *Early Study of Nigerian Languages*, 31–63.
[95] Peel, *Religious Encounter*, 26. N. A. Fadipe has been even more assertive, concluding that "the label, Yoruba, as that of an ethnic group could not have been long in vogue prior to 1856" and that "the present day people [c. 1939], particularly elderly persons in certain parts of the country, tend to distinguish their own local groups from the one they collectively referred to as Yoruba." N. A. Fadipe, *The Sociology of the Yoruba* (Ibadan: Ibadan University Press, 1970), 30–31.

While Yoruba speakers possessed no common name or common identity in their homelands, they often acquired both in diasporic settings when surrounded by the ethnolinguistic heterogeneity of the diaspora. Historians generally accept that an overarching identity among Yoruba speakers developed first in the diaspora, and was refracted back to Yorubaland by returning liberated slaves and missionaries.[96] This process is most commonly associated with Liberated Africans landed in Sierra Leone after 1807, though Robin Law has suggested this process may have been slightly foreshadowed by the return of liberated slaves from Brazil and Cuba.[97]

In the diaspora, processes of Yoruba ethnogenesis most often resulted in a term of self-identification other than Yoruba: Lucumí in Cuba and Nagô in Brazil and Saint-Domingue. João José Reis writes that Yoruba speakers of the Oyo, Egba, Ijebu, Ilesha, and Ketu kingdoms "became Nagôs in Bahia through complex exchanges and convergences of cultural signs with the help of a common language, similar divinities (Orishas), the unification of many under Islam, long experience as subjects of the Oyo *alafins* (kings), Yoruba urban traditions and, obviously a life of slavery in Bahia."[98] Robin Law has scrutinized the meanings of the terms "Nagô" and "Lucumí," concluding that neither term is unambiguously documented as a generic term for Yoruba speakers before the mid-nineteenth century. Rather, their general application in the diaspora reflects transformations in ethnic identities through displacement across the Atlantic.[99]

Aku as an ethnonym born of the slave trade has not received equal scrutiny as Lucumí or Nagô. Nor has the process by which a Yoruba identity was transferred back from Sierra Leone to present-day Nigeria been fully delineated, despite the historiographical consensus on these

---

[96] J. D. Y. Peel, "The Cultural Work of Yoruba Ethnogenesis," in Tonkin, McDonald, and Chapman (eds.), *History and Ethnicity*, 202; Michel R. Doortmont, "The Invention of the Yorubas: Regional and Pan-African Nationalism versus Ethnic Provincialism," in P. F. de Moraes Farias and Karin Barber (eds.), *Self-Assertion and Brokerage: Early Cultural Nationalism in West Africa* (Birmingham: Birmingham University African Studies Centre, 1990), 102.
[97] Robin Law, "Yoruba Liberated Slaves Who Returned to West Africa," in Falola and Childs (eds.), *Yoruba Diaspora*, 360–361.
[98] João José Reis, "'The Revolution of the *Ganhadores*': Urban Labour, Ethnicity and the African Strike of 1857 in Bahia, Brazil," *Journal of Latin American Studies*, 29.2 (May 1997): 361.
[99] Law, "Ethnicity and the Slave Trade," 205–219.

Aku

external origins of Yoruba identity.[100] The emergence of an "Aku nation" in Sierra Leone parallels the development of the Lucumí and Nagô nations of Cuba and Brazil. But identity formation is always a context-specific process and the development of the Aku nation was shaped by Liberated Africans' position of relative freedom and the nature of the colonial and missionary encounter in British West Africa.

The designation "Aku" derived from the commonest form of Yoruba greeting, *e ku*.[101] J. F. Ade Ajayi argues that the term was originally "Oku," from the salutation "Oku'o," and later corrupted by missionaries to "Aku." Ajayi adds that this term "shows that up till then the majority of them were Oyo," since it is a specifically Oyo–Yoruba greeting.[102] Sierra Leonean historians have argued that the term derives from the more specific Yoruba greeting "ẹ kuṣe" (lit. "good work" or "good job"), which persists to this day in Sierra Leone's Krio language as "Akushe O" or "Okushe O."[103] The Yoruba

---

[100] Thus far the only work to place Aku identity in comparative perspective is João José Reis, Flávio dos Santos Gomes, and Marcus J. M. de Carvalho, "Entre akus e males," in *O Alufá Rufino: Tráfico, escravidão e liberdade no Atlântico Negro (c. 1822–c. 1853)* (São Paulo: Companhia das Letras, 2010), 228–240.

[101] Law, "Ethnicity and the Slave Trade," 206.

[102] J. F. Ade Ajayi, *Christian Missions in Nigeria, 1841–1891* (London: Longmans, 1965), 21. Ade Obayemi has noted that the northeastern Yoruba communities of Oworo, Ijumu, Abini (Jumu), Ikiri, Igbede, and Iyagba (all beyond Oyo control) were referred to as "the 'O-kun' after a mode of salutation common, though not exclusive to them." Ade Obayemi, "The Sokoto Jihad and the 'O-kun' Yoruba," *Journal of the Historical Society of Nigeria*, 9.2 (June 1978): 61.

[103] C. Magbaily Fyle, "The Yoruba Diaspora in Sierra Leone's Krio Society," in Falola and Childs (eds.), *Yoruba Diaspora*, 369, 381. Fyle argues that the title actually derives from the Krio greetings, though this assumes that a creole language based at least partially on Yoruba had emerged by the late 1810s. John Raban, who published his pioneering *Vocabulary of the Eyo or Aku Language* in 1830, based on five years of discussions with Aku informants, recorded the following salutations among recaptives: "E-ku-du-ro?" (to an unknown persons standing), "O ku ye he?" (to a person walking), and "O ku om-le o?" (going to a house). It seems unlikely then that "aku" emerged specifically from "oku" than from the range of greetings beginning with "e ku" or "o ku" as overheard by those who did not necessarily understand the language. The earliest reference I have found to "Oku" is from John Ulrich Graf of the CMS, who commented in 1842 on starting his study "of the Ohku Language (pron. Awku)." Graf, Report for Quarter Ending March 25, 1842, CMS/CA1/O105/36. Despite this evidence, Gibril Cole has recently contended that the term "Aku" represented a missionary corruption of the term "Oku'o," adding that "neither the Liberated Africans nor their progeny in Krio society, including luminaries such as Mohammed Sanusie, Hadiru Deen, Sir Samuel Lewis, Bishop Samuel Adjai Crowther, and the Reverend Abayomi Cole,

language contains an array of greetings based on time of day, location, and speaker. The ethnonym "Aku" likely emerged from some combination of these greetings being overheard by non-Yoruba speakers. The external coinage of Aku may be comparable to the earlier term "Lucumí," which supposedly derived from the Yoruba greeting *oluku mi*, "my friend."[104] The historian and assistant district commissioner A. E. Tuboku-Metzger wrote in 1932 that "the people of whom the name 'Aku' is applied never call themselves 'Aku.' The other tribes (nations) first nicknamed them 'Oku' on account of their frequent use of that word which is a form of salutation in their language, and the members of the tribe accepted the nickname and then proceeded to call themselves by that name."[105]

The earliest mention of Aku appears to be the 1818 register of Liberated African children at Leicester Mountain, which identified 33 of the 176 children as "Accoo."[106] The earlier 1816 school roster of 250 students makes no mention of "Aku" or any other plausible term for Yoruba speakers.[107] This does not mean that Yoruba speakers were not present in the colony, only that none had been

identified themselves as Aku. Without equivocation they all consistently identified themselves as Oku." Cole, *Krio of West Africa*, 8. In fact, Crowther never referred to himself as either Oku or Aku, identifying himself in his earlier writings as an inhabitant of Oyo and later as Yoruba. Cole overlooked numerous instances in which Liberated Africans self-identified as Aku, many of which are presented here at the opening of Chapter 6. Conversely, Cole's assertion that anyone actually self-identified as "Oku" is unsubstantiated, with no reference to nineteenth-century sources.

[104] Law notes that this etymology of "Lucumí" is purely speculative. Law, "Ethnicity and the Slave Trade," 208. Henry Lovejoy and Olatunji Ojo have suggested that "Olukumi" likely originated as early as the sixteenth century as an Edo term at the height of Benin's imperial rule and referred to Benin's neighbors who spoke a foreign language, most likely "Yoruba." See Lovejoy and Ojo, "'Lucumí,' 'Terranova,' and the Origins of the Yoruba Nation," *Journal of African History*, 56 (2015): 353–372.

[105] A. E. Tuboku-Metzger, *History of the Colony Villages of Sierra Leone from the Earliest Time to about 50 Years Ago* (n.p., 1932). This account does seem to substantiate part of Gibril Cole's argument. However, this source is problematic for several reasons, not the least of which is that it was written in 1932. In this source, Tuboku-Metzger claims that Koelle was the first to misconstrue the "Oku" as "Aku"; in reality the opposite is true, and Koelle provides one of the first written renderings of the ethnonym as "Oku."

[106] List of Boys at the Christian Institution, Leicester Mountain in July 1818, CMS/CA1/E7/32.

[107] "A List of the Boys & Girls Supported by the Church Missionary Society at Leicester Mountain," CMS/CA1/E5A/68/N.

assigned to that school. The term was likely used within the colony for some time, gaining saliency by 1818 as a descriptive term for various Yoruba speakers. In total, 47 of the 691 Liberated African children attending the CMS schools between 1816 and 1824 were listed as Aku. The school registers show that until the 1820s, Yoruba speakers were one ethnolinguistic group among many in the colony, and that it was only over the course of the 1820s that they would become the largest and most conspicuous recaptive group.

The CMS school registers were modest attempts to differentiate recaptives based on ethnolinguistic grounds. It was through the systematic study of recaptive languages – particularly the language later called Yoruba – by which missionaries came to know more of the Aku, that the notion of Aku as a linguistic community was further elaborated. Hannah Kilham, who visited the colony in 1827, learned from missionaries such as Thomas Davy and W. K. Betts that the Aku language "is said to be spoken by more than half the Liberated Africans in Sierra Leone, and on this account important to cultivate." She added that Aku was "the name used for this nation in the Colony, but it appears from their information that the name of their country is E-i-o, and the term Aku only their word of salutation in meeting."[108] A year later, her *Specimens of African Languages Spoken in the Colony of Sierra Leone* included "Lessons in Aku, (or Eio) and English."[109] The pioneer of Yoruba language study, Rev. John Raban, also equated Aku with Oyo in his *Vocabulary of the Eyo or Aku Language, a Dialect of Western Africa* in 1830.[110]

In the 1820s, Aku primarily referred to those enslaved as a direct result of Oyo's collapse. As the Yoruba wars expanded beyond Oyo in the 1820s, documents in Sierra Leone began to reflect the shifting frontier of violence and enslavement as terms for other Yoruba subgroups appeared for the first time. Henry Gipps, a student at Gloucester village, is described in both 1821 and 1822 school registers as "Agba" (Egba), though later in 1822 and again in 1824 he is described as "Arcoo" (Aku). John Greig, also of Gloucester, is

---

[108] Kilham, *Report on a Recent Visit*, 9.
[109] See "Bibliography of Yoruba, to 1890," in Hair, *Early Study of Nigerian Languages*, 20–30.
[110] Raban subsequently noted that he was expanding his vocabulary "by intercourse with different individuals of the Eyo or Yoruba country." Raban, March 20, 1832, CMS/CA1/O180/52.

identified as "Agba" through 1821, 1822, and 1824. Beyond "Agba," the only possible reference to any Yoruba "subgroups" appears to be two boys, James Rumsey and Charles Prowett, identified as "Jasher" (Ìjèṣà) living in Charlotte and Leopold in 1822 and 1824, respectively. Egba and Ìjèṣà appear as the only "subgroups" identified by the missionaries before Koelle's careful linguistic study of recaptive language some three decades later.

While Yoruba speakers embraced the term "Aku," older, more localized identities were not fully subsumed. One elderly Aku recaptive, a native of "Ephee" (Ife) told Elizabeth Melville that "my country is to the other Aku countries what England is to this place."[111] Koelle was perhaps the most conscious European observer of this dynamic and his observations add a necessary degree of nuance to certain missionary and colonial documents that present an overly cohesive picture of *the* Aku. Among his informants, Koelle identified thirteen "Aku dialects, or the Aku language as spoken in different districts or countries": Ota, Egba, "Idsesa" (Ìjèṣà), Yoruba (Oyo), Yagba, Eki (Ekiti), Dsumu, Oworo, "Dsebu" (Ijebu), Ife, Ondo, "Dsekiri," and Igala.[112] Whereas Aku was once equated with Oyo, by mid-century it referred to "the whole nation" of Yoruba speakers. By contrast, Koelle deemed only those born in Oyo as "proper Yórūbans." His Yórūba ("proper") informant, Thomas Johnson, was born in Ogo a "day's journey" from New Oyo, and had been kidnapped by the Fulani some twenty-eight years prior. Johnson estimated that there were "several thousand proper Yórūbans in Sierra Leone."

Koelle was not alone in recognizing that the Aku nation encompassed more localized identities. Robert Clarke's 1843 *Description of the Manners and Customs of the Liberated Africans* included an entire chapter of "Notes on the Akoo Nation." Clarke noted that the Akoo were "better known by the term 'Eyeos,' or 'Yarribeans'" and were "distinguished into tribes, bearing the names of their native localities, Deholibah, or Joliba, Jebuh, Jessuh, Jffeh, and Ebghwa."[113] Clarke's

---

[111] Anonymous [Elizabeth Helen Melville], *A Residence at Sierra Leone: Described from a Journal Kept on the Spot, and Letters Written to Friends at Home* (London: John Murray, 1849), 257. Melville, who published her account anonymously as written "by a lady," was the wife of Michael Melville, Registrar of the Mixed Court, and wrote a series of letters to her cousin.
[112] Koelle, *Polyglotta Africana*, 5.   [113] Clarke, *Manners and Customs*, 147.

later 1863 account listed "Ifeh, Jebuh, Jessuh, Eyeo, Egbwa, Joliba, Yagwa."[114] These distinctions within the Aku community remained salient into the late nineteenth century, long after the arrivals of the last recaptives from the Bight of Benin. Reminders of these distinctions can be found in the form of memorials and gravestones to Liberated Africans in Freetown (see figure in Appendix D). In most cases, these memorials refer to the individual as Aku rather than Yoruba, and provide a more specific reference to their origins. For example, Isaac Benjamin Pratt, who became one of Freetown's leading merchants and property owners, is commemorated as a "native of the Ifeh section of the Aku tribe."

Beyond written references to Yoruba "subgroups" such as Egba, Yagba, and Ijebu, regional identities took on several other forms: names, dialect, and scarification. Within Africa and the diaspora, characteristics of ethnicity were often visual: cicatrization, tattooing, piercing of ears and lips, hairstyles, dress, jewelry, and cosmetics.[115] These important markers of identification have only recently been taken up as topics within studies of ethnicity and culture in the diaspora. Olatunji Ojo's discussion of scarification among the Yoruba characterizes cicatrices as being "like national passports" that needed to be uniform among citizens of a Yoruba state.[116] Yoruba *abaja* (markings) were associated with place of residence and political allegiance. Abaja scarifications were inscribed on the body, particularly the face, at an early age. Specialists, usually a devotee of Ògún, the Yoruba *orisa* (deity or spirit; see Chapter 6) of iron, manipulated sharp metal instruments and inscribed the markings.[117] These "national Passports" signified the origins of even the most acculturated Liberated Africans. Samuel Crowther had facial markings of the Osogun Yoruba, though not visible in his portraits. The Methodist missionary Thomas Dove observed that the Egba Joseph Wright "has all the

---

[114] Robert Clarke, *Sketches of the Colony of Sierra Leone and Its Inhabitants* (London: T. Richards, 1863), 329–330.
[115] Paul Lovejoy, "Scarification and the Loss of History in the African Diaspora," in Andrew Apter and Lauren Derry (eds.), *Activating the Past Historical Memory in the Black Atlantic World* (Newcastle: Cambridge Scholarly Publishing, 2010), 103.
[116] Olatunji Ojo, "Beyond Diversity: Women, Scarification, and Yoruba Identity," *History in Africa*, 35 (2008): 370.
[117] Lovejoy, "Scarification," 111.

162   *Liberated African Nations: Ethnogenesis in an African Diaspora*

1.—*Akoo National Mark.*   2.—*Jebu National Mark.*   3.—*Eyeo vel National Mark.*   4.—*Egwa National Mark.*

5.—*Ebgwa National Mark.—Woman.*   6.—*Yagwa National Mark.—Woman.*   7.—*Epha National Mark.*   8.—*Yarriba National Mark.—Woman.*

9.—*Joliba National Mark.*   10.—*Jessu National Mark.*

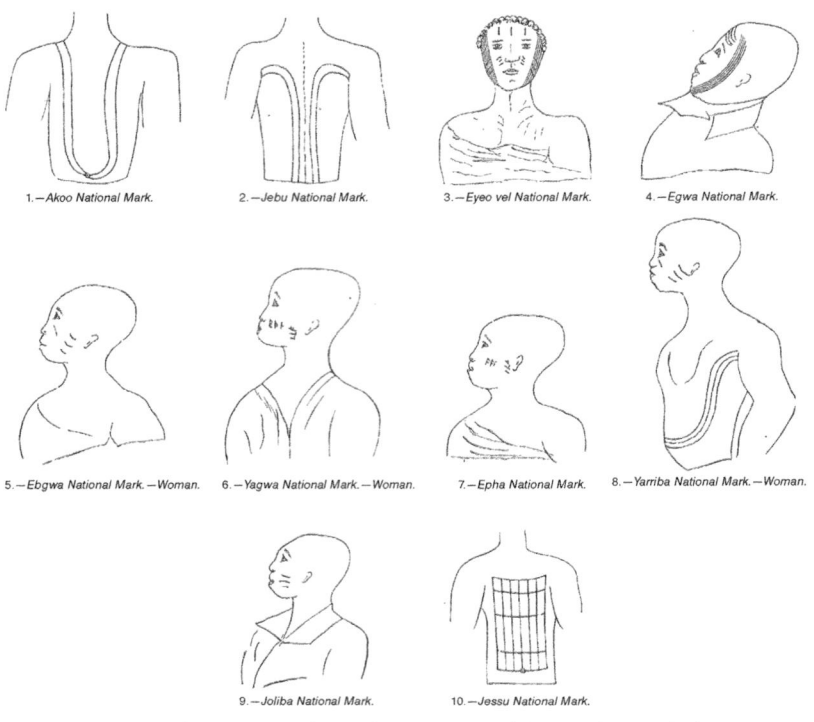

Figure 4.1 Yoruba "national marks" compiled by Robert Clarke, Senior Assistant Surgeon to the Colony of Sierra Leone, 1843
(Clarke, *Manners and Customs*, insert, 46–47)

marks and scars in his face indicative of the Akoo tribe to which he belongs."[118]

Robert Clarke, the chief medical officer at Kissy Hospital in the 1840s, provides the most complete catalogue of Yoruba scarification in Freetown, depicting what he saw as the distinctive marks of the Ijebu, Oyo, Egba, and Yagba (Figure 4.1). In 1863 he wrote that "nearly all the liberated Africans ... are distinguished by national marks upon the face, arms, or body" and that the practice "has not been entirely abandoned at Sierra Leone, as several of their children have cuts on the face exactly similar to the tribe to which their parents

---

[118] Dove to the General Secretaries, April 19, 1842, MMS Correspondence.

belong. This is particularly the case among the Akoos."[119] The largest and most cohesive nation of recaptive society was thus unified linguistically under a diasporic nickname, while dialect, scarification, and aesthetics spoke to the more local identities within the Aku nation.

Questions remain as to why this population in Sierra Leone referred to themselves as Aku, why their counterparts in their homelands came to identify as Yoruba, and why Yoruba never supplanted Aku as a term within Sierra Leone. The name "Yoruba" derives from the Hausa language, and referred to non-Muslim peoples to the south that the Hausa deemed permissible to enslave. Yoruba appears in Arabic language sources as early as the seventeenth century, though it is unclear whether the name referred specifically to Oyo or the wider ethnolinguistic group.[120] The earliest use of the term "Yoruba" in Sierra Leone appears to be Rev. John Raban's quarterly report for March 1832, in which he notes that he was collecting new vocabulary "by intercourse with different individuals of the Eyo or Yoruba country."[121] A year prior, Raban noted that he was consulting Hugh Clapperton's "vocabulary of the Yourriba tongue," from Clapperton's posthumous *Journal of a Second Expedition into the Interior of West Africa*. Clapperton, a Scottish explorer and diplomat, made two expeditions through Yoruba territories, providing linguistic samples within his published accounts. This suggests that Raban's adoption of Yoruba as a synonym for Oyo came from accounts published in England rather than because recaptives in Sierra Leone were using the term.[122]

The adoption of Yoruba as the CMS's term for the language was furthered by one of Raban's linguistic informants, Samuel Crowther.[123] John Peel argues that the decisive step for the final adoption of the term "Yoruba" by the CMS was Crowther's use of it

---

[119] Clarke, *Sketches of the Colony of Sierra Leone*, 329.
[120] Law, "Ethnicity and the Slave Trade," 206; Lovejoy contends that "Yoruba" originally referred to all speakers on the language, on the grounds that Oyo was only a minor polity when the term was first recorded in print in 1613. Paul E. Lovejoy, "The Yoruba Factor in the Trans-Atlantic Slave Trade," in Falola and Childs (eds.), *Yoruba Diaspora*, 41.
[121] Raban, Report, March 20, 1832, CMS/CA1/O180/52.
[122] Raban, Quarterly Report, Gloucester, March 22, 1831, CMS/CA1/O180/50.
[123] Samuel Crowther was likely one of Raban's informants since Crowther studied at the institution later named Fourah Bay until 1828 and was thereafter a schoolmaster in the district over which Raban had supervision. Hair, "The Contribution of Freetown and Fourah Bay College to the Study of West African Languages," 9.

in the title of his *Vocabulary of the Yoruba Language* (1843).[124] Crowther became the first to describe himself as Yoruba as it is understood today, primarily as a result of his experience on the Niger Expedition. In 1837 Crowther was still referring to "my (Eyo) country."[125] But during his preparation for the expedition in early 1841 he spoke of compiling a dictionary of "Yoruba, it being my native language."[126] On the expedition, both Crowther and James Frederick Schön spoke of "Yaruba" in reference to both the old "Yaruba kingdom" of Oyo and non-Oyo groups such as "the Yagba ... a dialect of Yaruba."[127]

In 1841 the African Civilization Society reprinted Raban's vocabulary of "The Aku, or Eyo" in their vocabulary of African languages compiled for use on the Niger Expedition. The vocabulary's headings reflected a language name in transition, identifying it as the "Ako, Eyo, Yabú, or Yarriba" language.[128] For a period, "Aku" and "Yoruba" were used interchangeably within the CMS. The journals of Christian Theophilus between 1842 and 1850 used "Aku" and "Yoruba" synonymously. So too did the German missionary Charles Gollmer, whose February 1844 letter stated that, "as regards my new appointment to the Aku mission ... I have commenced the study of the Yoruba language."[129] Four months later, Gollmer spoke of his "future abode in the Yoruba country" while noting "the returning Akus" who had made the journey before him. At the same time, Gollmer noted the arrival of "a large cargo of slaves, all Yorubeans," who informed him that there was presently no war in the interior.[130]

Other missionaries objected to the equating of Aku and Yoruba, and the projection of Yoruba to all speakers of the language. Writing in 1854, Koelle observed:

---

[124] Peel, *Religious Encounter*, 284.
[125] Crowther, Journal, February 22, 1837, CMS/CA1/079/2.
[126] Crowther, Journal extracts for the quarter ending June 25, 1841, CMS/CA1/O79.
[127] Schön and Crowther, *Journals*, 307, 317–318. At this time Crowther still primarily equated "Yoruba" with Oyo, giving a list of principal towns that is, with the exception of "Illah," purely Oyo.
[128] Edwin Norris (ed.), *Outline of a Vocabulary of a Few of the Principal Languages of Western and Central Africa; Compiled for the Use of the Niger Expedition* (London: John W. Parker, 1841), 2.
[129] Gollmer, Bathurst, February 20, 1844, CMS/CA1/O103/1.
[130] Gollmer, June 21, 1844, CMS/CA1/O103/2.

For the last few years they [missionaries] have very erroneously made use of the name "Yórūba" in reference to the whole nation, supposing that the Yórūban is the most powerful Aku tribe. But this appellation is liable to far greater objection than that of "Aku," and ought to be forthwith abandoned; for it is, in the first place, unhistorical, having never been used of the whole Aku nation by anybody, except for the last few years conventionally by the Missionaries; secondly, it involves a twofold use of the word "Yórūba," which leads to confusion of notions, for in one instance the same word has to be understood of a whole, in another, only of part; and, thirdly, the name being thus incorrect, can never be received by the different tribes as a name for their whole nation.

Arguing that Yoruba was a synecdoche, Koelle noted how "if, e.g., you call an Idṣébuan or a Yágban a Yórūban, he will always tell you, 'don't call me by that name, I am not a Yórūban.'" Indeed, many of the Aku would have objected on the grounds that Oyo "Yorubans" had been their enslavers. Sam Cole, born Idṣéṣa in Dṣéu, specified that he was "kidnapped by the Yórūbans" five years earlier, and would understandably not self-identify as Yoruba.[131]

If Koelle objected to the term "Yoruba" so too did most Aku recaptives. Memorial tablets and other sources show that most Aku were not receptive to the name change among missionaries, and few referred to themselves as Yoruba within the colony (see Appendix D). "Yoruba" was a term adopted primarily, and even then unevenly, by teachers, catechists, and clergymen. Most of Freetown's "Yoruba intelligentsia," as they have often been termed, never referred to themselves as such. Yoruba never supplanted Aku both because the latter had established itself over two decades of common usage and because of the narrower meaning of "Yoruba" within the Bight of Benin hinterland.

Conclusion

The recaptive nations of the nineteenth-century Sierra Leone peninsula were not simply recreations or "survivals" of African societies, nor were they colonial "inventions" imposed by mission and colonial agents. Recaptives brought certain assumptions about social relations that helped them navigate a new, alien setting in which there could be

---

[131] Koelle, *Polyglotta Africana*, 5.

many or few people of similar language, culture, and geographic origin. People reached out, made connections and bonds, both emotional and utilitarian, with people that they did not necessarily see as "their own" in their homelands. But this reappraisal of self-understanding did not necessitate abandoning or forgetting their specific regions of origin. Koelle's informants identified themselves in terms of small, kinship-based units, even several decades after they had left their homelands.

The mission and the colonial state played ancillary roles in the formation of receptive nations. Many national categories were those of the British slave trade and British American slave societies. Liberated Africans landed at Havana, often of similar origin, were assigned different ethnonyms based on local understandings in colonial Cuba.[132] But the fact that these were not terms of self-identity in African homelands did not preclude them becoming self-appellations in the diaspora. The actual names these groups took and their etymologies varied. Certain port designations came to have meaning because people gave them meaning. Other terms took on inertia based on common usage. Receptives were not credulous in utilizing monikers that made little sense in their homelands. Rather, the embrace of officially sanctioned "national" labels was an astute means of collective mobilization. As the next chapter will show, the receptive nations of Sierra Leone were at once ethnic communities and political constituencies.

---

[132] For *naciónes* found within the Cuban Mixed Court documents, see Henry Lovejoy, "Old Oyo Influences," 70–106.

5 | Kings and Companies
Ethnicity and Community Leadership

In September 1836, the CMS missionary James Schön watched anxiously as a large group assembled near the market in Bathurst village. The gathering "hoisted a flag and discharged several guns." Schön approached the commotion to see what was transpiring and "if possible to persuade them, to abstain from heathen positions." But the revelers greeted the interloper tersely. The missionary "was instantly told that I had no business with them; that they were Calabar people and made company and cared not for white man." When Schön tried to press one participant for answers, another grabbed him by the arm and said "come away, no court here, he no judge, what we want do we do we no care." After the crowds had dissipated, the curious missionary "learned from other persons that they came to make a queen, what they meant by it I do not know but certain it is that on their leaving they put a neatly dressed woman into a hammock, and carried her away amidst much shrilling and shouting."[1]

Schön witnessed a ceremony common in nineteenth-century Sierra Leone. Liberated Africans of various nations formed themselves into "companies" under the leadership of "headmen" and even "kings." Through these coronations, the title of "kings," and to a lesser extent "queens," entered the lexicon of receptive community leadership. Whether "Calabar" was a homeland for any Liberated African and whether that homeland possessed "queens" matters less than the fact that the Liberated Africans of Bathurst village elected their own national leader, a Calabar queen, in the context of the diaspora and Anglophone Christian colonial hegemony.

While the last chapter explored how ethnolinguistic backgrounds defined receptive nations, this chapter examines the forms of communal organizations and their inner hierarchies. Nations in Sierra Leone were organized along linguistic lines, but their purpose extended

---

[1] Schön, Journal entry for September 10, 1836, CMS/CA1/O195/48.

167

beyond perpetuating language and culture in the diaspora. National organizations were forms of communal welfare born out of the exigencies of displacement. These organizations assisted their members in times of distress, while forwarding the interests of the group. They filled the void left by a parsimonious colonial state and the absence of kin. As one attendee of the Calabar queen's coronation at Bathurst told Schön, "they were brought to this country to be starved to death; and that nothing was done for them to improve their condition."[2]

Scholars are now recognizing that diasporic identities were also political identities. Jessica Krug has argued that the terms of identity claimed by and ascribed to Africans and their descendants in the Americas "functioned less as claims of provenance than as complicated, shifting and highly contested languages of political logic."[3] This observation is particularly important for Sierra Leone because many recaptives came from regions experiencing revolutionary political change. Moreover, in Sierra Leone the political nature of these national organizations could be more fully expressed since recaptives could politically mobilize to a greater degree than enslaved Africans in the Americas. But voluntary associations in Sierra Leone often caught the ire of the church, while their leadership aroused suspicion and conflict with colonial and religious authorities. Over time, these political structures, comprising kings, companies, and headmen, became more elaborate. Recaptive nations were thus a compound of "horizontal," or egalitarian, relations based on shared language, culture, and experiences, and "vertical," or hierarchal, relations, based on leadership that mobilized these communities.

"To make company"

The most common forms of Liberated African social organization were mutual aid societies known as "companies." Their purpose and structure were much like societies commonly known in Cuba as *cabildos de nación*, as *cofradías* or *hermandades* in other Spanish colonies, and *irmandades* in Brazil. In the New World these associations, based primarily in cities and provincial towns, were organized by professed "nation" of origin. Such organizations could serve as a substitute for

---

[2] Ibid.   [3] Krug, "Social Dismemberment, Social (Re)membering," 1–22.

kinship and provide coherence for a group.[4] In Sierra Leone, the missionary Henry Townsend explained that "the companies were formed to help each other in cases of sickness or death and are not unlike the sick and death clubs of England but more strongly bound together." He added that they "made also rules to help each other if they should be fined or otherwise punished for offence against the laws of the land."[5] Like brotherhoods in the Americas, companies in Sierra Leone comprised a web of economic, sociopolitical, and religious connections.

The exact origins of the companies in the Sierra Leone peninsula are obscure. Christopher Fyfe and John Peterson suggest that the first company was organized among disbanded soldiers – recaptives enlisted during the Napoleonic Wars – who "returned" to the colony following their discharge. Disbanded soldiers and their family members numbered 1,216 in the 1820 colonial census, forming a substantial portion of the colony's population. In 1824, Abraham (or Abram) Potts, a former sergeant in the 4th West India Regiment, founded a benefit society by bringing together former soldiers and Liberated Africans to provide for members in times of need. The society collected funds via monthly subscription. It also exercised discipline over its members, imposing small fines for misconduct such as theft and fighting. The judicial function of the society was the first item recorded in its incorporating statutes, declaring that "this society is to be made with law and the law shall be read to the whole the Brethren of the said society."[6]

Potts took on the title of "headman." When the society grew in popularity and expanded to six of the colony's villages – each with its own headman – Potts, in Freetown, was given the title of "king," the first of many community leaders among recaptives to receive that title.[7] Governor Neil Campbell broke up the society in 1827, declaring it was exercising illegal jurisdiction. The "headmen" were tried in civil courts. Those who were discharged soldiers lost their pensions; Potts lost his minor government position. Potts's society had an influence long after it was disbanded, but it was likely not the only model for

---

[4] Thornton, *Africa and Africans*, 220.
[5] Townsend, Extracts ending December 25, 1838, CMS/CA1/O215/20.
[6] Enclosures in Governor Campbell's confidential dispatch of July 30, 1827, CO 267/82.
[7] Peterson, *Province of Freedom*, 210–211.

"companies."[8] Some forms of community organization – whether termed companies or not – were likely in place earlier, since recaptives had been residing in both planned and unplanned villages for more than a decade before Potts founded his society. Potts's group may have been the first to use the term "company," adopting military terminology they had become acquainted with as soldiers. But they likely gave a name to a form of group leadership that was already taking place. As Chapter 2 showed, the villages possessed "big companies" comprised of those speaking the same language, and "little companies" among those who had experienced the Middle Passage together.

In the Americas, Catholic powers in Spanish and Portuguese colonies more readily recognized and accepted the existence of African "nations" and allowed associations based on them a limited sphere of activity. The Catholic institution of the *cabildo* or religious fraternity further facilitated the survival of ethnic religious traditions. Thornton notes that these national organizations were particularly strong in urban America, where greater freedom of movement and less day-to-day supervision allowed nations to create semiformal and formal organizations.[9] In Sierra Leone, space and geography likewise shaped how companies functioned. Several companies emerged in each village to cater to the regionally diverse origins of the population. The Methodist Henry Badger observed that Liberated Africans sent to York were "not long located before they begin to develop the customs of the country to which they separately and formerly belonged."[10] The proximity of the different villages and the relative freedom of movement compared with slaves in the Americas also allowed those who had experienced the Middle Passage together to visit one another.

Many historians of Sierra Leone have attributed the functioning of companies in the colony to the Esusu credit system among the Yoruba.[11] In Yoruba territories, the Esusu pooled financial resources through fixed contributions and distributed them to members in times of need. As Samuel Johnson describes, "a fixed sum agreed upon is given by each at a fixed time (usually every week) and place, under a

---

[8] Fyfe suggests that companies spread following the death of Governor Campbell in December 1827, after his suppression of Potts's benefit society. Fyfe, *History of Sierra Leone*, 170–171.
[9] Thornton, *Africa and Africans*, 202.
[10] Badger, MMS Correspondence, Box 279, no. 1871, February 14, 1840.
[11] Magbaily Fyle, "The Yoruba Diaspora in Sierra Leone's Krio Society," 379.

president; the total amount is paid over to each member in rotation. This enables a poor man to do something worth while where a lump sum is required."[12] Certainly among Yoruba speakers in the colony Esusu was the blueprint for their national companies, even if the term does not appear in documents describing companies. By the mid-twentieth century, the term *asusu* was prevalent in Freetown for such associations.[13]

The prevalence of companies suggests a wider set of origins than Esusu alone, especially among non-Yoruba speakers. As we will see below, the Igbo are the group most commonly associated with companies in contemporary documents. Pooling financial resources was a main function of companies regardless of "nation." These savings provided for newly arrived recaptives of the same nation and furnished financial backing for more established members to move into Freetown trade. Companies in Sierra Leone served similar functions to savings associations in Bahia known as *juntas de alforria* (manumission pools) and *caixas de empréstimo* (boxes of loans).[14] A crucial difference, however, is that New World companies often financed the manumission of a certain number of slaves each year, a function not needed in Sierra Leone.

Given their primary role in conducting funerals, companies were often also religious institutions. Church officials saw them as particular challenges, for both their rival political leadership and their antithetical religious content. Missionaries expended a great deal of energy – and a great deal of their written reports – trying to disband these companies through co-option and coercion. Several missionaries came to the conclusion, whether independently or through discussions and emulation, of creating Christian companies to provide many of the same communal benefits but without the practices missionaries deemed reprehensible. The challenge for these new Christian companies was to offer incentives for membership while minimizing the costs of leaving their "heathen" companies.

---

[12] Johnson, *History of the Yorubas*, 119. See also William Bascom, "The *Esusu*: A Credit Institution of the Yoruba," *Journal of the Royal Anthropological Institute*, 82 (1952): 63–69.

[13] Kenneth Little, "Some Traditionally Based Forms of Mutual Aid in West African Urbanization," *Ethnology*, 1.2 (April 1962): 200.

[14] Nishida, *Slavery and Identity*, 55; Bastide, *The African Religions of Brazil*, 116.

W. A. B. Johnson created the first church-sanctioned company at Regent in 1817. Here, seventy communicants joined to care for sick and needy members.[15] Rev. William K. Betts emulated the strategy of co-option by forming his own church company at Gloucester in 1832. Betts had grown wary of a pre-existing Aku company, particularly the raucousness that accompanied its funeral observances. Betts noted that that his "benefit club amongst the communicants" had "arose from the following circumstance":

> One or two instances of gross intoxication having occurred of persons who had met together to feast after a funeral; & it having come to my knowledge that members of the church attend at such feasts which are very common; I spoke very strongly against the practice, & threatened to suspend any communicant who goes to such parties. They agreed "to make company" (as the current expression is) amongst themselves, to subscribe & assist each other in the event of any death occurring amongst them, but to have no feasting whatsoever, & separate from all other companies. When this began to be acted upon, the people from whom they had separated were much displeased; & came to me in a body to the number of about 20 to complain of this innovation.[16]

The strategy of founding church relief groups could be a potential wedge in the national communities of the recaptive villages.

Missionaries soon found that the stipulation to abandon non-church companies was a sacrifice that many were not willing to make. When attempting to found his own Christian relief company at Waterloo in 1843, Christian Theophilus Frey found that some recaptives were receptive, "while others finding it too hard to be thus cut off from their country-people raised objection."[17] In 1850 Rev. Nathaniel Denton similarly inquired with his communicants and candidates at Regent on the prospects of founding a "church relief company," indicating that the one formed by W. A. B. Johnson in 1817 had ceased to operate. Denton found that while many were interested, "when it came to the point whether or not they would become members they showed considerable hesitation." Denton concluded that "after the repeated attempts and failures to establish such a company here and the strong

---

[15] Minutes of half-yearly meeting, Freetown, November 5–6, 1817, CMS/CA1/E6/106.
[16] Betts, Quarterly Report, Gloucester, September 25, 1832, CMS/CA1/O42/45.
[17] Frey, Extracts for quarter ending September 25, 1843, CMS/CA1/O94.

hold which their corrupted heathen company have with them, I must act very cautiously and concede a good deal in order to gain any object."[18] Against his original intention, Denton conceded that those interested in the church relief company did not need to immediately abandon their prior companies.

Despite such concessions, missionaries knew the persistence of receptive companies threatened their efforts. Denton noted that at Regent the holdouts were primarily Igbo, and, given their large numbers in the village, the new Christian company would be hindered if he did not "supersede or reform those heathen companies ... of the Ebo tribe."[19] At Gloucester, Schön was irked by "a charge brought against several other members of the Church, all of the Ebo nation, of forsaking in part the company established among the people for supporting each other in case of sickness or decease of one of its members, and of associating with their own heathen countrymen for such purposes."[20] When Rev. Henry Rhodes assembled the members of Kent's "Christian Company" he found that his urging to give up rival companies went unheeded. Instead, three of his oldest female communicants responded with a letter on behalf of Kent's "Female Ebo Company" refusing to abandon their "Country Company." Rhodes also faced the exertions of "the heathen Ibo people, at the present time, [who] are speaking reproachfully & saying all manner of evil against their country people for leaving their Country Companies."[21]

Igbo is the ethnonym most often mentioned in regard to companies, as the complaints of Denton, Schön, and Rhodes highlight. References to Igbo companies are found in several missionary sources from various parts of the colony at different times. Rhodes's reference to Kent's "Female Ebo Company" is the only specifically gendered reference to companies of any nation. The Igbo cases make clear how ethnically aligned companies exerted pressure to prevent members from joining their Christian rivals. When Christian Ehemann founded a Christian company at York in 1849, he stipulated that "those who join it cannot belong to any other but this, as they have here as well as at other places, the evil practice that husband & wife & sometimes even their

---

[18] Denton, Journal extracts for half year to September 30, 1851, CMS/CA1/O87/34.
[19] Ibid.   [20] Schön, Quarter ending December 25, 1834, CMS/CA1/O195/36.
[21] Rhodes, Quarter ending June 25, 1843, CMS/CA1/O183/27. This is one of the few references to a company particularly for females.

children belong to 10 & more companies into which they pay annually from £2 to £3."²² Ehemann offered to compensate those willing to join his company for the loss they would incur in leaving their own. His overtures were undermined when lightning struck the house of a man who had taken up Ehemann's offer and his former compatriots publicly mocked the man for his decision.

Receptives saw the Christian societies as complementing, rather than replacing, their own companies. Company members acknowledged that success for a new Christian company might, with time, undermine and destroy their own. But they were willing to see what benefits dual membership might confer. Niels Christian Haastrup discovered this when he spoke to "members of the Aku nation in order to hear their views & what objections there were to the formation of a Christian Company." Haastrup found that the condition of abandoning non-Christian companies was "the greatest obstacle in our way; for many have for years been members of 4, 5, 6, or more of those companies that are formed by different tribes in this colony."²³

Dual membership in church companies and those organized by shipmates or ethnicity resulted in clashes, especially at the time of a member's death when companies arranged funerals, consoled the family members, and, in the absence of family, handled the deceased's property. The death of a receptive named Jenny Thomas led to a dispute between her shipmates and the CMS catechist Joseph Bartholomew, who wrote of the confrontation:

Her shipmate who were cruised in the slave vessel with her, sent to me that I should let them have her remains for burying, this I refused; especially as the head-man been a heathen. After I have buried her, as she has no husband, nor children to claim upon her articles, her shipmate demanded the Church Relief Company should deliver the late Jenny Thomas' articles to them.²⁴

The dispute became so heated that village manager of Hastings had to settle it, unsurprisingly, in favor of the church.

Over time, church companies found a measure of success. By the 1840s, "benevolent and improvement societies," as they became known, were a regular feature of the CMS's work, providing assistance

---

[22] Ehemann, Quarter ending June 25, 1849, CMS/CA1/O90/22.
[23] Haastrup, Quarter ending March 25, 1845, CMS/CA1/O107/20.
[24] Bartholomew, Journal for half year ending March 25, 1855, CMS/CA1/35/37.

from funerals to agriculture.[25] Nathaniel Denton wrote with particular satisfaction, "As the old heathen confederacies, or companies, have lost their strength & influence through the superior influence of a church company there have appeared fewer of those evils of which they were the principle sources." The success of Denton's company undermined the rival Igbo society, and "some who on the death of their friends have been entitled to assistance from the old Ebo Company have been kept in their houses for several weeks after the funeral, not being able to get money to buy a little mourning."[26]

Many recaptives remained adamant in their refusal to join. John Weeks, after eighteen years with the mission, lamented in 1843 that "this year I have had to learn by painful experience that only part of the evils existing in those 'companies' have been eradicated."[27] Weeks believed that there were "9 or 10 companies in Regent altogether," with one in particular having more than 200 members. John Ulrich Graf, who would later become archdeacon of Sierra Leone, likewise disparaged "how infatuated the natives are in their attendance to these clubs, and how hard it is to induce even professing Christians to break friendship with them."[28] As late as 1875 – more than a decade after the arrival of the last recaptives – the established church was struggling to impose its own vision to replace "heathen companies." A published pamphlet for the newly conceived Sierra Leone Diocesan Friendly Institutions acknowledged that "the great number and variety of Burial Companies and other Societies akin to this show that the principal of insurance is understood and liked in the Settlement; almost every body belongs to a Company of some sort or other."[29]

Wakes

The contest between missionary authority and companies was seen most explicitly in the practice of wakes. Wakes were the cultural practice among recaptives that drew the greatest ire of missionaries.

---

[25] Reports of Benevolent and Improvement Societies, 1848–1875, CMS/CA1/O18/1-15.
[26] Denton, Journal extracts for half year to September 30, 1851, CMS/CA1/O87/37.
[27] Weeks, Extracts, Regent, December 18, 1843, CMS/CA1/O219/76.
[28] Graf, Journal extracts for quarter ending September 25, 1844, CMS/CA1/O105/45.
[29] Sierra Leone Diocesan Friendly Institution: rules, 1875, Reports of Benevolent and Improvement Societies, CMS/CA1/O18/15.

Often spanning several days and nights, wakes were raucous affairs of mourning and celebration. One Sierra Leonean CMS schoolmaster of Oyo parentage described wakes as "a stronghold of Satan to be pulled down by the ministry."[30] Missionary suppression of wakes was an attempt to impose the veneer of a Christian populace. Their continued disruption of the Sabbath and drain on church attendance proved one of the greatest challenges to that veneer.

Missionaries described the events they saw – or more commonly simply heard – in their own terms. Missionary sources invariably describe the elaborate, spirited celebrations that took place for the death of recaptives simply as wakes. The challenge of analyzing wakes is that, for all the missionary complaints over their ubiquity, there are few eyewitness accounts of them. The descriptions we have are from missionaries occasionally intruding on or attempting to break up a wake, or from missionaries who subsequently interrogated wake participants. The latter occurred when a missionary gained word that communicants or candidates were attending a wake, seeing it necessary to question them on what the church – if not the celebrators – saw as a reversion from Christian piety. Protracted, celebratory wakes do not seem to have been more prevalent in certain villages over others. Some missionaries probably ignored their occurrence, or consciously excluded them from their reports. Others saw wakes as a central stumbling block to evangelization, and embarked on impassioned personal campaigns. The richest accounts often emerge when the animosity was mutual, and members of companies proved obdurate against missionary intrusion.

Vincent Brown has shown that in the African diaspora of eighteenth-century Jamaica wakes and funeral customs were events that solidified communal identity and group membership. Brown has coined the phrase "mortuary politics" to describe the importance of the beliefs and practices associated with death in social order and tension.[31] Similarly, wakes in Sierra Leone were key instances in which ethnic and religious inclusion and exclusion were demarcated. Though not a slave society like Jamaica, Sierra Leone was a tropical colony where the climate and lingering impact of the Middle Passage made death

---

[30] Charles Macaulay, Journal extracts for quarter ending September 1854, Bathurst, CMS/CA1/O140/5.
[31] Brown, *The Reaper's Garden*, 5.

omnipresent. Birth and death records show that the villages did not sustain their populations by natural reproduction, being repopulated by newly disembarked recaptives. Joseph Hume, a prominent Scottish radical who launched a scathing attack against the colony in 1830, noted that the annual death rate of 160 per 1,000 meant that a Liberated African population that should have been between 25,000 and 26,000 by the late 1820s was only an estimated 17,068 in 1828.[32] From the march to the coast, the voyage to Sierra Leone, and the conditions on the ship at anchor, and in the yard or hospital, recaptives were all too familiar with death.

Wakes were central to recaptive life because death was central to colonial life. As Christian aid societies attempted to subsume companies, the practice of wakes proved the greatest obstacle. Both Christian and non-Christian companies provided financially for burial and for the deceased's relatives. But Liberated Africans and missionaries disputed the tone and content of the burial proceedings, and the community that should be invited to attend. Wakes were unabashedly more festive send-offs for the deceased. Henry Townsend, the Exeter-born CMS missionary, recalled disapprovingly of one particular wake as "a scene of merriment and unnatural excitement instead of sorrow."[33] James Beale described the wake for a deceased child as "more like a house of feasting than a house of mourning."[34]

A newspaper article written a decade and a half after the arrival of the last recaptives references "[t]he 'keeping of the last wake' prevalent principally among the Congoes, but common to all alike."[35] In West Central Africa the *entambe*, a week-long burial ceremony celebrating the deceased, was observed in the Atlantic ports claimed by the Portuguese.[36] Wakes and funeral customs in Sierra Leone were and are often referred to as *awujo(h)*, a term of Yoruba origin.[37] Samuel Crowther,

---

[32] Drescher, *The Mighty Experiment*, 99.
[33] Townsend, Journal extracts to June 25, 1838, CMS/CA1/O215/18.
[34] Beale, Journal extracts for quarter ending June 25, 1841, CMS/CA1/O36/50.
[35] James A. Fitz-John, "Our Native Manners and Customs," *Sierra Leone Independent*, September 28, 1876, 1.
[36] Candido, *An African Slaving Port and the Atlantic World*, 128; John K. Thornton, "The Development of an African Catholic Church in the Kingdom of Kongo, 1491–1750," *Journal of African History*, 25.2 (1984): 147–167.
[37] Peterson, *Province of Freedom*, 236. For a description of Krio funeral customs in the later nineteenth century and twentieth century, see Spitzer, *Creole of Sierra Leone*, 33–36.

whose journal entries provide the most extensive record of Yoruba cultural practices in the colony, observed:

> For seven days together there is a continual drumming, dancing, and feasting in honour of the dead ... on the seventh day, what is called *separation of the dead, Iyakuh,* takes place ... When a profound silence is observed, one of the company calls aloud to the dead by his name three times, and tells him that they have removed him from their company according to the customs of their forefathers.[38]

Week-long periods of mourning such as this were common in many parts of Africa. Regardless of particular regional variations, funerals were defining occasions in the flow of community life.

In Sierra Leone, wakes were and are commonly followed by regular trips to the graves of the deceased. Visitors brought food and other gifts to the dead in order to "talk to them." An 1876 newspaper article arguing against "native manners and customs" deplored "the Akus depositing food either in their yards, in the streets, or ... 'on the tombs of their relatives and friends.'"[39] Missionary attempts to suppress and break up wakes thus faced the solidarity among those companies that had buried their dead, and between the living and the dead. George James Macaulay, the resident missionary at Murray Town, felt compelled to circulate a written tract to church attendees warning that he "would disconnect from class any of their members who unite with the people of the world to keep up wakes."[40] When the Wesleyans later in the century also threatened to expel church members who attended wakes, they found their congregations equally resistant. The Wesleyan missionary at Wilberforce in 1867 confessed that "amongst professing Christians I have found those who take delight in 'Oru,' Last Burying and other such ... relics of heathenism."[41]

---

[38] Crowther, Extracts of journal for quarter ending September 25, 1844, CMS/CA1/O79/13. By this time Crowther had returned from the Niger Expedition, and his account may well combine observations he made within both Yorubaland and Sierra Leone.

[39] Fitz-John, "Our Native Manners and Customs," 1. Wyse points out that later Krio custom involved celebrations on the third, seventh, and fortieth day, though economic realities led many Krio to celebrate on the fortieth day and the one-year anniversary. Wyse, *Krio of Sierra Leone*, 11.

[40] Macaulay, Half Yearly Report, Murray Town, September 30, 1860, CMS/CA1/O141/18.

[41] MMS, Fletcher to Boyce, Wilberforce, December 13, 1867, quoted in Peterson, *Province of Freedom*, 237.

Because funeral customs were central to communities, the intrusion of missionaries led to some of the most assertive responses from recaptives, even by members of the church. When John Weeks inquired why a church member had missed the previous Sunday's worship, the man coolly replied, "I attended the wake of my countryman's child, we sat up all Saturday night drinking rum and comforting the parents, we no sleep; on Sunday morning, I say, suppose I go to church I can't keep my eyes open, and that's the reason I no go."[42] George James Macaulay's attempts to preach against wakes were likewise "met with violent opposition from the people; and hatred from some of them."[43] Months later, Macaulay found that a member of his congregation had removed the pews from the church to provide seating for his younger brother's wake.[44]

While these disputes played out within the confines of the church, outside their walls the contest only grew. When attempting to infiltrate a wake at Hastings, Schön was told by a recaptive that "we were born in another country, this fashion we learned from our fathers. What they did we do too." The attendee added, "This fashion not fit for white man, white man's fashion not fit for black man, you do the fashion you see your fathers do we do the fashion we learn from our fathers."[45] This refusal to adhere to Christian expectations led some district manager in the villages to prohibit wakes. Edward Dicker, residing at Kissy, recounted how "at night we heard much noise and singing proceeding from the house of the deceased friends [sic], which folly proclaimed that a wake was being held there." It was only "by the interference of the manager of the district the wake was broken up: this made it necessary to bring the matter before the manager, wakes being prohibited by law."[46]

These prohibitions had little impact. Three years after the above attempt to ban wakes, the Nupe recaptive missionary Joseph Bartholomew was awoken at one in the morning by a wake at Hastings and proceeded "to tell the people to be quiet in shouting." But Bartholomew was greeted by a "man who was termed as a

---

[42] Weeks, Journal extracts for quarter ending September 25, 1842, CMS/CA1/O219/72.
[43] Macaulay, Half yearly report, Bathurst, September 30, 1854, CMS/CA1/O141/5.
[44] Macaulay, Half yearly report, Bathurst, April 1855, CMS/CA1/O141/6.
[45] Schön, Hastings, March 25 to June 8, 1837, CMS/CA1/O195/51.
[46] Dicker, Journal extracts for half year ending Michaelmas 1852, CMS/CA1/O88/10.

head-man among them" who "expanded both his hands over the door's mouth; as much as to say he will not permit me to enter in & deliver my message." From inside, a woman yelled "all missionaries are rascal, we do not thief, nor curse nobody."[47] The wake continued unabated until dawn.

Headmen and Kingship

Bartholomew's encounter with the headman at Hastings was the meeting of two forms of authority: missionaries sanctioned by the state, and leaders or "headmen" who functioned within receptive communities. Headmen emerged in the earliest receptive villages, settlements often bereft of any European oversight. Like "company" and "nation" it is far from obvious that all receptive communities should have embraced the Anglophone terminology of "headman." But there were antecedents. The Black Poor, even in London, had their own leadership and organization under "head men" and "corporals" and were organized into "companies."[48] And while receptives were drawn from societies with a great variety of political structures, the leadership of communities – at least as they appear in primarily European-written documents – was invariably recorded as being under headmen.

The language of "kings," "companies," "nations," and "headmen" represented the political idioms through which receptives engaged with the colonial state. In colonial Cuba the *cabildos de nación,* whether of West or Central African provenance, borrowed the titles of official state, church, and civic institutions, especially from the monarchy and military, to describe their offices.[49] It is perhaps not surprising then that a British colony that grew between the Napoleonic Wars and Queen Victoria's ascension should see its inhabitants embrace such terminology as king, company, and nation. Nevertheless, these homogenizing terms likely obscure differences between the leadership and organization that those of different ethnolinguistic backgrounds brought with them.

Headmen emerged in both planned and unsanctioned settlements, though there is more evidence for the former. One of the first was

---

[47] Bartholomew, Extracts for quarter ending September 25, 1847, CMS/CA1/O35/21.
[48] Braidwood, *Black Poor and White Philanthropists*, 91.
[49] David H. Brown, *Santería Enthroned: Art, Ritual, and Innovation in an Afro-Cuban Religion* (Chicago: Chicago University Press, 2003), 35.

Edward Brown, who came before the Governor's Council in 1819 as the "headman of Congo Town" in order to request official titles for property he occupied at White Man's Bay near Freetown.[50] Brown had been on the slave ship *Amelia* in 1811 when he and his shipmates successfully rose up against the ship's crew and diverted the vessel back to the West African coast (Chapter 2). He was then one of the founding residents of the village of New Cabenda, whose inhabitants thereafter moved to found Congo Town on the Freetown waterfront. The desire of recaptives to form some sort of internal leadership and guidance clearly pre-dated Potts's eponymous company by several years. As the case of Congo Town also suggests, headmen were often charter residents of particular villages, providing leadership in the formative stages of community development.

With the advent of the parish system, missionary superintendents encountered and tried to work through the system of recaptive leadership. The most explicit attempt came in 1823 when the recently arrived missionary at Wilberforce, George William Emmanuel Metzger, created a written contract for five of the village's headmen: "Thomas Decker, headman of the Coosoo people; Peter, headman of the Bandy people; Jack Davesen, headman of the Bassa people; Lucas, headman of the Congo people; Harry, leader of the Goolah people." Their signed declaration stated that they would "obey all his regulations, he should make," including to "keep holy the Sabbath day" and "leave off from performing any of our country fashions." In addition, "The drum or any thing to perform the heathen fashion with is to be destroyed in the presence of G.W.E.M."[51] The headmen conceded that their people could face fines or imprisonment for infractions ranging from making noise or trading on Sundays, walking the street during divine service, or firing a gun or banging a drum within the town. Moreover, their "respective country people [were] to settle themselves here orderly," and those who did not obey were given a fourteen-day warning, under threat of being expelled from the village. Those who complained to Freetown about Metzger's decisions would not be permitted to return. Against these theocratic stipulations to impose order,

---

[50] Petition of Edward Brown, March 9, 1819, CO 270/15.
[51] Metzger, "Contract between the Rev. G. W. E. Metzger and the Headmen," September 1, 1823, CMS/CA1/O150/76 and 77.

the signing headmen saw their authority within the village codified. They too could remove transgressors from the village, in return for acknowledging Metzger as "our chief headman." The respective "country people" could appeal any headman's decision to Metzger, who could in turn call on the headmen "in difficult matters."

Metzger's contract is a singular document within the archive for the exceptional powers the missionary gave himself within the village. For his indiscretion in claiming so much personal power – and for the wave of complaints that did reach Freetown – Governor Charles MacCarthy removed Metzger from his post. Yet if Metzger's contractual co-option of headmen was an exceptional case, missionary superintendents invariably saw the indispensable role headmen played in mobilizing and governing segments of the village.

Headmen only grew in importance when the CMS gave up their secular duties in overseeing the villages in 1826. Hannah Kilham, visiting the colony's villages in late 1827, recounted that

> the first place which we visited was Wellington, of which Thomas Macfoy, a native of the West Indies, is Superintendent ... T. Macfoy experiences an evident advantage in the large village in which he lives, from classing his people according to their tribes, and placing one of the older residents of the same tribe over each company. These Overseers (who have the name of Constables) communicate with the people more fully and easily than T. Macfoy could do himself, knowing their language and their habit of thought. They endeavor to settle for them what are called "small palavers," or little difficulties and contests; but subjects of more importance, or any that they cannot satisfactorily settle, are brought to T.M. as their Superintendent, to decide.[52]

While Kilham spoke of Macfoy "classing his people according to their tribes, and placing one of the older residents of the same tribe over each company," the opposite was generally true. While the colonial and missionary establishment increasingly recognized the role of headmen as intermediaries, there are few other examples in which they chose or imposed headmen on a population.

Joseph Bartholomew noted in 1849 that the headmen's "superiority & influence over the rest does not come from either any personal claim or pre-eminent qualification, but from the choice of others, & from his

---

[52] Kilham, *Report of a Recent Visit*, 15–16.

own offer to help the parties."[53] Headmen were generally older and had spent more time in the colony. The Aku headman at Murray Town was, according to Rev. Henry Rhodes, "an aged man ... who has hitherto been a regular worshipper of Ifa, the god of palm nuts."[54] Thomas Tob of Freetown, Koelle's informant of the Bomboma language (in present-day Democratic Republic of the Congo), had "been in Sierra Leone forty years, where he now fills the office of Kongo headman."[55] That there were "still about twenty Mimboma people in Sierra Leone" shows how Tob's authority extended beyond those speaking his language of birth and to a larger community of West Central Africans in Sierra Leone.

Headmen were intermediaries between their people and the colonial government. This role could both further receptives' interests by making claims on the colonial state, while at times placing headmen in a position of conflicting demands. The most conspicuous example of the former occurred in 1835 when the headmen of Wilberforce and Waterloo congregated to sign two petitions against the dismissal of the manager and magistrate in their district. The Wilberforce petition included Josh Allen, "Chief of the 'Akoos'"; "James Johnson, Chief of the 'Calibars'"; and "John Nugent, chief of the 'Hiboos.'" A similar petition from the larger village of Waterloo had eleven signatories:

> John Bull, chief of the Hiboo nation
> Sergt Richard Martin, chief of the "Akoos"
> Pagit Baillie, chief of the "Calibars"
> James Sewell, chief of the "Kana Kays"
> John, chief of the "Cussoos"
> William, chief of the "Ranakays"
> John Sampson, chief of the "Connors"
> John Cox, chief of the "Tarpars"
> John Carew, chief of the "Papaws"
> Sergt John Moor, chief of the Houssas"
> Papua, chief of the "Brassas"

Not all of these terms are easily recognizable as ethnic groups, but they reflect the plurality of ethnic leadership within larger villages such as

[53] Bartholomew, Journal extracts for quarter ending June 25, 1849, CMS/CA1/O35/27.
[54] Rhodes, Journal for half year to March 1853, CMS/CA1/O183/45.
[55] Koelle, *Polyglotta Africana*, 13.

Waterloo. The petition is unique in its reference to local leaders as "chiefs" rather than "headmen." As these petitions also suggest, the constituency for headmen was shaped by the composition of a particular village. For example, at Aberdeen in the 1850s, there were enough Egba among the Aku to have their own headman.[56]

Headmen petitioned the government partly because the government and missions devolved a degree of power to them. Theoretically, the laws of England were in force across the colony. However, their implementation and execution across the peninsula was varied. In 1838, the Liberated African Department officially sanctioned the village overseers at Hastings and Wellington to ensure headmen were placed over every ten neighboring families in the village and "centenaries" above them who would convey information to the government. The new headmen would arbitrate disputes and have the authority to punish crimes. The department concluded that "all complaints and petitions in being presented through their own headmen are rendered more congenial to their feelings by bringing the cause of dispute before one of their own nation, with the power of appeal both to the secretary and manager."[57] To an extent, this policy of co-option prefigured British customary law in their latter nineteenth-century African empire, as headmen were able to impose justice and fines for crimes, so long as they did not contravene British law.[58] But more often than not, headmen could be sources of rival political and religious authority.

The Aku King

If "headman" was the most common title among Liberated African companies, other community leaders took on more regal titles. Jacob Boston Hazeley, a superintendent at Wellington, reported that one of the companies in the village had written regulations stipulating a "King, Queen, King's Son, Governor, Judge, Macaulay, Raffell, Commissary Dougan, Savage, Constable" (the proper names being those of

---

[56] Rhodes, Half year ending September 30, 1851, CMS/CA1/O183/42.
[57] Terry to Thorpe, August 28, 1838, LADLB 1837–1842.
[58] The literature on law in British colonial Africa is extensive, but see Martin Chanock, *Law, Custom, and Social Order: The Colonial Experience in Malawi and Zambia* (Cambridge: Cambridge University Press, 1985); Kristin Mann and Richard Roberts (eds.), *Law in Colonial Africa* (Portsmouth, NH: Heinemann, 1991).

The Aku King

notable colonial figures).[59] The most conspicuous example of monarchical titles among recaptives was the "Aku King" a prominent position that existed for several decades under three different monarchs.

Kingship was common in the African diaspora. Historians have debated whether such royalism derived from African backgrounds, where kings were the rule, or from a European implanted idea.[60] Little is known about kingship in the diaspora despite its apparent ubiquity. In Brazil, the "Kongo nation" elected a king and queen since the early seventeenth century, a time when central African slaves dominated the Brazilian trade.[61] But even in Brazil, a lack of clarity hampers uncovering the origins of the practice of naming Afro-Brazilian kings and the context in which this occurred.[62] Were diasporic kings a conscious attempt to preserve African customs or were they intended to invert social order in slave societies? How was the adoption of European terms symbolic in terms of emulation or critique?

In Sierra Leone the Aku kingship was an acknowledgment of financial success. Those who held the post during the nineteenth century were all leading Liberated African merchants within Freetown. This was certainly true of the first Aku King, Thomas Will, who built a fortune in trade and resided in prime downtown real estate once occupied solely by settlers. Little is known about Thomas Will's early life, when he arrived as a recaptive, or at what point he emerged as the first Aku king. Will emerged as a leading trader on Pa Demba Road, one of Freetown's main thoroughfares. Like many recaptive traders, he began by purchasing items at the prize auctions of captured slave vessels. Starting in 1826, he bid on whatever unsold items a slave vessel might have on board in order to resell them. By 1836, with the assistance of financial backers, he was able to bid up to £60 for spirits,

---

[59] Hamilton, "Sierra Leone and the Liberated Africans," 35. Macaulay is likely a reference to Kenneth Macaulay, the leading Freetown merchant in the 1820s. Joseph Reffell had been in charge of the Liberated African Department. Robert Dougan was an Afro-West Indian businessman and lawyer. W. H. Savage was a prominent trader of part European descent. Christopher Fyfe, *Sierra Leone Inheritance* (London: Oxford University Press, 1964), 142.

[60] John Thornton, "'I Am the Subject of the King of Kongo': African Political Ideology and the Haitian Revolution," *Journal of World History*, 4 (1993): 181–182.

[61] Thornton, *Africa and Africans*, 203.

[62] Elizabeth W. Kiddy, "Who Is the King of Kongo? A New Look at African and Afro-Brazilian Kings in Brazil," in Heywood (ed.), *Central Africans*, 154.

tobacco, or bales of cotton.[63] A year later, he purchased a home from a bankrupt European for £307. Will's authority and stature derived from his prowess in trade and his long residence in the colony. Robert Clarke wrote admiringly that "the influence of their headman or king, as they call him, is so great, that no Akoo dare disobey him." Disobedience meant "he would be shunned by his countrymen, and be denied the Akoo ceremonies which take place at their burial; the bare thought of which is associated in their minds with degradation and the worst disgrace."[64]

On Thomas Will's death in 1840, John Macaulay assumed the title of Aku king. Interestingly, Macaulay was likely Hausa rather than Yoruba and a Muslim until he converted to Christianity five years before his death. A later newspaper article described him as being "a Housa, of the pure Bornu tribe." The article continued:

His native name was Mama. The name Atapa – which in this Colony is pronounced wrong – is historical, and should be A-tàpa, instead of Atapa. The word Atapa means the kicker, and King Mama received this appellation from being very famous on board vessels more as an adept in the use of his legs in fighting than he was with his fists. There were many Mamas among the Liberated Housas; so to distinguish King Mama, he was always known by the name of Mama Atapa, or Mama the kicker.[65]

Like his predecessor, Macaulay had spent many years in the colony becoming a successful trader and alderman of Freetown. The above article placed his date of arrival as 1822. James Johnson, who undertook a concerted and eventually successful effort to convert the prominent Muslim receptive, wrote in 1863 that "John Macaulay, alias King Macaulay, a popular man in the city ... was born and brought up a Mahomedan, has resided in the colony for about 48 years," suggesting an arrival date around 1815.[66] By various accounts, he had spent between eighteen and twenty-five years in Sierra Leone by the time of his election in 1840.

Macaulay expanded the powers of kingship, forming his own governing council. He may have earlier been a member of King Potts's

---

[63] Fyfe, *History of Sierra Leone*, 204.
[64] Clarke, *Sketches of the Colony of Sierra Leone*, 330.
[65] Inaugural Address on the Installation of Mr. G[eorge] M. Macaulay, *Sierra Leone Weekly News*, April 18, 1891.
[66] Johnson, Journal for half year ending March 1863, CMS/CA1/O123/13.

"secret society" – as a John Macaulay was listed as a headman of that organization in 1827 – and adopted that society's concept of a king and council.[67] King John's deputy was Isaac Benjamin Pratt, an Ife-born shopkeeper who reached Sierra Leone as a teenager in 1825.[68] The other council members were the Egba recaptives Christopher Taylor (or Agidimo) and William Lewis.[69] The council heard disputes, rendered judgments, and imposed fines. To be boycotted by King John's court was a very serious matter for a merchant.[70] He also enjoyed the recognition of acting Governor Benjamin Pine, who appointed Macaulay as head overseer in the Liberated African Department yard.

Isaac Benjamin Pratt, Macaulay's deputy, assumed the title of king after his predecessor's death in late 1867. Pratt too had built his wealth, first buying up items at prize auctions before purchasing his own vessel in 1845 to trade along the coast. Pratt was "of the Ifeh section of the Aku tribe," part of the smaller population of Aku born in the more easterly Ife territory of Yoruba speakers (see top left part of figure in Appendix D). Though most Aku were of Oyo, Egba, Ijebu, and Ìjẹ̀sà origin – all, with the exception of the Ìjẹ̀sà groups living in western Yoruba territory – Pratt's Ife origins, like his predecessor's Hausa origins, were no barrier to his ascension to the throne. Pratt ruled until his death in 1880, at which time the institution of Aku King faded away. Kingship thus endured beyond the arrival of the last captured slave ship in 1863, passing from the era of recaptives to their Krio descendants. The three men who held the title of "Aku King" were all recaptives, but their divergent origins reflect the broad linguistic, religious, and even ethnic umbrella of what it meant to be Aku in Sierra Leone.

The Seventeen Nations

Receptive community leadership reached its fullest articulation with the founding of the "Seventeen Nations," a government-sanctioned

---

[67] Peterson, *Province of Freedom*, 224; citing CO 267/82, Enclosure number 1 in Campbell to Goderich, July 20, 1827.
[68] Memorial tablet to Isaac Benjamin Pratt, St. George's Cathedral, Freetown; Obituary, Isaac Benjamin Pratt, *West African Reporter*, July 28, 1880.
[69] Fyfe, *History of Sierra Leone*, 292.
[70] Harrell-Bond et al., *Community Leadership*, 121–122.

council of "national" headmen, at Waterloo in 1843. The immediate impetus behind the Seventeen Nations was a violent confrontation between the village's Igbo and Calabar on one side, and the Aku on the other. Christian Frey, the resident missionary, recorded that the hostilities broke out when "Calabar woman" bathed in a local well "where different tribes use to fetch water from." The incident was only the catalyst for an expression of underlying grievances. The Aku claimed that the Igbo and Calabar regularly accosted their countrymen: "The Calabar & Ibos said the Akus were the favorite of the whitemen, always preferred in office, whilst they themselves were overlooked." During the altercation, the Waterloo Aku mobilized their countrymen in the nearby village of Benguema. Frey reported that

> they joined the Akus at Waterloo, whilst the Ibo united with the Calabars, & at 2 O'clock P.M. they began a regular fight in the midst of the village ... when almost all the Ibos & Calabars were driven out of town into the mangroves. The Akus now placed sentinels around the lawn to prevent their enemies from entering in at night. Whilst doing this some got shot by the Ibos, who had hid themselves in their houses, & now the Akus began breaking the fronts of the Ibo & Calabar houses, destroying, at the same time, all what was found inside.[71]

Ultimately, six were killed and thirty-nine wounded before troops from Freetown intervened.

In response to these events the government called on John Macaulay, Freetown's Aku King of Hausa birth, to mediate the dispute. Macaulay's solution was to formalize the leadership systems that had emerged in the villages over the previous decades. Leaders of the seventeen largest nations in Waterloo were mandated to settle disputes, led by an elected president. An 1886 edition of the *Sierra Leone Weekly News* identified its succession of presidents over the ensuing four decades as "Sulay of the Howsa tribe ... Camandoe of the Eboe tribe, Tom Coker of the Aku tribe, and Olnwole of another Aku tribe."[72]

The Seventeen Nations spread from Waterloo to other villages. John Peterson notes that this was a natural progression of community

---

[71] Christian Theophilus Frey, Extract ending March 25, 1844, Waterloo, CMS/CA1/O94.

[72] "A President Elected for the 'Seventeen Nations,'" *Sierra Leone Weekly News*, December 25, 1886. By this time – in the immediate aftermath of the Scramble for Africa – "tribe" emerged as a common term, whereas it was not commonly used during the period in which recaptives reached the colony.

leadership, with roots in the longer history of social welfare among those of common ethnolinguistic origins.[73] But who were the Seventeen Nations that formed the eponymous group? Why were these particular seventeen chosen? To what extent were these groups in existence before the officially sanctioned onset of the seventeen nations? What was the relationship between these nations, the national categories of colonial and missionary documents, and how people self-identified? Given that Koelle uncovered some 154 languages spoken within the colony, the emergence of "seventeen nations" reflects the complex interplay of language, culture, habitation, and local politics that shaped ethnogenesis in the Sierra Leone peninsula.

The only source to list the purported original members of the seventeen nations is A. E. Tuboku-Metzger's 1932 *History of the Colony Villages of Sierra Leone from the Earliest Time to about 50 Years Ago*. The source is problematic for being written by a retired assistant district commissioner some eighty-nine years after the founding of the Seventeen Nations. Tuboku-Metzger identified the Seventeen Nations of Waterloo as Oku (Aku), Ibo, Popo, Moko, Hausa, Takpa (Nupe), Kakanda, Krabar, Congo, Aja, Atam, Kossoh (Mende), Soso (Susu), Temne, Fula, Maninka or Madinga (Mandinka), and Lokkoh. As the previous chapter showed, most of these designations were common ethnonyms in the colony by the 1840s. Thirteen of these seventeen nations – including the nine largest – appear as categories in the 1848 census (Table 5.1). Conversely, of the nineteen categories of the 1848 census, only six (Kromantees, Binnees, Bassas, Sherbros, Mozambiques, Jolofs) did not form one of the Seventeen Nations, suggesting that these groups were not a significant presence at Waterloo.

Tuboku-Metzger noted that "there were a few members of some tribes who united with other kindred tribes in their representation e.g., Kperesheh united with Atam, Sherbro with Lokko, Limba with Timne, Krankoh (Kurankoh) with Maninka, etc." The composition of the Seventeen Nations likely changed over time through these strategic alliances and incorporations. An 1886 newspaper article on the Waterloo institution noted how "some of the old tribes have either died out or have amalgamated with other tribes by intermarriage; as the Attam,

---

[73] Peterson, *Province of Freedom*, 220; see 224–226 for a discussion of the operations of the Seventeen Nations in other Liberated African villages.

Table 5.1 *Ethnic designations of "Seventeen Nations" and 1848 census*

Members of the Seventeen Nations (c. 1843)	Designation in 1848 census
Oku (Aku)	Akoos (1)
Ibo	Eboos (2)
Popo	Paupahs (3)
Hausa	Housas (4)
Kossoh (Mende)	Koosoos (5)
Moko	Mokos (6)
Congo	Congos (7)
Krabar	Calabahs (8)
Maninka or Madinga (Mandinka)	Mandingoes (9)
Kakanda	Kakanjas (11)
Soso (Susu)	Soosoos (14)
Fula	Foulahs (18)
Temne	Timnehs (19)

the Crabbah, and the Mocoh tribes."[74] The 1886 article is the only source stating the members of the Seventeen Nations while it still existed; the roster shows both continuity and evolution compared with those listed by Tuboku-Metzger (Table 5.2).

The national names within the Seventeen Nations were also terms that appeared frequently in other colonial documents, including the 1835 petition of Waterloo headmen and the CMS school rosters from 1816 to 1824. Terms were agreed on over time, in a dynamic process that combined self-recognition, the missionary study and classification of languages, and certain colonial presuppositions about African social organization. Through this process, the 154 languages uncovered by Koelle could congregate into only seventeen nations.

Conclusion

Receptive community leadership emerged from the necessity of providing for one another in an alien colonial landscape whose authorities could scarcely manage the human impact of abolition. Over time,

---

[74] "A President Elected for the 'Seventeen Nations,'" *Sierra Leone Weekly News*, December 25, 1886.

Table 5.2 *Members of the "Seventeen Nations"*

Metzger 1932 [1843]	1886
Oku (Aku)	Ijesha, Egba, Yoruba, Yagba
Ibo	Ebo
Popo	Popo
Hausa	Howsa
Krabar	"amalgamated with other tribes"
Moko	"amalgamated with other tribes"
Maninka or Madinga (Mandinka)	Mandingo
Fula	
Soso (Susu)	
Temne	Timneh
Atam	"amalgamated with other tribes"
Aja	
Kakanda	Kakanda
Loko	Lokkoh
Takpa (Nupe)	Tagpa
Congo	Congo
Kossoh (Mende)	Mendi

recaptive society formed a spectrum of "horizontal" relations based on shared language, culture, and experiences, and "vertical," relations, based on leadership that mobilized these communities. Africans who found themselves in a new context did not consciously recreate the institutions and leadership structures that they left behind; these diasporic organizations grew out of the immediate need for social welfare and mutual assistance. Many of these institutions reflected those found elsewhere in the African diaspora, such as mutual aid societies and kingship. Yet the absence of a slave labor regime as in the Americas allowed for a fuller expression of these relationships. At times these organizations and their leadership claimed the sanction of government, even as they became the voice of receptive concern and discontent. While kings, companies, and nations were pervasive across the African diaspora, their power and prominence in Sierra Leone were inextricably tied to the unique context of an evangelizing post-slave society on the West African coast.

6 Religion, Return, and the Making of the Aku

I Joseph B May of the Colony of Sierra Leone was born in Aku Country.
—Joseph Boston May, 1838[1]

I James Will, was born in the land of Akue.
—James Will, March 1839[2]

I Charles Harding was born in Western Coast of Africa ockue nation.
—Charles Harding, 1839[3]

I George Thompson, was born in the west africa, in acoo nation.
—George Thompson, undated[4]

In 1838 and 1839, the Methodist Missionary Society compiled testimonies of life experiences from Liberated African members of their church. The narrators of most accounts declared they were from the "Aku Country" or of the "Acoo nation" of West Africa. As we have seen, these converts were not alone in asserting an Aku identity. The 1848 the colonial census listed 7,114 "Aku," a majority of the 13,273 Liberated Africans in Freetown. Despite the diffuse origins of Liberated Africans, and the plurality of ethnonyms used to describe them, colonial and missionary officials in Sierra Leone concluded by the mid-nineteenth century that the Aku nation eclipsed all others in terms of their size, conspicuousness, and unity within recaptive society. By 1853, Governor Kennedy believed that the "Akoo race" constituted

---

[1] "The Life and Experience of Joseph Boston May," MMS, Sierra Leone Correspondence, fiche box 25, box no. 280, "Sierra Leone Odds papers," fiche no. 1879, no. 3.
[2] MMS, Special Series, Biographical, Various Papers, Anti-Slavery Papers 1774–1891, fiche box 44, box 662(1)
[3] MMS, Sierra Leone Correspondence, fiche box 25, box no. 280, "Sierra Leone odd papers," fiche no. 1880, no. 6.
[4] Ibid., no. 34.

two-thirds of the population. This was certainly an overstatement, but one that reveals colonial perceptions of the population they oversaw. Kennedy added the common colonial trope that the Aku "may be termed the Jews of Africa (bearing all the strong characters of that race in Europe) are so clan-ish and so bounded together."[5]

Most historians have reiterated this colonial narrative of the Aku as the largest and most cohesive receptive nation. Moreover, scholars have spoken of the cultural legacy of recaptives on Krio society in terms of vocabulary, diet, religious customs, and social organizations of almost exclusive Yoruba provenance. Previous studies of Sierra Leone have attributed the conspicuousness and influence of the Aku to their demographic preponderance, treating the Aku either implicitly or explicitly as a majority among recaptives. Chapter 1 complicated this interpretation by showing that perhaps one-third of all recaptives spoke dialects of Yoruba. They were thus the largest ethnolinguistic group in the colony, but far from the majority that they are often portrayed as. What, then, made the Aku the most successful recaptive nation in asserting their influence on the social life and history of the colony? Why have contemporary observers and subsequent historians placed a singular emphasis on the Aku element of recaptive society?

In most New World diasporas Yoruba speakers were one ethnolinguistic group among many. But as Eltis points out, wherever they have gone in the diaspora the Yoruba have had an impact out of all proportion to their relative demographic weight.[6] Perhaps in no other diaspora did Yoruba speakers form such a large percentage of the population as they did in Sierra Leone. But while demographics were undeniably important, the scale of the Yoruba-speaking migration from the Bight of Benin alone does not explain the predominance of the Aku in colonial life and the ubiquity of references to the Aku within travel narratives and colonial and missionary documents. Nor does it explain the supposedly unique degree of unity within the Aku

---

[5] Kennedy to the Duke of Newcastle, July 18, 1853, CO 267/233.
[6] Eltis, *The Rise of African Slavery in the Americas*, 253. Some scholars have attributed this influence to the relatively late entry of large numbers of Yoruba-speaking slaves in the final decades of the transatlantic slave trade. This chronological argument is less relevant for Sierra Leone since all recaptives arrived within a period of only fifty-six years. See Pierre Verger, *Trade Relations between the Bight of Benin and Bahia, 17th to 19th Century* (Ibadan: Ibadan University Press, 1976), 1.

community, comprised of victims of a period of unprecedented *disunity* and warfare in their homelands. There is no mono-causal explanation for the pre-eminence of the Aku nation in colonial Sierra Leone; rather, there are a number of related and overlapping factors. Beyond demographics, the role of common experience through war and enslavement, settlement patterns in Sierra Leone, the missionary study of language, the role of returnees to the Bight of Benin, and the tenacity of Yoruba religious practices combined to shape the image of the Aku as the dominant element in receptive society.

As Chapter 3 showed, captives from the Bight of Benin had a substantial presence in each of the major Liberated African villages, and communities of Yoruba speakers existed in all the colony's larger settlements. The scale of their presence meant that the CMS took particular interest in studying the "Aku language." Through the missions, recaptives and their offspring became the first Western-educated Yoruba, helping to reduce the language to writing and produce the first "national" histories. The Aku were also unique in their political organization, possessing their own king who, in the reign of King John Macaulay (1840–1867), extended their powers over the committees of the Seventeen Nations in the Liberated African villages.

Two other factors contributed to the enduring perception of Aku prominence and influence: the bilateral linkages that developed between homeland and diaspora and the resiliency of "Yoruba traditional religion" within the colony. This chapter argues that religion and return help account for the conspicuousness, coherence, and longevity of Aku identity and their cultural influence among receptives and their descendants. It first traces the opening of commercial relations between Freetown and the Bight of Benin, showing how this movement of people, goods, and information strengthened the connections between diaspora and homeland while magnifying the perception of the Aku as a dynamic force in coastal West Africa.

The chapter then considers the role that religion played both in defining the Aku nation and as a symbol of their cultural influence over the receptive community. As Peel notes, the Yoruba possess "an indigenous religious culture of unusual vitality, adaptiveness, and tenacity" reflected in its survival in Brazil and Cuba compared with religions of most other enslaved groups.[7] Yoruba religious practices

---

[7] Peel, *Religious Encounter*, 8.

were adhered to with a particular vigor, as they were in Brazil, Cuba, and throughout the Yoruba diaspora. Yet they were also uniquely commented on in missionary journals, including those that were subsequently published in CMS and MMS publications.

The irony is that in attempting to extirpate Yoruba religious practices, missionaries, particularly Yoruba converts, catalogued and highlighted their resilience in the diaspora. Aku clergymen and Krio churchmen of Aku parents observed, intruded on, and vociferously debated with those they saw practicing the most intractable set of African religious practices that recaptives brought with them from their homeland. Beyond simply reporting on such practices, the ubiquity and detail of their accounts unintentionally reified *orisa* worship as the preeminent "pagan" (as they termed it) religion in the colony and one that lay at the core of Aku identity. The result, as Matory points out, was that "the premise of Yorùbá religious superiority to other African ethnic groups appeared at the very 19th-century origins of the pan-Yorùbá ethnic identity."[8]

Sàró Returnees

In Sierra Leone, Yoruba speakers embraced a broader linguistic and political identity as Aku while retaining markers and memories of more specific homelands, as evinced through dialect, scarification, and specific references to "subethnic" identities such as Oyo, Egba, Ìjẹ̀sà, and Ijebu. But these localities were not simply remembered. What it meant to be Aku was further shaped by the opening of commercial links back with coastal Yorubaland from the late 1830s onward, as well as the 1841 Niger Expedition and subsequent Yoruba mission commencing in 1846.

By 1839, successful Aku merchants in Freetown had purchased vessels to trade with the Bight of Benin. Though the British government did not sponsor these endeavors, they did not prevent recaptives from trading and emigrating. The first voyage departed Freetown on April 1, 1839, with sixty-seven passengers destined for Badagry.[9] On their successful return Freetown's merchants petitioned the British government to form a protected British enclave at Badagry. The original petition was not an exclusively Aku project. The signatories included

---

[8] Matory, *Black Atlantic Religion*, 62.   [9] Fyfe, *History of Sierra Leone*, 212.

the Aku King Thomas Will and several other Aku, but also the Nupe John Ezzidio and the Hausa Emmanuel Kline.[10] The petition surprised Governor Doherty, as no interest in emigration or return had ever been expressed before. The governor later postulated that the "arrival from Trinidad of some Hausa natives [in 1837], who were sent hither on their return to that country, in a freight ship from England, suggested the idea to many of the hawkers."[11] Yet as Jean Herskovits Kopytoff points out, this interpretation overemphasizes the impression made by this brief encounter.[12] By this period, some recaptive merchants had acquired enough wealth to extend their trading down the coast, purchasing captured slave ships to trade European goods and Sierra Leone's produce for palm oil and other goods.

Governor Doherty noted in March of 1840 that two hundred recaptives "belonging chiefly to the Housa Country and the Kingdom of Yarriba" had pooled money to purchase a captured slave ship "in which it was their intention to proceed to Badagry, and from thence to seek their native homes at a distance of some hundred miles inland."[13] Five voyages sailed from Freetown between October 25, 1839, and April 30, 1841, to "Badagry and the Leeward Coast" with 273 emigrants. In July 1844, Lieutenant-Governor Fergusson reported to Lord Stanley that "between 600 and 800 persons, liberated Africans from Sierra Leone, are now established in the Yarriba or Aku country."[14] The movement was not exclusively a Christian undertaking, as Crowther noted that the Aku Muslim community at Foulah Town owned a vessel called *The Maria* on which many had emigrated to

---

[10] Enclosure, November 15, 1838, in Doherty to Russell, November 30, 1839, CO 267/154.

[11] Doherty to Russell, October 3, 1839, CO 267/160. For the case of returning Trinidad Muslims to the Bight of Benin, see David V. Trotman and Paul E. Lovejoy, "Community of Believers: Trinidad Muslims and the Return to Africa, 1810–1850," in Lovejoy (ed.), *Slavery on the Frontiers of Islam*, 219–231.

[12] Jean Herskovits Kopytoff, *A Preface to Modern Nigeria: The "Sierra Leoneans" in Yoruba, 1830–1890* (Madison: University of Wisconsin Press, 1965), 40.

[13] Doherty to Russell, March 20, 1840, CO 267/159. Doherty intervened against this particular venture, noting the presence of "some one hundred children" traveling with their parents. Passports were limited to those without children, though this did not hinder the growth of emigration.

[14] Kuczynski, *Demographic Survey*, 137, quoting *Reports Made in 1844 and 1845 by Butts*, 131.

Badagry.[15] For Yoruba Muslims, religious repression in the colony was a major impetus for departure, as Chapter 7 will show.

By 1844, recaptives owned four vessels traveling regularly between Freetown and Badagry. One of the earliest owners was the Egba trader William Johnson, a signatory to the original 1839 petition. Johnson started as a trader in the early 1830s and by 1841 was wealthy enough to buy the condemned Brazilian slave ship *Donna Elliza* at auction for £205.[16] In March 1843 he purchased the Bahian brig *Bon Fim* for £395 followed by the Rio de Janeiro brig *Izabel* for £210 in August 1844.[17] With his fleet of reappropriated Brazilian slave vessels, Johnson established a regular service between Freetown and Badagry (and later Lagos), taking emigrants and trade goods while returning with produce.[18]

This movement is often referred to as a "return" to "ancestral lands." But Aku desires to reach the Bight of Benin were initially less focused on their natal communities than on coastal ports, including where many had been sold as slaves. The earliest contacts and settlements were made at Badagry, Lagos, and Ouidah, cumulatively where the majority of recaptives from the region had embarked.[19] These connections were as much about commercial enterprise as they were about nostalgia or longing for return, but the two impulses were interwoven. As early as 1842, one clergyman noted how "frequent information has been received from there with the most pressing invitations from their relatives to many of the people to return to their country." Through these early contacts "long parted relatives

---

[15] Crowther, Extract for June 25, 1844, CMS/CA1/O79. An additional recaptive-owned vessel had been recently shipwrecked. Crowther, Freetown, February 26, 1844, CMS/CA2/O31/1.

[16] Account of sale of the Brazilian Brigantine *Donna Elliza*, August 3, 1841, FO 84/345.

[17] Account sales of the Brazilian Brig *Bon Fim*, March 6, 1843, FO 84/449; Account sales of the Brazilian Brig *Izabel*, August 21, 1844, FO 84/506.

[18] Christopher Fyfe, "Four Sierra Leone Recaptives," *Journal of African History*, 2.1 (1961): 82.

[19] Cole has suggested that the initial focus on Badagry was "partly because it was the point of embarkation for many taken across the Atlantic following their capture and subsequent sale into slavery." Cole, *Krio of West Africa*, 135. However, only an estimated 3,163 recaptives entered the Atlantic trade at Badagry, far less than at either Lagos or Ouidah. The early focus of returnees on the port likely had more to do with their initial reception there and the possibilities to navigate inland.

supposing one another long dead and hearing each other's circumstances seem to have aroused each other's natural affections."[20] The movement of returnees from the coast inland to Abeokuta brought many – particularly the Egba – closer to their places of birth, though the human geography of the region had been transformed by conflict. Between 200 and 300 recaptives resided in Abeokuta by 1842, rising to 3,000 by 1850.[21]

The arrival of the steamship to West Africa from 1852 onward greatly impacted the region's commerce and the bilateral linkages between Yorubaland and Freetown.[22] Steamships allowed for easier movement along the coast, escalating the recaptive diaspora into what Christopher Fyfe termed an "exodus."[23] The voyage to Lagos was cut to eleven days, at a cost of £5 for males to travel "deck class."[24] The British occupation of Lagos in 1851, combined with this faster and cheaper transport, made the port through which the most recaptives had been sold a desirable destination for relocation. Returnees became known as Sàró, based on the local pronunciation of Sierra Leone in Lagos. By 1870, approximately 1,500 made their homes in Lagos.[25]

The mission followed the merchants. The 1841 Niger Expedition, organized by the Society for the Extinction of the Slave Trade and for the Civilization of Africa in London, was a calamitous failure. But its instigation further awakened Liberated Africans' sense of connectivity with their regions of birth. The Methodist Thomas Dove witnessed how "the arrival of the expedition bound for the great Golliba, or

[20] Graf, Quarter ending December 25, 1842, CMS/CA1/O105/39.
[21] These estimates were made by the Methodist missionary Thomas Birch Freeman and Royal Navy Commander Forbes, respectively. Kopytoff, *Preface to Modern Nigeria*, 50–51. Sarah Tucker adds that "between the years 1839 and 1842 no less than five hundred had left the colony," including more than 300 to Badagry, "most of whom proceeded on to Abbeokuta." Sarah Tucker, *Abbeokuta; or Sunrise within the Tropics: An Outline of the Origin and Progress of the Yoruba Mission* (New York: Robert Carter and Brothers, 1854), 45–48.
[22] Martin Lynn, "Technology, Trade, and a 'Race of Native Capitalists': The Krio Diaspora of West Africa and the Steamship, 1852–95," *Journal of African History*, 33.3 (1992): 421–440. Matory similarly stresses the importance of direct steamship travel between Lagos and Bahia in forging a transatlantic Yoruba identity. Matory, *Black Atlantic Religion*, 64–65.
[23] Fyfe, *History of Sierra Leone*, 317.
[24] Lynn, "Technology, Trade, and a 'Race of Native Capitalists,'" 426.
[25] Kristin Mann, *Marrying Well: Marriage, Status and Social Change among the Educated Elite in Colonial Lagos* (Cambridge: Cambridge University Press, 1985), 17.

Niger, excited in our colony of Sierra Leone extraordinary interest."[26] Trade and the Christian mission coalesced to pique the interest of many recaptives. In 1842, the Wesleyan Mission sent Thomas Birch Freeman, one of its agents on the Gold Coast, to investigate the potential for a mission in Abeokuta. At Badagry, Freeman organized a recaptive congregation and ventured inland. On reaching Abeokuta they were warmly received by the town's ruler, Sodeke.[27] Meanwhile, prospective emigrants at Hasting requested a CMS agent to accompany them. The CMS chose Henry Townsend to start a station at Abeokuta, based on his experiences in studying the "Aku language" and was given free passage by three Aku who owned a trading vessel. He was joined by Andrew Wilhelm Dasalu, an Egba recaptive and Aku class leader from the Hastings church, whose voyage was paid by church members. Dasalu had been enslaved when his town of Kesu-Egba fell in 1823; Townsend noted how he "has been from his country twenty years & was best a youth when he left."[28]

Both the CMS and MMS took steps to establish a mission presence at the Egba capital after 1842, though Abeokuta's military operations kept the road to the interior largely closed to Europeans until 1846.[29] In 1847 the church leaders of Gloucester village met with the local CMS agent, William Parkin, "to know what they could do toward erecting a church for their brethren in Abbeokuta."[30] Enough money was raised throughout the colony to erect a "Freetown Church" in what would become the missions' epicenter in Yorubaland.[31] Sierra Leoneans also sent less pious donations. The missionary Isaac Smith noted in his journal in late 1851 the arrival at Ake of a "large quantity of gun powder & flints sent by the Akoo Benevolent Committee" for the defense of the town against Dahomey.[32] By the 1860s, the presence

---

[26] Thomas Dove, July 27, 1841, MMS Sierra Leone, box 1841–1847, file 1841–42.
[27] See E. A. Ayandele, *The Missionary Impact on Modern Nigeria, 1842–1914: A Political and Social Analysis* (London: Longmans, 1966), 3–26.
[28] Townsend, Journal while on a mission of research to Badagry and Abeokuta, January 7, 1843, CMS/CA1/O215/34.
[29] Kopytoff, *Preface to Modern Nigeria*, 57.
[30] Parkin, Journal for quarter ending September 25, 1847, CMS/CA1/O171/6.
[31] Fyfe, *History of Sierra Leone*, 236.
[32] Smith, Journal extracts for quarter ending December 25, 1851, CMS/CA2/O82/23.

of returnees and missionaries was such that James Africanus Beale Horton dubbed Abeokuta the "metropolis of Aku."[33]

Our interest here is not in fully tracing the actions of these returnees or the inchoate Yoruba mission. Much has been written on the influence of Sàró returnees and their impact on a coastal Yoruba identity.[34] Less attention has been given to how this movement instigated a reciprocal process of cultural influence and identity formation. From the onset, returnees sent back news of the reorganization of the old Oyo kingdom and the growing prosperity of Abeokuta. The movement of individuals and information sparked an interest and engagement with Yorubaland among those with no means or ambition to make the journey. Mission agents returning from Yorubaland – both Africans and Europeans – drew attention for the information they could relay. Henry Townsend, on a "mission of research" as the first CMS missionary to Abeokuta, spent a January morning in 1843 "writing notes for people of Abbeokuta for their long lost relatives in S. Leone."[35] On his return to Sierra Leone, he was met with a church meeting "larger than any that I have seen in Hastings" eager to hear of his experience. Townsend realized he was "since my return from Badagry, an object of general interest among the Akus; when meeting them in the streets or roads of S. Leone I frequently hear them remarking to each other, that I am the white man that has been to their country."[36] Archdeacon Graf was even more emphatic in declaring: "The news of our friends' favourable reception at Understone [Abeokuta] flew speedily from village to village and filled everyone belonging to the Egba tribe of Akus with the fondest anticipation of a speedy return to their country."[37]

The pulpit became a link between the Yoruba homeland and the Aku diaspora. This link became even stronger, as an unintended consequence of missionary language preparation for the Niger Expedition and the Yoruba mission was the use of the Yoruba language by

[33] Horton, *West African Countries and Peoples*, 167.
[34] See Kristin Mann, *Slavery and the Birth of an African City: Lagos, 1760–1900* (Bloomington: Indiana University Press, 2007); Bronwen Everill, "Bridgeheads of Empire? Liberated African Missionaries in West Africa," *Journal of Imperial and Commonwealth History*, 40.5 (2012): 789–805.
[35] Townsend, Journal while on mission of research to Badagry and Abeokuta, November 1842–April 1843, CMS/CA1/O215/34.
[36] Townsend, Journal entries for May 18 and June 23, 1843, CMS/CA1/O215/32.
[37] Graf, Quarter ending September 25, 1843, CMS/CA1/O105/41.

mission agents within the colony. Vernacular preaching and teaching in Yoruba had never been pursued in Sierra Leone, despite the large percentage of the population who could understand the language, the pioneering role of the mission in Yoruba language study, and the number of missionaries and catechists trained as CMS and MMS agents who could speak it.[38] It was only in January 1844, following his return from the Niger Expedition, that Samuel Crowther presented the first Yoruba sermon in Sierra Leone, reading from the first chapter of St. Luke before a crowded mission church. Crowther recognized the significance of the moment and how "the novelty of the thing brought a large number of people together, both Yorubas, Ibos, Calabars, &c. to witness the reading and preaching of the gospel of Christ in a native language in an English Church."[39] As J. D. Y. Peel notes, the event was in many ways the symbolic inauguration of the modern Yoruba language.[40]

Joseph Wright, the Egba Methodist preacher, noted that since Crowther "last year commenced preaching in Ackoo language every Tuesday in the Church, the Akoo people so delighted to hear that many of the members of our society flocked there."[41] The "Aku preacher" soon became a fixture of the CMS and Methodist services, and those who could preach in the language, such as Wright himself, rotated between the village churches. Missionary journals depicted their sermons as the best-attended and liveliest services. George James Macaulay, a Krio pastor of Egba and Ijebu parents, described how, during an Aku sermon at Murray Town, "[t]he church was full to overflowing, many were obliged to remain outside, and the children were made to sit on the floor."[42] Sermons in Yoruba became moments of public excitement, whether given by the Oyo-born Crowther, the Egba Wright, or his Methodist compatriot Joseph May, born in the village of Iware near the Ogun River. The production of a standard

---

[38] Hannah Kilham did make an attempt in 1831 to teach in Yoruba to a class of "Aku girls." However, it seems that she found little success and no further attempts were made until the 1840s. Hair, *Early Study of Nigerian Languages*, 8.
[39] Crowther, Journal extracts for quarter ending March 25, 1844, CMS/CA1/O79/11.
[40] Peel, "The Cultural Work of Yoruba Ethnogenesis," 202–203.
[41] Wright, July 1, 1844, MMS Correspondence, fiche box 25, box 281, no. 12.
[42] Macaulay, Journal for half year ending March 1861, CMS/CA1/O141/19.

language understandable to Yoruba speakers of varied dialects helped reify the ethnic unity of the Aku population.[43]

Yoruba language services drew those with little interest in the Christian message. Crowther's inaugural sermon attracted many Aku Muslims, especially those interested in emigrating to Badagry. When the Ibadan-based missionary David Hinderer visited Freetown, the bishop jubilantly wrote to his sister: "You should have seen the Moslems at Fourah Bay Road listening to Hinderer preach in Ako yesterday evening."[44] Trade vessels and missionary reports from Yorubaland did more than stir memories of an unchanging past. Rather, congregations – and interested non-Christians – were tied to their homeland through reports of war, migration, new towns and cities, and missionary successes and failure. These connections were epitomized in the reaction of Crowther's visits to the villages of Wellington, Waterloo, Hastings, Kent, and the Banana Islands in February 1852, where he relayed news of Britain's bombardment of Lagos and expounded "the success of the gospel among our countrymen in Abeokuta." In these visits the most striking reaction "was the expression of the Yoruba tribe when they learned that Lagos was destroyed ... and the English flag was flying at last in that stronghold of the slave trade."[45]

The growth of missionary publications further articulated the linkages and dispersal of information from homeland to diaspora. The publication of Crowther and Schön's account of the Niger Expedition (1842), distributed through the missionary establishment, instigated a further level of connectivity through letters and missionary publications.[46] From 1844 onward, the *Sierra Leone Watchman*, the official publication of the Methodists, ran stories reporting on developments at "Badagry and Understone [Abeokuta]."[47] The CMS *Church*

---

[43] James Lorand Matory, "The English Professors of Brazil: On the Diasporic Roots of the Yorùbá Nation," *Comparative Studies in Society and History*, 41.1 (January 1999): 85. See also Peel, "The Cultural Work of Yoruba Ethnogenesis," 198–215; J. F. Ade Ajayi, "How Yoruba Was Reduced to Writing," *Odu: A Journal of Yoruba and Related Studies*, 8 (1960): 49–58.

[44] *Memoirs of John Bowen by His Sister*, 1862, 526, 587, quoted in Hair, *Early Study of Nigerian Languages*, 18.

[45] Crowther, letter, Freetown, February 11, 1852, CMS/CA2/O31/18.

[46] Schön and Crowther, *Journals of the Rev. James Frederick Schön and Mr. Samuel Crowther*.

[47] "News from Badagry," *Sierra Leone Watchman*, May 1844.

Missionary Gleaner (from 1841) and *Church Missionary Intelligencer* (from 1844) brought similar stories. Charles Davies noted how his class was "very much interested in reading from one of our Church Missionary Gleaners ... With profound silence they listened to hear something of their country."[48] There were less sanguine reports too. At Regent, Nathaniel Denton called together the congregation in June 1850 when "tidings having reached us, through the medium of the 'Intelligencer' & by private letters from Abbeokuta, of the afflictions which the Xtians there have been called, for the truths' sake, to endure."[49]

At the most symbolic level, these publications provided details of improbable reunions. In 1847 James Beale and Thomas King spread the word in Freetown "of the joyful tidings that has just come from England of the Abbeokuta mission." At the prayer meeting Beale read to those assembled a published account "of that mission's proceedings, their agricultural enterprise at Badagry, the kind of reception they met with at Abbeokuta, and the heartsheering [sic] account of the Revd. S. Crowther's finding his mother and other relatives at that place."[50] Ten years later, William Moore Odusina published an account of his return to Abeokuta, where he was reunited with his relatives from whom he had been separated when their town of Isaga fell in 1824.[51] Missionary activity thus connected people in Sierra Leone with those whom they saw as their own people within Yorubaland. The dual missions in Sierra Leone and Yoruba territory, the linguistic studies they engendered, and the spread of information by individuals and through mission publications informed conceptions of Aku identity among listeners and readers, even those disinterested in the evangelizing content of these sources.

"Traditional Religion" and Aku Identity

As the narrative above makes clear, the ethnolinguistic community and the religious community interacted in complex ways. It may seem

---

[48] Davies, Journal for half year ending March 31, 1857, January 15, CMS/CA1/O81/2.
[49] Denton, Journal for half year ending September 30, 1850, CMS/CA1/O87/35.
[50] King, Journal for quarter ending June 25, 1847, CMS/CA1/O130/7.
[51] William Moore Odusina, Journal in Mary Barber, *Oshiele or Village Life in the Yoruba Country* (London: James Nisbet & Co., 1857), 55.

counterintuitive, then, to suggest that religion – specifically the religious practices of the Yoruba homeland – explains the conspicuousness and unity of the Aku nation. Gibril Cole has recently argued along these lines, stating that it was because Yoruba speakers "coalesced around shared beliefs" that they "provided the polyglot Liberated Africans with crucial cultural elements to anchor their shared historical experience and forge a cohesive community."[52] Cole's work is primarily on Islam among the Krio and their forebears, though his analysis wavers regarding whether these "shared beliefs" in question refer to Islam or what he refers to as "Yoruba traditional culture." The real question is what role religion played in Aku identity given that they *did not* all hold "shared beliefs." In their homeland, Yoruba speakers followed a number of deities, many tied to specific regions or lineages. Moreover, the spread of jihad precipitated the enslavement of many recaptives, while other Aku recaptives were born Muslims or had converted to Islam prior to their enslavement. Finally, in Freetown a perception emerged of the Aku, among the entire recaptive population, as disproportionately Western-educated, literate, Christian, commercially active, and prosperous.[53]

Yoruba speakers have thus been variously described within the historiography on Sierra Leone as particularly influential converts to Christianity, as staunch adherents to Islam, and as those who most tenaciously held on to their "traditional" religious customs.[54] These characterizations are not as contradictory as they appear. We know more about Yoruba religious practices in Sierra Leone specifically because more Yoruba converts to Christianity rose within the ranks of the missionary establishment. Moreover, Muslim Aku did not clash with or look down on their non-Muslim counterparts, but often found common cause in solidarity against the colony's evangelical mission.

The role of Christianity in the making of the Aku is evident through this and the previous chapters: the mission's concept of language and "nation" being coterminous and the reduction to writing of a standardized "Yoruba" text. Islam, whose arrival in Yoruba territory long pre-dated Christianity and spread over the course of the nineteenth century, provided a form of unity for its adherents in Yorubaland and

---

[52] Cole, *Krio of West Africa*, 6.   [53] Matory, *Black Atlantic Religion*, 53–54.
[54] On the strong association of Islam and Aku identity, see Spitzer, *Creoles of Sierra Leone*, and Gibril Cole, *Krio of West Africa*. For the role of "traditional" religion, see Peterson, *Province of Freedom*.

"Traditional Religion" and Aku Identity

the diaspora, as Chapter 7 will show. The decisions of influential Christian such as Crowther and Samuel Johnson to adopt a Muslim term – Yoruba – for both the language and the territory may have been partly an acknowledgment of the role Islam played in shaping ethnic cohesion.[55]

The impact of these two world religions in the emergence of an Aku identity in Sierra Leone and of a Yoruba identity in the future Nigeria are well established. Less attention has been placed on how indigenous cosmologies played a role in community cohesion within the diaspora. Yoruba beliefs and worship were the single most important element of Yoruba culture and played a unifying role, despite regional variations and local practices. The belief in Olodumare as the Supreme Being, a panoply of deities known as *orisa*, and ancestor worship were the defining elements of Yoruba "traditional" religion. Ifá and other forms of divination were consulted everywhere before important decisions were made.

Still, one cannot simply claim that a "traditional religion" lay at the foundation of Aku identity. As Peel points out, the problem of referring to "Yoruba traditional religion" is both that important Yoruba *orisa* (e.g., Ifá, Ògún, Esu-Elegba) were widely found among neighboring non-Yoruba peoples, and even more significantly, that local cult-complexes varied so much from town to town and from West to East. These complexes comprised an ensemble of cults that likely combined *orisa* found widely and those of more local currency. Kingdoms under Oyo military domination came to practice forms of worship deeply indebted to Oyo ritual and mythology, and the cult of Sàngó in particular. People therefore had identities as members of their communities and as initiates of the cult groups of *particular* deities, but were not adherents of a generalized religion.[56]

The standard historiographical interpretation is that it was in the diaspora where worshippers of various *orisa* converged to create a pantheon that did not exist within Yorubaland. Olatunji Ojo has recently suggested that this process had parallels and even antecedents in the homeland. Ojo argues that in the nineteenth century – a period of population movement and admixture and of urbanization – *orisa* were transformed from local to regional symbols. Warfare created

---

[55] Lovejoy, "The Yoruba Factor in the Trans-Atlantic Slave Trade," 41.
[56] Peel, *Christianity, Islam, and the Orisa*, 217.

greater population mixture, new cities, and interethnic marriages. The geography of *oriṣa* worship therefore changed as people moved and brought with them ritual practices to regions where they had not been before. Ojo concludes that by the mid-nineteenth century, "Yorubaland had evolved into a unified Orisa world," and *oriṣa* worship should therefore be considered alongside Christianity and Islam as the third religion that made the Yoruba.[57] This included the unity found in pan-ethnic religious fraternities and cults such as Oro, Ifá, Egungun, and Ogboni. Since these groups had members from all over Yorubaland, their membership could transcend local ethnic and political hostilities.[58]

John Peterson, more than any other scholar, recognized the importance of *oriṣa* worship in nineteenth-century Sierra Leone. Yet he characterized these practices in Herskovits-like terms as "older survivals in a Christian context" and attributed their persistence primarily to the recently landed.[59] The reality was more complex and dynamic; most references to specific *oriṣa* in the CMS and MMS papers appear after the fall of Oyo in c. 1836. There were, of course, barriers to the transposition of Yoruba practices to Sierra Leone. Religious practitioners crucial to the transportation of particular *oriṣa* may not have arrived in the colony in large numbers. Nor was it certain that devotees of a particular *oriṣa* would be settled near one another within the Liberated African villages. The large number of children among recaptives meant that a significant percentage of the Aku community had limited experience of the religious traditions of their homeland. Finally, law and order campaigns by governors passed ordinances repressing "country fashion" and "heathen custom," purging "idols" and "greegrees" from houses and compounds. Despite these impediments,

---

[57] Olatunji Ojo, "The Root Is Also Here: The Nondiaspora Foundations of Yoruba Ethnicity," in Toyin Falola and Aribidesi Usman (eds.), *Movements, Borders, and Identities in Africa* (Rochester: University of Rochester Press, 2009), 62–64. Yet Apter notes that in contemporary times "òrìṣà cults do preserve indigenous (and carefully archived) records of former migrations and allegiances to rival kings – in their praises, songs, iconography, dialects of spirit possession, and even in their talking-drum texts." Andrew Apter, *Black Critics and Kings: The Hermeneutics of Power in Yoruba Society* (Chicago: University of Chicago Press, 1992), 9.

[58] Olatunji Ojo, "'Heepa' (Hail) Òrìṣà: The Òrìṣà Factor in the Birth of Yoruba Identity," *Journal of Religion in Africa*, 39.1 (2009): 30–59.

[59] Peterson, *Province of Freedom*, 234.

Yoruba *orişa* devotion displayed a tenacity that made it a defining feature of the Aku community. If a form of unified *orişa* devotion was developing in nineteenth-century Yoruba territory, this process was accelerated in the diaspora.

It was the prominence of "traditional" religion and its interaction and, at times, collision with Christianity and Islam that was central to perceptions – including self-perceptions – of the Aku as the largest and most cohesive nation in Sierra Leone. This is not to treat "traditional" religion uncritically as the vehicle par excellence of ethnic and community identity, but to look historically at how changes in nineteenth-century Yorubaland and the transferal of devotees to the diaspora began to recognize and celebrate the resiliency of their religious institutions in a new setting.

Documenting an *Orişa* Diaspora

The major premise of all Yoruba religious practice is that the material, phenomenal world is continuously affected by unseen powers of various kinds and indefinite number.[60] Yoruba *orişa* worship is a practical religion that "feeds" deities with offerings and sacrifices in return for requested services.[61] Most *orişa* are either deified ancestors or personified natural forces. Yet *orişa* are difficult to adequately define as "spiritual beings." As Apter points out, this is due to the pact of secrecy (*imulè*) with the earth that all initiatives swear, proscribing them from openly divulging what they know and preventing noninitiates from finding out. The secrecy that shielded the uninitiated public means that we cannot know very much about the *orişa* historically, though the CMS agents in Sierra Leone embarked on the earliest inquiries into what is now one of the most studied forms of African religion on the continent and around the Atlantic world.[62]

While some aspects of *orişa* practice demanded secrecy, others were public-oriented affairs. Drumming and singing, animal and other sacrifices, and the earthly manifestations of the *orişa* in their chosen human vessels through possession are public events whose effectiveness depends on the community of believers.[63] Rather than a religion

---

[60] Peel, *Religious Encounter*, 93. [61] Apter, *Black Critics and Kings*, 98.
[62] Ibid., 150.
[63] David V. Trotman, "Reflections on the Children of Shango: An Essay on the History of Orisa Worship in Trinidad," *Slavery & Abolition*, 28.2 (2007): 220.

of solitude, *orisa* worship is a community religion based on cooperative praise and veneration.[64] This made *orisa* devotion the most conspicuous form of "traditional" worship across the Sierra Leone peninsula, and partly what drew missionaries to so frequently comment on it.

Despite some divergent interpretations of the origins and relationship between *orisa*, there is a general consensus that there are 401 deities in total.[65] Yet only a small number had a pan-Yoruba following, namely, Ifá, Esu, Ògún, Ṣàngó, Osun, and the *orisa funfun* (Obatala, Orisanla, Orisa Alaye, etc.) complex. Other *orisa* operated mostly as local ritual complexes, each having its adherents concentrated on a town or kingdom.[66] Broadly, *orisa* can be classified into one of two broad categories as either hot, temperamental deities (*òrìṣà gbígbóná*) or cool, temperate, symbolically white deities (*òrìṣà funfun*). This characterization of "hot" and "cold" does not reflect a dichotomy between good and evil, but rather the particular powers and temperance of individual *orisa*.

Even as *orisa* possessed distinct qualities, they were expected by their devotees to provide many of the same benefits in terms of protection, health, and guidance. Cults worked analogously to communities as their members thought of themselves as together the children of a deceased or more-than-mortal person.[67] A cult's unique identity is expressed by the name of the dominant *orisa* that it serves and is elaborated with specific *oriki* (praise poetry) that refer to the deity's attributes and origins. Ritual houses (*ilé òrìṣà*) served as meeting places of these literal and figurative communities. During the celebration of its *orisa*, the "house" qua town shrine (*ilé òrìṣà*) invokes its forebears and literally occupies the town.[68]

---

[64] Toyin Falola and Ann Genova (eds.), *Orisa: Yoruba Gods and Spiritual Identity in Africa and the Diaspora* (Trenton, NJ: Africa World Press, 2005), 7.

[65] Cornelius O. Adepegba, "Associated Place-Names and Sacred Icons of Seven Yorùbá Deities: Historicity in Yorùbá Religious Traditions," in Jacob K. Olupona and Terry Rey (eds.), *Òrìṣà Devotion as World Religion: The Globalization of Yorùbá Religious Culture* (Madison: University of Wisconsin Press, 2008), 109. Adepegba notes that no one source convincingly lists all 401, and that many *orisa* are known by multiple names in different communities. Tishkin, Falola, and Akinyemi note that this count should be treated more as a sacred metaphor than a scientific list. "Introduction," in Joel E. Tishken, Toyin Falola, and Akintunde Akinyemi (eds.), *Ṣàngó in Africa and the African Diaspora* (Bloomington: Indiana University Press, 2009), 1.

[66] Ojo, "'Heepa' (Hail) Òrìṣà," 34.   [67] Peel, *Religious Encounter*, 58.

[68] Andrew Apter, "Yoruba Ethnogenesis from Within," *Comparative Studies in Society and Culture*, 55.2 (2013): 366–367.

The period of the disintegration of Oyo and the subsequent Yoruba wars was commonly referred to by mission agents – including many who had been enslaved in these conflicts – as an "age of confusion." This experience of the "world being spoiled" (aiye bajẹ) was a time of paramountcy for "hot," angry deities such as Ògún (god of war), Ṣopona (god of smallpox), and above all Esu (the intemperate trickster deity) whom the Christians identified as Satan.[69] Even before the upheavals of the nineteenth century, individuals could move between cults, which were competitive and expansionist in character. It is therefore impossible to demarcate a "baseline" against which developments in the diaspora are measured. The orișa who traveled with recaptives were those that had been spreading within Yorubaland itself through migrations, displacements, and trade. In the diaspora, adherents modified orișa worship based on local exigencies and made it attractive to outsiders.

Most of what we know of orișa devotion in Sierra Leone comes to us through the archives and publications of the CMS and the MMS. Far from impartial observers, the corpus of mission documents nevertheless records in detail a diasporic religious community. For most of the nineteenth century, agents were expected to keep journals or "journal extracts" for dispatch to headquarters in London, in order to inform policy decisions and provide excerpts for publication in CMS periodicals. Every CMS missionary was instructed to send home regular journals to the parent committee, a practice that began with the discouraging accounts of Melchior Renner and Peter Hartwig among the Susu in the early nineteenth century.[70] But the CMS operated for nearly two decades within the colony before the journal extract system was fully settled in the 1830s and was further elaborated on during the years when the Rev. Henry Venn was clerical secretary (1841–1873).[71]

In total, 210 individuals wrote letters and journals for the CMS mission, now contained within the incoming "original papers" series

---

[69] Peel, "The Cultural Work of Yoruba Ethnogenesis," 203.
[70] Fyfe, *History of Sierra Leone*, 94–95.
[71] Journals were kept beforehand and published in the annual reports of the CMS, most famously in the case of W. A. B. Johnson's accounts of Regent. However, the practice of sending regular journal extracts only appeared at this later date. The documents that exist within the archive today are journal "extracts," likely copied from actual journals, though the exact conditions of production are not known and the original journals are not extant.

of the CMS archive (CA1/O). Unlike colonial sources and travel narratives, African agents of the mission composed a large percentage of the journals. Recaptives composed some 30 percent of the 5,115 individual documents in the archive, including much of the most valuable and detailed material. Though it has not been possible based on CMS Register of Missionaries to identify place of birth for all 210 who contributed to the archive, it is possible to identify eighty-five "native agents" of the mission. This includes five Aku mission agents, and seventeen Krio offspring with at least one Aku parent. Whereas European-born missionaries were often content to describe undifferentiated "idolatry," "greegrees," or "country fashion," recaptive converts were more likely to give the specific name and provenance of religious practices. In particular, the papers of the Oyo-born Samuel Crowther and James Johnson (born in Sierra Leone to Ijebu and Ondo parents) provide perhaps the most sustained descriptive tracts of *orisa* devotion in the nineteenth-century Yoruba diaspora.

The movement of missionaries back and forth from the Yoruba mission meant that mission agents – including those who had left those regions enslaved years earlier – had additional reference points to draw on. The level of detail in these records and the number of references to specific *orisa* significantly increases following the 1841 Niger Expedition – of which Crowther was a participant – and the onset of the Yoruba mission. In fact, I have uncovered only one document prior to the Niger Expedition in which a particular *orisa* is referred to by name.[72] By contrast, most named references to *orisa* occur in the period 1843–1851 as the missionary field in Yoruba territories expanded and agents moved between both mission fields.

The development of the journal system plus this greater familiarity means that the "traditional" religion of recaptives is discussed with greater frequency and detail over the middle decades of the nineteenth century. This evidence takes several forms. At times it involved engaging with an individual adherent; engagements with practitioners such as *babalawos* (priests of Ifá divination) and other religious specialists were recorded with particular vigor. At other times, missionaries recounted how they intruded on and broke up religious ceremonies. This included entering recaptives' properties and households, or

---

[72] Weeks, Report of Hastings for quarter ending September 25, 1831, CMS/CA1/O219/44.

executing government decrees to purge "idols." In these instances, descriptions primarily pertain to material embodiments and materials such as the ritual ceramic bowl of the thunder god (*ikoko Ṣàngó*).[73]

While it is not surprising that missionaries should mention religious customs of Yoruba origin more than those of other ethnic groups, what is striking is that mission agents commented almost exclusively on practices of Yoruba origin. Those deities most referenced within CMS documents were primarily those with a pan-Yoruba following or those associated with Oyo, most notably Ṣàngó and the Egungun.[74] Cults associated with the Egba and Ijebu – Ogboni/Osugbo – are mentioned far less, despite the large numbers of Egba recaptives.

Orìṣa in Sierra Leone were also worshipped in close proximity to one another. Waterloo – the village for which there are the most missionary references to particular *orìṣa* – was home in the middle third of the nineteenth century to Ṣàngó devotees, Ifá diviners, and common sightings of the Egungun. There is no evidence that these deities "came together under the same roof," as was the case with the emergence of *Candomblé* in nineteenth-century northeastern Brazil. *Orìṣa* were worshipped separately, which likely meant their adherents were still defined based on their regional origins. But in Sierra Leone there was an awareness of commonalities across regional origins and these cults endured with a unique degree of success.

The Repression and Persistence of *Orìṣa* Devotion

By 1831 Governor Alexander Findlay had grown tired of the persistence of "superstitious practices." A circular to the village managers stated that they were to administer warnings "to repress such vicious practices, which are calculated only to insult the supreme being, and with that view you will consider yourselves authorized in all cases of like nature coming before you, in future, where parties act in contempt of that warning to punish the offenders either by fine or imprisonment."[75] The subsequent idol purges – often undertaken by missionaries – both underscored the ubiquity of *orìṣa* worship and provide some

---

[73] Robert Farris Thompson, *Flash of the Spirit: African and Afro-American Art and Philosophy* (New York: Vintage, 1984), 6.
[74] See Adepegba, "Associated Place-Names and Sacred Icons of Seven Yorùbá Deities," 106–127; Thompson, *Flash of the Spirit*, xv.
[75] Cole to managers, May 11, 1831, LADLB 1830–1831.

of the most detailed accounts. Ultimately, rather than destroy such forms of worship, purges simply revealed the full magnitude of non-Christian practices that had heretofore been clandestine.

In August 1831, six recaptives were brought before Rev. John Wills Weeks for breaking Governor Findlay's prohibition of sacrificing to idols. The accused had killed several fowls in offering "to an idol, whose name was Headon (the meaning of which is 'one of the twins').''[76] Weeks was startled to learn from the constable who apprehended these six that "there were plenty of greegrees in Hastings." The reverend asked the constable to round up "all the idols to whom any a sacrifice was offered," and was presented with four filled baskets within the same evening. Weeks summoned the idol owners the following day. They were, from his vantage, "all of the Aku nation." Weeks quickly found some 150 Aku crowded on his piazza. Through an interpreter he chastised them for not repaying their "debt" to the English government by conforming "both to English laws, and to the laws of the great God." Weeks questioned one of those present, an Aku recaptive named Fagboo, "to explain to me the nature of these gods, which were then placed before them." In response,

Fagboo commenced the history of his god by saying (through an interpreter for he did not know any thing of the English language) he had worshipped him eight years, during this period, Fagboo sacrificed colars [*sic*], fowls, and occasionally a ram sheep; Shangoo (the name of his god) was first good to him when he had been sick eight months, he sacrificed a ram sheep to Shangoo who make him well. If Fagboo wanted employment he would offer a fowl to Shangoo who would be sure to bless him.

The account of this interaction reflects the missionary campaign to simultaneously document and extirpate *orişa* devotion, a campaign that for at least a generation had ambiguous results.

The proclamations against "superstition" and the greater familiarity with those practices as gleaned through the Niger Expedition and subsequent Yoruba mission had the dual impact of bringing "Yoruba traditional religion" in the colony into the open and documenting the ubiquity of such practices. At times missionary journal entries betray the very narrative of success they try to substantiate, and explicit

---

[76] Weeks, Report of Hastings for quarter ending September 25, 1831, CMS/CA1/O219/44.

disavowals of "paganism" became more pronounced over time. The consistent reporting of religious practices of almost exclusively Yoruba origin magnified popular perceptions of the Aku as the largest and most culturally influential ethnic group in the colony. The numerous writings and publications on the subject had the effect – quite unintentionally – of reifying the persistence and centrality of *orisa* worship to the Aku community.

What follows is not a complete discussion of Yoruba religious practice in the colony. Rather, the discussion emphasizes both the role of *orisa* devotion as central to the communal life of its adherents and how missionary reporting unintentionally reinforced contemporary perceptions of the Aku's singular cultural imprint. To do so, the analysis looks at the three deities most commonly mentioned in missionary sources: Ṣàngó (the *orisa* of thunder and lightning), Ifá (the *orisa* of wisdom and divination), and the Egungun (an ancestral masquerade). In Sierra Leone, even the most ardent Christian converts – including and especially Aku clergymen – acknowledged the role these manifestations of "Yoruba traditional religion" played in shaping Aku identity and ethnic consciousness.

Orisa in Sierra Leone: Ṣàngó, Ifá, and Egungun

The deity most often mentioned within the CMS archive is Ṣàngó, the Yoruba *orisa* of thunder and lightning.[77] The Onishango (Ṣàngó devotees) proved a particular menace to missionary eyes and ears through their drumming and reveling. The 1847 annual report of the acting-governor noted: "Among them [recaptives] the worshippers of thunder and lightning are remarkable."[78] Three decades later, an article in the *Sierra Leone Independent* stated: "The 'worship of thunder' by the most benighted of the Akus, who firmly believe, its roar the

---

[77] This is based on an analysis of 3,326 documents in the CMS archive written by ninety-six mission agents. Though it has not been possible to read the entirety of the CMS original papers for the Sierra Leone mission, I have consulted a majority of documents composed by mission agents, particularly those of African birth. I have uncovered thirteen documents focused on describing some aspect of Ṣàngó devotion in the colony, while an additional fourteen documents refer less precisely to "thunder worship."

[78] Benjamin Pine, Annual Report, enclosed in dispatch no. 88 of October 27, 1848, CO 267/204.

voice of some powerful divinity, is another of the many dark practices so numerous in this place."[79]

In Oyo tradition, the cult of Ṣàngó was strongly associated with royal power. Most historical traditions place Ṣàngó as the fourth Aláàfin (emperor) of Oyo, who ascended to the status of a god on his death.[80] The Ṣàngó cult played an important role in securing the loyalty of Oyo's provinces to the Aláàfin. Resident *ajele* (king's resident overlords) at Oyo Ile traveled from the capital, while Ṣàngó priests from the provinces traveled to the metropole for final initiation and instruction. The Ṣàngó cult was thus fused with Oyo's imperial administration to distribute the Aláàfin's ritual power and political authority.[81]

Ṣàngó spread into non-Oyo districts, first as a symbol of Oyo authority and militarism and later through the out-migration of Oyo refugees following the empire's disintegration. The cult spread to the Egba and southwest Yoruba territories in the period of Oyo's political ascendance.[82] After the fall of the Oyo Empire, the Oyo-ethnic military leaders of Ibadan, controlling an even larger territory than the former empire, employed Oyo gods as potent sources of symbolic power.[83] As J. F. Ade Ajayi points out, the royal cult spread more rapidly in the days of Oyo decline than in the days of Oyo hegemony.[84] It is not surprising then that worshippers of Ṣàngó were and are found everywhere Yoruba people have had a cultural or demographic influence.

References to Ṣàngó or "thunder worship" comprise almost half of all mentions of *orisa* within CMS documents. Many documents speak only of "worshippers of thunder" or the "worship of thunder," while others specifically mention Ṣàngó by name. The latter documents are primarily composed by Aku receptives or their Krio offspring, though some interested European observers took the care to name that which they were condemning. Ṣàngó is not the only thunder deity among the Yoruba, especially in western Yorubaland where the thunder deity Àrá

---

[79] James A. Fitz-John, "Our Native Manners and Customs," *Sierra Leone Independent*, September 28, 1876, 1.
[80] Law points out that the first four *Aláàfin*, including Ṣàngó, were all *orisa* and are likely to be humanized gods, rather than deified mortals. Law, *Oyo Empire*, 50.
[81] Apter, *Black Critics and Kings*, 25.   [82] Peel, *Religious Encounter*, 109.
[83] Matory, *Black Atlantic Religion*, 51.
[84] Ajayi, "Aftermath of the Fall of Old Oyo," 146–147.

co-existed with Ṣàngó cults.[85] Oramfe is worshipped as a thunder deity at Ife, while Agbona is worshipped as such in Ketu.[86] Mentions of "thunder worship" are therefore not unambiguous references to Ṣàngó. Explicit mentions of Ṣàngó worship are, however, recorded in the Liberated African villages of Waterloo, Hastings, and Aberdeen, as well as Freetown, between 1831 and 1871. In addition, references to "thunder worship" are seen in these locations as well as Kissy, Wellington, Leicester, Wilberforce, and Tumbo.

Ritual processes to Ṣàngó in Africa and the diaspora are of two types: periodic and annual rituals. Periodic rituals usually take place once a week, on Jàkúta day (the last day of the traditional four-day week) in Nigeria, and usually on Thursday or Friday in the diaspora.[87] Samuel Crowther and Joseph Bartholomew both observed that "Friday is kept secretly in the Colony by the Shango worshippers of the Yorubah tribes."[88] Crowther recorded in his journal on one Friday:

This day is sacred to *Shango*, the god of thunder and lightning. This morning ... I visited a party of worshippers of this god, when I was received rather to be thundered upon, than listened to. On my entering the yard, I found three drummers sitting in front of the house, opposite the representation of Shango, which was placed in a conspicuous place in the house.

Crowther described the "seat of Shango" as "a bank of earth raised a few inches in a semicircular form about two or three feet from the center in circumference, touching the walls at both ends." Inside was "a wooden mortar bedeviled with blood, on the top of which was placed a large calabash whitewashed with chalk, covered up." The earth was "with two broad ribbands of red clay and white chalk not very much unlike those of a new painted ship" and surrounded by calabashes, pots, and bottles. Crowther explained:

---

[85] Marc Shiltz, "Yorùbá Thunder Deities and Sovereignty: Àrá versus Ṣàngó," in Tishken et al. (eds.), *Ṣàngó in Africa and the African Diaspora*, 78–108.

[86] William Bascom, *Shango in the New World* (Austin: University of Texas African and Afro-American Research Institute, 1972), 3.

[87] Tishkin, Falola, and Akiyemi (eds.), "Introduction," in *Ṣàngó in Africa and the African Diaspora*, 3.

[88] Crowther, Journal ending March 25, 1847, CMS/CA2/O35/18.

Every Shango worshipper has such a furniture set up in his house. They commenced their worship on Thursday night, when they drum and dance till Friday morning. Occasionally they offer a ram, an animal particularly dedicated to him.[89]

When Joseph Bartholomew attempted to infiltrate a Ṣàngó compound, the attendees taunted that they would attend church on Sundays if Bartholomew would continue to attend their worship on Fridays.[90]

Ṣàngó devotees traveled to attend worship. Bartholomew visited a female devotee at Hastings who "set out from thence to Freetown once every week, about five hours travel, for the purpose of worshipping thunder and lightning."[91] These networks mobilized particularly after Ṣàngó struck the property of his followers. After a strong storm in which a house was burned by lightning, Christian Frey watched as afterward,

we were for a period of four weeks annoyed by the thunderworshippers ... These people, all Yorubans, have, instead of humbling themselves before Him who has life & death under his disposal tried their uttermost to appease their god of thunder, who, as they said, was vexed because many left to serve him. Numbers from the adjacent villages came to join in the ceremonies.[92]

The combination of impromptu and calendrical worship made Ṣàngó devotion the most conspicuous African religious practice in the colony.

At Mountain Cut, a community lying behind central Freetown, the Rev. James Beale noted that "the tomtom never ceases among the thunder worshippers."[93] Drumming often drew church officials to compounds in Freetown and the villages. The Methodist missionary Henry Badger recorded in his journal for February 6, 1841, that when visiting Wilberforce,

in a certain part of town I heard a noise and went to see, some men and women were together. I asked them what they were doing, they answered "we are praying." To whom I said. "To thunder" they said. I said "where is he" and pointing to the hut a women said "he dere," and there he was, and

---

[89] Crowther, Extracts ending March 25, 1844, CMS/CA1/O79/11.
[90] Bartholomew, Extracts ending March 25, 1847, CMS/CA1/O35/18.
[91] Bartholomew, Extracts for half year to March 25, 1854, Hastings, CMS/CA1/O35/35.
[92] Frey, Journal extract, Waterloo, quarter ending September 25, 1844, CMS/CA1/O94.
[93] Beale, quoted in *Church Missionary Paper*, no. 151, Michaelmas 1853.

the alter on which they sacrifice to him, shortly after a woman came by, and prostrated herself to the ground before the hut. So I left them and went to preach in our little chapel.[94]

Christian Frey was similarly drawn to "noise being made in that direction of the village which is chiefly occupied by the Thunderworshippers" where he found "the same people assembled with whom I had in former years many a dispute about the folly of idolatry."[95]

The numerous references to Ṣàngó in the CMS archive was partly due to the fact that Ṣàngó's followers were so uncompromisingly conspicuous in the colony. The reverberations of the Ṣàngó bata drum were such that "bata" became the Krio term for drum.[96] The community of Ṣàngó worshippers in Sierra Leone also marked themselves aesthetically. Bartholomew noted that the "Shango worshippers generally distinguish themselves by wearing white beads on their necks especially the women."[97] Ṣàngó's ubiquity was such that Henry Townsend declared "the usual badge of heathenism, a string of small white beads."[98] Ṣàngó proved so pervasive that Crowther found it necessary to write in detail to the CMS's parent committee in London, expounding Ṣàngó's origins and powers.[99] Yet this was an epistemological battle in which Crowther and other missionaries found ambivalent results. The tangibility of thunder and lightning, in contradistinction to the noninterventionist Christian God, proved a stumbling block for missionaries. Crowther went so far as to suggest that "a small electrified machine would be very serviceable in this Colony, and in our mission on Abbeh-Okuta," in order to show that thunder and lightning were natural phenomena that could be contained.

These natural phenomena also worked against missionaries, at times in embarrassing and ironic ways. Such was the case when James Johnson attempted to admonish Eliza Coker, "a long time resident in the colony" on Freetown's Pa Demba Road, who was also "an

---

[94] Badger, Journal beginning October 18, 1840, MMS/17/02/03/5, MMS Biographical.
[95] Frey, Extracts, March 25, 1848, CMS/CA1/O94.
[96] A. T. von S. Bradshaw, "A List of Yoruba Words in Krio," *Sierra Leone Language Review*, 5 (1966): 65.
[97] Bartholomew, Extracts for quarter ending December 25, 1846, CMS/CA1/O35/17.
[98] Townsend, Quarter ending March 25, 1842, CMS/CA1/O215/29.
[99] Crowther, Extracts of journal ending March 25, 1844, CMS/CA1/O79/11.

idolatress – a thunder-worshipper." Coker was emphatic in her response, declaring, "I am a thunder-worshipper, would always worship it, my God above; you hear his voice often.... My parents have ever worshipped it, and I will on no account, give up worshipping it." Johnson pressed on attempting to explain the cause of thunder before leaving her. Unfortunately for his argument, before he could reach home "it thundered very loudly and I was overtaken by a heavy shower of rain. I fear that that would appear to the idolaters as the vengeance of her god."[100] Ṣàngó's influence persisted in Sierra Leone through his large number of adherents and because many found him and *oriṣa* of continued relevance and use. Yet Ṣàngó's presence as one of the most conspicuous deities in the African diaspora was magnified in Sierra Leone by reports by Yoruba converts such as Crowther and Johnson, who saw this symbol of Oyo authority as the most prevalent of all deities among recaptives.

Ifá

The challenge of the cult of Ṣàngó to the colonial Christian establishment was matched by systems of Yoruba divination, of which Ifá was the most prevalent. Ifá, an omniscient deity, is known as the god of wisdom and divination. Ifá's cult is believed to have originated at Ile-Ife and was by far the most widespread cult across Yoruba territories.[101] Ifá divination differed significantly from other *oriṣa* worship as a primarily masculine domain led by *babalawo* (lit. "father of mysteries") or diviners. *Babalawos* possessed a set of techniques and body of knowledge that allowed them to divine the unseen forces affecting an individual's well-being, making them important religious guides and counselors.

Ifá experienced varying fortunes in the diaspora, virtually dying out in Brazil while flourishing in Cuba. This divergence is surprising given the number of enslaved Yoruba sent to Bahia and the greater connectivity between Yorubaland and Brazil in the nineteenth century. Part of Ifá's success in Cuba, where it became solidly established in Havana in

---

[100] Johnson, Journal, half year ending September 1863, CMS/CA1/O123/14.
[101] See William Bascom, *Ifa Divination: Communication between Gods and Men in West Africa* (Bloomington: Indiana University Press, 1969), and Bascom, *Sixteen Cowries: Yoruba Divination from Africa to the New World* (Bloomington: Indiana University Press, 1980).

Ifá

the late nineteenth century, came through the efforts of five Yoruba-born *babalawos*, who are recognized as the founders of the main branches of the entire *Regla de Ifa* in Cuba and the Cuban diaspora down to today.[102] Though we know less about the individual *babalawos* in Sierra Leone, their role was likely equally instrumental.

In Sierra Leone, *babalawos* caught the ire of many missionaries. They presented evangelicals with a particular challenge: to convert a religious specialist. But missionaries also viewed them as particularly egregious frauds, not only propagating a rival "false" religion but also benefiting financially for these services. When Henry Rhodes visited a candidate for baptism at Kent, he found the man acting as a diviner for two other recaptives. Rhodes "afterwards found, [that they] had come to consult him as the diviner of their country-god 'Fang or Efah' & that the man had practiced this previous to his becoming a candidate for baptism."[103] Besides specializing in divination, the *babalawo* also possessed knowledge of medicines, *ogun*.[104] When Crowther confronted a *babalawo* in Freetown "on the folly of worshipping Ifah the god of palm nuts," the diviner answered his Christian critic by stating that "it was necessary he should do this because he was a doctor, that he could not consent to give up his medicine to any one who applied to him without consulting his god whether he should give or not, and according to the direction of Ifah, so he acts."[105]

Missionaries viewed diviners as fraudulent, but also obdurate defenders of their faith. Despite obvious feelings of animosity, missionaries often acknowledged a level of deference toward these religious specialists.[106] For their part, *babalawos* and other individuals justified *orişa* worship and divination to critical missionaries by explaining how these deities were intermediaries between ordinary people and the

---

[102] Peel, *Christianity, Islam, and the Orişa*, 11. On the complexities of the cultural passage of Ifá from Nigeria to Cuba, see Michael Marcuzzi, "The Ipanodu Ceremony and the History of Orisa Worship in Nigeria and Cuba," in Falola and Genova (eds.), *Orişa: Yoruba Gods*, 183–208.

[103] Rhodes, Quarter ending June 25, 1843, CMS/CA1/O183/27.

[104] This term has no etymological connection with the *orişa* Ògún. In Freetown, the terms *oogun* and *juju* persist as terms for medicines within secret societies. See John W. Nunley, *Moving with the Face of the Devil: Art and Politics in Urban West Africa* (Urbana: University of Illinois Press, 1987), 61.

[105] Crowther, Journal for quarter to June 1844, CMS/CA1/O79/12.

[106] For similar dynamics in Yoruba territories, see J. D. Y. Peel, "The Pastor and the *Babalawo*: The Interaction of Religions in Nineteenth-Century Yorubaland," *Africa*, 60.3 (1990): 338–369.

supreme power. Diviners were of central importance since the success of the religious community in the African diaspora was in part contingent on the presence of ritual guides. Raimundo Nina Rodrigues argued in the 1930s that "Yoruba superiority" in Brazil was due to a highly organized priesthood.[107] Pierre Verger similarly postulated that the predominance of Yoruba religious institutions in northeastern Brazil was partly due to "the presence among them of many prisoners of war of high social class and also of priests, aware of the value of their institutions, and firmly attached to the precepts of their religion."[108] This assertion is difficult to prove or disprove concretely based on evidence from Sierra Leone, though *babalawos* are the only particular rival religious figures mentioned in missionary sources (along with Muslim *alufa*), and the multiple references to these individuals suggests that many arrived on board captured slave vessels.

Egungun

The persistence of the cult of Ṣàngó and the intransigence of the *babalawos* were not the only form of Yoruba religious praxis to continually frustrate the efforts of the Christian mission in Sierra Leone. One of the most commonly cited Yoruba religious practices in nineteenth-century Sierra Leone was the Egungun, a masquerade of ancestor reverence. References to the Egungun in the CMS archive exceed all other aspects of Yoruba cosmology, other than the cult of Ṣàngó.

The Yoruba make a distinction between "gods" and "ancestors," a common division in the cosmologies of West African peoples.[109] Ancestors began as known individuals, quite different from *orişa*. In life, as elders, they were credited with a great deal of power; but funerals greatly elevated the powers of the deceased. Egungun in Yorubaland did not represent a specific deceased individual, but the embodiment of a particular lineage's ancestors returned to earth. The Egungun (lit. "powers concealed") is a representation of the dead that is given its own name, and is regarded as the collective spirit of ancestors known as Ara Orun (dwellers of heaven). Ancestral spirits

---

[107] Raimundo Nina Rodrigues, *Os Africanos no Brasil* (São Paulo: Companhia Editorial Nacional, 1932).
[108] Verger, *Trade Relations*, 1.   [109] Peel, *Religious Encounter*, 93.

are seen to be closer to the living than the oriṣa, and are called on to protect the community against various evils and maladies. The appearance of the Egungun is thus a rededication of closeness with ancestors, though it is regarded as dangerous for ancestral spirits to dominate daily life.[110]

Given the importance of ancestors in many African religions, comparatively little is known of how first-generation enslaved Africans in the diaspora imagined their relationship to their deceased forebears.[111] But the persistent manifestation of the Egungun in Sierra Leone (first recorded by missionary witnesses in 1844) to the present day underscores the centrality of ancestors and a community of the living and the Ara Orun across generations. A. B. Ellis, the soldier and writer who spent much of his career in West Africa, wrote in 1894, that

> a large proportion of the slaves landed at Sierra Leone, at the beginning of the present century, from slave-ships captured by British cruisers, were Yorubas, and their Christian descendants have preserved the practice of Egungun, who may often be seen performing his antics in the streets of Freetown ... Spectators soon gather round him, and though, if asked, they will tell you that it is only "play," many of them are half-doubtful, and whenever the Egungun makes a rush forward the crowd flees before him to escape his touch.[112]

Ellis's observations say a great deal about the aesthetics, theatrics, and importance of the Egungun, some thirty-five years after the last Aku recaptives reached Sierra Leone. Ornamentally, the Egungun consists of multiple layers of cloth, and the ensemble itself acts as the medium for the masker's transformation into his ancestors. Based on his travels, Ellis observed how in Sierra Leone "his disguise is less elaborate than in Yoruba country, and he appears in a long robe of cotton-print, with a piece of cloth, having apertures for the eyes, covering the face and head." Crowther explained: "The Egung appears always covered with a cloth like a pair of sheets sewn together lengthways, and ornamented

---

[110] S. O. Babayemi, *Egungun among the Oyo Yoruba* (Ibadan: Board Publications, 1980), 1.
[111] Kristin Mann, "Shifting Paradigms in the Study of the African Diaspora and of Atlantic History and Culture," in Kristin Mann and Edna G. Bay (eds.), *Rethinking the African Diaspora: The Making of a Black Atlantic World in the Bight of Benin and Brazil* (London: Frank Cass, 2001), 4.
[112] A. B. Ellis, *The Yoruba-Speaking Peoples of the Slave Coast of West Africa* (London: Curzon Books, 1974 [1894]), 109.

with different kinds of coloured cloth which make the whole dress appear like a patchwork. The face is made of net and decorated with cowries that the Egung might see the more easily when he parades about the streets."[113]

Egungun in Yorubaland sometimes adopted a style of provocative confrontation, especially toward missionaries.[114] This proclivity carried over to Sierra Leone. One such incident reached the pages of the CMS publications in England. In 1853 James Beale responded vociferously to "an egugu, or Aku (Yoruba) devil, with a party of heathen ... [who] went drumming and dancing by my church, and in front of my house" while he was preparing for an evening service (Figure 6.1). Beale explained that "these grotesque figures – which the people believe to be the spirits of their departed forefathers, and which they therefore greatly fear – come out six or seven together." He lamented that "these open exhibitions of idolatry have become much bolder than before" and "determined to expose the cheat on the first opportunity, so that, if the people *would* continue to follow it, they should not do so ignorantly." When the Egungun passed Beale, the missionary attempted to unmask the performer. The altercation escalated as followers of the Egungun surrounded the intruder:

In a short time a large crowd gathered round; but none, not even my servants, dared for some time to help me.... Finding, however, that I could not hold out longer against so many, I tore off his upper garment in shreds, and then, seizing his under garments at the bottom, drew them over his head, and so stripped him before all the people. Underneath were many charms, and other badges of superstition. When the crowd saw that the egugu was not only a human being like themselves, but known to many, they raised a loud shout – the heathen in derision, and the Christians in thankful exultation – upon which his defenders slipped off and left him alone in my hands.[115]

For his supposed indiscretion the Egungun dancer was handed over to the constable, before Beale offered clemency if he agreed to attend church.

The encounter between Beale and the Egungun highlights several aspects of the contest between representatives of the official church and

---

[113] Crowther, June 25, 1844, CMS/CA1/O79/12.
[114] Peel, *Religious Encounter*, 58.
[115] Beale, quoted in *Church Missionary Paper*, no. 151, Michaelmas 1853.

Figure 6.1 "Mr. Beale Seizing the Egugu"
(*Church Missionary Paper*, No. 151, Michaelmas, 1853)

figures that the Aku took to be the physical manifestation of their forebears. The CMS journals of the 1840s and 1850s describe Egungun processions more commonly than prior decades. More significant was Beale's observation that the Egungun and its followers "have become much bolder than before." Crowther similarly noted in 1844 how the Egungun "are growing bold, not only openly in the villages do they parade, but also in Freetown, and have become stumbling blocks to many newly arrived liberated Africans of the Yoruba nation."[116] Charles Davies, a Krio pastor of Aku parentage, lamented how one Egungun procession was "so daring as not to content themselves with disturbing us at some distance, but to proceed so far as to be coming to the church gate, loudly beating and dancing; and *that* whilst we were engaged in our Thursday evening service."[117] As Matory points out, Aku masking societies modeled on the Egungun became a "cultural diacritic," marking and reinforcing group identity in emphatic fashion.[118]

---

[116] Crowther, June 25, 1844, CMS/CA1/O79/12.
[117] Davies, Journal for the half year ending March 31, 1857, CMS/CA1/O81/2.
[118] Matory, "The English Professors of Brazil," 92.

As Chapter 5 showed, funeral rites were central to community because death was an omnipresent reality in the colony. One these occasions, the Egungun often featured prominently. George James Macaulay provides the most detailed account of Aku funeral customs in this period. In a diatribe entitled "Heathen Custom," Macaulay described how "the custom of going to the grave yard to ascertain from the dead, the locality assigned them in the other world, is prevalent among them." Macaulay continued:

On the night of the seventh day after the death of an individual, women and men proceed to the burial ground, headed by Agea,[119] an Egugu or devil supposed to be an inhabitant of the nether regions, to know from him his present state, as an inhabitant of the other world. Previous to their going hither, a man is sent to conceal himself in the bush, dressed all in white, to personify the dead & respond to whatever questions might be put to him by the people who stood at a certain distance, whilst the Agea who holds a midway between the living and the dead returns the answer in an audible tone, as the dead generally speak in soft tones & cannot be directly heard.[120]

Crowther noted how in these ceremonies "[t]he Egung speaks with a deep hoarseness quite different from the natural voice of man," adding that "this is the voice of the spirit of dead men not to be imitated under a severe penalty."[121]

Among the Aku, Egungun became a pan-ethnic fraternity that transcended ethnopolitical divisions among Yoruba speakers.[122] The Egungun tied Liberated Africans and their descendants with their deceased forebears. It was also a reaction against Anglo-Christian cultural chauvinism. For these reasons, the Egungun continued to parade the streets of the Sierra Leone peninsula long after the era of receptive arrivals. At Wellington in 1871, George James Macaulay disparaged "a notorious class of young people in the village who were resolved to perpetuate the heathen practices of their parents" and had "formed themselves into a club with a view to keep up the Egugu dance ... for which in years gone by Wellington was very remarkable."[123]

---

[119] Perhaps *alágbàá,* an *Egungun* priest/family elder who presides over the ancestral rites.
[120] Macaulay, Half yearly report, September 1861, CMS/CA1/O141/20.
[121] Crowther, Extracts of journals for the quarter ending June 25, 1844, CMS/CA1/O79/12.
[122] Ojo, "'Heepa' (Hail) Òrìṣà," 39.
[123] Macaulay, letter, Wellington, March 13, 1871, CMS/CA1/O141/6.

Egungun masquerades continued into the twentieth century, by which time their name had morphed to *agugu*, and were also known as the "Yoruba Club" or *oje*.[124] *Agugu* seems to have been particularly strong in the village of Hastings, as well as the Fourah Bay community of Freetown. At Fourah Bay many of the followers were also Muslim, despite Islam's objections to worshipping the dead. Within this community *agugu* rituals were timed to coincide with the three major Muslim holy days, underscoring how Islam and "traditional religion" were not always mutually exclusive in quotidian practice.[125] The persistence of the Egungun was such that "Egungun" is sometimes used as the shorthand for retained Yoruba religious customs in Sierra Leone, much the same way that in Trinidad "Sango" is synecdoche for customs of Yoruba origin.

Conclusion

Yoruba speakers remained uniquely visible wherever they went in the diaspora, and in Sierra Leone they perhaps formed a larger segment of the population than in any slave society of the Americas. Yet the ubiquitous references to "Aku" as the largest, most cohesive, and most influential "nation" among recaptives cannot be reduced to numerical dominance. Compared with other ethnic groups in the colony, there was a conscious effort by educated Christian Yoruba to forge a pan-Yoruba/Aku identity based on common language. These ethnic entrepreneurs engaged in what J. D. Y. Peel has referred to as the "cultural work" of Yoruba ethnogenesis.[126]

The scale of the Yoruba migration to Sierra Leone and the conscious effort to promote an Aku identity based on a codified common language were complemented by the movement of Yoruba speakers between Freetown and the Bight of Benin. Robin Law and Kristin Mann have adopted the phrase "Atlantic community" to describe the similar transoceanic social and cultural connections between the coastal communities of the Bight of Benin, the Americas (especially Brazil), and Europe. This conceptualization moves past assessing the influence of West Africa on the diaspora and vice versa, focusing on

---

[124] Peterson, *Province of Freedom*, 264; *Sierra Leone Weekly News*, September 20, 1924.
[125] Harrell-Bond et al., *Community Leadership*, 111.
[126] Peel, "The Cultural Work of Yoruba Ethnogenesis."

reciprocal cultural influences, often involving the same persons. If anything, the bilateral connections between the Bight of Benin and Sierra Leone were even greater than those with Brazil, in terms of proximity, the demographic scale of the movement, receptive involvement in trade and ship ownership, and the movement of returnees and the accompanying Christian missions inland from the coast.[127]

Finally, nineteenth-century Sierra Leone was part of a much broader Atlantic diaspora of *orisa* devotees. Perhaps in no other diasporic setting did *orisa* devotees comprise such a large segment of the population. Yet Sierra Leone has been conspicuously omitted from recent historiographical discussions of *orisa* devotion as a transatlantic and even global religion.[128] This occlusion within the scholarship likely derives from the fact that Sierra Leone did not produce a syncretized religion, such as *Santería* in Cuba or *Candomblé* in Brazil, in which Yoruba elements persist to the present. But the fact that *orisa* cults in Sierra Leone have fared poorly compared with their New World counterparts over the last century and a half should not lead us to overlook how they formed a central aspect of communal life in the nineteenth century.

J. Lorand Matory has observed that "diasporas are often studied as though time had stopped in the homeland" and that all too often for historians "homelands are to their diasporas as the past is to the present and future."[129] Matory has called for a nonlinear interpretation of diasporas, in which a dialectical approach is taken to the relationship between diasporas and homelands around the Atlantic perimeter. Certainly, what it meant to be Aku in Sierra Leone and what it meant to be Yoruba in Yorubaland were defined and reinforced through a dialogue along the Atlantic coast of West Africa.

---

[127] Law and Mann, "West Africa and the Atlantic Community," 307–334.
[128] The essays in Olupona and Rey make only one reference to Sierra Leone, while neither recent volumes on Ṣàngó and Ògún mention Sierra Leone as an important place of worship for these *orisa*. See Olupona and Rey (eds.), *Òrìsà Devotion as World Religion*; Sandra T. Barnes (ed.), *Africa's Ogun: Old World and New* (Bloomington: Indiana University Press, 1997); Falola and Genova (eds.), *Orisa: Yoruba Gods and Spiritual Identity*; Tishken et al. (eds.), *Ṣàngó in Africa and the African Diaspora*.
[129] Matory, *Black Atlantic Religion*, 3.

7 | The Cobolo War
Islam, Identity, and Resistance

In November 1832, alarm quickly spread through Freetown and the peninsular villages. A group of "Mahommedan Aku" recaptives who had previously vacated the colony were now assembling near a location called Cobolo, seemingly poised to attack the colony's eastern villages of Waterloo, Hastings, and Wellington. When the Aku began to accost local traders, colonial troops were dispatched to patrol the area. A brief skirmish between the soldiers and their Muslim adversaries left one British soldier killed. In response, Lieutenant-Governor Alexander Findlay ordered an attack on the Aku settlement of Cobolo, located along the Ribi River (Map 3.1). Findlay estimated the Aku force to be 1,000 and feared more would join.[1] Later he would admit there was only 100 Aku, 50 of whom were killed or drowned trying to escape.[2]

The Cobolo War – as colonial officials labeled the skirmish – has been described by John Peterson as the first organized opposition to Britain's colonial government.[3] But what were the motivations of those whom colonial officials identified as Muslims, Yoruba speakers, and rebels? The "war" was contemporaneous with a pattern of violent resistance to colonial oppression instigated by Yoruba speakers around the Atlantic world in the 1830s and 1840s. In the aftermath of the collapse of Oyo, the spread of jihad, and the ensuing Yoruba wars, the diffusion of Yoruba-speaking slaves to Cuba and northeastern Brazil led to a series of rebellions involving captives from the Bight on Benin.

This chapter situates the Cobolo War in a comparative, Atlantic perspective, looking at the role of ethnicity and religion in mobilizing the Cobolo militants and how this compares with the famed 1835 Malê Rebellion in Brazil and a series of Yoruba-led rebellions in Cuba

---

[1] Findlay to Crawford, November 17, 1832, Governor's Letter Book, 1827–1832, SLPA.
[2] Findlay to Goderich, May 15, 1833, LADLB 1831–1834.
[3] Peterson, *Province of Freedom*, 212.

in the 1830s and 1840s. Was the Cobolo War analogous to these New World slave rebellions? And, if so, what does the event tell us about the interaction with ethnic and religious identity among Liberated Africans? The chapter traces the buildup, instigation, suppression, and ultimate defeat of the Cobolo community. It then examines the ensuing government campaign of intimidation and repression, toppling mosques that Muslim Liberated Africans had built as they moved into communities to ensure their religious autonomy. Finally, it explores the legacies of the Cobolo conflict for Muslim and ethnic identity in the colony. The legacy of the Cobolo War was ultimately far more significant than the event itself. Its aftermath had implications for the contours of Aku identity through the remaining decades of the nineteenth century as after Cobolo, and well into the twentieth century, "Aku" became increasingly associated with Islam and subversion.

Lovejoy has argued that for Muslims in the diaspora, ethnic identity was subordinated to the religious community.[4] Islam could be a unifying identity that transcended ethnicity, a bridge in community formation between Liberated Africans from regions of Islamic practice such as the Bight of Benin, with fellow recaptives, as well as traders and other free people from the vicinity of the Sierra Leone colony. But the Islamic reform movements of nineteenth-century West Africa produced a complex interplay between religious and ethnic identities.[5] Religion and ethnicity offered related but contrasting mechanisms for group identity, and Muslim communities in the diaspora often retained a series of ethnic/religious layers.[6] This chapter explores how Islam provided a path to empowerment and symbolic resistance to colonialism, while also exploring the tensions of group consciousness among those who identified as Muslim and as Aku. The chapter further delineates the process of Aku ethnogenesis described in Chapter 6.

Islam and the Sierra Leone Peninsula

As Chapter 1 showed, the Liberated African population included a visible contingent of Muslims, particularly those identified in colonial and missionary sources as "Hausa," "Tapa" (i.e., Nupe), and

[4] Paul Lovejoy, "Trans-Atlantic Transformations," 127.
[5] Nugent, "Putting the History Back into Ethnicity," 922.
[6] Paul E. Lovejoy, "Slavery, the Bilād al-Sūdān, and the Frontiers of the African Diaspora," in Lovejoy (ed.), *Slavery on the Frontiers of Islam*, 5.

"Borno." The large population of Yoruba speakers would also have included a proportion of Muslims. However, a range of evidence – the prevalence of Muslim names in the Liberated African registers, colonial census data, and contemporary qualitative observations – all suggests that the total number of Liberated African Muslims was small. While Islam had long influenced Yoruba societies, it is unlikely that at the beginning of the nineteenth century Islam had been adopted by more than a small minority of the Oyo–Yoruba and hardly at all by non-Oyo.[7] Yoruba societies had long absorbed elements of Islamic culture without any requirement of conversion. Still, many recaptives who left Oyo enslaved did so before the conversion of that population, while many other Yoruba speakers such as the Egba arrived in the colony with little introduction to Islam. The population derisively termed "Mahomedan Aku" or "Aku Mahomedans" by colonial officials was therefore relatively small, especially compared with the amount of time and energy officials spent monitoring their movements and proscribing their activities.

Liberated African Muslims would have been used to being a minority in West Africa, having lived in enclaves in towns along trade routes and the capitals and main towns of the non-Muslim states near the coast. In Sierra Leone, they were a minority in a British colony with the explicit goal of Christian evangelization in Africa. As elsewhere in the diaspora, they struggled to sustain the institutions of their faith and reconstitute the Muslim *jamā'a* (community) in ways that fitted into an existing pattern of group identity and cultural survival.[8] Sustaining the five pillars of the faith – literacy in Arabic, dietary restrictions, and religiously sanctioned customs of naming, marriage, and death – required Liberated Africans to interact with Muslims beyond the peninsula and to retrench themselves within a hostile social environment.

Aku Muslims were an increasing presence in the easterly villages of the peninsula, such as Waterloo, Hastings, and Wellington. These villages grew in the period coinciding with the collapse of Oyo and the large-scale arrival of enslaved Yoruba on intercepted slave vessels. According to the Liberated African Registers, some 4,306 Liberated Africans had been sent to Waterloo and Hastings by the end of 1832.

---

[7] Peel, *Christianity, Islam, and the Oriṣa*, 151.
[8] Lovejoy, "Slavery, the Bilād al-Sūdān, and the Frontiers of the African Diaspora," 3.

Among these individuals, 1,833 had embarked at ports of the Bight of Benin, of whom 949 had been sold as slaves at Lagos.[9] The populations of these villages were far from static. While the colonial government sent many individuals of similar backgrounds to the same Liberated African villages, others subsequently moved voluntarily to be in closer proximity to those of the same faith. The 1831 census of the colony enumerated 3,324 inhabitants in the district of Waterloo, 2,663 inhabitants in the Hastings district, and 2,812 in the district of Wellington.[10]

On the eve of the Cobolo War, the villages of Waterloo and Hastings had a large Yoruba-speaking population and a visible contingent of Muslims among them. Much like in Salvador de Bahia, the close physical distance between Muslims was fundamental to community, religious observance, and, ultimately, resistance to colonial repression. The arrival of captives from the Bight of Benin in the aftermath of these villages' founding in 1819 means that the concentration of Muslims in these villages was likely greater than in most regions of the Americas, and comparable to the situation in Bahia after 1804. In Sierra Leone, like Bahia, the number of Muslims was substantial enough to develop a sense of community that was impossible in most parts of the diaspora.

A key factor in the coalescence of Muslim Liberated Africans and resistance to colonial oversight was that Yoruba and Hausa speakers were disembarking in a region of long-standing Islamic practice. This was a unique feature of Sierra Leone's African diaspora, since Muslims in the New World were far removed from societies that followed the Islamic faith. The colony bordered regions long influenced by Muslim merchants, teachers, and political elites. The "yula tribes" (*jūla*: Mande merchant families, from the Arabic *jaulah*, "circuit/travel") along with Muslim scholars and powerful political/military leaders had established Islam in territories adjacent to the Sierra Leone peninsula well before the eighteenth century.[11]

---

[9] Despite the strong association between these villages and Yoruba Liberated Africans, the data show that for the period of 1820–1832, more Liberated Africans sent to Waterloo came from the Bight of Biafra (869) than the Bight of Benin (761).

[10] 1831 Census of Population and Liberated Africans, CO 267/111.

[11] For this broader history, see Alusine Jalloh and David E. Skinner (eds.), *Islam and Trade in Sierra Leone* (Trenton, NJ: Africa World Press, 1997); David E. Skinner, "The Influence of Islam in Sierra Leone History: Institutions, Practices, and Leadership," *Journal of West African History*, 2.1(2016): 27–72.

The political and economic contacts between the colony and surrounding Muslim communities intensified in the period after the 1807 declaration of the Crown Colony. In the 1810s, Muslim migrants constructed the residential areas of Bambara Town and Foulah Town. Sarakuli, Susu, Temne, and Limba immigrants formed other Muslim communities on and near the peninsula. Muslim scholars and traders were regular visitors to and, eventually, residents of the colony. Koelle's informants included Mohammadu, a Fulbe trader from Futa Jallon, and Abdallahi Serif, born in Timbuktu and a "teacher of Arabic in Freetown, in which capacity he earns a comfortable living."[12] This population, referred to by colonial officials as both immigrant "natives" and "strangers," was modest and transient. But they formed the nuclei of emerging communities, which included prominently among them those who taught the Qur'an, led prayers, and manufactured amulets.[13]

Though colonial censuses could not properly enumerate such a shifting population, their numbers were estimated at 1,009 in 1817 and 3,113 in 1826, consisting primarily of traders drawn to Freetown. They were a sizable presence alongside a colonial population of 13,020.[14] The Sierra Leone peninsula was therefore a meeting point of two internal African diasporas: Muslim traders extending their economic and educational networks and Muslims from the Bight of Benin and Upper Guinea who reached the colony's shores on intercepted slave vessels.

Members of these two overlapping diasporas carved out new spaces and opportunities to practice their faith. Much like nineteenth-century Bahia, Sierra Leone became a diaspora in which Islam not only persisted but found new converts. The Rev. John Gerber lamented that "in my present sphere of labour, I have as yet at least at Waterloo and Campbell Town very little encouragement." Gerber believed that there were "upwards of 100 Mohammedons residing" at Waterloo in 1828, "who also endeavor to make proselites [sic] and who not unfrequently succeed."[15] Familiarity with Arabic facilitated Islamic conversion. Henry Townsend of the CMS lamented how "the Mohammedans are

---

[12] Koelle, *Polyglotta Africana*, 17.
[13] Harrell-Bond, Howard, and Skinner, *Community Leadership*, 44–48.
[14] 1827 Commission of Enquiry, CO 267/91.
[15] Gerber, Waterloo, July 16, 1828, CMS/CA1/O101.

able to teach in their own tongue their religion, and thus, often, before newly liberated Africans can acquire enough English to receive instructions from us, they are laid lots of by the Mohammedans and instructed and made proselytes to their faith, before they have an opportunity of hearing the gospel of Christ."[16] Missionaries and colonial officials looked on with suspicion at Islam's seeming advantages and success in a manifestly Christian colony.

Premonitions of Violence

The 1832 Cobolo War had a long prelude amid a context of official distrust of Muslims. Fears of an Aku attack on the settlement emerged as the British observed many receptives leaving the villages they had been assigned to. Since at least 1826 many Aku Muslims were removing themselves outside the colony's boundaries and beyond British jurisdiction. They settled at a location called Cobolo, previously a Sherbro village situated beyond Waterloo where the Sierra Leone peninsula met the Upper Guinea coast. In December 1826, Rev. J. G. Wilhelm, the Waterloo superintendent, warned of "many runaways and vagrants from other stations of the Colony passing through Waterloo, armed with cutlasses, and some also with firearms." More worrying to the missionary was "an alarming report raised among the inhabitants here, that those stragglers were gathering together somewhere for the purpose of attacking and plundering this station." Leaders of a village near Waterloo had informed him that "about 20 men of the Accoo nation had just passed his village, all armed with cutlasses, and when he asked them whither they wanted to go, they said, 'into the Sherbro country.'"[17]

Thomas Cole, Chief Superintendent of the Liberated African Department, visited the area soon after and, like Wilhelm, became convinced that a Muslim rebellion was imminent. Cole informed his superiors that:

A rumour has spread, by some persons unknown, that a great number of Ackoos, from the different villages have assembled on a new road near Maharra where they have built two large houses, and armed themselves,

[16] Townsend, Extracts for quarter ending December 25, 1839, CMS/CA1/O215/24.
[17] Wilhelm, Report of Waterloo for Christmas 1826, CMS/CA1/M4.

Premonitions of Violence 233

for the purpose of coming down, to plunder Waterloo, destroy all the houses, and murder all who offer resistance.[18]

Wilhelm feared that a Christmas attack was probable since the villages' discharged soldiers – the bulk of his militia – would be in Freetown to collect their pensions. When Cole mustered the Waterloo Liberated Africans, he found that some were missing and concluded that they too had joined the incipient rebellion.[19] In response to Cole's report, Governor Campbell dispatched fifteen soldiers and twenty-six militia men "and muskets and a great quantity of cartridges were furnished in store." When thirteen Yoruba recaptives entered Waterloo, Rev. Wilhelm questioned the "armed vagabonds" before sending them to jail in Freetown.[20]

Six years before the Cobolo War, rumors of insurrection were unsettling wary colonial officials. After Governor Campbell came to Waterloo to survey the scene in late 1826, he reassigned Wilhelm to York. Campbell's private Secretary noted that Wilhelm's removal from Waterloo was ultimately due to his paranoia and fear.[21] After Wilhelm's departure no missionary was stationed in Waterloo for the next six years, meaning there was opportunity for non-Christian cultural and religious practices to flourish. The tense climate in the eastern villages only escalated in the period after Wilhelm's removal. A newly appointed Lieutenant-Governor, Alexander Findlay, arrived in 1830 and embarked on a campaign of surveillance, restricting movement and non-Christian religious expression within the colony. Findlay anxiously believed that Mandinka and Fulbe Muslims had converted the Aku to Islam. Suspicion of itinerant Muslims led Thomas Cole to suggest to the governor "to cause measures to be adopted for interdicting the Mandingoes and the people denominated 'Book Men' from coming into the villages."[22]

Findlay replaced the missionary superintendents in the villages with secular managers, appointing J. Auguin to Wilhelm's old post at Waterloo. The Liberated African Department instructed Auguin to curtail the movement of those who would "abscond from the places

---

[18] Extract from Mr. Cole's letter, Waterloo, December 8, 1826, CO 267/81.
[19] Peterson, *Province of Freedom*, 213.
[20] Wilhelm, Report of Waterloo for Christmas 1826, CMS/CA1/M4.
[21] Rishton to Haensell, July 21, 1827, Governor's Letterbook 1825–1827, SLPA.
[22] Cole to Gerber, September 11, 1830, LADLB 1830–1831.

where they were first located."[23] He was given the authority to fine or arrest those seeking to relocate, those who harbored runaway Liberated Africans, and "all strangers who they may find within the district who cannot give a satisfactory account of themselves."

Findlay's heavy-handedness continued when, annoyed at the pace of Christian conversion in the colony, he prohibited sacrifices to "idols" in August 1830. The proclamation was not targeted specifically at Muslims; if anything, it was directed at the intransigence of devotees of Ṣàngó, Ifá, and the Egungun. But Findlay's stance was a reiteration of Christian hegemony in a British colony, and led in turn to a ramping-up of official repression of Muslims in and around Freetown. John Peterson notes that whenever a government official attempted to enforce the order, another wave of Aku flight resulted and the dissident community outside the colony swelled.[24]

Colonial officials and missionaries nervously monitored the movement of Liberated Africans navigating into and out of British territory. In September 1830 John Gerber, the resident missionary at Hastings, wrote to colonial authorities that he was "apprehensive that a great number of Ackoos are about to leave the colony in an unlawful manner" and that they were "making preparations to carry their seditious project into action."[25] Gerber was sanctioned to apprehend the ringleaders for unlawful movement. The testimony of three apprehended men – identified as Ogubah, Odohdoo, and Soko – stated that

> they are of the Mahomedan faith in their own country and never having received any interruption since they were brought to this Colony, in the performance of their religious duties, they imagined that it was tolerated, but they declared that none of them have been made proselytes through the intervention of the Mandingoes and Foulahs.[26]

No account is given of what happened to the three men following their interrogations. But the questions posed to them reflected a half-decade of colonial anxieties: a disbelief that Liberated African Aku had been Muslims prior to their enslavement and a certainty that Mandinka and Fulbe "book men" were winning many converts among discontented colonists.

---

[23] Cole to Auguim, April 1, 1831, LADLB 1830–1831.
[24] Peterson, *Province of Freedom*, 214.
[25] Cole to Gerber, Hastings, September 4, 1830, LADLB 1830–1831.
[26] Cole to Gerber, Hastings, September 11, 1830, LADLB 1830–1831.

An atmosphere of suspicion and hearsay prevailed in the aftermath of Findlay's prohibitions. By January 1831, Thomas Cole was confident that "there were no grounds for apprehending that any serious riot was about to take place on the part of the Akoos who were stated to have assembled on the Maharrah road" and cautioned against being constantly "kept in alarm by a set of miscreants who appear to have nothing else to do than to excite a commotion among the more peaceable inhabitants of the villages."[27] But by October the alarm was palpable. Frederick Campbell, Cole's colleague in the Liberated African Department, instructed the village manager at Waterloo to swear in seven special constables with strict orders to apprehend "all strangers in the village" and make sure that all disbanded soldiers in the village had their weapons in serviceable condition for any potential altercation.[28]

The attack did not materialize. Over the next year reports nevertheless persisted, warning that "there is a certain insurrection setting on foot by those evil disposed and discontented Mahommandan Ackko." Reports trickled in that those based at Cobolo were plundering nearby farms and probing south into Sherbro territory. Sierra Leonean traders operating in Sherbro country warned that the Aku had seized their canoes and property.[29] The colonial government informed Thomas Caulker, the chief of the neighboring Plantain Islands, that the Aku had moved into his territory and had "committed several depredations on the other subjects of this Colony who have been trading there." Findlay requested that Caulker apprehend the interlopers, adding that "they are all of the Ackoo Nation ... Consequently your people can have no difficulty in finding the parties."[30] Christopher Fyfe has suggested that it was Caulker who had in fact secretly induced the Aku to help him in a conflict with the Temne, and promised that if they did he would show them a route back to their own country.[31]

Even as the Aku moved beyond the peninsula, Findlay, Cole, and others were as convinced as ever that an attack on the eastern villages was imminent. In November 1832, informants spotted a force of one

---

[27] Cole to Coker, January 15, 1831, LADLB 1830–1831.
[28] Campbell to John Thorpe, Manager, Waterloo, October 21, 1831, LADLB 1830–1831.
[29] Findlay to Goderich, December 5, 1832, CO 267/115.
[30] Campbell to Thomas Caulker, October 21, 1832, LADLB 1831–1834.
[31] Fyfe, *History of Sierra Leone*, 186.

hundred Liberated Africans from Hastings, Waterloo, and Campbell Town assembled on the Maharra Road waiting for others to arrive from Wellington, Kissy, and York.[32] C. B. Jones, the assistant superintendent of the Liberated African Department, sent an urgent message to John Dougherty, the manager at Hastings, instructing him to call up all of the militia volunteers of Hastings and Waterloo and to arm them in preparation for "intercepting those who are reported will pass Waterloo tonight."[33] Once again the invasion was illusory, but Findlay and his subordinates had now settled on attacking and apprehending the recalcitrant Aku.

The "War"

Six years had elapsed since the first whisperings of Aku restlessness. What transpired next – the chronology of this "war" – comes to us entirely through colonial documents designed to justify the capture, incarceration, and potential execution of the accused. Under Dougherty and Waterloo manager Jacob Hazeley, the combined village volunteer forces marched on Cobolo. Marching from Waterloo they arrived at dusk on November 14 and prepared for a dawn attack. Hazeley formed an advanced guard of sixty men, pushing forward through grass fields and mangrove swamps. They reached the higher ground of Cobolo to find the Aku waiting in the bush. Findlay had given "strict orders not to fire upon the Ackoos unless they resisted" and to take them prisoner if possible.[34] Later in court, witnesses – all sided with the British – were adamant that the Aku fired first.[35] Six volunteers and a bugler died in the melee; Findlay estimated that sixteen Aku had died.[36] In the midst of the firefight the British volunteer force panicked and fled, retreating down the road toward Waterloo.

Dougherty was now convinced that the Aku would rather die than be taken alive. He knew that they were well stocked with muskets,

---

[32] Hazeley to Jones, November 11, 1832, CO 267/115.
[33] Jones to Dougherty, November 12, 1832, LADLB 1831–1834.
[34] Findlay to Goderich, December 5, 1832, CO 267/115.
[35] Secretary's Office Letter Book Private & Confidential Police Record Book, SLPA.
[36] Findlay to Goderich, December 5, 1832, CO 267/115.

bows and arrows, cutlasses, and ammunition.[37] Findlay, frustrated by "this unfortunate disaster and the shameful conduct of the volunteers," called up the Wellington Company of the Sierra Leone Militia and the Hastings company of volunteers. The governor also requested that Lieutenant Crawford, the commander of HMS *Charybdis*, proceed to the Ribi River and attack the Cobolo militants from the rear, stopping along the way to pick up the York village volunteers. At this time Findlay falsely believed that the Cobolo Aku had been "augmented to the number of 1000" and discharged his two-pronged attacking force to apprehend them.[38]

Before Findlay's offensive could assault Cobolo they found that their enemy had vanished. In the time it had taken the British to reassemble their forces, the local Loco and Temne people had exacted revenge on the Cobolo Aku for having displaced them and plundered their farms. Perhaps taking advantage of the Aku's debilitated state, the Loco and Temne attacked and dislodged the Aku from their fortifications. More than fifty Aku were killed or drowned as they attempted to flee and cross the river.

Surviving documents identify the leader of the Cobolo Aku as "Ojoe Corrie," possibly a corruption of Kure, a praise name or alias for the name "Ojo" in the Yoruba language.[39] Following his defeat at Cobolo, Ojoe Corrie fled south to the Sherbro territory. He found no safety in the territory of Chief Thomas Caulker, especially as Findlay had earlier requested that Caulker comply in apprehending all Aku who entered his jurisdiction. Caulker led his men against the fleeing Aku, killing the Cobolo leader and two others. He then personally delivered five Aku prisoners to Freetown, bringing with him the right ear of Ojoe Corrie.[40] With the Aku routed, the British troops returned to Freetown. A detachment of the 2nd West India Regiment remained at Waterloo to surveil the movements of Muslims in the Liberated African villages.[41]

---

[37] Dougherty to Findlay, November 15, 1832, CO 267/115.
[38] Findlay to Crawford, November 17, 1832, Governor's Letter Book, 1827–1832, SLPA.
[39] Personal correspondence with Olatunji Ojo, May 30, 2017. "Ojo" is the name given to a male child born with the umbilical cord around his neck.
[40] Findlay to Goderich, December 5, 1832, CO 267/115.
[41] A. B. Ellis, *The History of the First West India Regiment* (London: Chapman and Hall, 1885), 185–187.

In a lengthy correspondence to the Secretary of State not long after the event, Governor Findlay confidently concluded:

> By the evidence which has come out in the examinations of some of the prisoners, there is strong reason to suppose that a deep concerted rebellious plan had been laid by the Mahommadan Ackoos, and that Christmas was the time fixed for an attack on Freetown, the only reason which has as yet been assigned as the cause of this rebellion on the part the Ackoos, is, that by killing all the white men they would be able to get back to their country.[42]

But the actual intention of the Yoruba Muslim contingent was less obvious than the official narrative Findlay perpetuated. As was often the case, colonial governments chose the terminology to describe what occurred, perhaps consciously inflating its severity. The historiography on Sierra Leone has tended to accept uncritically the depiction of these events as a "war" or "rebellion," thereby reifying the colonial interpretation of events. F. Harrison Rankin suggested as such in 1836 when referring to the "Akoo rebellion, as it has been humorously called."[43] Much like in colonies of the Americas, an attempt at armed and violent escape was termed a "war" and its instigators "rebels" by European observers.

It is unlikely then that the conflict developed the way documents portray it. Rather than fomenting a rebellion or "war" to overthrow the colonial order, the motivation of those who left the colony was likely to practice their Islamic faith or their devotion to the *orișa* outside the confines of colonial control and oversight in the villages. Findlay postulated based on little evidence that "a parcel of Mandingo Mahomedans" had tempted the Aku to leave the colony with the promise to guide them to their "Native homes," a supposed subterfuge to re-enslave the Liberated Africans.[44] The Cobolo rebels were more likely simply engaged in a form of *marronnage*, or what Barry Gaspar has termed "avoidance protest."[45] Their actions may also reflect the teachings of Uthmān dan Fodio in his *jihād fi sabīl Allāh* (jihad in the path of Allah) that military confrontation was a last resort and that commitment to the faith was based initially on withdrawal and

---

[42] Findlay to Goderich, December 5, 1832, CO 267/115.
[43] Rankin, *White Man's Grave*, vol. 1, 212–213.
[44] Findlay to Goderich, May 15, 1833, LADLB 1831–1834.
[45] David Barry Gaspar, "Runaways in Seventeenth Century Antigua, West Indies," *Boletin de Estudos Latinoamericas y del Caribe* (June 1979): 3–13.

avoidance of confrontation.[46] Cobolo may therefore be more analogous to fugitive communities of *quilombos* and *mocambos* in Brazil and *palenques* in Cuba.

Cobolo was likely a community of escape, rather than an encampment for attack. Findlay himself praised Cobolo's defensive qualities. Several of his officers told him that Cobolo was "situated on a rising ground almost surrounded by swamps with only two admissible small passes which were barricaded with doors from the huts, and covered with green hides." He concluded that "a more advantageous position could not have been taken by the most scientific general."[47] Elizabeth Helen Melville provides the most complete first-hand description of the Cobolo settlement. Melville described how "the village itself was neatly laid out" and that the inhabitants had erected a stockade, a key feature of Yoruba settlement. She incorrectly surmised that the village "had probably been founded on the site of some old English or Portuguese slave-factory, as there were regular rows of fine orange trees down the centre and at the sides of the street; and otherwise the spot bore marks of former occupation by people more enlightened than these runaway negroes."[48] This condescending observation nevertheless paints Cobolo as more of a community than a war camp.

Another important factor was the presence of female recaptives. In the African diaspora, resistance was gendered. Armed resistance and violence were often instigated by men, while women were more conspicuous in runaway communities. While most accounts of Cobolo have focused on the male leadership of the runaway community, women were clearly present in the settlement. One farmer spotted about thirty men and eight women passing through his farm on the Maharra Road about six weeks prior to the war.[49] Another witness reported that fifty men and eight women were spotted sneaking through Hastings three days before the first altercation with the village's volunteer force. They allegedly carried with them guns tied up in mats.[50]

---

[46] Lovejoy, *Jihād in West Africa*, 15.
[47] Findlay to Goderich, December 5, 1832, CO 267/115.
[48] Melville, *A Residence at Sierra Leone*, 216.
[49] Testimony of Henry Cavallah, CO 267/118.
[50] Testimony of Barbaree, Secretary's Office Letter Book Private & Confidential Police Record Book, SLPA.

The notion that Cobolo refugees wanted to attack the colony comes only through rumor and suspicion. One witness to the initial skirmish with the Waterloo and Hastings volunteers claimed that one of the celebrating Aku "fired a gun 3 times as a rejoicing at the event and told the people that in the dry season, they would make war upon Sierra Leone." Another witness suggested that the entire population of Freetown's Foulah Town would join the Cobolo contingent when the dry season arrived.[51] There is circumstantial evidence that the inhabitants of Cobolo were procuring supplies to stage an offensive; by all accounts they were well armed. One witness, held in jail for the security of his evidence, had been sent to Bompee with three cutlasses and two kegs of gunpowder. The man testified that "Abdulyi residing in the grassfield had manufactured bows and arrows of sharpened iron points."[52] At trial the prosecution argued that the Aku had "arrayed in a warlike manner, that is to say with guns, muskets, blunderbusses, cutlasses, bows and arrows, and other weapons."[53] We are left with contradictory and circumstantial evidence: on the one hand, unsubstantiated rumors of immediate invasion had gripped the colony for six years without coming to fruition, and conflict came about only when colonial forces descended on the Aku. On the other hand, the Aku were clearly well armed and had a colony-wide network of abettors and potential recruits.

Diasporic Comparisons

The date of the Cobolo War and the identity of its participants as Yoruba and Muslim places the conflict within a broader pattern of Yoruba armed resistance around the Atlantic in the 1830s and 1840s. As slave ships departing the Bight of Benin dispersed the combatants and victims of the Sokoto jihad and Yoruba wars to Sierra Leone, Cuba, and Brazil, a succession of violent insurrections transpired in these three corners of the Black Atlantic. In Bahia, a series of revolts from 1807 to 1835 occurred in the years after the Fulani jihad,

---

[51] Since the events at Cobolo escalated during the dry months of November and December, it is likely that these references were to January and February, the driest months of the year due to the Harmattan winds.

[52] Testimony of George, Secretary's Office Letter Book Private & Confidential Police Record Book, SLPA.

[53] Finldlay to Hay, January 19, 1833, CO 267/118.

declared in 1804, which resulted in the arrival of Hausa prisoners of war and recently converted Yoruba Muslims to northeastern Brazil.[54] An aborted 1807 Hausa conspiracy in Bahia was followed by at least another ten revolts and conspiracies prior to the famous 1835 rebellion.[55] João José Reis has examined the 1835 rebellion in terms of the class (slave/free), ethnic (Nagô [Yoruba], Hausa), and religious (Islam, *oriṣa* devotion) mobilization.[56] For Cuba, Manuel Barcia has identified fifteen revolts and conspiracies between 1832 and 1844 associated with Yoruba speakers, though few if any of the participants were Muslims.[57]

Manuel Barcia has posed the question of to what extent were these series of conspiracies and insurrections in Bahia and western Cuba "the result – or the continuation – of events that occurred in and around Oyo in the same period?"[58] Lovejoy has called for an extension of Barcia's comparative framework of revolts in Bahia and Cuba to include the contemporaneous Cobolo War in Sierra Leone. Lovejoy argues that the jihad movement and the events that created the Sokoto Caliphate had a profound impact, shaping the pan-Atlantic pattern of resistance among Yoruba and Hausa.[59] But any comparison between the Aku militants and their Nâgo and Lucumí counterparts in Brazil and Cuba must be mindful of the contextual differences between the Sierra Leone, Brazil, and Cuba and, more importantly, in the distinct nature of the conflicts. As I argue here, the Cobolo War cannot be treated as a comparable conflict to slave rebellion in Bahia or Cuba; it was not the "war" colonial officials and subsequent historians have taken it to be. The archival evidence simply does not support an interpretation that the intentions and goals of those at Cobolo were

---

[54] Verger, *Trade Relations*, 286; Schwartz, *Sugar Plantations*, 468–488.
[55] João José Reis, "Slave Resistance in Brazil: Bahia, 1807–1835," *Luso-Brazilian Review*, 25.1 (1988): 111–144. See also Verger, *Trade Relations*, chapter 9, "Slave Revolts and Uprisings in Bahia, 1807–1835."
[56] João José Reis, *Slave Rebellion in Brazil: The Muslim Uprising of 1835 in Bahia* (Baltimore: Johns Hopkins University Press, 1995).
[57] Barcia, *West African Warfare*, 161–65. Also see Barcia, "West African Islam in Colonial Cuba," *Slavery and Abolition*, 35.1 (2014): 1–14; Barcia, "An Islamic Atlantic Revolution: Dan Fodio's *Jihād* and Slave Rebellion in Bahia and Cuba, 1804–1844," *Journal of African Diaspora, Archaeology, and Heritage*, 2.1 (2013): 6–18.
[58] Barcia, *West African Warfare*, 6.
[59] Paul Lovejoy, *Jihād in West Africa*, 22, 27, 204–205, 242.

analogous to those who instigated the Malê uprising in Bahia or Lucumí slave revolts in Cuba.

Though Findlay dreaded that the goal of the Aku was "killing all the white men," the conspiracy to attack the colony was likely a colonial fiction.[60] Still, we cannot discount that the experiences of many Liberated Africans with warfare in their homelands – either as combatants or as victims – played a part in the history of Cobolo. Much like in Bahia, resistance in nineteenth-century Sierra Leone was concentrated in two overlapping groups of people: those who identified as Yoruba and those who identified as Muslim.[61] Moreover, while Liberated Africans were not slaves and Sierra Leone was not a slave society, the colonial oppression and prohibitions on movement, assembly, and worship were in many ways analogous to slave societies. Prohibitions against Muslim worship in Freetown were similar to those in place in Rio de Janeiro or Salvador de Bahia during the same period, while Findlay's decrees against "unlawful" movement mirrored the close monitoring of New World slaves in urban settings.

Scholars such as Barcia have observed how Islam survived and even spread in Bahia, whereas references to it in Cuba are almost totally lacking. The case of Freetown, the Liberated African villages, and Cobolo therefore provides a closer comparison to northeastern Brazil than Cuba, even though Liberated Africans were brought to Sierra Leone on intercepted vessels that were originally intended for either destination. Indeed, of the 1,987 recorded Liberated Africans sent to the village of Waterloo from 1820 to 1832, 545 had originally been destined for Bahia while 513 had been traveling toward Havana.

At trial, court officials referred to the accused as the "Alla Accou Barras," possibly a very corrupted rendering of Allahu Akbar ("Allah is Greater"). Various witnesses testified that "the prisoners are Alla Accou Barra," that "all the Alla Accou Barras possess cutlasses," and that "the Alla Accou Barras rendezvous at Allie's house" where they would "talk of the war." The court and witnesses were thoroughly convinced of the centrality of Islam to the "war." The ignorant clerk

---

[60] Following slave rebellions in the Americas, "killing all the whites" was often given as a reason for fighting by captured rebels and by key witnesses, even though the reality was more complex. Manuel Barcia, "'To Kill All Whites': The Ethics of African Warfare in Bahia and Cuba, 1807–1844," *Journal of African Military History*, 1 (2017): 72–92.

[61] Lovejoy, "Background to Rebellion," 155.

who recorded the testimony referred not only to the accused as the "Alla Accou Barra" but also to the creation and dissemination of the "Alla Accou Barra book," perhaps a peculiar reference to the Qur'an.[62] Unwittingly, these trials reveal that part of the clandestine activities of the accused was simply the sale of religious texts. The same witness who stated that the Aku met at Allie's home in Hastings to "talk of the war" also acknowledged that a "Mahomadoo Mandingo man makes books for the people." These meetings may have been partly to purchase Islamic texts away from the surveillance of the Hastings village manager.

Alberto da Costa e Silva has traced the illicit sale of Qur'ans in nineteenth-century Rio de Janeiro, a trade also apparent in Bahia and Recife in this period.[63] In Sierra Leone the trade in Islamic texts was generally much more licit, though less so in this period of heightened suspicion toward Muslims. Thomas Eyre Poole, the colonial and garrison chaplain, was impressed by Wolof traders who sold "Greegrees or charms, consisting of part of the Koran, which they copy and transcribe very beautifully and accurately, and enclosed in cases of leather of different sizes, variously ornamented."[64] After the termination of hostilities at Cobolo, Findlay went so far as to suggest that the Aku had initially defeated his volunteers due to "the faith which the delinquents put in their gregries and fetishes purchased from their Mahomedan teachers."[65]

Religion was obviously a source of unity among the Cobolo community, and colonial officials were certain that Muslims – the "Alla Accou Barras" – were the sole plotters in the rumored attack on the colony. The documentation we have for the Cobolo War paints the event as an exclusively Yoruba and Muslim affair. Extant documents do not mention the presence of Hausa recaptives, for example, or Muslims from regions adjoining the colony. Findlay, for one, was certain that his enemies were "all of the Ackoo Nation."[66]

---

[62] Testimony of Ackroo, Secretary's Office Letter Book Private & Confidential Police Record Book, SLPA.
[63] Alberto da Costa e Silva, "Buying and Selling Korans in Nineteenth Century Rio de Janeiro," *Slavery and Abolition*, 22.1 (2001): 83–90.
[64] Thomas Eyre Poole, *Life, Scenery, and Customs in Sierra Leone and the Gambia*, vol. 1 (London: R. Bentley, 1850), 20.
[65] Findlay to Goderich, May 15, 1833, LADLB 1831–1834.
[66] Campbell to Thomas Caulker, October 21, 1832, LADLB 1831–1834.

A discharged solider at Hastings who joined the village volunteers testified that "the people witness saw were all Ackoos" because he "knows them by their marks and their language."[67] Further hints come from the name of defendants listed in court documents. Some individuals had identifiable Yoruba names, such as Callanko (Killanko), Ododoo (Odudu), and Hyenah (Aina). Most, however, had Muslim names: Allie (Ali), Salloo (Salu/Sallau), Abdulyi (Abdullahi), and Mahomadoo (Muhammadu).[68]

The Aku on Trial

On November 30, 1832, twenty-five defendants appeared at Freetown's courthouse. On December 4 an additional thirty-nine prisoners were brought up on charges after being apprehended by Jacob Hazeley "upon suspicion ... they intend to join the Accous in the vicinity of Cobolo." Findlay reported to Whitehall that the legal proceedings had been brought up against eighty-nine individuals in total, "charged with riotously & seditiously assembling with the intent of urging and creating disturbance among the Accous under the Colonial Government."[69] While forty-two had their cases dismissed, thirty-three had by that time been sent to the house of correction for three months. A further nine had been committed for trial, while five remained under examination.[70]

None of the accused was forced to take the stand, and those that did offer a defense often simply denied the accusations against them. We are thus left without the detailed interrogations that have informed analyses of events such as the 1835 Malê Rebellion, sources that are invaluable despite being extracted under duress. Historians' interpretations of what actually transpired at Cobolo have relied on a limited number of documents.[71] Much of the sworn testimony relied on

[67] Testimony of Henry Grattan, CO 267/118.
[68] Secretary's Office Letter Book Private & Confidential Police Record Book, SLPA. The interpretation of names is based on those found in African Origins database (www.african-origins.org). Additional name interpretation was provided thanks to Ibrahim Hamza and Olatunji Ojo, personal correspondence, June 4, 2017.
[69] Secretary's Office Letter Book Private & Confidential Police Record Book, SLPA.
[70] Findlay to Hay, December 6, 1832, CO 267/115.
[71] Chief among these are the Colonial Office correspondence (CO 267/115–119) of this period, Letterbooks of the Liberated African Department for the years

witnesses who had supposedly overheard the plotting of the accused or observed clandestine meetings; many had also participated as militiamen in the attacks on Cobolo.

The highest profile legal action against the Cobolo militants was a treason trial instigated by the stringent Findlay. At the Quarter Sessions of Oyer and Terminer he sought indictments for high treason against six prisoners whom he identified as the rebel leaders. The grand jury found a true bill against four of them, throwing out the case against the other two. On trial were "William Cole of Cobolo, in the country of Sierra Leone, labourer, otherwise called Atala, William Cole, late of the same place, labourer, otherwise called Lalayah, George Cole, late of the same place, labourer, and George, late of the same place, labourer."[72] The charge against them was that they had "unlawfully, maliciously, and traitorously assembled and gather together ... to stir up, move, and excite insurrection, rebellion, and war against our said Lord the King."[73]

Since the four men could not afford legal counsel, Acting Chief Justice M. L. Melville appointed William Henry Savage to represent the defendants. Savage was born in England to an African father and an English mother. He first came to Sierra Leone in 1810 as a schoolteacher before Governor Columbine's cost cutting ended his appointment.[74] In 1820 he traveled back to England and took out papers to become a notary public. On his return to Sierra Leone he was admitted to the bar on the basis of his notary papers. He became only the second lawyer in 1820s Freetown, the other being a white Englishman. His clients included both naval claimants and Havana commercial firms in cases before the Mixed Commission Courts.[75] He also prospered in

---

1830–1833, and the reports of resident Church Missionary Society missionaries. The analysis here draws on these sources in conjunction with a previously unused volume in the Sierra Leone Public Archives, which is variously described on its cover as "Secretary's Office Letter Book Private & Confidential" or "Police Record Book." Secretary's Office Letter Book Private & Confidential Police Record Book, SLPA.

[72] Kalendar of Prisoners Tried at the General Quarter Sessions of the Peace, December 17–20, 1832, January 3–4, 1833. CO 267/118.
[73] Finldlay to Hay, January 19, 1833, CO 267/118.
[74] Peterson, *Province of Freedom*, 217.
[75] Critics who later tried to discredit Savage pointed out a five-month period in the 1810s in the employ of notorious slave trader John Ormond in the Rio Pongo. In the 1820s Savage and Ormond established an arrangement whereby American traders, restricted from Freetown by the Navigation Acts, could acquire goods

business, entering a commercial partnership with the Nova Scotian merchant Samuel Gabbidon. Savage owned a home on Cross Street as well as a country estate near Fourah Bay. By the time he came to represent the Cobolo Aku he was a prosperous figure in Freetown's top social circles, though one who felt the constant racial antipathy from British officials toward a wealthy and influential man of mixed heritage.

Savage crafted a compelling defense for the accused Aku. A pained Findlay wrote to Under-Secretary of State Hay that Savage had "succeeded in creating a doubt as to Cobolo being within the jurisdiction" and had then "endeavoured to impress on the minds of the court and jury that, Liberated Africans not being British born subjects, did not owe allegiance to His Majesty, but only so long as they chose to remain within the limits of the Colony."[76] Findlay sent the Colonial Office a map placing Cobolo squarely within British territory, but Savage had planted sufficient doubt in the mind of the court that Britain had any authority over this place.

The actual location of Cobolo was a moot point. The second prong of Savage's defense was more factual and logically irrefutable: Liberated Africans were not British subjects, they owed no allegiance to the Crown, and therefore could not be tried with treason. Findlay considered this "a dangerous argument in a Colony like this" and one that "ought to have been put down at once by the court." Instead, the Chief Justice conceded Savage's point and the jury acquitted the four men of the charge of high treason.

A despondent Findlay immediately sought a retrial, hoping that a charge of willful murder of militia members would avoid more legal complications. But a lack of witnesses for the Crown and the court's questionable jurisdiction outside the colony meant that the jury again acquitted the four Aku. The second acquittal ended Findlay's court campaign against the Cobolo Aku. His suggestion for a third trial in an Admiralty Court, this time for a charge of piracy, was quickly shot down by his colonial legal team, who pointed out that piracy pertained

---

from Savage via John Ormond. George E. Brooks, *Yankee Traders, Old Coasters, and African Middlemen: A History of American Legitimate Trade with West Africa in the Nineteenth Century* (Brookline, MA: Boston University Press, 1970), 173–174; Bruce Mouser, "Trade and Politics in the Nunez and Pongo Rivers, 1790–1865," PhD dissertation, Indiana University, 1971, 174.

[76] Finldlay to Hay, January 19, 1833, CO 267/118.

only to "offences committed upon the sea, or in any haven, river, creek & where the Admiral has powers."[77]

The acquittals did little to calm the state's antipathy toward the Muslim Yoruba. Defeated in court, Findlay turned to legislation. In March 1833 he released a proclamation stating that because of the "numerous instances of Liberated Africans leaving their locations and settling themselves in various parts of the Colony" a new order in council sanctioned fines on all those who would "harbor or entertain any runaway Liberated Africans in his or their houses." The order in council also declared that "no Stranger professing the Mahomedan Faith shall, in future, be permitted to settle in any of the Towns, Villages, or Places within this Colony, over which we have jurisdiction except at Freetown, without having the permission of the Colonial Secretary." Additionally, District Managers and Justices of the Peace were to prohibit recaptives from "assuming any other dress than that usually adopted by Europeans." The proclamation laid bare the governor's contempt for the "wicked and evil-disposed Persons professing the Mahomedan Religion" who had "introduced themselves at various times, in a clandestine manner, in certain Liberated-African Towns and Villages within this Colony, for the purpose of carrying on their lucrative and diabolical Trade in the sale of Fetishes and Charms."[78]

Aftermaths

After the trial, Savage let several of the Cobolo Aku settle on his estate at Fourah Bay. They established a Muslim community that persists to this day. Savage assured the Aku that Findlay's proclamation against the mobility and refuge of Liberated Africans was illegal. Findlay took this stance as proof that Savage meant "to sow the seeds of discontent and rebellion among a large population."[79] Savage's predisposition to aiding the Aku Muslim community pre-dated the events of Cobolo. According to traditions Michael Banton recorded in 1952–1953, Savage had employed an Aku servant, who

---

[77] The Acting King's Advocate reasons for not trying Mr. Cole 1st under the Royal Commission, enclosure no. 1 in Findlay to Hay, April 15, 1833, CO 267/119.
[78] Proclamation, March 1, 1833, enclosure in Findlay to Hay, March 2, 1833, CO 267/119.
[79] Findlay to Hay, March 2, 1833, CO 267/119.

used to ask his employer on Fridays for leave to go and visit his friends. Savage inquired after these people, so his servant brought some of them to meet him; these men formed an association known as *arota* – the friends – who held meetings in part of Savage's property known to this day as "Yardee." Some of them, it is said, were already Muslims. When visiting the prison, Savage found a number of Muslims there who had been committed for following the practices of their religion; he had them released and they took his name in gratitude. Many Yoruba settled in the neighbourhood of his house, where one of the principal streets is now named Savage Square.[80]

In the years after the failed treason trial, the Aku Muslims congregated at Fourah Bay, Foulah Town, and the village of Aberdeen on the western edge of Freetown. The Muslim communities at Foulah Town and Aberdeen had pre-dated Savage's 1833 land grant, and their communities attracted other Aku as well as Muslim scholars from the region. By the middle of the decade the Aku at Foulah Town outnumbered the Fula population who had founded the settlement on Freetown's eastern limits in 1819.[81] At Fourah Bay, the Aku farmed plots and sold their produce at the local Cline Town quay. John Peterson recorded oral histories in the 1960s recounting how, a century before, men would spend their days farming in the field before gathering at Fourah Bay in the evening in groups of fifteen to twenty around a fire to learn long passages from the Qur'an.[82]

The Fourah Bay, Foulah Town, and Aberdeen Muslim communities attracted the settlement of Muslim clerics, already in the Liberated African villages despite Findlay's best efforts. Mandinka and Fula clerics, in particular, played important roles in establishing these villages' mosques (*jami*) and schools (*karanthe*) for teaching the Qur'an. They were also the teachers (*karamoko/cherno*) and religious specialists (*alfa*, *fode*, imam, *alimami*) who provided the leadership of these institutions.[83] The Aku at first relied on these Mandinka and Fula *alfas* and imams for their religious instruction and ceremonies, acknowledging their knowledge and training. While their enslavement had interrupted their religious education, their arrival at Sierra Leone brought them to a region of active Muslim teachers. Charles Augustus Reichardt of the CMS observed how several of his Fula translators were

---

[80] Banton, *West African City*, 5.   [81] Peterson, *Province of Freedom*, 164.
[82] Ibid., 219.   [83] Harrell-Bond et al., *Community Leadership*, 107.

influential among the Aku Muslims, including Alfa Sulaiman, the imam of the Foulah Town mosque.[84]

With time, these communities developed their own religious specialists, institutions, and leadership. Alfa Muhammad (Momodu) Yadda became the first *alimami* at Fourah Bay, where the Muslim community erected their first mosque in 1836 and drew in many Aku from Waterloo and Hastings.[85] The Muslim Aku formed themselves into three self-contained *jamā'a* (communities), each with its own *alimami*, imam, and alfas.[86] The concentration of Yoruba Muslim communities within the colony was the unintended and ironic outcome of Findlay's efforts to destroy an unsanctioned Yoruba Muslim settlement outside colonial jurisdiction. These flourishing Muslim communities remained a persistent blot on British attempts to erect the edifice of a Christianized colony.

Findlay's immediate successors did not share his level of paranoia toward these communities. But Richard Doherty, who arrived as governor in June 1837, certainly did. Doherty was a former soldier and Irish Catholic who had converted to Protestantism. He shared Findlay's concerns over Islam among the Liberated Africans and "the more open and ostentatious observance of its rites by persons of that class, which has arisen from the increased confidence they have thereby acquired."[87] Doherty focused his ire on the Fourah Bay and Foulah Town communities, whom he alleged lived "in the open contempt or violation of the quiet and decency of the Christian Sabbath" and "send out their emissaries into the town and into the country districts, where they propound and insinuate their faith."

Doherty's complaints to the Secretary of State were informed by an alarmist petition signed by eight prominent members of the CMS, including John Weeks (by now fourteen years in the colony) and John Ulrich Graf (the future archdeacon of Sierra Leone). Their appeal to the governor lamented "the rapid increase of the Mahomedans, and the bold practice of their imposing ceremonies," polygamy, and implicated Muslims in the continuing slave trade from the

---

[84] David E. Skinner, "Islam and Education in the Colony and Hinterland of Sierra Leone (1750–1914)," *Canadian Journal of African Studies*, 10.3 (1976): 514.

[85] Harrell-Bond et al., *Community Leadership*, 107–108.

[86] Skinner, "Islam and Education," 514–515.

[87] "Extension of the Mahomedan Faith among the Liberated Africans," Doherty to Lord John Russell, December 4, 1839, CO 267/154.

region.[88] Doherty was a student of Findlay; he read his predecessor's correspondence and was particularly taken by Savage's defiant community at Fourah Bay. As if paraphrasing Findlay, he referred to Islam as a "religion as *adopted* by these persons, since their arrival in the colony, because the statement which they themselves make that they were born and bred in its tenets, must be considered as having no foundation in fact."[89]

In 1839 the police pulled down the Foulah Town mosque.[90] The governor explained away the event as a mistake, rather than the apotheosis of more than a decade of state-sanctioned repression. While the mosque had been "destroyed through a mistake of some officers of police," Doherty did not regret its destruction.[91] Not everyone agreed. The Irish abolitionist Richard Robert Madden, sent to the colony as commissioner of inquiry not long after, concluded that "if the measures taken to prevent the diffusion of a false religion had been limited to a prohibition to erect other places of worship of this kind, I think it would have been better than the pulling down of those which already existed."[92]

From 1839, Doherty passed a series of Alien Acts to curtail the "evil consequences" of Muslim "strangers" on the minds and morals of the liberated.[93] He suggested to the Secretary of State a concomitant policy of expulsion, "breaking up the establishment in that quarter, and removing its numbers in a body to a more distant part of the colony – a measure which might be effected without any infringement of the

---

[88] Enclosure no. 1 in Doherty to Lord John Russell, December 4, 1839, CO 267/154.

[89] Doherty ignorantly believed that "the Mahomedan faith is scarcely known in the southern countries of Africa, to which they great majority of these persons belonged." "Extension of the Mahomedan faith among the liberated Africans," Doherty to Lord John Russell, December 4, 1839, CO 267/154.

[90] The archival record for this event is, perhaps consciously, scarce. Some scholars have placed the event in 1839, and others in 1840. Some have stated that two mosques were destroyed. See, e.g., Skinner, "The Influence of Islam in Sierra Leone History," 32. Doherty's own correspondence makes clear that the event occurred in 1839 as does the colonial surgeon, Robert Clarke. Doherty to Lord John Russell, December 4, 1839, CO 267/154; Clarke, *Manners and Customs*, 29–30.

[91] Doherty to Lord John Russell, December 4, 1839, CO 267/154.

[92] Commissioner Dr. Madden's Report, 1841, CO 267/172.

[93] "An Act to Regulate the Residence of Aliens within the Colony of Sierra Leone, Passed in Council, 19th September, 1840," replicated in Report of Commissioner of Inquiry, CO 267/172, 40.

rights of property." The governor justified his course of action by stating that the Muslims resided on Crown land. The irony that these people had previously sought to live beyond Crown territory was lost on him.

Robert Vernon Smith, the Under-Secretary of State for the colonies, was hesitant. He annotated Doherty's letter, opining that "to banish them from their houses merely because they will not think as we do … seems to me nothing less than persecution, which, at whatever risk, I would abstain from." But Smith proposed to instead "eject these people as bad tenants not as bad Xtians." Doherty singled out Savage's original claim to the land that the Aku had resided on since 1832 and called on the colonial surveyor, Frederick Pyne, to investigate. William Henry Savage had died two years earlier. Pyne predictably found that the Fourah Bay Aku and their mosque stood on Crown land originally granted to Nova Scotian Settlers.[94]

Faced with eviction, the leaders of the Fourah Bay community, in addressing Doherty, called themselves "Your Excellency's most dutiful and loyal Liberated African subjects" and politely requested the end of his "melancholy mandate" to expel them from their homes.[95] The signatories, including Mammado Savage, Henry Macaulay, and James MacCarthy, pointed out that governors between Findlay and Doherty had approved their settlement at Fourah Bay, even if the now-deceased Savage did not have a deed to the land. They pled with the governor to remain and attested that "prior to our being brought to this colony as slaves, and subsequently made liberated, we were taught in our own country, to adopt the Mahammodan Faith, which we have strictly followed from our childhood up to the present period."

Ultimately, Doherty's plan fizzled. Within the Colonial Office, James Stephen and Vernon Smith prevaricated on the legality and morality of religiously motivated removals. Doherty himself left the colony in 1840 before he could implement his policy. But six years later his successor, Norman Macdonald, again proposed to expel the Muslim Aku from the colony. The catalyst was an attack on the settlement of

---

[94] Enclosure no. 3, Report of the Colonial Surveyor on the Mahomedan Settlements at Fourah Bay, in Governor Doherty's despatch no. 77 of the 4th of December 1839, CO 267/154.
[95] Enclosure no. 4, the Fourah Bay Mahomedans deprecating their removal from their settlements at that place, Enclosure in Governor Doherty's despatch no. 77 of the 4th of December 1839, CO 267/154.

Clarkson, a small outpost across the Sierra Leone estuary on the Bullom Shore founded by Macdonald's immediate predecessor, William Fergusson, to resettle Liberated Africans who had moved across the estuary to farm. A small group of Liberated Africans, described in official sources as "Accoo," were placed on a small, square-mile tract of land that the governor and his council knew had been rented from local chiefs from the era of the Sierra Leone Company onward, but had remained largely unclaimed since 1792.

Recaptive occupation of the territory, and the failure of colonial officials to notify any indigenous leaders, put the colonists on a collision course with the local populations. The area was nominally ruled by the aged Be Sherbro, though he had surrendered his power to the Susu leader of Lungi, Amara. When Macdonald sent Be Sherbro's nephew – the England-educated Peter Wilson – to be overseer at Clarkson, the Susu at Lungi were incensed at the installation of a Bullom man in such a position of power.[96] In May 1846, reports came in that a force of two hundred Susu had descended from Medina on the Bullom Shore, driving Wilson from the settlement, and ransacking and burning recaptive houses.

The attack was the result of Macdonald's interference in Bullom–Susu politics and an attempt to extend British territory without consultation of local rulers. Macdonald deflected blame. In a patently false dispatch to the Colonial Office, he argued that the attack was long planned and that "the worst feature in the matter, [is] that Amarah and his people would be backed and aided in this villainy by some of our own people Liberated Africans who have embraced Mahomedanism." The accusation against the "Mahomedan Ackoos" was spurious but tapped into a long line of scapegoating. Macdonald's rambling fifty-six-page dispatch drew a direct line to "the remnants of the rioters at Cobolo in 1831 and 32" and declared that the Aku would be the first to aid anyone who might wish to attack the colony. His long list of grievances included the Muslim Aku's propensity for "continually obtaining proselytes to their faith, particularly amongst newly imported Africans" and their desire to "live apart from the rest of their countrymen and under rules, laws & regulations of their own."[97]

---

[96] Fyfe, *History of Sierra Leone*, 242.
[97] Macdonald to Gladstone, July 13, 1846, CO 267/193.

Macdonald lamented that his predecessors – Doherty excluded – had "tacitly permitted this most grievous evil" and that "there has always existed some legal or technical objection to taking measures for removing them." Calling the Muslim Aku "blisters on the face of our society," Macdonald concluded that it was "highly desirable to get rid of such a *bed of serpents.*" Macdonald proposed expulsion at the government's expense, this time suggesting the Bight of Benin. Macdonald's superiors responded to his effusive dispatches and irresponsible behavior by censuring his extension of British territory and its potential to cause a needless war in the region. The Colonial Office threatened Macdonald's recall, but he remained. So too did the Muslim Aku.

Recurrent state persecution, culminating in the destruction of property and threats of eviction, did fuel the desire for many Muslim Liberated Africans to emigrate. They seized the opportunity to return home via the commercial and mission ties with the Bight of Benin. Prominent Muslims organized return voyages for themselves and others. Foulah Town's Aku Muslims traveled between and emigrated to Badagry in their own vessel, *The Maria*. In July 1843, Alfa Mohammadu Savage, the imam and leader of the Muslim community at Fourah Bay, purchased the captured Brazilian slave schooner *Esperança* at auction after it had been captured on a failed voyage from Bahia to Ouidah.[98] At least fifty members of the Fourah Bay community sailed soon after on a very different voyage to the Bight of Benin.[99] Salu Shitta, who had moved from Waterloo to Fourah Bay in 1831, became the imam of the Fourah Bay Muslim community. In 1844 he, his family, and a group of about fifty followers departed for Badagry. Larger numbers still went to Lagos where they became known as the Fourah Bay or Sàró Muslims.[100]

Other Muslims tried to use the CMS mission to the Yoruba territory to their advantage. Crowther wrote in his journal on December 17, 1843:

This morning the Mahomedan headman in the neighbourhood of Fourah Bay sent four men to Bathurst, about seven miles distant, to ask after my health and to learn for certain whether I was going to the Yoruba country....

---

[98] Account sales of the Brazilian Schooner "Esperança," August 11, 1843, FO 84/449.
[99] Fyfe, *History of Sierra Leone*, 228; Cole, *Krio of West Africa*, 134.
[100] Gbadamosi, *Growth of Islam among the Yoruba*, 28.

He is a clever Yoruba man, and a very strict Mahomedan, has a very great influence over those who profess Mahomedanism. He speaks the Haussa like a native.[101]

Crowther's Aku CMS compatriot Thomas King eventually grew frustrated with how the Muslim Aku "ingratiated with the Abbeokuta mission for employment or free passage to the country."[102] Three years later he gave up preaching in Yoruba because "none ever did attend with a view to be benefitted by it."[103]

Yoruba Muslims continued to arrive on intercepted slave vessels for more than two decades after the events of Cobolo. Christian Frey recorded the account of one Liberated African, identified only as J. Vincent, who told the missionary in 1849 that he "was born in the Aku country" and had worshiped the "God of Iron" (Ògún) as did his parents, "until I was sold to Mahomedans, who obliged me to adopt their religion. They sold me again & 4 years ago I was brought to this colony."[104] Thomas Cole, the author of many panicked reports about the Aku in the 1820s, wrote in 1840 that "Mahommedanism is unfortunately making rapid strides in Africa, in proof we find a vast number of captured negroes from the Akoo nation (near the equator) of that persuasion, and all attempt in the colony to convert them to the true faith, have hitherto wholly failed." The man who had a decade earlier called for the banishment of Muslim "book men" now commented on how Muslims "formed themselves into isolated bodies, and hold little to no intercourse with those of the opposite creed."[105]

By 1848, Acting Governor Pine estimated (likely underestimated) that there were 2,000 Muslims in a colonial population of 45,006, most of whom were "Mandingoes, Sousous, and other people from the adjacent country who have settled in the Colony." But Pine, like his predecessors, believed that this number included many Aku "a part of whom have in their own country been converted to that religion by Foulah and Mandingo priests." Pine added that these "mahomedans generally reside together in the suburbs of the town and, except in the way of trade, hold little intercourse with the other people of the

---

[101] Report for quarter ending December 18, 1843, CMS/CA1/O79/10.
[102] King, Journal extracts for quarter to June 25, 1845, CMS/CA1/O130/2.
[103] King, Journal extracts for quarter to June 25, 1848, CMS/CA1/O130/11.
[104] Frey, Journal extracts for quarter ending March 25, 1849, CMS/CA1/O94/25.
[105] Cole to John Russell, August 11, 1840, CO 267/162.

Colony."[106] Robert Clarke noted in the 1860s, "The Mahomedans, Akoos, Mandingoes, &c., reside generally together in the suburbs of the city, and, except in the way of business, hold little intercourse with the rest of the people."[107] Almost a century later, Olumbe Bassir estimated that out of a population of about 100,000 along the colony's peninsula, the Aku community at Fourah Bay was about 5,000 with half that number again at Foulah Town and Aberdeen. Bassir, born in Senegal to Aku parents and raised in the Fourah Bay community, found it "remarkable that these Yoruba people should have maintained their group solidarity and social cohesion over the last 150 years."[108]

Aku, Islam, and Identity

The Muslim Aku formed tightly bound communities in response to persistent government persecution. Researching and writing in the 1950s, the British sociologist Michael Banton observed how "Muslim Akus are still very conscious of the religious discrimination from which they suffered in the last century." Banton stated that Aku was by this time "used to describe Muslim descendants of liberated Africans of Yoruba origin."[109] Jean Herskovits Kopytoff similarly concluded that in the twentieth century, "Aku" referred only to Muslim descendants of recaptives of Yoruba origin.[110] To some observers, then, "Aku" went from being a broad term encompassing all Yoruba speakers in the colony (as well as others who associated themselves) during the nineteenth century to a term more narrowly associated with Yoruba Muslims and their descendants into the twentieth century. In terms of diasporic comparisons, "Aku" may have transitioned from being a close cognate of the term "Nâgo" used in northeastern Brazil to describe Yoruba speakers, to the term "Malê" used in the same region to describe Yoruba Muslims. Yet John Peterson, who conducted research in Sierra Leone in the decade after Banton and Kopytoff,

---

[106] Pine, Annual Report, enclosed in dispatch no. 88 of October 27, 1848, CO 267/204.
[107] Clarke, Sketches of the Colony of Sierra Leone, 324.
[108] Olumbe Bassir, "Marriage Rites among the Aku (Yoruba) of Freetown," Africa: Journal of the International African Institute, 24.3 (July 1954): 251.
[109] Banton, West African City, 5, 7.
[110] Kopytoff, Preface to Modern Nigeria, 21–22.

criticized their equating of Aku with Muslim. Peterson observed how as late as 1960, Freetonians always placed the adjectives "Christian" or "Muslim" before "Aku."[111] Certainly in the late nineteenth century, Liberated African Christians were still self-identifying as Aku, as the memorials to prominent Aku in Freetown's churches attest (Appendix D).

"Aku" was not synonymous with "Muslim," just as it had never been simply synonymous with "Yoruba." Religious affiliation and even ethnic origin did not determine membership in the Aku community, as the Aku king John Macaulay (a Hausa Muslim) exemplified. In the official mind, however, "Aku" became closely associated if not synonymous with "Muslim." The colonial state created a false binary between Muslim and non-Muslim Aku.[112] At the community level, this religious distinction and antipathy did not exist between Aku of different faiths. Intermarriage and conversion were both common. Among Yoruba speakers in the Bight of Benin hinterland, conversion to Islam and later Christianity was always underpinned by a level of pragmatism. Yoruba speakers tended to view religious attachments as provisional on their capacity to deliver benefits, reflecting the pragmatism that had guided membership in the *orisa* cults.[113] King John

---

[111] Peterson, *Province of Freedom*, 238.

[112] Gibril Cole argues that British officials progressively created a category of "Aku Mahomedan" and that "colonial authorities and the European missionaries developed the colonial constructed Oku as an ethno-religious entity separate from other Liberated Africans, and subsequently the Krio, in order to create and maintain a dichotomy between Muslims and Christians within Freetown society." Cole has conjectured that it was a colonial ordinance – Ordinance no. 19 of 1905 – that marginalized and "tribalized" non-Christians by creating a new tribe known as the "Aku" under the headship of their alimani. This new epithet, rendered as "Aku Mahommean," was, according to Cole, a convenient obfuscation on the part of the colonial state. Cole, *Krio of West Africa*, 7–8, 64. Cole's interpretation is difficult to substantiate. The colonial state never considered the Aku – whether Liberated Africans or their descendants – as outside the colonial and Liberated African population. The colonial censuses for 1891, 1901, and 1911 all made the distinction between "Liberated Africans and their descendants," "natives" (a euphemism for the "children of strange tribes"), and a taxonomy of West African "races" or "nations," which included local ethnic groups from the "Mandingoes" and "Timaness" but never included the Aku. See Colonial reports – Annual, No. 64, Sierra Leone, Annual report for 1891, Command Paper, C.6857-14; Schedule, Census of Sierra Leone, 1901 in CO 269/6; Colonial reports – annual, No. 724, Sierra Leone, Report for 1911.

[113] Peel, *Christianity, Islam, and the Orisa*, 132–133.

Macaulay converted from Islam to Christianity five years before his death, following the concerted efforts of the Rev. James Johnson, the son of Aku parents from Ijebu and Ondo.[114] Elizabeth Shaw, married at Pa Demba Road church in the 1840s, later converted to Islam when her husband died and she remarried and moved to Foulah Town.[115]

Aku of different faiths attended each other's social functions, weddings, and funerals. Aku of all religious persuasions attended the dedication of mosques, the opening of *madrasa* (religious schools), and the weddings and funerals of prominent Muslims.[116] At the same time, Aku preachers drew Yoruba speakers regardless of their affiliation to the Christian church. While presenting the first sermon in the Yoruba language in 1844, Crowther "observed three of my Mahomedan friends, sent by their headmen to attend the service" who "followed me to my house after service, and expressed their satisfaction at what they had heard."[117]

By mid-century, decades of official suspicion and repression gave way to greater accommodation from the colonial state. Governor Benjamin Pine, deviating from Findlay and Doherty, described the Aku as a "very industrious, and enterprising people" whose "exertions have materially tended to the advancement of the prosperity of the colony." He added, in an observation that would have bemused his predecessors, that the Aku were "a very orderly people and exhibit great respect for constituted authority."[118] Colonial governors came to acknowledge Islamic festivals and other events and in some cases to participate directly in them. During the 1840s, Muslims began parading through Freetown's streets at the end of the Ramadan fast, approaching Government House in a symbolic procession of détente with the colonial state.[119] A decade later the CMS missionary Edward Dicker watched "a large assemblage of Mahomedans in a field opposite the Female Institution to celebrate the conclusion of their fast Ramadan." That morning:

[114] James Johnson, Journal for half year ending March 1863, CMS/CA1/O123/13.
[115] "The Mohammedan Burial Ground," *Sierra Leone Church Times*, 2 (September 16, 1885): 10, 4.
[116] Harrell-Bond et al., *Community Leadership*, 122.
[117] Crowther, Journal extracts for quarter ending March 25, 1844, CMS/CA1/O79/11.
[118] Report on the Annual Blue Book of Sierra Leone for the year 1847, in CO 267/204.
[119] Fyfe, *History of Sierra Leone*, 228.

A drum summoned the faithful to the spot, who came clothed in many different colours, red, white, and blue being prominent. All came well armed with swords, daggers, spears, and a few with muskets. I should think there were present about five hundred. They arranged themselves in long ranks facing the rising sun. Their Mullah, clothed in white under garments, with a scarlet cloak over them, stood in front.[120]

For Dicker, "It was truly painful to witness so much apparent devotion" to the Islamic faith in a Christian colony.

Conclusion

The Cobolo War was a seminal event in the legal history of Sierra Leone, bringing to the forefront questions of British territoriality and control. Liberated Africans were meant to be obedient, pliant, and grateful. Compliance was embedded in a series of acceptable sociocultural practices: western dress, the English language, and observation of the Sabbath. The endurance of a distinct Muslim and Aku identity beyond the era of the slave trade was the result of colonial policies ostracizing Muslims and a concomitant pattern of resistance and exclusivity among Muslim receptives. Muslims displayed the same recalcitrance that they showed elsewhere in the diaspora of the Atlantic slave trade, buttressed by residing in a region of Islamic influence and growth.

Gibril Cole has argued that "African Muslims played a crucial role in the evolution of Krio society," of which there can be no doubt.[121] The development of an overarching Krio identity in the late nineteenth and early twentieth century did not deny entry to Muslims; Krio identity could transcend ethnicity, religion, and class. Yet as Paul Lovejoy has pointed out, Muslims in the diaspora "maintained a sense of continuity with the African past that was impervious to the process of 'creolization.'" Lovejoy contends that "[s]ituations in which people resisted incorporation to such an extent that they developed a separate subculture should be distinguished from those in which people produced 'creole cultures.'"[122] Muslims within the colony of Sierra Leone,

---

[120] Dicker, Journal extract, July 16, 1854, CMS/CA1/O88/12.
[121] Cole, *Krio of West Africa*, 2.
[122] Lovejoy, "Slavery, the Bilād al-Sūdān, and the Frontiers of the African Diaspora," 8.

like elsewhere around the Atlantic, resisted the assimilation, and many Muslims, Aku and otherwise, consciously chose to not be a part of the hegemonic imperial culture.

The legacies of Cobolo were felt over the ensuing decades and into the twentieth century. Over the course of the nineteenth century, the term "Aku" became increasingly associated in the official mind with Islam and dissent, even as the Aku community embraced a membership of multiple religious, linguistic, and regional origins within the Bight of Benin hinterland. In the African diaspora writ large, Muslims faced challenges in sustaining their faith and reconstituting the Muslim *jamā'a*. In Sierra Leone, this challenge resulted in an enduring urban Muslim community that outlived the colonial state.

Conclusion

Retention or Renaissance? Krio Descendants and Ethnic Identity

On Christmas Day 1863, the last intercepted slave vessel entered Freetown harbor. Its arrival concluded one of the largest forced migrations of the nineteenth-century Black Atlantic. A decade before, the British Parliament passed an act declaring, "All Liberated Africans domiciled or resident in the Colony of Sierra Leone or its Dependencies shall be deemed to be, and to have been for all purposes, as from the date of their being brought into, or their arrival in, the said colony, natural-born subjects of Her Majesty."[1] By the time of this declaration the colony-born descendants of recaptives were beginning to outnumber their forebears who had experienced the Middle Passage.[2] With the passing of one generation to another the imperative of identifying and organizing based on linguistic and ethnic heritage changed accordingly.

The dominant narrative of Sierra Leonean history in the latter half of the nineteenth century is the emergence of an overarching creole (or Krio) identity, which subsumed the panoply of earlier ethnic identities. This process is usually attributed to the emergence of a colony-born majority, intermarriage, and socialization and tutelage in a westernized, Christian culture.[3] This process is assumed to be linear as Liberated Africans passed on and subsequent generations of their offspring felt less attachment to their ancestral homelands.

Within this unidirectional narrative, scholars have identified certain aspects of recaptive culture as persisting or being retained, particularly

---

[1] Crooks, *History of Sierra Leone*, 189.
[2] Censuses taken in the 1840s did not distinguish Liberated African and their descendants. The 1850 census was the first that clearly showed that the 20,766 descendants of Liberated Africans born in the colony outnumbered the 20,243 Liberated Africans counted. By 1860 the number of Liberated Africans had dropped to 15,782, while their offspring were 22,593. Kuczynski, *Demographic Survey*, 162.
[3] See, among many examples, Porter, *Creoledom*.

Conclusion: Retention or Renaissance?

those of Yoruba origin. These legacies of Liberated African identity and culture of late nineteenth- and twentieth-century Freetown have often been framed in a Herskovits-like discussion of "survivals." Hence many scholars have pointed to the importance of Yoruba vocabulary in Sierra Leonean Krio. Related to this are naming practices known in Sierra Leone as *komojade*, similar both phonetically and in practice to the Yoruba *ako konjade* ceremony for the naming of a child. Others have looked at the Krio *awujo* feast, deriving from the Yoruba word for "an assembly of persons." The feast is said to comprise primarily Yoruba-derived dishes, taking place in the home or yard of a person wishing to invoke the assistance of their ancestors.[4]

Today, more than two centuries later, the existence of a number of esoteric societies in and around Freetown has similarly been taken as proof of the persistence of certain aspects of receptive cultural retention. John Nunley's excellent study on art and performance in post-colonial Freetown highlighted how secret societies are the primal component of the city's cultural organization.[5] Societies such as Ode-lay, Ojeh, Gelede, Egungun, and Hunting draw members from across the city. Masquerading "devils" bare the aesthetic imprint of the earlier Egungun while co-opting the pejorative term that colonial missionaries used to describe these masked figures. Like their nineteenth-century counterparts, these cultural presentations invoke ancestors and draw members regardless of religious affiliation.

Nunley notes that elements of the "ancestral religions" of receptive descendants survived in Sierra Leone, among which Yoruba traditions were by far the most influential.[6] Nunley, who conducted extensive fieldwork in Freetown prior to Sierra Leone's civil war, concludes that "the origins of Ode-lay organization are found in the Yoruba-based Hunting, Gelede, and Egungun traditions, as well as in general concepts of Yoruba religion."[7] Yet with the exception of Egungun, none of these societies is actually named in missionary documents from the era of recaptives. It falls beyond the scope of this study to fully explain why those practices most referenced within the CMS journals – the cult of Ṣàngó and Ifá divination – have largely fallen by the wayside, while institutions not mentioned within the archive – Odelay, Gelede, and

---

[4] Spitzer, *Creoles of Sierra Leone*, 27; Magbaily Fyle, "The Yoruba Diaspora in Sierra Leone's Krio Society," 376.
[5] Nunley, *Moving with the Face of the Devil*, xvii. [6] Ibid., 14. [7] Ibid., 61.

Ojeh – have thrived for the last century. These discrepancies do suggest that the latter organizations, all of which are clearly of Yoruba derivation, did not simply "survive" and may have been the product of post-slave trade movements of people between Sierra Leone and the Bight of Benin.

Other attempts to search for "survivals" attributed various cultural features to a "Yoruba" origin. Michael Banton observed during research in the 1950s that "some descendants of liberated Africans still describe themselves as Yoruba, Ibo, Ejesa, Ijebu, Popo, Egba, Tarkpa, etc., but Yoruba is the only language to survive out of the multitude which were once heard among the liberated Africans."[8] The fact that the descendants of recaptives still referred to themselves by these designations almost a century later was not simply a claim to ancestral provenance. Often, they remained political identities, invoked at particular times for particular reasons. In the years following the Scramble for Africa, many educated recaptive descendants found that the possibilities for government employment established over previous decades were now being circumscribed by racist attitudes and the increase of Britons in lower administrative posts. The response was the re-establishment of many of those national institutions that had been so central to recaptive life. The Seventeen Nations, which had disbanded in the 1870s, was reformed in 1886, with leaders representing the "Mendi, Ebo, Ijesha, Egba, Yoruba, Yagba, Popo, Congo, Kakanda, Tagpa, Howsa, Timneh, Limbah, Mandingo, Creoles, Ottah, Lokkoh."[9] As in prior decades, these nations were dynamic constructs. Some of those nations that existed in the 1840s had faded away. Others, most notably the Ìjèṣà, Egba, Yoruba, and Yagba, were subgroups of what was often perceived as a singular "Aku" nation.[10]

The Aku and their descendants were particularly vocal in this reinvigoration of national identity. In many respects their response mirrors the better-known resurgence of Yoruba cultural practices in

---

[8] Banton, *West African City*, 4–5.
[9] "A President Elected for the 'Seventeen Nations,'" *Sierra Leone Weekly News*, December 25, 1886.
[10] Akintola Wyse, *Searchlight on the Krio of Sierra Leone: An Ethnographical Study of a West African People* (Freetown: Institute of African Studies, University of Sierra Leone, 1980), 34 note 48. The Seventeen Nations persisted until the institution was officially abolished in 1903.

Conclusion: Retention or Renaissance? 263

and around Lagos in the late nineteenth century, commonly termed "cultural nationalism."[11] The Aku kingship, another abandoned institution, was refounded in 1887. The candidate elected was George Metzger Macaulay, son of the long-standing and influential King John Macaulay. By this time – a period of scientific racism and the expansion of British rule over much of the continent – the context was different. The Rev. J. Augustus Cole, who addressed the inauguration, prefaced his remarks by stating, "To think of installing a king in a British colony, under the British flag, is an absurdity equal to madness. It is insurrection against the Crown." Cole assured the crowd:

Neither the Government, who is not ignorant of our movement to-day, nor our good friend Mr. Macaulay, nor the great multitude who are here to give us their moral support, understand that we are setting up a King, that is in the English meaning of the word King. A Chief Leader, or Headman would better express the African or Yoruban synonym; hence such words as Oba-ile, King of the house, Oba-Ologun, King of war, Oba-ileh, king of land, etc.[12]

The speaker concluded his remarks by affirming, "We are here then, today, to install Mr. George Metzger Macaulay to the office of Chief Leader of his people, or if you like, in the loose translation of the word Oba, call him King.... We are Kingdoms within a Kingdom."

The Aku kingship was part of a broader renaissance. There was also a resurgence in Yoruba naming patterns and dress. This shift was symbolized by an 1887 advertisement in the *Sierra Leone Weekly News* in which the purchaser stated that "the public are hereby informed that from and after this date Mr. W. J. Davis, Senior Resident Master of the Wesleyan High School, Freetown, and 1st B.A. of the University of London, will henceforth be called and known by the name of Orishatukeh Faduma. All communications should be

---

[11] On "cultural nationalism" in Nigeria, see J. F. Ade Ajayi, "Nineteenth Century Origins of Nigerian Nationalism," *Journal of the Historical Society of Nigeria*, 2 (1961): 196–211; Ayandele, *The Missionary Impact on Modern Nigeria*, esp. chapter 8; Robin Law, "Local Amateur Scholarship in the Construction of Yoruba Ethnicity, 1880–1914," in Louise de la Gorgendière, Kenneth King, and Sarah Vaughan (eds.), *Ethnicity in Africa* (Edinburgh: Center for African Studies, University of Edinburgh, 1996).

[12] Inaugural Address on the Installation of Mr. G[eorge] M. Macaulay, *Sierra Leone Weekly News*, April 18, 1891.

addressed accordingly."[13] Faduma, the son of Aku recaptives, readopted the surname of his parents while choosing a forename that acknowledged the importance of the *oriṣa* despite being himself a Methodist.[14]

Faduma became founding member of the Reform Movement, a self-reflective effort to inculcate and promote an African identity in the face of racial discrimination. Following Davis's lead, A. E. Metzger became Kufileh Tuboku-Metzger, while Claude George assumed the name Esu Biyi, and Isaac Augustus Johnson became Algerine Kefallah Sankoh.[15] Many other offspring of Aku Liberated Africans joined Faduma, and one respondent in the *Sierra Leone Weekly News* recalled how

> every one of our Liberated Negro Parents had a name given to them in the land of his nativity by which he was called and known from his birth up to the time he arrived in the land of his exile. He had a name full of meaning, and explaining his family connection, the manner of his birth, and any peculiar circumstances attending it; a name significant of the religious ideas of his parents and preserving a tribal or racial individuality.[16]

These sentiments reflect the fact that recaptive national identities – and Aku identity in particular – were not simply retained in the generations after the Middle Passage but consciously revived and invoked. This was not, for the most part, a rejection of Christianity, western education, and British values. It was rather a reassertion of African identities at a moment of disillusionment with imperialism.

Much like the Aku kingship and the Seventeen Nations, many of the "Yoruba-isms" identified and celebrated within Sierra Leonean historiography as having "survived" into the twentieth century and to the present were in fact revived – and in some cases possibly first introduced to the colony – following the demise of the transatlantic

---

[13] *Sierra Leone Weekly News*, September 24, 1887.
[14] Faduma's parents, John and Omolofi Faduma, were Egba recaptives first brought to British Guiana rather than Sierra Leone. The family took on the name Davis, and William J. Davis was born in1857. His parents later opted to move to Waterloo, Sierra Leone. Moses N. Moore, *Orishatukeh Faduma: Liberal Theology and Evangelical Pan-Africanism, 1857–1946* (Lanham, MD: American Theological Library Association; London: Scarecrow Press, 1996); Rina L. Okonkwo, "Orishatukeh Faduma: A Man of Two Worlds," *The Journal of Negro History*, 68.1 (1983): 24–36.
[15] Bangura, *Temne of Sierra Leone*, 46–47.
[16] Anonymous letter to the editor, *Sierra Leone Weekly News*, September 24, 1887.

slave trade. A. T. von S. Bradshaw observed in 1966 that while "it is alleged that Yoruba has 'survived' in Freetown among Aku families isolated for more than a century from the mother country," the reality by that time was that it was spoken "only by Nigerians or Sierra Leoneans who have had personal or family contacts with Nigeria in their own lifetime."[17] T. D. P. Dalby similarly noted, "Aku has survived in the Freetown area for over 150 years, but it appears to have been kept alive by constant contact with Nigeria."[18] In Sierra Leone, vestiges of Liberated African ancestry did not simply survive in the face of colonial and missionary disapproval, though they did so to a remarkable degree. Rather, they were sustained and revived by these connections between homeland and diaspora, and the conscious choice of descendants to invoke and revive such customs and identities.

Conclusion: African Colony, African Diaspora

The history of early colonial Sierra Leone has often been treated as a particular, parochial history. Established as a colony in 1787, almost a century before the Scramble for Africa, its colonial and mission history does not fit the chronology of most other regions of sub-Saharan Africa. But while the colony's history was singular, and the journeys of its inhabitants remarkable, it was a part and product of a larger history of forced migration in the Black Atlantic world. This study has situated Sierra Leonean history within the historiography of precolonial Africa and its Atlantic diaspora, as one stream of the largest forced migration in human history. Recaptives were a small fraction – perhaps 3.5 percent – of the 2.8 million Africans who survived the Middle Passage in the decades after Britain's 1807 Abolition Act. Sierra Leone resembled Africa's New World diaspora as men, women, and children sought to comprehend their new environment, establish connections with those with whom they could communicate, and re-establish some sense of community. This was never a conscious project to "re-create" the societies they came from, but an imperative born

---

[17] A. T. von S. Bradshaw, "A List of Yoruba Words in Krio," in *Sierra Leone Language Review*, 5 (1966): 61.

[18] T. D. P. Dalby, "Language Distribution in Sierra Leone 1961–2," *Sierra Leone Language Review*, 1 (1962): 62–67. Dalby also noted that Krio fishermen at the village of Kent in 1961 sang a Yoruba song without knowing the meaning of the words.

from circumstance. The specific context that recaptives found themselves in was Britain's first colony in sub-Saharan Africa, the site of one of the earliest Protestant missions in Africa, and one of the first locations in Africa in which Anglicanism met Islam and the *oriṣa*.

The narrative arc of this book has followed recaptives from enslavement through liberation and their subsequent lives in their new colonial context. Britain's naval intervention against the transatlantic slave trade was one of the earliest examples of what would later be termed "humanitarian intervention." Like many subsequent interventions, its human impact was ambiguous. Liberation brought with it a range of lived experiences, some falling far short of the lofty aspirations of abolitionists in the imperial metropole. Yet the unintended consequence of this naval interdiction against the slave trade was to create in Sierra Leone one of the most heterogeneous and cosmopolitan societies of the nineteenth-century Atlantic world.

Appendix A

"Nations" of children in CMS school rosters by probable coastline of embarkation, 1816–1824 (n = 1066)[a]

Upper Guinea	316	Windward and Gold Coasts	69
Bullom	7	Banda/Banty [Bandi]	4
Cassinkah [Kasanga]	2	Bassa Kroo	2
Connah [Kono]	7	Bussay [Loma/Toma]	2
Cosoo/Cossoh [Mende+]	189	Foy [Vai]	2
Foulah/Fowlah [Fula]	11	Gola [?]	24
Jaloff/Jallof [Wolof]	12	Kroo [Kru]	9
Kissy/Kissey [Kisi]	21	Passa/Pessah/Pessay [Kpelle]	17
Mandingo [Mandinka]	18	Aquimah [? Akyem/Akwamu]	1
Maeendee [Mende]	1	Bandah [? Avikam]	1
Rio Pongos	3	Cromantine/Cromanty [Akan+]	7
Sherbro	10		
Soulamah [Yalunka]	2		
Sulima Susoo	1		
Suso [Susu]	28	**Northern Nigeria**	73
Timne [Temne]	4	Bassa	40
		Haussah/Housah [Hausa]	21
Bight of Benin	124	Tagbah/Taquah [Nupe]	12
Adjah [Aja]	2		
Agba [Egba]	5	**Bight of Biafra**	377
Akoo [Yoruba]	75	Baccumcum [Lundu/Mbo]	25
Bacco [Boko]	1	Bayong [Bate/Duala]	57
Barabah [Bargu/Bariba]	1	Brookham [Tikar]	13
Cowrie [Kabre]	3	Calabar [Ibibio/Efik]	68
Egorah [Igara/Igbira]	1	Crabbah [Elem Kalabari = Ijo]	2
Jasher [Ìjèsà]	2	Effee/Epheck [Efik]	3
Papa/Paupau [Ewe]	33	Ethcer [Etche = southern Igbo]	1
Uquai/Uquae [Ukwuale]	1	Ebo [Igbo]	205
		Hi-Foot [Bafia/Bafut]	1

267

(cont.)

Upper Guinea	316	Windward and Gold Coasts	69
West Central Africa	33	Mocko [Efik+]	2
Congo [Bakongo+]	32		
Roonga/Roongo [Rungo]	1	**Unidentified**	74

[a] Compiled from "A List of the Boys & Girls Supported by the Church Missionary Society at Leicester Mountain," 1816, CMS/CA1/E5A/68/N; List of Boys at the Christian Institution, Leicester Mountain in July 1818, CMS/CA1/E7/32; CMS/CA1/E8/13, /15, /17-19 (1819); CMS/CA1/O13–14 (1821, 1822, 1824); List of African children named after benefactors, made out by Mr. James Norman, up to December 29, 1821, CMS/CA1/M1.

Appendix B

1848 Sierra Leone census[a]

Name in census	Modern equivalents	Population
Akoos	Yoruba	7,114
Eboos	Igbo	1,231
Paupahs (Popo/Ewe)	Adangme, Adja, Hueda or Aizo, Fon, Mahi	1,075
Housas	Hausa	657
Koosoos	Mende et al.	609
Mokos (Ibibio-speakers, possibly the Anang in particular)	Isuwu. Duala. Rungu, Bayon, Bakom, Bagba, Beli, Bamum, Nwala, Bamenyam, Bafia, Bamileke, Ngoteng, Bongkeng, Kossi, Seke	470
Congos (Bakongo+)	Vili, Mboma, Ntandu (Kongo), Tege, Kaniok, Teke, Tsaye, Boma, Mbeti, Imbangala, Yombe, Nsudi, Ambundu, Ovimbundu, Kimbundu, Lunda, Songo, Kisama	421
Calabahs	Efik or Efik-Ibibio	319
Mandingoes	Mandinka	188
Kromantees	Akan et al.	168
Kakanjas	Nupe et al.	163
Binnees (Benin)	Urhobo, Etsaka, Edo, Ishan, Olomo	107
Bassas	Bassa et al. (Windward Coast)	60
Soosoos	Susu	51
Sherbros	Sherbro/Bullom	38
Jolofs	Wolof	16
Mozambiques	East Africa unspecified (Yao, Cuabo, Maravi, Medo, S. Makwa, Inhambane [Tonga])	18

(*cont.*)

Name in census	Modern equivalents	Population
Foulahs	Fula/Fulbe	14
Timnehs	Temne	5
"Other small tribes"		549
Total		13,273

[a] CO 267/209. Parliamentary Papers, "Report on the Annual Blue Book of Sierra Leone for the year 1848," November 2, 1849, 1849 [1126], 304–305. Modern equivalencies taken from Curtin, *Atlantic Slave Trade*, 245; Adam Jones, "Recaptive Nations"; and Northrup, "Becoming African," 10.

Appendix C

Koelle's Aku informants[a]

Names of informant	Place of origin	Language in Koelle [Yoruba dialect]	Years in Sierra Leone	Number present	Means of enslavement	Age at enslavement
Odogu/John Davis	Elogbo	Ota [Egbado]	15	~20	"kidnapped by Egbas"	~20
Odso/Henry Macauley	Dseu	Egba [Egba]	22	"great many"	"taken in war"	~24
Gbiludso/Thomas Cole	Igbore	Egba [Egba]	25	"great many"	"taken by the Dsebus"	~15
Degbite/Sam Cole	Ilesa	Idsesa or Igesa [Ijẹsa]	6	"great many"	"kidnapped by the Yorubans"	?: [w/kids]
Ogbaleye/Thomas Johnson	Ogo	Yoruba [Oyo]	~28	"several thousand"	"kidnapped by the Phula"	~25
Aboyade/James Cole	Ogbomaso	Yoruba [Oyo]	17	"several thousand"	"sold by a war-chief"	?: [married, w/kids]
Robo/George Macaulay	Eri	Yagba	15	?	"captive in war by the Nupes"	?: [w/kids]
Aeta/Joseph Wilhelm	Lasa	Yagba	15	?	"Taken in war by Yorubans"	?: [w/kids]
Arogu/James Jones	Irele	Yagba	14	?	"taken in war by Phula"	?: [w/kids]

Adsofe/William Davis	Ebila	Ki, Eki [Ekiti]	14	3	"kidnapped on a trading journey"	? [w/kids]
Magu/William Hambleton	Taki	Ki, Eki [Ekiti]	18	?	"kidnapped by the Kupas"	~23
Odiemi/James Wilhelm	Dsumu	Jumu	?	?	"War with the Phula"	~28
Elifo/Peter Mamma	Oworo	Aworo	~30	3	"sold by a supposed friend"	~25
Olukoko/Peter Wilhelm	Dsebu, Idsebu	Ijebu	~20	"many"	"war with the Egbas"	~25
Lagegu/William Isaak	Ife	Ife	24	6	"kidnapped by Yorubans"	~17
Maku/William Harding	Ondo	Ondo	8	~30	kidnapped by Dsesas while trading	~18-20
Owonaka/George Mackenzie	Dsekiri,	Itsekiri	~26	3	"adultery"	~24

[a] Koelle, *Polyglotta Africana*, 5–6.

Appendix D

Liberated African memorials in Freetown churches[a]

Top left:
Isaac Benjamin Pratt
(Native of the Ife Section of the Aku)
Merchant and Member of the Legislative
Council of Sierra Leone
He arrived in this colony in 1825, and
in after years filled the important
post of king or headman among his
Countrymen in the city.

Top right: Benjamin Syble Boyle
(Liberated African of the Egba tribe in the Yoruba country)
Member of the Legislative Council and Merchant of this city

Bottom left:
Henry Benjamin Cummings
Native of the Yagba Section of the Aku Tribe

Bottom right:
Imbora alias Nancy Bishop Eboe
of the Isworma tribe

[a] I am grateful to the custodians of the following churches for their assistance with this research: St. George's Cathedral, Freetown; Wesley Methodist Church, Lamina Sankoh Street, Freetown; and Ebenezer Methodist Church, Circular Road, Freetown. Thanks also to Sierra Leone government archivist Albert Moore for guiding me toward these sources.

Select Bibliography

Manuscripts

Church Missionary Society Archives, University of Birmingham (CMS)

Sierra Leone Mission
    Early Correspondence, CA1/E5–E8
    Mission Books (Incoming), CA1/M1–M22
    Original Papers (Incoming), CA1/O1–O235
Yoruba Mission
    Original Papers (Incoming), CA2/O31, CA2/O61, CA2/O86

Methodist Missionary Society Archives, SOAS (MMS)

Sierra Leone/Gambia Correspondence
Special Series: Biographical

The National Archives, Kew (TNA)

Colonial Office Papers
    Sierra Leone Original Correspondence, CO 267
    Sierra Leone: Acts, CO 269
    Sierra Leone Sessional Papers, CO 270
Foreign Office Papers
    Slave Trade Department and successors: General Correspondence FO 84
    Archives of Sierra Leone Slave Trade Commission, FO 315
High Court of Admiralty Papers
    Vice-Admiralty Courts: Proceedings, HCA 49

Royal Naval Museum, Portsmouth (RNM)

Binstead, Cheesman Henry. *Memorandum of Remarks on Board HM Ship Owen Glendower Commodore Sir Robert Mends, from England, and along the Western Coast of Africa.* 2005.76/1. January 21, 1823–May 9, 1823.

Sierra Leone Public Archives (SLPA)

Colonial Secretary's Letter Books
 1831–1833
Governor's Letter Book/Local Letters
 1808–1811, 1825–1827, 1827–1832
Liberated African Department Letter Books
 1820–1826, 1828–1830, 1830–1831, 1831–1834, 1834–1837, 1837–1842, 1842–1847
Liberated African Department Miscellaneous Return Books
 1845–1861
Liberated African Department Statement of Disposals
 1821–1833
Liberated African Registers and Duplicate Registers
 1–3772 (1808–1812), 3773–6274 (1812–1814), 4684–7507 (1814–1815), 6289–8528 (1814–1816), 7508–9758 (1815–1816), 8529–9758 (1816–1817), 9759–11908 (1816–1819), 10115–15143 (1816–1822), 11909–15967 (1819–1822), 15144–19888 (1822–1825), 19889–24205 (1825–1827), 20514–25422 (1827), 25423–30708 (1827–1829), 30709–37429 (1829–1830), 37430–43537 (1829–1833), 50762–54382 (1835–1836), 54157–57571 (1837), 57572–64406 (1837–1839), 64407–67635 (1839), 75378–84307 (1845–1848)
Secretary of State's Despatches
 1816–1821
Secretary's Office Letter Book Private & Confidential Police Record Book
 1832

Dissertations and Theses

Anderson, Richard. "Recaptives: Community and Identity in Sierra Leone, 1808–1863." PhD dissertation, Yale University, 2015.

Lovejoy, Henry. "Old Oyo Influences on the Transformation of Lucumí Identity in Colonial Cuba." PhD dissertation, University of California, Los Angeles, 2012.

Misevich, Philip. "'On the Frontier of 'Freedom': Abolition and the Transformation of Atlantic Commerce in Southern Sierra Leone, 1790s to 1860s." PhD dissertation, Emory University, 2009.

Mouser, Bruce. "Trade and Politics in the Nunez and Pongo Rivers, 1790–1865." PhD dissertation, Indiana University, 1971.

Scanlan, Padraic. "MacCarthy's Skull: The Abolition of the Slave Trade in Sierra Leone, 1792–1823." PhD dissertation, Princeton University, 2013.

Spitzer, Manon Lily. "The Settlement of Liberated Africans in the Mountain Villages of the Sierra Leone Colony 1808–1841." MA thesis, University of Wisconsin, 1969.

Published Contemporary Sources

Newspapers

Sierra Leone Church Times
Sierra Leone Independent
Sierra Leone Watchman
Sierra Leone Weekly News
Church Missionary Society
    Annual Reports
    Church Missionary Gleaner
    Church Missionary Intelligencer
African Institute
    Annual Reports

Books and Articles

Buxton, Thomas Fowell. *The African Slave Trade and Its Remedy*. London: J. Murray, 1840.

Clarke, Robert. *Sierra Leone: A Description of the Manners and Customs of the Liberated Africans; With Observations upon the Natural History of the Colony, and a Notice of the Native Tribes*. London: J. Ridgway, 1843.

    Sketches of the Colony of Sierra Leone and Its Inhabitants. London: T. Richards, 1863.

Hamilton, William. "Sierra Leone and the Liberated Africans." *The Colonial Magazine and Commercial-Maritime Journal*, Robert Montgomery Martin (ed.), vol. 6, September–December 1841, 327–334; vol. 7, January–April 1842, 29–42.

Horton, James Africanus. *West African Countries and Peoples*. Edinburgh: Edinburgh University Press, 1969 [1868].

Johnson, W. A. B. *Memoir of Rev. W. A. B. Johnson, Missionary of the C.M.S. Regents Town, Sierra Leone, AD 1816–1823*. London: 1852.

Kilham, Hannah. *Report on a Recent Visit to the Colony of Sierra Leone*. London: William Philipps, 1828.

Koelle, S. W. *Polyglotta Africana, or, A Comparative Vocabulary of Nearly Three Hundred Words and Phrases in More than One Hundred Distinct African Languages*. London: Church Missionary House, 1854.

Leonard, Peter. *Records of a Voyage to the Western Coast of Africa in H.M.S. Dryad*. Edinburgh: William Tait, 1833.

Melville, Helen Elizabeth. *A Residence at Sierra Leone: Described from a Journal Kept on the Spot, and Letters Written to Friends at Home*. London: John Murray, 1849.

Rankin, F. Harrison. *White Man's Grave; A Visit to Sierra Leone in 1834*. 2 vols. London: R. Bentley, 1836.

Schön, James Frederick, and Samuel Crowther. *Journals of the Rev. James Frederick Schön and Mr. Samuel Crowther Who, with the Sanction of Her Majesty's Government, Accompanied the Expedition Up the Niger, in 1841, in Behalf of the Church Missionary Society*. London: Hatchard and Son, 1842.

Secondary Sources

Ajayi, J. F. Ade, and Michael Crowder, eds. *History of West Africa*, vol. 2. New York: Columbia University Press, 1973.

Anderson, Richard, Alex Borucki, Daniel Domingues da Silva, David Eltis, Paul Lachance, Philip Misevich, and Olatunjo Ojo. "Using African Names to Identify the Origins of Captives in the Transatlantic Slave Trade: Crowd-Sourcing and the Registers of Liberated Africans, 1808–1862." *History in Africa*, 40.1 (2013): 165–191.

Apter, Andrew. *Black Critics and Kings: The Hermeneutics of Power in Yoruba Society*. Chicago: University of Chicago Press, 1992.

Ayandele, E. A. *The Missionary Impact on Modern Nigeria, 1842–1914: A Political and Social Analysis*. London: Longman, 1966.

Bangura, Joseph J. *The Temne of Sierra Leone: African Agency in the Making of a British Colony*. Cambridge: Cambridge University Press, 2017.

Banton, Michael. *West African City: A Study of Tribal Life in Freetown*. London: Oxford University Press, 1957.

Barcia, Manuel. *West African Warfare in Bahia and Cuba: Soldier Slaves in the Atlantic World, 1807–1844*. Oxford: Oxford University Press, 2014.

Bastide, Roger. *The African Religions of Brazil: Towards a Sociology of the Interpretation of Civilizations*. Baltimore: Johns Hopkins University Press, 1978.

Bethell, Leslie. "The Mixed Commissions for the Suppression of the Transatlantic Slave Trade in the Nineteenth Century." *Journal of African History*, 7.1 (1966): 79–93.

Biobaku, Saburi O. *The Egba and Their Neighbours, 1842–1872*. Oxford: Clarendon Press, 1957.

Braidwood, Stephen J. *Black Poor and White Philanthropists: London's Blacks and the Foundations of the Sierra Leone Settlement 1786–1791*. Liverpool: Liverpool University Press, 1994.

Brown, Christopher Leslie. *Moral Capital: Foundations of British Abolitionism*. Chapel Hill: University of North Carolina Press, 2006.

Brown, Vincent. *The Reaper's Garden: Death and Power in the World of Atlantic Slavery*. Cambridge, MA: Harvard University Press, 2010.

Byrd, Alexander X. *Captives and Voyagers: Black Migrants across the Eighteenth-Century British Atlantic World*. Baton Rouge: Louisiana State University Press, 2008.

Candido, Mariana. *An African Slaving Port and the Atlantic World: Benguela and Its Hinterland*. Cambridge: Cambridge University Press, 2013.

Cañizares-Esguerra, Jorge, Matt D. Childs, and James Sidbury, eds. *The Black Urban Atlantic in the Age of the Slave Trade*. Philadelphia: University of Pennsylvania Press, 2013.

Chambers, Douglas B. "'My Own Nation': Igbo Exiles in the Diaspora." *Slavery and Abolition*. 18.1 (1997): 72–97.

Christopher, Emma. *Freedom in Black and White: A Lost Story of the Illegal Slave Trade and Its Global Legacy*. Madison: University of Wisconsin Press, 2018.

Christopher, Emma, Cassandra Pybus, and Marcus Rediker, eds. *Many Middle Passages: Forced Migrations and the Making of the Modern World*. Berkeley: University of California Press, 2007.

Cole, Gibril. *The Krio of West Africa: Islam, Culture, and Colonialism in the Nineteenth Century*. Athens: Ohio University Press, 2013.

Cooper, Frederick. *Colonialism in Question: Theory, Knowledge, History*. Berkeley: University of California Press, 2005.

Crooks, John Joseph. *A History of the Colony of Sierra Leone, Western Africa; With Maps and Appendices*. Dublin: Browne and Nolan, 1903.

Curtin, Philip D, ed. *Africa Remembered: Narratives by West Africans from the Era of the Slave Trade*. Madison: University of Wisconsin Press, 1967.

Curtin, Philip D, ed. *The Atlantic Slave Trade: A Census*. Madison: University of Wisconsin Press, 1969.

Curtin, Philip D., and Jan Vansina. "Sources of the Nineteenth Century Atlantic Slave Trade." *Journal of African History*, 5.2 (1964): 185–208.

Curto, José C., and Paul E. Lovejoy, eds. *Enslaving Connections: Changing Cultures of African and Brazil during the Era of Slavery*. Amherst, NY: Humanity Books, 2004.

Dalby, David. "Provisional Identification of Languages in the *Polyglotta Africana*." *Sierra Leone Language Review*, 3 (1964): 83–90.

Dixon-Fyle, Mac, and Gibril Cole, eds. *New Perspectives on the Krio of Sierra Leone*. New York: Peter Lang, 2006.

Domingues da Silva, Daniel B., David Eltis, Philip Misevich, and Olatunji Ojo. "The Diaspora of Africans Liberated from Slave Ships in the Nineteenth Century." *Journal of African History*, 55.3 (November 2014): 347–369.

Domingues da Silva, Daniel B., David Eltis, Nafees Khan, Philip Misevich, and Olatunji Ojo. "The Transatlantic Muslim Diaspora to Latin America in the Nineteenth Century." *Colonial Latin American Review*, 26.4 (2017): 528–545.

Drescher, Seymour. *The Mighty Experiment: Free Labor versus Slavery in British Emancipation*. Oxford: Oxford University Press, 2002.

Eltis, David. *The Rise of African Slavery in the Americas*. Cambridge: Cambridge University Press, 2000.

Eltis, David, and David Richardson. *Extending the Frontiers: Essays on the New Transatlantic Slave Trade Database*. New Haven, CT: Yale University Press, 2008.

Eltis, David, and G. Ugo Nwokeji. "The Roots of the African Diaspora: Methodological Considerations in the Analysis of the Names in the Liberated African Registers of Sierra Leone and Havana." *History in Africa*, 29 (2002): 365–379.

Falola, Toyin, and Raphael Chijioke Njoku, eds. *Igbo in the Atlantic World: African Origins and Diasporic Destinations*. Bloomington: Indiana University Press, 2016.

Falola, Toyin, and Matt D. Childs, eds. *The Yoruba Diaspora in the Atlantic World*. Bloomington: University of Indiana Press, 2004.

Falola, Toyin, and Ann Genova, eds. *Orisa: Yoruba Gods and Spiritual Identity in African and the Diaspora*. Trenton, NJ: Africa World Press, 2005.

Fyfe, Christopher. *A History of Sierra Leone*. London: Oxford University Press, 1962.

Gbadamosi, T. G. O. *The Growth of Islam among the Yoruba 1841–1908*. London: Longman, 1978.

Gomez, Michael A. *Exchanging Our Country Marks: The Transformation of African Identities in the Colonial and Antebellum South*. Chapel Hill: University of North Carolina Press, 1998.

Hair, P. E. H. "The Contribution of Freetown and Fourah Bay College to the Study of West African Languages." *Sierra Leone Language Review*, 1 (1962): 7–18.

"The Enslavement of Koelle's Informants." *Journal of African History*, 6.2 (1965): 193–203.

The Sierra Leone Settlement – The Earliest Attempts to Study African Languages." *Sierra Leone Language Review*, 2 (1963): 5–10.

"The Spelling and Connotation of the Toponym 'Sierra Leone' since 1461." *Sierra Leone Studies*, New Series, 18 (1966).

Hall, Gwendolyn Midlo. *Slavery and African Ethnicities in the Americas: Restoring the Links*. Chapel Hill: University of North Carolina Press, 2003.

Haour, Anne, and Benedetta Rossi, eds. *Being and Becoming Hausa: Interdisciplinary Perspectives*. Leiden: Brill, 2010.

Harrell-Bond, Barbara E., Allen M. Howard, and David E. Skinner. *Community Leadership and the Transformation of Freetown (1801–1976)*. The Hague: Mouton Press, 1978.

Hawthorne, Walter. "'Being Now, as It Were, One Family': Shipmate Bonding on the Slave Vessel *Emilia*, in Rio de Janeiro and throughout the Atlantic World." *Luso-Brazilian Review*, 45.1 (2008): 53–77.

Heywood, Linda M., ed. *Central Africans and Cultural Transformations in the American Diaspora*. Cambridge: Cambridge University Press, 2002.

Higman, Barry W. *Slave Populations of the British Caribbean*. Baltimore: Johns Hopkins University Press, 1984.

Jones, Adam. "Recaptive Nations: Evidence Concerning the Demographic Impact of the Atlantic Slave Trade in the Early Nineteenth Century." *Slavery & Abolition*, 11.1 (1990): 42–57.

Klein, Herbert S. *The Atlantic Slave Trade*. Cambridge: Cambridge University Press, 1999.

Konadu, Kwasi. *The Akan Diaspora in the Americas*. New York: Oxford University Press, 2010.

Kopytoff, Jean Herskovits. *A Preface to Modern Nigeria: The "Sierra Leonians" in Yoruba, 1830–1890*. Madison: University of Wisconsin Press, 1965.

Krug, Jessica A. "Social Dismemberment, Social (Re)membering: *Obeah* Idioms, Kromanti Identities, and the Trans-Atlantic Politics of Memory, c. 1675–Present." *Slavery & Abolition*, 35.4 (2014): 537–558.

Kuczynski, Robert R. *Demographic Survey of the British Colonial Empire, West Africa*, vol. 1. London: Oxford University Press, 1948.

Law, Robin. "Ethnicity and the Slave Trade: 'Lucumi' and 'Nago' as Ethnonyms in West Africa." *History in Africa*, 24 (1997): 205–219.

  The Oyo Empire c. 1600–c. 1836: A West African Imperialism in the Era of the Atlantic Slave Trade. Aldershot: Gregg Revivals, 1991.

Law, Robin, and Kristin Mann. "West Africa and the Atlantic Community: The Case of the Slave Coast." *William and Mary Quarterly*, Third Series, 56.2 (April 1999): 307–334.

Lovejoy, Paul E. "Background to Rebellion: The Origins of Muslim Slaves in Bahia." *Slavery and Abolition*, 15.2 (1994): 151–180.

Lovejoy, Paul E. ed. *Identity in the Shadow of Slavery*. London: Continuum, 2000.

——— ed. *Jihād in West Africa during the Age of Revolutions*. Athens: Ohio University Press, 2016.

——— ed. "Scarification and the Loss of History in the African Diaspora," in Andrew Apter and Lauren Derry, eds., *Activating the Past Historical Memory in the Black Atlantic World*. Newcastle: Cambridge Scholarly Publishing, 2010.

Lovejoy, Paul E. ed. *Slavery on the Frontiers of Islam*. Princeton: Marcus Weiner, 2004.

Lovejoy, Paul E., and Suzanne Schwarz, eds. *Slavery, Abolition, and the Transition to Colonialism in Sierra Leone*. Trenton, NJ: Africa World Press, 2014.

Lovejoy, Paul, and David Vincent Trotman, eds. *Trans-Atlantic Dimensions of Ethnicity in the African Diaspora*. London: Continuum, 2003.

Lynn, Martin. "Technology, Trade, and a 'Race of Native Capitalists': The Krio Diaspora of West Africa and the Steamship, 1852–95." *Journal of African History*, 33.3 (1992): 421–440.

Mabogunje, Akin L., and J. D. Omer-Cooper. *Owu in Yoruba History*. Ibadan: Ibadan University Press, 1971.

Mann, Kristin. *Slavery and the Birth of an African City: Lagos, 1760–1900*. Bloomington: Indiana University Press, 2007.

Mann, Kristin, and Edna G. Bay, eds. *Rethinking the African Diaspora: The Making of a Black Atlantic World in the Bight of Benin and Brazil*. London: Frank Cass, 2001.

Matory, James Lorand. *Black Atlantic Religion: Tradition, Transnationalism, and Matriarchy in the Afro-Brazilian Candomblé*. Princeton: Princeton University Press, 2005.

Misevich, Philip, and Kristin Mann, eds. *The Rise and Demise of Slavery and the Slave Trade in the Atlantic World*. Rochester: Rochester University Press, 2016.

Mullin, Michael. *Africa in America: Slave Acculturation and Resistance in the American South and the British Caribbean, 1736–1831*. Urbana: University of Illinois Press, 1992.

Nishida, Mieko. *Slavery and Identity: Ethnicity, Gender, and Race in Salvador, Brazil*. Bloomington: Indiana University Press, 2003.

Northrup, David. *Africa's Discovery of Europe: 1450–1850*. Oxford: Oxford University Press, 2002.

——— "Becoming African: Identity Formation among Liberated Slaves in Nineteenth-Century Sierra Leone." *Slavery and Abolition*, 27.1 (April 2006): 1–21.

"Igbo and Myth Igbo: Culture and Ethnicity in the Atlantic World, 1600–1850." *Slavery & Abolition*, 21.3 (2000): 1–20.

"New Light from Old Sources: Pre-colonial References to the Anang Ibibio." *Ikenga Journal of African Studies*, 2.1 (January 1973).

Trade without Rulers: Pre-colonial Economic Development in Southeastern Nigeria. Oxford: Clarendon Press, 1978.

Nugent, Paul. "Putting the History Back into Ethnicity: Enslavement, Religion, and Cultural Brokerage in the Construction of Mandinka/Jola and Ewe/Agotime Identities in West Africa, c. 1650–1930." *Comparative Studies in Society and History*, 50.4 (October 2008): 920–948.

Nunley, John W. *Moving with the Face of the Devil: Art and Politics in Urban West Africa*. Urbana: University of Illinois Press, 1987.

Ojo, Olatunji. "'Heepa' (Hail) Òrìṣà: The Òrìṣà Factor in the Birth of Yoruba Identity." *Journal of Religion in Africa*, 39.1 (2009): 30–59.

"The Organization of the Atlantic Slave Trade in Yorubaland, ca. 1777 to ca. 1856." *International Journal of African Historical Studies*, 48.1 (2008): 77–100.

Olupona, Jacob K., and Terry Rey, eds. *Òrìsà Devotion as World Religion: The Globalization of Yorùbá Religious Culture*. Madison: University of Wisconsin Press, 2008.

Peel, J. D. Y. *Christianity, Islam, and the Orisa: Three Traditions in Comparison and Interaction*. Oakland: University of California Press, 2016.

"The Cultural Work of Yoruba Ethnogenesis," in Elizabeth Tonkin, Maryon McDonald, and Malcolm Chapman, eds., *History and Ethnicity*. London: Routledge, 1989, 198–215.

Religious Encounter and the Making of the Yoruba. Bloomington: University of Indiana Press, 2000.

Peterson, John. *Province of Freedom: A History of Sierra Leone, 1787–1870*. London: Faber and Faber, 1969.

Porter, Arthur T. *Creoledom: A Study of the Development of Freetown Society*. Oxford: Oxford University Press, 1963.

Reis, João José. *Slave Rebellion in Brazil: The Muslim Uprising of 1835 in Bahia*. Baltimore: Johns Hopkins University Press, 1995.

Rucker, Walter C. *Gold Coast Identities: Identity, Culture, and Power*. Bloomington: Indiana University Press, 2015.

Scanlan, Padraic X. *Freedom's Debtors: British Antislavery in Sierra Leone in the Age of Revolution*. New Haven, CT: Yale University Press, 2017.

Schuler, Monica. "Liberated Central Africans in Nineteenth-Century Guyana," in Linda M. Heywood, ed., *Central Africans and Cultural Transformations in the American Diaspora*. Cambridge: Cambridge University Press, 2002.

Schwartz, Stuart B. *Sugar Plantations in the Formation of Brazilian Society: Bahia, 1550–1835*. Cambridge: Cambridge University Press, 1985.

Schwarz, Suzanne. "Reconstructing the Life Histories of Liberated Africans: Sierra Leone in the Early Nineteenth Century." *History in Africa*, 39 (2012): 175–207.

Skinner, David E. "The Influence of Islam in Sierra Leone: Institutions, Practices, and Leadership." *Journal of West African History*, 2.1 (Spring 2016): 27–71.

Smith, Robert. *The Kingdoms of the Yoruba*, 3rd edition. Madison: University of Wisconsin Press, 1988.

Spitzer, Leo. *The Creoles of Sierra Leone: Responses to Colonialism, 1870–1945*. Madison: University of Wisconsin Press, 1974.

Strickrodt, Silke. *Afro-European Trade in the Atlantic World: The Western Slave Coast c. 1550–c. 1885*. Woodbridge: James Currey, 2015.

Thompson, Robert Farris. *Flash of the Spirit: African and Afro-American Art and Philosophy*. New York: Vintage: 1984.

Thornton, John. *Africa and Africans in the Making of the Atlantic World, 1400–1800*, 2nd edition. Cambridge: Cambridge University Press, 1998.

Tishken, Joel E., Toyin Falola, and Akintunde Akinyemi, eds. *Ṣàngó in Africa and the African Diaspora*. Bloomington: Indiana University Press, 2009.

Tonkin, Elizabeth, Maryon McDonald, and Malcolm Chapman, eds. *History and Ethnicity*. London: Routledge, 1989.

Turner, Michael J. "The Limits of Abolition: Government, Saints, and the 'African Question', c. 1780–1820." *The English Historical Review*, 112.446 (April 1997): 319–357.

Verger, Pierre, *Trade Relations between the Bight of Benin and Bahia, 17th to 19th Century*. Ibadan: Ibadan University Press, 1976.

Walker, James St. G. *The Black Loyalists: The Search for a Promised Land in Nova Scotia and Sierra Leone, 1783–1870*. London: Longman, 1976.

Wilson, Ellen Gibson. *The Loyal Blacks*. New York: Capricorn Books, 1976.

Wyse, Akintola. *The Krio of Sierra Leone: An Interpretive History*. Washington, DC: Howard University Press, 1991.

Index

Note: Page entries in italics refer to illlustrations.

Abeokuta, 57, 198–203
Aberdeen, village, 111, *118*, 184, 248, 255
Abolition Act (1807), xii, 1–3, 25, 101–103, 107
Afonja, Are ona Kakamfo, 52–54, 63, 71
African Origins Project, 40–41, 59
Akan, 26, *267*
Aku
  ethnonym in Sierra Leone, 10, 36, *38*, 39, 127, 143, 155, 158–159, 163, *267*, *269*
  etymology of term, 133, 157–158
  identity, 20–21, 74, 160–163, 192–195, 204–205, 255–257
  Liberated Africans, 50, 58–59, 183–184, 188–191
  missionaries, 195, 201, 210, 214
  Muslims, 63, 196, 202, 227–229, 248–249
Aku King, 185–188, 196, 263
Aláàfin of Oyo, 52–53, 58, 214
alfas, 248
Ali Eisami Gazirmabe
  arrival in Sierra Leone, 113, 120
  enslavement of, 54, 63, 69–72, 75, 77
  Kanuri informant of Koelle, 39
alimami, 249
Allen Town, 117, *118*
Amelia (slave ship), 93–94, 107, 136, 181
Anang, *38*, 46, 147, *269*
Angola, 136–138
Anomabu, *116*
apprenticeship, 25, 96, 99–103, 106
Arabic language and literacy, 229–231
Arabic names, 61

Arabic sources, 153, 163
Attarra, John, 75

babalawo, 41, 210, 218–220
Badagry, 63, 149
  port of embarkation, 27, 114, *116*
  returnees to, 195–203, 253
Badger, Henry, 170, 216
Bahia
  African population of, 156, 171, 218, 230–231
  slave resistance in, 89, 154, 240–243
  slave trade to, 2, 31
Baikie, William Balfour, 143, 145
Bambara, 13, 105, 107, 119
Bambara Town, 108, 231
Banana Islands, 111, *112*, *118*
Barber, James, 56
Bartholomew, Joseph, 174, 179, 182
Bassa
  ethnonym in Sierra Leone, 108, 119, 122, 127, 181
  of present-day Liberia, 36, 109, *267*, *269*
  of present-day Nigeria, *267*
Bathurst (village), 88, 111, 113, *118*, 119, 167–168
Bathurst, Henry, Secretary of State, 83–84, 110, 123
Beale, Rev. James, 177, 203, 216, 222–223
Benguela, 137, 149
Benguema (village), 188
Benin, 39, 132
Benin, Republic of, *38*
Betts, Rev. William, 122, 159, 172
Bickersteth, Rev. Edward, xii, 110

Index

Bight of Benin
  ethnic groups of, 36, 39, 149, 161, 267
  Liberated Africans from, 27, 31–34, 50–59, 114, *116–118*
  Muslims from, 60–62, 228–231, 240, 256, 259
  returnees to, 193–197, 226, 253
  voyages from, *80–81*
Bight of Biafra
  ethnic groups of, 36, 39, 139–147
  Liberated Africans from, 18, 32–34, 50, 97, 116, 267
  voyages from, 49, 79, 88
Bissau, 70, *116*
Black Loyalists, 22, 26, 28. *See also* Nova Scotians
Black Poor, 22, 24, 26, 28, 180
Bones, Lieutenant, Robert, R.N., 107
Bonny
  Liberated Africans brought from, 97, 127
  mortality on ships from, 49, 88
  port of embarkation, 27, 34, 44–47, *48*, *116*, 140
Borno, 60, 62, 132, 229
Boyle, Benjamin Syble, *275*
Brazil
  Africans in, 89, 151–153
  comparisons with Sierra Leone, 168, 185, 211, 218, 227, 239–242
  slave trade to, 2, 31
  Yoruba in, 51, 156, 194, 220, 226, 255
British Guiana, 125
Bullom (people), 105, 131, 252, 267, *269*
Bullom Shore, 252
Bunce Island, 24, 42
Buxton, Thomas Fowell, 50, 94

Cabinda, 27, 65, 93, 107, *116*, 137
Cacheu, *116*
Calabar. *See also* Elem Kalabari; Old Calabar
  ethnonym in Sierra Leone, 10, 36, 39, 47–50, *48*, 145–148, 167–168, 267
  meanings in diaspora, 45–47, 141
Calmont (village), *118*

Cameroon, *38*, 65, *116*, 146
Campbell, Sir Neil, Governor, 122, 124, 169, 233
Campbell Town, 231, 236
Candomblé, 211, 226
Cape Mount, xiii, 65
Captured Negro Department. *See* Liberated African Department
Captured Negroes, xii, 2. *See also* Liberated Africans
Caulker, George Stephen, 110, 121
Caulker, Thomas, 111, 235, 237
census, colony, 108, 230–231
  1848, 38–43, 49, 60, 64, 189, *269*
Charlotte (village), 111, *118*, 160
Christian Institution, Leicester, 134, 136, 140, 151, 158
Christianity, 20
church benefit and welfare societies, 171–174
Church Missionary Gleaner, 86, 203
Church Missionary Society (CMS)
  and adoption of "Yoruba" ethnonym, 165
  African converts, 66, 69, 109, 201, 210
  founding of Sierra Leone mission, 110
  journal system, 209
  and *orişa* devotees, 206–211, 213–214, 217
  and parish plan, 88, 105, 111, 124, 182
  relationship with Muslims, 231, 248–249, 253, 257
  schools, 35, 43, 47, 159, 267
  and translation of African languages, 19, 35, 131, 155, 163, 194
Clapperton, Hugh, 163
Clarke, Dr. Robert, 91, 119, 152, 160–162, 186, 255
Clarkson (settlement), 252
Clarkson, Lieut. John, R.N., 23
Cobolo
  Cobolo "War," 21, 227–228, 236–237, 240
  settlement, 232, 235, 238–239
  trial of Cobolo inhabitants, 243–246
Cole, Thomas, 49, 123, 232–235, 254
Colonial Office, 125, 246, 251–253

Columbine, Captain Edward Henry, R.N., 106–107
Committee for the Relief of the Black Poor, 22
companies (Liberated African), 167–175
Congo
  ethnonym in Sierra Leone, 10, 36, 119, 127, 136–138, 181, 189, *191*, *268–269*
  meanings in diaspora, 136–137
Congo Town, 94, 136, 138, 181. *See also* New Cabenda
Coromantee, 26, 127. *See also* Akan
Cosso. *See also* Mende
  etymology and meaning of term, 133–135
  Liberated Africans, 10, 36, 43, 105, 127, 190, *191*, *267*, *269*
  settlements in colony, 108, 119, 122
Courts of Mixed Commission. *See* Mixed Commission Courts
creole, 7–10, 258, 260
creolization, 7–9
Cross River, 45, 147
Crown Colony, 25
Crowther, Rev. Samuel Ajayi
  arrival in Sierra Leone, 88, 119
  enslavement, 6, 54, 69–72, 75, 78, 90
  on Islam, 205, 253, 257
  on Niger Expedition, 203
  translation work, 143, 163, 201–202
  on Yoruba customs, 177, 210, 215, 217, 224
Cuba
  Africans in, 89, 151, 166
  comparisons with Sierra Leone, 168, 180, 226–227, 239–242
  slave trade to, 2, 64
  Yoruba in, 51, 156–157, 194, 218

Dahomey, 151–152
Dasalu, Andrew Wilhelm, 199
Davies, Charles, 223
Decker, Rev. Charles, 117
Denton, Rev. Nathaniel, 118, 172–175, 203
Derwent, HMS, 102–103
Dicker, Edward, 179, 257
disbanded soldiers, 112, 169

Doherty, Col. Richard, Governor, 196, 249–251
Dove, Rev. Thomas, 161, 198
Düring, Rev. Henry, 88, 113

Eboe, Nancy Bishop, 144, *275*
Efik, 18, 28, 45, 48, 145–146
Egba
  in Yoruba wars, 56–57, 72, 114
  Liberated Africans, 51, 59, 66, 155, 159–162, 184, *191*, *267*, 272
  returnees, 198–200
Egungun, 211, 213, 220–225, 261
Ekiti, 132, 155, *273*
Elem Kalabari, 45–46, *116*, 140, 143, 145, *267*
Emẹrẹ, 57, 66
emigration, 32, 98
  to Bight of Benin, 196–197, 202, 253
  to West Indies, 49, 125
enlistment, 87, 101, 103, 106
Esusu, 170
Ewe, 39, 151, *267*, *269*
Ezzidio, John, 196

Faduma, Orishatukeh (William James Davis), 263
Fergusson, Dr. William, Governor, 196
Findlay, Alexander, Lieutenant-Governor, 85, 87, 123, 211, 227, 233–239, 242–249
Fon, 151–152
Foulah Town, 196, 231, 240, 248–250, 253, 255
Fourah Bay, 225, 246–251, 253, 255
Fourah Bay College, 131
Freeman, Rev. Thomas Birch, 199
Freetown
  connections with Bight of Benin, 195–203, 225
  esoteric societies, 261
  founding, 23, 42
  merchants, 185–186
  Muslim population, 234, 240, 242, 248, 257
  orisa worship in, 215–217, 219
  population of, 9, 24–25, 37, 39, 49, 62, 101, 111, 124, 127, 134, 139, 152, 155, 169, 171, 192, 225, 231, 256

Index

and suppression of slave trade, 1–2, 6, 17–18, 25, 30, *31*, 34, 40, 79, *80*, 82–85, 87–88, 96–98, *116*, 260
Yoruba population, 161–162
Frey, Rev. Christian Theophilus, 91, 172, 188, 216, 254
Fulani jihad, 54, 58, 71–72
Fulbe (Fulani, Fula), 13, 60, 132, 231, 234, *267*, *270*

Gabon, *116*, 147
Gallinhas, 27, 34, 42, 76, 104, *116*
Gbe, 18, 28, 149–152
Gelede, 261
Gerber, Rev. John, 231, 234
Gloucester, village, 111–113, 117, 144, 159, 172–173, 199
Gold Coast, *31*, *33*, *80–81*, *116*, *267*
Gollmer, Rev. Charles, 164
Graf, Rev. John Ulrich, 175, 200, 249
Grand Bassa, *116*
Grand Popo, 149–152
Granville Town, 23, 26
Guinea-Bissau, xiii, 120

Harding, Charles, *55*, 192
Hastings (village)
  Aku Muslim population, 229, 236, 243, 249
  CMS and population of, 174, 179, 199–200, 215
  founding, 112
  Liberated African population, 40, 115–118, 120, 124, 184, 225
Hausa
  in Bahia, 241
  ethnonym in Sierra Leone, 10, 36, 62–63, 127, 153–155, *267*, *269*
  language, 18, 28, 132
  Liberated Africans, 39, 48–49, 186, 188–191, 228
  slave revolt in Oyo, 53–54, 58, 71
Havana, 2, 32, 43
Hazeley, Jacob Boston, 91, 184, 236, 244
headmen (of Liberated African communities), 122, 167, 169, 180–184
Hogbrook, 106, 108. See also Regent
Horton, James Africanus Beale, 144–145, 200

Ibibio, *38*, 46–49, 145–146
Ifá, 63, 183, 205, 210–211, 213, 218–219
Igbo
  debates over "Igbo" identity, 44, 139–143
  ethnonym in Sierra Leone, 10, 36, 39, 44, 49, 143–144, *267*, *269*
  language, 18, 28, *38*, 47, 50, 132, 146
  Liberated Africans, 97–98, 117, 127, 171, 173–175
Ijebu, 56–57, 66, 155, *273*
  Liberated Africans from, 51, 59, 161–162
Ìjẹ̀sà, 51, 59, 155, 160, 187, *191*, *267*
Ile-Ife, 55–57, 155, 160–161, 187, 218
Ilorin, 52–54, 58
Islam, 6, 8, 61
  in Bight of Benin hinterland, 54, 58, 63–64, 154, 156, 229
  and Liberated African identity, 20–21, 204–205, 225, 228, 255–259
  in Sierra Leone region, 230

Jamaica, 1, 17, 23, 26, 125
jihad, 53, 58, 63, 71, 154, 240. *See also* Fulani jihad
Johnson, Rev. James, 186, 210, 217, 257
Johnson, Rev. Samuel, 40, 52, 170, 205
Johnson, Rev. W. A. B., 75, 88, 97–98, 172

Kakanda, *38*, 132, 189, *190–191*
Kano, 75, 153, 155
Katsina, 71, 155
Kennedy, Sir Arthur, Governor, 192
Kent (village), 92, 111, *118*, 124, 173
Kilham, Hannah, 50, 117, 131, 151, 159, 182
King, Thomas, 57, 66–69, 203, 254
King Jimmy, 22
King's Yard (from 1837, Queen's Yard), 49, 86–87, 125
kingship, 180, 185. *See also* Aku King

Kingston-in-Africa, 106, 108
Kissi (people), 36, 43, 108, *267*
Kissy (village), 108, 111, *118*
Kissy Hospital, 85
Kline, Emmanuel, 196
Koelle, Sigismund Wilhelm
  on CMS adoption of "Yoruba" ethnonym, 160, 164
  enslavement of informants, 70, 74
  on "Igbo" ethnonym, 44, 142–143
  informants, 39, 43, 58–60, 92, 120, 147, 153, *155*, 166, 183, 231, *272*
  on "Kálaba" ethnonym, 46, 145–146
  on "Kongo-Ngola languages," 135, 137
  Polyglotta Africana, 36–37, 131–133
Kongo, 135–138. *See also* Congo
Kono, 43
Koranko, 24, 43, 105
Kossoh/Kosso/Kusso. *See* Cosso
Krio, 7–10, 193, 258, 260–261
  language, 157, 217
Kru, 119, *267*

Lagos
  port of embarkation, 27, 34, 41, 51, 58, 76, 114–119
  returnees to, 197–198, 202
Leicester (village), 105, 110–111, *118*
Leicester Mountain, 47. *See also* Christian Institution, Leicester
Leopold (village), 92, 111, *118*
Lewis, William, 187
Liberated African Department, xii, 97, 110
  "disposal" policies, 99, 113, 115
  facilities, 84, 87
  officials, 121, 123
  policies, 184, 236
  reduction of, 125
Liberated African registers, 17, 40, *59*, 61, 99, 103–104, 111, 125
Liberated Africans
  adoption of term, xii, 2
  and British subjecthood, 246, 260
  estimates of numbers of, 1, 18, 30, *31*, *33*, 50, 98, 125
  and identity, 6–10
  and settler society, 26–28
Liberia, *38*, 109

Limba, 43, 189, 231
Little Bassa, *116*
Little Popo, 149–152
Loango, 137
Loko, 43, 105, *191*, 237
London, 17, 22
Luanda, 137
Lucumí, 156–158
Ludlam, Thomas, Governor, 102–106
Lungi, 252

Macaulay, George Metzger, Aku King, 263
Macaulay, John, Aku King, 186–188, 194, 256–257
Macaulay, Kenneth, 84, 120
Macaulay, Rev. George James, 179, 201, 224
Macaulay, Zachary, 102
MacCarthy, Sir Charles, Governor, 83, 109–110, 115, 123
MacDonald, Norman, Governor, 251–253
Madden, Richard Robert, 250
Malembo, *116*, 137
Mandingo. *See* Mandinka
Mandinka, 13, 238
  Liberated Africans, 43, 127, *190–191*, *267*, *269*
  religious leaders in colony, 233, 243, 248, 254
Maroons, 23–28
Maxwell, Charles William, Governor, 107
May, Rev. Joseph Boston, 41, 114, 192
Melville, Elizabeth Helen, 239
Melville, Michael Linning, 245
Mende. *See also* Cosso
  language, 18, 28, *38*
  Liberated Africans, 36, 43, 134, 191
Mendi Mission, 134
Methodists. *See* Wesleyan Methodist Missionary Society
Metzger, George William Emmanuel, 114, 181–182
Mixed Commission Courts, 2, 25, 82–83, 85, 110, 245
Moko
  ethnonym in Sierra Leone, 10, 39, 49, 127, 145, *190–191*
  meanings of, 145–148

Index

mortality
  shipboard, 76, 79–81
  in Sierra Leone, 39, 49, 88
Mozambique, *117*, 127, *269*
Murray Town (village), 114, *118*, 178
Muslims, 21
  diaspora in Atlantic, 240–243
  emigration of, 197, 202, 253–254
  Liberated Africans, 60–64, 117, 228–230, 247–249, 254
  migrants to colony, 230, 248
  repression of, 244–247, 249–253
  resistance, 227–228, 232–238

Nagô, 143, 156–157, 241
nations (Liberated African), 10, 19–20, 35–39, 58, 117–119, 127–133, 165–166
New Brunswick, 22–23
New Cabenda, 93, 108, 136, 181.
  See also Congo Town
New Calabar. *See* Elem Kalabari
Newlands (village), 114, *118*
Niger Expedition, 130, 132, 143, 155, 164, 195, 198
Niger River, 45, 132
Nigeria, 20, 34, 37, 45, 74, 265
Noah, David, 109
Nova Scotia, 1, 17, 22
Nova Scotians, 23–28, 251
Nupe, 52–54, 57, 59, 62
  language, *38*, 132
  Liberated Africans, 39, 60, 63, 120, 179, 189, *191*, 196, 228, 267
Nylander, Gustavus, 111

Ògún, 161, 205, 208–209, 254
Ojoe Corrie, 237
Okrafor-Smart, John Weeks, 41
Old Calabar
  and "Calabar" identification, 46, 145–146
  and "Moko" identification, 147
  port of embarkation, 27, *34*, 44, 47–48, 85, *116*, 140
Oldendorp, C. G. A, 147
oriṣa, 8, 20, 161, 195, 205–214, 226
Osogun, 54, 71

Ouidah
  Liberated Africans brought from, 74, 114
  port of embarkation, 27, 34, *52*, *116*
  returnees to, 197
Owen Glendower, HMS, 77, 82
Owu, 55–59, 63
Oyo Empire
  collapse of, 51–60
  Liberated Africans from, 18, 41, 71, 114, 155–156, 159–162, 229
  Muslims in, 63, 71
Oyo Ile (Old Oyo), 58, 63, 71, 75, 214

parish plan, 123
Pernambuco, Brazil, 2
Peters, Thomas, 22
Pine, Benjamin, Governor, 39, 64, 187, 254, 257
Plantain Islands, 121, 235
Popo
  ethnonym in Sierra Leone, 10, 39, 127, 151–152, 189–191, *269*
  meanings in diaspora, 149–151
Porto Novo, 63, 71–72, 149
Portugal, 31
Potts, Abraham/Abram, secret society, 169–170, 181, 186
Pratt, Isaac Benjamin, Aku King, 161, 187, *275*
Pratt, William Benjamin, 135
prize auctions, 185, 187, 197, 253
Province of Freedom (1787–1791), 22

Qur'an
  teaching in Sierra Leone colony, 248
  trade in Brazil, 243

Raban, Rev. John, 55, 131, 159, 163
Rankin, F. Harrison, 85, 91, 127
recaptives. *See also* Liberated Africans
  anachronism, xii
  preferability of term over "Liberated Africans," xii
Reffell, Joseph, 113–114, 122
Regent (village)
  CMS and population of, 171–173, 175
  founding, 108–109
  Liberated African population, 93, 97–98, 112, 117–118, 124

Rhodes, Rev. Henry, 173, 183
Ribi River, 227, 237
Rio de Janeiro, 2, 43, 90, 243
Rio Nun, 76, *116*
Rio Pongo, 42, 104, *116*, 267
Royal African Corps, 96
Royal Navy, 1, 25, 42, 62, 76–79, 96

Salvador de Bahia. *See* Bahia
Sandoval, Alonso de, 45, 147
Sàngó, 52, 205, 211–218
Santería, 226
Sàró, 198
Savage, William Henry, 245–248
scarification, 152, 161–163
Schön, Rev. James Frederick, 132, 143, 164, 167–168, 173
Senegambia, *33*, *80–81*, *116*
settlers, 17, 24–29, 123
Seventeen Nations, 187–190, 194, 262
Sharp, Granville, 1, 22
Sherbro (people), 43, 104–105, 127, 189
Sherbro (territory), 24, 42, 108, *116*, 232, 235, 237
shipmates, 18, 89–94, 107, 111, 120
Sierra Leone, coastline, *31*, *33*, 36, 42–43, *116*
Sierra Leone, disambiguation, xiii
Sierra Leone Company, 23, 252
Sierra Leone River, 42
Sierra Leone Watchman, 85, 202
Sierra Leone Weekly News, 148, 188
Somerset, James, 84
Southeast Africa, *31*, *33*
St. Paul River, 109
Susu
  CMS mission to, 110, 131
  Liberated Africans, 43, 104–105, 127, *190–191*
  residents of Sierra Leone peninsula, 231

Temne
  language, 131
  Liberated Africans, 43, 104–105, *189–191*
  relations with colony, 22–23, 231, 235–237
Thompson, Thomas Perronet, 102–106

Townsend, Rev. Henry, 169, 177, 199–200, 217, 231
Trinidad, 125, 196, 225
Turner, Charles, Governor, 123–124

Upper Guinea, 36, 41–43, 62, *80–81*, 105, 108, 267
Uthmān dan Fodio, 53, 60, 71, 238

Vai, 43, *267*
Venn, Rev. Henry, 209
Vernon Smith, Robert, 251
Vice-Admiralty Court, 2, 25, 102

wakes, 175–179
Waterloo (village)
  Aku Muslim population, 229–231, 236, 249
  founding, 112
  Liberated African population, 115–118, 172, 184, 188–190
Weeks, Rev. John Wills, 117, 175, 212, 249
Wellington (village), 124
  Aku Muslim population, 229, 236
  founding, 112
  Liberated African population, 92, 117, 147, 184
Wesleyan Methodist Missionary Society, 6, 69
  and Abeokuta, 198–199
  African clergy, 73, 114, 192, 201
West Central Africa
  coastline of embarkation, 31–34, *80–81*, *116*
  Liberated Africans from, 65, 125, 135–138, 183
West India Regiments, 112, 237
West Indies, migration to, 49, 99, 125. *See also* emigration
Wilberforce (village), 110, 112, *118*, 178, 181
Wilberforce, William, 24, 102
Wilhelm, Rev. J.G., 232–233
Will, James, 73–74, 192
Will, Thomas, Aku King, 185–186, 196
Windward Coast, *31*, *33*, *80–81*, *116*, *267*
Wolof, 105, 243, *267*, *269*
Wright, Rev. Joseph, 6, 57, 72–74, 78, 161, 201

Index

Yagba, 160–164
Yamsey, Josiah, 75
York (village), 91–92, *112*, 115, *118*, 124
Yoruba
  CMS adoption of name, 163–165
  culture in diaspora, 28, 170, 178, 193–195, 225–226, 261–262
  language, 9, 18, *38*, 131, 157, 159, 201–202, 265
  Liberated Africans, 21, 50–59, 63–65, 72–73, 114–117, 155, 159–162
  naming practices, 40, 263
  term in diaspora, 143, 156
Yoruba Mission, 195, 199–200